PHILOSOPHY OF MIND IN THE EARLY AND HIGH MIDDLE AGES

Philosophy of Mind in the Early and High Middle Ages provides an outstanding overview of a tumultuous 900-year period of discovery, innovation, and intellectual controversy that began with the Roman senator Boethius (*ca.* 480–524) and concluded with the Franciscan theologian and philosopher John Duns Scotus (*ca.* 1266–1308). Relatively neglected in philosophy of mind, this volume highlights the importance of philosophers such as Abelard, Duns Scotus, and the Persian philosopher and polymath Avicenna to the history of philosophy of mind.

Following an introduction by Margaret Cameron, twelve specially commissioned chapters by an international team of contributors discuss key topics, thinkers, and debates, including:

- mental perception,
- Avicenna and the intellectual abstraction of intelligibles,
- Duns Scotus and the will,
- soul, will, and choice in Islamic and Jewish contexts,
- perceptual experience,
- the systematization of the passions,
- the complexity of the soul and the problem of unity,
- the phenomenology of immortality,
- morality, and
- the self.

Essential reading for students and researchers in philosophy of mind, medieval philosophy, and the history of philosophy, *Philosophy of Mind in the Early and High Middle Ages* is also a valuable resource for those in related disciplines such as religious studies and history.

Margaret Cameron is Canada Research Council Chair in the Aristotelian Tradition (Tier II) and an associate professor in the Department of Philosophy at the University of Victoria, Canada. She works in the Aristotelian tradition of logic and philosophy of language, as well as the history of the philosophy of language more broadly, and has published articles in *The Cambridge Companion to Boethius*, *The Oxford Handbook of Medieval Philosophy*, *Vivarium*, *History of Philosophy Quarterly*, *American Catholic Philosophical Quarterly*, and the *Archives d'histoire doctrinale du moyen âge grec et latin*, as well as in a number of other book publications.

The History of the Philosophy of Mind
General Editors: Rebecca Copenhaver and Christopher Shields

The History of the Philosophy of Mind is a major six-volume reference collection, covering the key topics, thinkers and debates within philosophy of mind, from Antiquity to the present day. Each volume is edited by a leading scholar in the field and comprises chapters written by an international team of specially commissioned contributors.

Including a general introduction by Rebecca Copenhaver and Christopher Shields, and fully cross-referenced within and across the six volumes, *The History of the Philosophy of Mind* is an essential resource for students and researchers in philosophy of mind, and will also be of interest to those in many related disciplines, including Classics, Religion, Literature, History of Psychology, and Cognitive Science.

VOL. 1 PHILOSOPHY OF MIND IN ANTIQUITY
edited by John E. Sisko

VOL. 2 PHILOSOPHY OF MIND IN THE EARLY AND HIGH MIDDLE AGES
edited by Margaret Cameron

VOL. 3 PHILOSOPHY OF MIND IN THE LATE MIDDLE AGES AND RENAISSANCE
edited by Stephan Schmid

VOL. 4 PHILOSOPHY OF MIND IN THE EARLY MODERN AND MODERN AGES
edited by Rebecca Copenhaver

VOL. 5 PHILOSOPHY OF MIND IN THE NINETEENTH CENTURY
edited by Sandra Lapointe

VOL. 6 PHILOSOPHY OF MIND IN THE TWENTIETH AND TWENTY-FIRST CENTURIES
edited by Amy Kind

PHILOSOPHY OF MIND IN THE EARLY AND HIGH MIDDLE AGES

The History of the Philosophy of Mind, Volume 2

Edited by Margaret Cameron

LONDON AND NEW YORK

First published 2019
by Routledge
2 Park Square, Milton Park, Abingdon, Oxon OX14 4RN

and by Routledge
711 Third Avenue, New York, NY 10017

Routledge is an imprint of the Taylor & Francis Group, an informa business

© 2019 selection and editorial matter, Margaret Cameron; individual chapters, the contributors

The right of Margaret Cameron to be identified as the author of the editorial material, and of the authors for their individual chapters, has been asserted in accordance with sections 77 and 78 of the Copyright, Designs and Patents Act 1988.

All rights reserved. No part of this book may be reprinted or reproduced or utilised in any form or by any electronic, mechanical, or other means, now known or hereafter invented, including photocopying and recording, or in any information storage or retrieval system, without permission in writing from the publishers.

Trademark notice: Product or corporate names may be trademarks or registered trademarks, and are used only for identification and explanation without intent to infringe.

British Library Cataloguing-in-Publication Data
A catalogue record for this book is available from the British Library

Library of Congress Cataloging-in-Publication Data
Names: Cameron, Margaret (Margaret Anne), editor.
Title: Philosophy of mind in the early and high middle ages /
   edited by Margaret Cameron.
Description: New York : Routledge, 2018. | Series: The history of the
   philosophy of mind ; Volume 2 | Includes bibliographical references and index.
Identifiers: LCCN 2017060251 | ISBN 9781138243934 (hardback : alk. paper) |
   ISBN 9780429508196 (e-book)
Subjects: LCSH: Philosophy of mind—History—To 1500.
Classification: LCC BD418.3 .P4842 2018 | DDC 128/.20902—dc23
LC record available at https://lccn.loc.gov/2017060251

ISBN: 978-1-138-24393-4 (Vol II, hbk)
ISBN: 978-0-429-50819-6 (Vol II, ebk)

ISBN: 978-1-138-24392-7 (Vol I, hbk)
ISBN: 978-0-429-50821-9 (Vol I, ebk)
ISBN: 978-1-138-24394-1 (Vol III, hbk)
ISBN: 978-0-429-50817-2 (Vol III, ebk)
ISBN: 978-1-138-24395-8 (Vol IV, hbk)
ISBN: 978-0-429-50815-8 (Vol IV, ebk)
ISBN: 978-1-138-24396-5 (Vol V, hbk)
ISBN: 978-0-429-50813-4 (Vol V, ebk)
ISBN: 978-1-138-24397-2 (Vol VI, hbk)
ISBN: 978-0-429-50812-7 (Vol VI, ebk)
ISBN: 978-1-138-92535-9 (6-volume set, hbk)

Typeset in Times New Roman
by Apex CoVantage, LLC

CONTENTS

Notes on contributors   vii
General introduction   ix
REBECCA COPENHAVER AND CHRISTOPHER SHIELDS

Introduction to volume 2   1
MARGARET CAMERON

1 **Peter Abelard on mental perception**   18
MARGARET CAMERON

2 **The problem of intellectual cognition of material singulars between 1250 and 1310**   35
DAVID PICHÉ

3 **Avicenna and the issue of the intellectual abstraction of intelligibles**   56
RICHARD C. TAYLOR

4 **Duns Scotus on freedom as a pure perfection: necessity and contingency**   83
CRUZ GONZÁLEZ-AYESTA

5 **Soul, will, and choice in Islamic and Jewish contexts**   103
SARAH PESSIN

6 **Perceptual experience: assembling a medieval puzzle**   134
JUHANA TOIVANEN

CONTENTS

7 **The systematization of the passions in the thirteenth century**   157
HENRIK LAGERLUND

8 **Soul and agent intellect: Avicenna and Aquinas**   178
KARA RICHARDSON

9 **The complexity of the soul and the problem of unity in thirteenth-century philosophy**   197
ANDREW ARLIG

10 **The phenomenology of immortality (1200–1400)**   219
CHRISTINA VAN DYKE

11 **Morality**   240
PETER S. EARDLEY

12 **The self**   257
JOHN MARENBON

Index   279

CONTRIBUTORS

Andrew Arlig is Associate Professor of Philosophy at Brooklyn College, City University of New York. He specializes in medieval philosophy, ancient philosophy, and metaphysics. His work focuses primarily on medieval theories of parts and wholes, and his research has been published in *Oxford Studies in Medieval Philosophy*, *The Oxford Handbook of Medieval Philosophy*, and *The Stanford Encyclopedia of Philosophy*.

Margaret Cameron is Canada Research Council Chair in the Aristotelian Tradition (Tier II) and an associate professor in the department of philosophy at the University of Victoria, Canada. She works in the Aristotelian tradition of logic and philosophy of language, as well as the history of the philosophy of language more broadly, and has published articles in *The Cambridge Companion to Boethius*, *The Oxford Handbook of Medieval Philosophy*, *Vivarium*, *History of Philosophy Quarterly*, *American Catholic Philosophical Quarterly*, and the *Archives d'histoire doctrinale du moyen âge grec et latin*, as well as in a number of other book publications.

Peter S. Eardley is Associate Professor of Philosophy at the University of Guelph. A specialist in the area of later medieval thought in the Latin tradition, Eardley focuses particularly on the work of Thomas Aquinas, Giles of Rome, and Henry of Ghent. In addition to a number of articles on ethics, metaphysics, and theology, Eardley has recently published the *Brill Companion to Giles of Rome*.

Cruz González-Ayesta is Profesor Titular of Philosophy at the Universidad de Navarra. She has published widely on Duns Scotus' philosophy, including "Duns Scotus on the Natural Will" and "Duns Scotus on Synchronic Contingency and Free Will: The Originality and Importance of His Contribution". González-Ayesta is also co-editor of *Causality in Early Modern Philosophy*.

Henrik Lagerlund is Professor of the History of Philosophy at Stockholm University. He is editor of the Springer books series *Studies in the History of Philosophy of Mind* and was the editor-in-chief of the *Encyclopedia of Medieval Philosophy*. Lagerlund specializes in the areas of medieval philosophy of mind and metaphysics and is the author of twelve books and numerous articles.

CONTRIBUTORS

John Marenbon is a Fellow of the British Academy, Senior Research Fellow of Trinity College, Cambridge, and an Honorary Professor of Medieval Philosophy and Visiting Professor at the Philosophy Department of Peking University. He is the author of many books on medieval philosophy, including *Pagans and Philosophers. The Problem of Paganism from Augustine to Leibniz* and *Medieval Philosophy: An Historical and Philosophical Introduction*.

Sarah Pessin is Professor of Philosophy and Judaic Studies and Interfaith Director of the Center for Jewish Studies at the University of Denver. Among her many publications, she recently published *Ibn Gabriol's Theology of Desire*.

David Piché is Professor of Philosophy at the Université de Montréal. His work primarily focuses on the epistemic and psychological status of acts of faith in the thirteenth and fourteenth centuries, as well as on ontological issues that bear on the problem of universals. From among his many contributions to the field, he has recently published *La théorie de la connaissance intellectuelle de Gérard de Bologne*.

Kara Richardson is Associate Professor of Philosophy at Syracuse University. Richardson is a specialist in the area of the history of metaphysics in the medieval modern period, with a particular focus on the topic of causality. Among her publications, Richardson has written on natural teleology, efficient causality, formal causality, and the principle of sufficient reason.

Richard C. Taylor is Professor of Philosophy at Marquette University. His wide-ranging interests include religious studies, ancient and medieval metaphysics, philosophical psychology, and the interaction of medieval religious and philosophical thought. He is translator of Averroes' *Long Commentary on the De Anima of Aristotle* and organizer of *Aquinas and 'the Arabs' International Working Group*.

Juhana Toivanen is an Academy Research Fellow with the University of Jyväskylä, Finland and a postdoctoral researcher at the University of Gothenburg, Sweden, in the Department of Philosophy, Linguistics and Theory of Science. He published *Perception and the Internal Senses: Peter of John Olivi on the Cognitive Functions of the Sensitive Soul*, as well as other articles on medieval philosophy.

Christina Van Dyke is Professor of Philosophy at Calvin College. She has published many articles on medieval mysticism and the metaphysics and epistemology of human embodiment and death. Van Dyke is editor of the forthcoming four-volume series, *Medieval Philosophy* (Routledge), and is co-editor and co-translator of Thomas Aquinas' *The Treatise on Happiness and The Treatise on Human Acts* (with T. Williams).

GENERAL INTRODUCTION

Rebecca Copenhaver and Christopher Shields

How far back does the history of philosophy of mind extend? In one sense, the entire history of the discipline extends no further than living memory. Construed as a recognized sub-discipline of philosophy, philosophy of mind seems to have entered the academy in a regular way only in the latter half of the twentieth century. At any rate, as an institutional matter, courses listed under the name 'Philosophy of Mind' or 'The Mind-Body Problem' were rare before then and seem not to have become fixtures of the curriculum in Anglo-American universities until the 1960s.[1] More broadly, construed as the systematic self-conscious reflection on the question of how mental states and processes should be conceived in relation to physical states and processes, one might put the date to the late nineteenth or early twentieth century.

One might infer on this basis that a six-volume work on *The History of Philosophy of Mind* extending back to antiquity is bound to be anachronistic: we cannot, after all, assume that our questions were the questions of, say, Democritus, working in Thrace in the fifth century BC, or of Avicenna (Ibn-Sînâ), active in Persia in the twelfth century, or of John Blund, the Oxford- and Paris-trained Chancellor of the see of York from 1234–1248, or, for that matter, of the great German philosopher and mathematician Leibniz (1646–1716). One might on the contrary think it *prima facie* unlikely that thinkers as diverse as these in their disparate times and places would share very many preoccupations either with each other or with us.

Any such immediate inference would be unduly hasty and also potentially misleading. It would be misleading not least because it relies on an unrealistically unified conception of what *we* find engaging in this area: philosophy of mind comprises today a wide range of interests, orientations, and methodologies, some almost purely *a priori* and others almost exclusively empirical. It is potentially misleading in another way as well, heading in the opposite direction. If we presume that the only thinkers who have something useful to say to us are those engaging the questions of mind we find salient, using idioms we find congenial, then we will likely overlook some surprising continuities as well as instructive discontinuities across these figures and periods.

Some issues pertinent to mental activity may prove perennial. Of equal importance, however, are the differences and discontinuities we find when we investigate questions of mind assayed in earlier periods of thought. In some cases, it is true, we find it difficult to determine without careful investigation whether difference in idiom suffices for difference in interest or orientation. For instance, it was once commonplace to frame questions about mental activity as questions about the soul, where today questions posed about the nature of the soul and its relation to the body are apt to sound to many to be outmoded or at best quaintly archaic. Yet when we read what, for instance, medieval philosophers investigated under that rubric, we are as likely as not to find them reflecting on such core contemporary concerns as the nature of perception, the character of consciousness, the relation of mental faculties to the body, and the problem of intentionality – and to be doing so in a manner immediately continuous with some of our own preoccupations.

That said, even where upon examination we find little or no continuity between present-day and earlier concerns, this very difference can be illuminating. Why, for instance, is the will discussed so little in antiquity? Hannah Arendt suggests an answer: the will was not discussed in antiquity because it was not discovered before St. Augustine managed to do so in the third century.[2] Is she right? Or is the will in fact discussed obliquely in antiquity, enmeshed in a vocabulary at least initially alien to our own? On the supposition that Arendt is right, and the will is not even a topic of inquiry before Augustine, why should this be so? Should this make us less confident that we have a faculty rightly called 'the will'? Perhaps Augustine not so much discovered the will as *invented* it, to give it pride of place in his conception of human nature. A millennium later Thomas Aquinas contended that the will is but one power or faculty of the soul, as an intellectual appetite for the good (*ST* I 82, resp.). Is he right? Is the will as examined by Augustine and Aquinas the same will of which we ask, when we do, whether our will is free or determined?

A study of the history of philosophy of mind turns up, in sum, some surprising continuities, some instructive partial overlaps, and some illuminating discontinuities across the ages. When we reflect on the history of the discipline, we bring into sharper relief some of the questions we find most pressing, and we inevitably come to ask new and different questions, even as we retire questions which we earlier took to be of moment. Let us reflect first then on some surprising continuities. Three illustrations will suffice, but they could easily be multiplied.

First, consider some questions about minds and machines: whether machines can be conscious or otherwise minded, whether human intelligence is felicitously explicated in terms of computer software, hardware, or functional processes more generally. Surely such questions belong to our era uniquely? Yet we find upon reading some early modern philosophy that this is not so. In Leibniz, for instance, we find this striking passage, known as 'Leibniz's mill':

> Imagine there were a machine whose structure produced thought, feeling, and perception; we can conceive of its being enlarged while maintaining the same relative proportions, so that we could walk into it as we can walk into a mill. Suppose we do walk into it; all we would find there

are cogs and levers and so on pushing one another, and never anything to account for a perception. So perception must be sought in simple substances, not in composite things like machines. And that is all that can be found in a simple substance – perceptions and changes in perceptions; and those changes are all that the internal actions of simple substances can consist in.

(*Monadology* §17)

Leibniz offers an argument against mechanistic conceptions of mental activity in this passage, one with a recognizably contemporary counterpart. His view may be defensible or it may be indefensible; but it is certainly relevant to questions currently being debated.

Similarly, nearly every course in philosophy of mind these days begins with some formulation of the 'mind-body problem', usually presented as a descendant of the sort of argument Descartes advanced most famously in his *Meditations*, and defended most famously in his correspondence with Elisabeth of Bohemia. Centuries before Descartes, however, we encounter the Islamic polymath Avicenna (Ibn-Sînâ) wondering in detail about the question of whether the soul has or lacks quantitative extension, deploying a striking thought experiment in three separate passages, one of which runs:

One of us must suppose that he was just created at a stroke, fully developed and perfectly formed but with his vision shrouded from perceiving all external objects – created floating in the air or in space, not buffeted by any perceptible current of the air that supports him, his limbs separated and kept out of contact with one another, so that they do not feel each other. Then let the subject consider whether he would affirm the existence of his self. There is no doubt that he would affirm his own existence, although not affirming the reality of any of his limbs or inner organs, his bowels, or heart or brain or any external thing. Indeed he would affirm the existence of this self of his while not affirming that it had any length, breadth or depth. And if it were possible for him in such a state to imagine a hand or any other organ, he would not imagine it to be a part of himself or a condition of his existence.

(Avicenna, '*The Book of Healing*')

Avicenna's 'Floating Man' or 'Flying Man', reflects his Neoplatonist orientation and prefigures in obvious ways Descartes' more celebrated arguments of *Meditations* II. Scholars dispute just how close this parallel is,[3] but it seems plain that these arguments and parables bear a strong family resemblance to one another, and then each in turn to a yet earlier argument by Augustine,[4] more prosaically put, but engaging many of the same themes.

The point is not to determine who won the race to this particular argument, nor to insist that these authors arrive at precisely the same finish line. Rather, when we study each expression in its own context, we find illuminating samenesses and differences, which in turn assist us in framing our own questions about the character of the quantitative and qualitative features of mind, about the tenability of solipsism, and about the nature of the human self. One would like to know, for instance, whether such a narrow focus on the internal states of human consciousness provides a productive method for the science of mind. Or have our philosophical forebears, as some today think, created impediments by conceiving of the very project in a way that neglects the embodied characteristics of cognition? From another angle, one may wonder whether these approaches, seen throughout the history of the discipline, lead inexorably to Sartre's conclusion that 'consciousness is a wind blowing from nowhere towards objects'?[5] One way to find out is to study each of these approaches in the context of its own deployment.

For a final example, we return to the birthplace of Western philosophy to reflect upon a striking argument of Democritus in the philosophy of perception. After joining Leucippus in arguing that the physical world comprises countless small atoms swirling in the void, Democritus observes that *only* atoms and the void are, so to speak, really real. All else exists by convention: 'by convention sweet and by convention bitter, by convention hot, by convention cold, by convention colour; but in reality atoms and void' (DK 68B9). This remark evidently denies the reality of sensible qualities, such as sweetness and bitterness, and even colour. What might Democritus be thinking? By judging this remark alongside his remaining fragments, we see that he is appealing to the variability of perception to argue that if one perceiver tastes a glass of wine and finds it sweet, while another perceiver tastes the same glass and finds it bitter, then we must conclude – on the assumption that perceptual qualities are real – that either one or the other perceiver is wrong. After all, they cannot both be right, and there seems little point in treating them as both wrong. The correct conclusion, Democritus urges, is that sensible qualities, in contrast to atoms and the void, are not real. The wine is neither sweet nor bitter; sweetness and bitterness are wholly subjective states of perceivers.

Readers of seventeenth- and eighteenth-century British philosophy will recognize this argument in Locke and Berkeley. Locke presents the argument to support his distinction between primary and secondary qualities: primary qualities being those features of objects that are (putatively) *in* objects, independently of perception, such as number, shape, size, and motion; secondary qualities being those features of objects subject to the variability of perception recognized by Democritus. Locke struggles with the reality of secondary qualities, sometimes treating them as ideas in our minds and other times as dispositions of the primary qualities of objects that exist independently of us. Democritus, by contrast, aligning the real with the objective, simply banishes them to the realm of convention. And Berkeley appeals to the same phenomenon on which Locke founds his famous distinction – the variability of perception – to argue that the distinction is unsustainable and thus embraces the anti-Democritean option: the real is the ideal.

We may ask which if any of these philosophers deserves to be followed. As an anecdotal matter, when beginning philosophy students grasp the point of arguments from the variability of perception, they become flummoxed, because before having their attention focussed on the phenomenon of variability, most tend to think of sensible qualities as intrinsic monadic properties of the external objects of perception. This issue in the philosophy of perception, straddling as it does different periods and idioms, remains a live one, proving as vivid for us as it was for Democritus and Locke.

When we find similar philosophical arguments and tropes recurring in radically different periods and contexts throughout the history of philosophy, that is usually at least a strong *prima facie* indication that we are in an area demanding careful scrutiny. Unsurprisingly, arguments concerning the nature of perception and perceptible qualities offer one telling illustration. Still, we should resist the temptation to find continuities where none exist, especially where none exist beyond the verbal or superficial. We should moreover resist, perhaps more strongly still, the tendency to minimize or overlook differences where they appear. One of the intellectual joys of studying the history of philosophy resides precisely in uncovering and appreciating the deep discontinuities between disparate times and contexts.

On this score, examples abound, but one suffices to illustrate our point. The title of a widely read article written in the 1960s posed a provocative question: 'Why Isn't the Mind-Body Problem Ancient?'.[6] This question, of course, has a presupposition, namely that the mind-body problem is in fact *not* ancient. It also seems to betray a second presupposition, namely that there is *a* mind-body problem: a single problem that that engages philosophers of the modern era but that escaped the ancients. This presupposition raises the question: what *is* the single, unified, mind-body problem that the ancients failed to recognize? In fact, when we turn to the range of questions posed in this domain, we find a family of recognizably distinct concerns: the hard problem, the explanatory gap, mental causation, and so on. Not all these questions have a common orientation, even if they arise from a common anxiety that the mind and the body are at once so dissimilar that inquiring into their relationship may already be an error, and yet so similar in their occupation and operation as to obliterate any meaningful difference.

We might call this anxiety *categorial*. That is, it has seemed to various philosophers in various eras that there is some basic categorial distinction to be observed in the domain of the mental, to the effect that mental states belong to one category and physical states to another. That by itself might be true without, however, there being any attendant problem. After all, we might agree that there is a categorial distinction between, say, biological properties and mathematical properties, and even that these families of properties are never co-instantiable. After all, no number can undergo descent with modification, and no animal can be a cosine. That is hardly a problem: no one expects numbers to be biological subjects, and no one would ever mistake an organism for a mathematical function. The problem in the domain of the mental and physical seems to arise only when we assume that some objects – namely ourselves – exhibit both mentality and physicality, and do so in a way that is systematic and unified. Bringing these thoughts together we arrive at a mind-body problem: if mental and physical properties are categorially exclusive while we ourselves are mental and physical at once, we must be what we cannot be, namely subjects of properties that cannot coincide.

In this sense, Cartesian dualism might be regarded as a solution to the mind-body problem, at least *this* mind-body problem, one which simply concedes its conclusion by affirming that minds and bodies are irredeemably different sorts of substances displaying different sorts of properties. Needless to say, this 'solution' invites a series of still more intractable problems concerning the interaction of these postulated disparate substances, about the location of the mental, and so forth. Even so, when the Cartesian expedient is rejected on these or other grounds, the old problem re-emerges, in one guise yielding an equally desperate seeming sort of solution, namely the total elimination of the mental as ultimately not amenable to a purely physicalistic characterization.[7] Eliminativism, no less than Cartesianism, solves the mind-body problem by effectively by concession.

One should accordingly look afresh at the problem as formulated. In fact, when one asks *what* these purportedly mutually excluding properties may be, several candidates come to the fore. Some think properties such as *being conscious* are mental and cannot possibly be physical, perhaps because conscious states are ineliminably subjective, whereas all physical properties are objective, or because mental properties are essentially qualitative, whereas physical properties are only quantitative. Descartes' own reasons, though disputed, seem to have been largely epistemic: possibly one can doubt the existence of one's body, whereas it is impossible, because self-defeating, to doubt the existence of one's own mind or mental states (*Meditation* II). If these property-differences obtain in these domains and are in fact such as to be mutually exclusive, then we do now have the makings of a mind-body problem.

Returning, then, to the question pertinent to our study of the ancient period, we may ask: do the ancients draw these sorts of categorial distinctions? If so, why do they fail to appreciate the problems we find so familiar and obvious? Or do they in fact fail to draw these categorial distinctions in the first place? If they do not, then one would like to know why not. One can imagine a number of different options here: one could fault the ancients for failing to pick up on such starkly categorial differences; one could credit them for astutely avoiding the conceptual muddles of Cartesianism. Some argue, for instance, that Aristotelian hylomorphism embraces a framework of explanation within which Cartesian questions simply cannot arise, thereby obviating an array of otherwise intractable problems.[8] Although we do not attempt to litigate these issues here, one can appreciate how an investigation into ancient approaches to philosophy of mind yields palpable benefits for some modern questions, even if and perhaps precisely because such questions were not ancient.

Needless to say, we never know in advance of our investigations whether the benefits of such study are forthcoming. To make such discoveries as can be made in this area, then, we need ask a set of questions similar to those we asked regarding the mind-body problem, *mutatis mutandis*, for other philosophical problems in the mental domain, broadly construed, as they arise in other periods of philosophy beyond ancient philosophy as well.

If we proceed in this way, we find that the study of the history of philosophy of mind offers the contemporary philosopher perspectives on the discipline which, however far below the surface, may yet guide our own inquiries into the mental and physical, and into the character of mental and physical states and processes. This is, of course, but one reason to engage the studies these six volumes contain. Other researchers with a more purely historical orientation will find a wealth of material in these pages as well, ranging across all periods of western philosophy, from antiquity to that part of the discipline that resides in living memory. Our historical and philosophical interests here may, of course, be fully complementary: the history of philosophy of mind takes one down some odd by-ways off some familiar boulevards, into some dead-ends and cul-de-sacs, but also along some well-travelled highways that are well worth traversing over and again.

Notes

1 A perusal of the course offerings of leading universities in the US tends to confirm this. To take but one example, which may be multiplied, a search of the archives of the University of Notre Dame lists one course in 'Philosophy of Mind' offered as an advanced elective in 1918 and 1928, 1929, but then no further course until 1967, when 'The Mind-Body Problem,' began to be offered yearly off and on for two decades. In the 1970s, various electives such as 'Mind and Machines' were offered intermittently, and a regular offering in 'Philosophy of Mind' began only in 1982. This offering continues down to the present. While we have not done a comprehensive study, these results cohere with archive searches of several other North American universities.
2 Arendt sees prefigurations in St. Paul and others, but regards Augustine as 'the first philosopher of the will and the only philosopher the Romans ever had' (1978, vol. ii, 84).
3 For an overview of these issues, see Marmura (1986).
4 On the relation between Descartes and Augustine, see the instructive treatment in Matthews (1992).
5 Sartre (1943: 32–33).
6 Matson (1966). Citing Matson's question, King (2007) went on to pose a continuing question of his own: 'Why Isn't the Mind-Body Problem Medieval?'. In so doing, King meant to oppose Matson, who had claimed that the one should not assume that medieval philosophers, although writing in a recognizably Aristotelian idiom, similarly failed to engage any mind-body problem. After all, he noted, in addition to their Aristotelianism, they accepted a full range of theistic commitments alien to Aristotle.
7 Eliminativism about the mental has a long a chequered history, extending at least as far back as Broad (1925) (who rejects it), but has its most forceful and accessible formulation in Churchland (1988).
8 Charles (2008) has advanced this sort of argument on behalf of hylomorphism.

Bibliography

Arendt, Hannah. 1978. *The Life of the Mind*, vols. i and ii. New York: Harcourt Brace Jovanovich.
Broad, C. D. 1925. *The Mind and Its Place in Nature*. London: Routledge & Kegan.

Charles, David. 2008. "Aristotle's Psychological Theory". *Proceedings of the Boston Area Colloquium in Ancient Philosophy* **24**: 1–29.

Churchland, P. M. 1988. *Matter and Consciousness*. Cambridge, MA: MIT Press.

King, Peter. 2007. "Why Isn't the Mind-Body Problem Medieval?" In *Forming the Mind: Essays on the Internal Senses and the Mind/Body Problem From Avicenna to the Medical Enlightenment*, 187–205. Berlin: Springer.

Marmura, Michael. 1986. "Avicenna's Flying Man in Context". *The Monist* **69**(3): 383–395.

Matson, Wallace. 1966. "Why Isn't the Mind-Body Problem Ancient?" In *Mind, Matter, and Method: Essays in Philosophy and Science in Honor of Herbert Feigl*, 92–102. St. Paul: University of Minnesota Press.

Matthews, Gareth. 1992. *Thought's Ego in Augustine and Descartes*. Ithaca: Cornell University Press.

Sartre, Jean-Paul. 1943. "Une Idée fondamentale de la phénomenologie de Husserl: L'intentionalité". In *Situations I*. Paris: Gallimard.

INTRODUCTION TO VOLUME 2

Margaret Cameron

1 Introduction

The historical period covered in this volume begins with the Neoplatonic translator and commentator and Roman senator Boethius (*ca.* 480–524) and concludes with the Franciscan theologian and philosopher John Duns Scotus (*ca.* 1266–1308). What we find during the nine hundred intervening years is an exciting, tumultuous, and philosophically robust period of discovery, rediscovery, innovation, and intellectual controversy taking place in multiple languages over large territories, stretching from ancient Rome, through England and France, into Alexandria, Baghdad, Spain, and eventually throughout Europe. Philosophy of mind during this period is in fact much broader and often stranger than it is taken to be in contemporary philosophical circles. Discussions took place within a wider context of investigation into and debate over what is better termed "philosophical anthropology", or the study of the human soul and its relation to other living things, to God, and to the material world, including human bodies. No introduction to the historical context of the period could do justice to the sheer volume, let alone complexity, of these topics; many excellent studies of various portions of this extensive historical period have been done (and will be noted throughout). Instead, this introduction is intended for those who are more or less unfamiliar with what happened in the history of the philosophy of mind from the end of the ancient period to the start of the fourteenth century. For those already familiar with this period and this material, jump ahead and read the chapters themselves.

This period in the history of philosophy has its roots the ancient world, to Plato, to Aristotle, to the medical writer Galen (129–*ca.* 200), to the Neoplatonist Plotinus (*ca.* 204–270) and other Neoplatonic commentators, and to Augustine (354–430) and other Christian writers. It also branches forward, past the end of the thirteenth century, by means of the theoretical authority acquired by many of its figures, such as Thomas Aquinas (1225–1274), his teacher Albert the Great (*ca.* 1200–1280), and John Duns Scotus (1265/66–1308), as well as the Arabic philosophers Ibn Sina (*ca.* 970–1037), known in the Latin West as "Avicenna", Ibn Rushd (1126–1198), known as "Averroes", and Jewish thinker Moses

Maimonides (*ca.* 1135–1204), just to mention some of the most influential names. It would be a great mistake to think that the years covered by this volume mark off any natural period in intellectual history. Rather, by being set in this series of volumes on the history of philosophy of mind, it should be thought of as part of a continuous history, impossible fully to appreciate and understand without recognizing the relationship of its major achievements to the work that came before and after.

Even so, some periodization within this 900 year stretch can be helpfully marked off. In what follows, we will examine four overlapping periods. We start with Boethius and his intellectual context and examine some of the major achievements that followed in what is called the "Latin West" (roughly, at this time, northern Europe and parts of England) up until the eleventh century theologian Anselm of Canterbury (*ca.* 1033–1109). Second, we will turn to the development of philosophy, particularly the philosophy of mind in Arabic-speaking centres of learning, turning our focus to two towering figures: Avicenna and Averroes. Third, we mark off the twelfth century in the Latin west as a major turning point in intellectual history, as a period of intense recovery and translation of parts of ancient as well as Arabic philosophy. Within this century, running alongside the new developments prompted by the availability of new material, we find an avid fascination – little explored in the history of philosophy – with topics in the philosophy of mind. Fourth, and finally, we turn to the study of the philosophy of mind taking place in the new intellectual world of the university, both in Paris and Oxford, and then beyond. Since no one list of topics could be generated to characterize the study of philosophy of mind during this long, multifaceted period, we will instead highlight some of the most pressing topics along the way.

2 Between Boethius and Anselm in the Latin West

Boethius served as the first conduit for the transmission of ancient Greek philosophy into the Latin language, which remained the language of academia in the West throughout this period (and beyond). Boethius set out to translate and comment on all the works of Plato and Aristotle, the two philosophers who, in his day, were regarded as authoritative and – rather surprising from a present-day perspective – doctrinally compatible along most philosophical dimensions.[1] His early death made this ambitious plan impossible, although he managed to translate the majority of Aristotle's logical writings, two of which were transmitted into the medieval period, namely the *Categories* and *On Interpretation*. Boethius' commentaries on these works, as well as on Porphyry's *Isagoge* (usually taken as an introduction to logic), link more than just Aristotle to the future: in his lengthy commentaries on these works, Boethius reports the views of a host of ancient commentators, such as Alexander of Aphrodisias (*fl.* late second and early third centuries) and Plotinus' student Porphyry (*ca.* 234–*ca.* 305), among others. Boethius' reliance on and interest in the ancient commentators not only gave medieval readers insight into this rich ancient tradition but primed them to be open to, indeed eager for, the assistance those commentators would provide once their works were translated into Latin in the thirteenth century and beyond.

In addition to this achievement, Boethius also provided a work on logical division, *On Division*, in which of the three main ways of dividing parts and wholes provided a mereological framework for later thinkers, who tackled (for example) the question of the division of the soul into its parts (see Chapter 9). But it was Boethius' best-selling *Consolation of Philosophy*, a philosophical reflection about the true nature of being human and about the question of whether, in a universe providentially governed by an omnipotent God, humans can have free will, that provided a major resource for thinking about philosophy of mind. Read continuously throughout this period in the Latin West and included on the prescribed curriculae of study in the universities, the *Consolation* provided a basic psychological vocabulary and a description of the relationship between various mental processes/acts, for example, sensing, imagining, estimating, reasoning, and understanding, as well as the differences between animal, human, and divine cognition. Like Augustine, Boethius was a Christian and a Neoplatonist: this spiritual and intellectual orientation was enormously attractive to many Western thinkers, and Boethius' authority remained secure throughout this period (see Chapter 2).

What happened after the death of Boethius in the Latin West? As D. Gutas dramatically explained, "Philosophy died a lingering death before Islam appeared" (Gutas 2010, 11). Chronologically, this is mostly correct: after the pagan philosophical schools were closed by edict of the Emperor Justinian in 529, it was only in Baghdad in the ninth century that we find any major philosophical activity taking place (see section 3, Introduction). In the Latin West, a period of philosophical silence also ensued, to be picked up again only in the late eighth century's court of Charlemagne. Intellectuals and politicians were stimulated by theological controversies (such as the production of religious images, the nature of the Trinity, predestination, and so on) to turn to logical works, specifically those inherited from Boethius, to solve problems. Immediately, however, philosophically minded intellectuals turned to questions in the philosophy of mind: Alcuin (active *ca.* 780), the leading political thinker, wrote *On the rational soul* (*De animae ratione*), and the leading philosopher John Scottus Eriugena (*ca.* 800–*ca.* 877) penned the masterful five-part *On nature* (*Periphyseon*), the fourth and fifth parts of which put forward his views on human nature within the perspective of a mystically oriented theophany (see Chapter 12). A speculative idealist, Eriugena held the bold position that human nature, which uniquely mediates between worldly and other-worldly realms, transcends this material reality and exists as a concept made eternally in the divine mind.[2] The activity of this period set into motion a period of theologically motivated philosophical inquiry, inspired in part by mystical theology of the Greek Pseudo-Dionysius (the sixth century Neoplatonist trying pass himself off as Dionysius the Areopagite,[3] thereby cashing in on Christian credentials), but in the main by the thought of St. Augustine.[4]

Among the early medieval Latin thinkers that followed, Anselm of Canterbury towers in importance both for his philosophical ingenuity and legacy. To contemporary readers, Anselm is best known for his ontological proof for the existence of God presented in the *Proslogion*, that is, of "that than which nothing greater can be thought". For the history of philosophy of mind, Anselm's *On Truth* and *On Free Will*, two books in a three book collection which also includes *On the Fall of the Devil*, are more important. By his own description:

> One of the three is *On Truth*, what it is and in what things it is customarily said to be found; and what is justice. The second is *On Free Will*, what it is, and whether a man always has it, and how many different ways there are of having and not having rectitude of will, the preserving of which is the task of the rational creature. In it I showed how great the natural strength of the will is for preserving rectitude once acquired, not how necessary grace may be for it.
>
> (Anselm 1998, 151)

It helps to situate Anselm in his own environment, noting that while some philosophical texts (e.g., Aristotle's *Categories* and *On Interpretation*, as well as the Pseudo-Augustinian *Ten Categories*) were in use, the logical schools organized around the teaching of a master were only just getting started in Paris. Anselm was not untouched by this work, but he was mainly motivated by another type of school – the secular theological schools, especially that of Laon, in which controversies were rapidly boiling over and motivating a new generation of intellectuals to inquire after human nature. We will pick up on this development in section 4.

3 Development of the Arabic tradition in the history of the philosophy of mind

Arguably, the most influential philosopher in the Arabic tradition is Avicenna, whose philosophical output would not have been possible without the momentous translation of Greek intellectual writings into Arabic beginning in the eight century. Not only were Aristotle's writings made available through this initiative, which was broadly supported in Baghdad by the political and religious elite (see Gutas 1998), but so too were the writings of Plato, the ancient Greek Neoplatonic commentators, and medical works by Galen and others. Philosophical interest in philosophical psychology meshed with interest in biology and other natural sciences and must be reviewed as being continuous with physiological inquiry (Gutas 1998; Harvey 2006). This meant that, for example, in the process of identifying and determining the functions of various activities of the soul, such as nutrition, perception, and memory (to name just a few), philosophers in this tradition were also keen to associate these activities with locations and operations of the physical body. In addition, many philosophical arguments and theories of the Arabic-speaking philosophers were advanced against the background of, and oftentimes in direct debate with, Muslim theologians, the *Mutakallimûn*.

What we are calling "philosophy of mind" here was known as the science of the soul in the Arabic tradition. There was a religious motivation for engaging in this study; according to philosopher and theologian al-Ghazali (1058/9–1111), there are "only two starting points for attaining knowledge of God: knowledge of the human soul and knowledge of the visible world". Coming to know the human soul was a teleologically driven rational inquiry, with the goal of attaining human perfection. Aristotle's *On the soul* provided the starting point of inquiry, lending a philosophical vocabulary and psychic schema to this project. Consequently, philosophers in the Arabic tradition operated within a more or less hylomorphic metaphysical framework in which Aristotle's definition of the soul was "the first actuality of a natural body that has life potentially" (*On the soul* 412a27).

While accepting a broadly Aristotelian perspective, Avicenna was also strongly influenced by Plato as well as Neoplatonic currents. In brief, Avicenna did not accept Aristotle's theory of the soul. Instead, he held a substance-dualist view, an approach more congenial to Plato, according to which body and soul are discrete substances that nonetheless operate closely together. His view is supported by an ingenious and famous thought experiment known as the "flying man":

> We say, therefore, that one of us must imagine himself as created all at once and perfect but with his sight veiled from seeing external things, and created as moving in the air or in the void so that the density of the air, which he could perceive, would not touch him, and with his limbs separate in such a way that they neither meet nor touch each other. He must then see if he affirms the existence of his essence. For, he would not hesitate to affirm that he exists, but he would not affirm anything external about his members, anything hidden about what is inside him, neither his mind nor his brain, or anything external whatsoever. But he would affirm that he exists without affirming his length, width, or density. If he were able at that time to imagine a hand or some other member, he would not imagine it to be a part of him or necessary to his existence. Now, you know that what is affirmed is different from what is not affirmed and what is granted is different from what is not granted. And because the essence that he affirms to exist is proper to him in that it is himself and in addition to the body, he who is attentive has the means to be awakened to knowing that the being of the soul is different from the being of the body; indeed, he does not need the body in order to know and perceive the soul.
> (Avicenna *On the soul* 1.1, 36–7)[5]

Consequently, Avicenna was able to argue for the soul's continued existence after bodily death.[6]

Avicenna's interest in the soul and psychological phenomena is remarkably wide ranging. Of particular importance are his theories of the five internal and five external senses. The internal senses are common sense, imagery, imagination, estimation, and memory; the external are vision, hearing, smell, touch, and taste.

Avicenna was particularly interested in sense perception in order to explain how individual objects of perception are able to be intellected by the soul. Avicenna posited that there are in fact two objects of sense perception: in addition to the images of the sensible objects, which are their sensible forms, Avicenna added that the faculty of estimation is capable of grasping intentions (*ma'naa*), which he took to be meanings. The intention thus grasped enables the sensible to be intelligible, having ultimately emanated from the Active Intellect, which is the source of all understanding (see Chapters 3 and 8).

Avicenna's influence carried on continuously in the subsequent Arabic tradition[7] and was a major factor in thirteenth-century theories of the soul in the European West. So, too, was the philosophy of Averroes, whose many commentaries on Aristotle's *On the soul* demonstrate his ongoing efforts to interpret Aristotle's views correctly. His views evolved throughout his lifetime, and with regard to cognition Averroes moved away from an early commitment to an emanationist theory to the view that the Agent Intellect illuminates by means of efficient causation both the potential subject and object of cognition. Averroes' focus was on the role and operation of the material intellect, which is the principle of potential intellection for human beings. The question is: how can this potential for thought become actualized? In his *Middle Commentary on On the Soul*, Averroes thought the material intellect had an incidental connection to a human soul but was effectively "on loan" from the Agent Intellect, which is wholly separate from human beings:

> It has thus been explained that the hylic [i.e., material] intellect is something composed of the disposition found in us and of an intellect conjoined to this disposition. As conjoined to the disposition, it is a disposed intellect, not an intellect in act; though, as not conjoined to this disposition, it is an intellect in act; while, in itself, this intellect is the Agent Intellect, the existence of which will be shown later.
>
> (Averroes 2002, 284)[8]

In his *Longer Commentary on On the Soul*, however, Averroes famously sheds this view, along with the view that each individual human being has his or her own material intellect. If this were the case, then among the many unwanted implications would be that each received intelligible would be unique to its thinker, and consequently there could be no common or shared understanding of what is understood. Instead, there is one material intellect shared by the entire human species:

> For just as light is the actuality of the transparent [medium], so the agent intellect is the actuality of the material [intellect]. Just as the transparent [medium] is not moved by color and does not receive it except when there is light, so too that intellect does not receive the intelligibles which are here except insofar as it is actualized through that [agent] intellect

and illuminated by it. Just as light makes color in potency to be in act in such a way that it can move the transparent [medium], so the agent intellect makes the intentions in potency to be intelligible in act in such a way that the material intellect receives them. This, then, is how the material intellect and the agent [intellect] should be understood.

(Averroes 2009, 3.5, 411)

This theory, which raised a great deal of controversy in the Latin West, became known as the doctrine of the unicity of the intellect (although Averroes' own views were often misunderstood). Among the controversies pursuant to this view were its implications for personal immortality.

There were many other exciting developments in Averroes' thinking about the soul and its operations, including his views on estimation, imagination, memory, and many other topics.[9] We will return to Avicenna and Averroes in section 5.

4 Twelfth century in the Latin West

Most histories of philosophy demarcate the "early medieval period" from "late" or "high medieval period" with the advent of the rise of the universities in the early thirteenth century. This periodization, however, obscures the considerable developments of the twelfth century in the Latin West. Moreover, even those historians who have turned their sights on the twelfth century have overwhelmingly focused on the developments in logic, as well as the influence of logic on theology. There may be an explanation of sorts for this neglect: philosophers in the twelfth century were without the benefit of access to Aristotle's *On the Soul*, and so were left to recover theoretical bits from the writings of the Church Fathers, from Boethius' commentaries on logic, and other resources. The history of philosophical anthropology at this time, however, with its strong inclination toward Platonic philosophy, demands greater attention, given the intense attention given to all sorts of questions about the human soul. The turn to serious investigation of the nature of the soul and its place in the cosmos (and, ultimately, its relationship to God) can perhaps be explained by the cultural and political tumult of the period. According to medieval historian G. Constable (1996, 4), "The eleventh and twelfth centuries, and especially the years between about 1040 and 1160, were a period of intense, rapid, and to a high degree self-conscious change in almost all aspects of human thought and activity." At the same time, stability afforded by growing social cohesion and the communities of monastic scholarship enabled the production of significant pieces of scholarship. The pulse and productivity of this period is made all the more thrilling given what is taking place in the background: the recovery and translation into Latin of the bulk of Aristotle's philosophical corpus, along with the first translations of commentaries and studies by Arabic philosophers.

If anything, the twelfth century is known to non-specialists because of the life and work of Peter Abelard (1079–1142), justly famed as a great logician and made popular because of his scandalous life, as he himself presented it in his autobiographical *History of my calamities*. At this time students were moving *en masse* to Paris, attracted by the presence of paid masters specializing in the study of Aristotelian logic.[10] None of the available philosophical treatises being taught at this time in Paris directly addressed topics in the philosophy of mind; indirectly, however, the philosophy of mind demanded attention, given the nature of the logical topics most hotly debated. For instance, their logic concerned itself with the theory of signification, according to which "to signify" is "to generate an understanding" of something in someone. How spoken words connect with the things about which we speak and how they generate understandings in the mind were topics of serious concern. It is not surprise, then, that such concerns prompted Abelard to investigate the psychology behind the activity of signifying. In a similar way, logic deals with concepts and properties and so equally gives way to a second free-standing interest in the problem of universals: are universals to be found in reality or only in our words and understanding? Again, it is the connection to the role of understanding in explaining one's position on this philosophical question that generated new theories of cognition. But as for other anthropological questions – about the nature of the soul, its connection to the body, and so on – these remained mostly untouched by the logical communities. If anything, a basic commitment to Augustine's substance dualism (in which the body is one substance and the immaterial soul another), which hewed much closer to Plato's conception of the relationship between body and soul than to Aristotle's, along with religious faith seemed to render these questions unimportant to these young philosophers.

Outside the logic classrooms, however, there was intense interest in all sorts of anthropological issues, motivating the production of a number of treatises on the soul. The ancient texts around which many of their discussions were framed paint a clear picture of the importance of Platonism to these thinkers: for example, *The Marriage of Mercury and Philology* by the fourth century Martianus Capella, Boethius' *Consolation of Philosophy*, not to mention all of the available works by Augustine. These authors were self-consciously both Christians and Platonists, and explicit efforts to work out a synthesis between Christian and Platonic doctrines can be found throughout their writings. Three broad traditions of Platonic anthropology (which could equally be called "Platonic cosmology", since human beings were often depicted as microcosms of the universe) will be briefly noted, although these are research areas to which historians of philosophy today have not paid much attention.[11] Nonetheless, to display the breadth of philosophical interest in these issues, they deserve brief mention.

The first, centred around the monastery of St. Victor, developed an Augustinian-inspired substance dualism to account for the nature of human beings. According to Richard of St. Victor (d. 1173) in his treatise *On the Trinity*:

> What is man if not a "rational mortal animal"? This formula carries a primary and a secondary [consignified] meaning. "Animal" means, in effect, substance. Not substance absolutely, but substance blessed with

sensibility. "Man" does not signify sensitive substance absolutely, but sensitive substance blessed with rationality.

(Richard of St. Victor 1958 IV.6)

The second is centred around the city of Chartres[12] and is represented by the figures of William of Conches (*ca.* 1090–*ca.* 1154), Gilbert of Poitiers (*ca.* 1085–1154), and John of Salisbury (*ca.* 1120–1180). A good example of the effort to identify both differences and common ground between Christian Scripture, the Church Fathers, and Platonism can be found in William of Conches' dialogue between a Duke and a Philosopher on the topic of natural philosophy called *Dragmaticon*. In a discussion about the human soul, William investigates the location of the soul in the body:

DUKE: If the soul as a whole is in one's hand, then when one's hand is cut off the soul will be separated from the body.
PHILOSOPHER: If the soul as a whole were in the hand in such a way that it was not as a whole in another organ as well, your objection would hold. Although the hand, therefore, in which the soul resides entirely, is cut off, it remains, however, in the other organs in which it also was entirely before.
DUKE: Whose opinion do you support? That which holds that all souls were created at the same time or that which claims that new souls are created daily?
PHILOSOPHER: I am a Christian, not an Academic [i.e., not a member of Plato's school]. With Augustine, therefore, I believe and hold that new souls are created daily, that they are created not by transmission, not from some other material, but from nothing, by the sole command of the Creator. . . . Many, however, conjecture that the soul is joined on as soon as the body has become ready to receive it, because the Creator *blew the breath of life upon the face of Adam* [Genesis 2.7] after he had formed his body. Plato seems to agree with this opinion when he says, "Therefore, they [that is, the gods] bound the circuits of the soul to the ready material, [namely,] the wet and fluid body. [*Timaeus* 43A, in Calcidius' translation]."

(William of Conches 1997, 170)

The third is centred around the monastic order of the Cistercians and is represented by the figures of William of St. Thierry and Isaac of Stella. According to B. McGinn, their "technical questions of psychology were . . . directly related to a wider anthropological and spiritual program designed to provide a theoretical basis for man's return to God" (McGinn 1977, 20–21). Concerned primarily to systematize the operations of the soul, these thinkers also explored the soul's connections to physiology and medicine. William of St. Thierry (*ca.* 1075–1148) began his work *The Nature of Body and Soul* with facts he had gathered from available literature on subject such as the four bodily humours and the processes of digestion and concludes his treatise on the dynamism of the soul's ascent and descent.

Another point of interest for this albeit brief and patchy history is the all-important set of writings called the *Sentences* of Peter Lombard (*ca.* 1105–*ca.* 1160). This four-volume work contains an organized compendium of themes emerging from biblical texts and quotations from Church Fathers. First assembled by Peter Abelard in his *Yes and No* (*Sic et Non*), these types of compendia were fashionable, and several were produced in the twelfth century. Lombard's *Sentences* gained the strongest foothold, however, and became the authoritative source for theologically motivated questions and topics. Many topics, from angelic cognition to the nature of the Eucharist, elicited philosophical speculation. Every university-educated person would have been familiar with the material, since in the Christian tradition, the *Sentences*, it has been claimed, is second only to the Bible in the numbers of commentaries written on it (Grabmann 1911, 392, repeated in Rosemann 2004, 3).

5 The heyday of thirteenth-century philosophy of mind

The thirteenth century in the European West was vibrant, eclectic, and transformative. Universities in Paris, Bologna, and England had become firmly established by the start of that century, complete with discipline-specific curriculae grounded – not always uncontroversially[13] – in the works of Aristotle, which had only recently become widely available to the Latin-speaking scholars of this period. As was the case for Avicenna and Averroes, the study of the science of the soul was situated in the context of natural philosophy, i.e., physics, as one of its branches. Focus on the soul, considered in Aristotle's sense as the principle of living things, entailed that it encompassed not just human but also animal and plant souls. But the science of the soul was also a subject for metaphysical speculation: questions about its essence, parts, unity, relation to the body, to God, and to eternity were answered in nearly countless commentaries on *On the Soul* and other treatises. What follows will be a mere sketch of some of the highlights, and the reader can be guided by footnote references to more comprehensive studies on this complicated and rich period.

After Aristotle's *On the Soul* was first translated into Latin, it did not enjoy immediate attention. When it was first translated in the mid-twelfth century by James of Venice, philosophically minded theologians were occupied writing their own treatises on the soul envisioning human beings as microcosms of the universe, as we saw earlier. The first person to incorporate some Aristotelian elements into his treatise on the soul was Dominicus Gundissalinus (*ca.* 1115–*ca.* 1190), who was also the first to translate Avicenna's work on the soul from *The Healing*; in fact, much of Gundissalinus' treatise consists of long passages copied from Avicenna's text.[14] Commentaries on Aristotle's *On the Soul* did not begin to appear until nearly one hundred years after James' translation,[15] and by this time in the late mid-thirteenth century, the Avicennian influence had worn off in favour of that of Averroes. This was partly a consequence of the availability of Averroes' *Long Commentary on the De Anima* in Latin translation by the 1220s, as well as an accompanying Latin translation of the Arabic translation of *On the Soul*.[16] It was also a consequence of changing intellectual tastes for topics that were not covered by Avicenna.

In order to appreciate the development of thinking about the soul during this period, it is important to note the double appearance of Aristotle's *On the Soul* on the university curriculum: it was first read and studied by students in the first cycle of a bachelor's degree alongside the study of logical and grammatical works. It was then studied again in a course containing Aristotle's *Physics* and *Metaphysics*:

> the book *On the Soul*, if it is read with the works on natural philosophy [should be read] at the feast of the Ascension Day, but if it is read with the books on logic [it should be read] at the feast of the Annunciation of the holy Virgin.[17]

This double placement is evidence of the dual character of Aristotle's treatise as a work of both epistemology and natural science. In addition, many of the topics covered in Aristotle's *On the Soul* were explored in the context of metaphysics, thereby lending it a tri-disciplinary character. It is epistemic in the sense that thirteenth-century philosophers inquired whether we can know the soul with certainty, and how such knowledge is possible. (It was also epistemic in the sense that the soul was something so obviously felt by every thinker.) It was a subject for natural science since its relation to other parts of the body and their operations were treated as topics of biology and physiology. Additionally, it is treated in metaphysical writings in the sense that they investigated the soul's definition, its nature or essence, its parts, the way in which it hylomorphically exists, the nature of its matter, whether its matter contains any actuality of its own, and so on. Study of the soul was complex and expansive and, following the first lines of Aristotle's treatise, was regarded to be difficult.[18]

Just as Avicenna marked a major turning point in the tradition of Arabic philosophy, so too did Thomas Aquinas for the period considered here. We have already mentioned that, prior to the mid-century, study of the soul was largely Avicennian-inspired. This entailed that the soul was defined, following Avicenna, as the *perfection* of the body. It was also more deeply infused with religious aims, which raised questions about what the proper discipline for a metaphysical study of the soul should be, as this passage from John Blund (*ca.* 1175–1249) demonstrates:

> The theologian has to inquire how the soul may earn merit and demerit and what leads to salvation and what to damnation. But it is not his task to inquire what the soul is, to what category it belongs, and how it is infused into the body. Consequently, knowledge of these things pertains to someone of another faculty [i.e., the Arts Faculty]. Therefore, since the theologian only has to teach how to earn merit and demerit, it is not his proper task to teach what the soul is and what its essence is.
>
> (*Tractatus de anima* 2, 7.14)[19]

Long quotations and paraphrases taken from Avicenna's *On the Soul* all but disappear in the first commentaries on Aristotle's treatise. Averroes' *Long Commentary* became the model for a new approach to Aristotle, which provided not only "a hermeneutical framework, a model of interpretation based on the search for logical consistency between the propositions of a given text using principles of the whole philosophical system of which that text is a part" (Bazán 2005, 596), but also answers to new questions about the unicity of the soul, the plurality of forms, and other metaphysical matters.[20] With regard to the unicity of the soul, Aquinas took the line that every substance can have but one substantial form (see Chapter 9). Consequently, the intellective soul was no longer defined as the perfection of the body but rather as its substantial form.[21] Aquinas' thesis was amplified by the work of the so-called "Radical Aristotelians", such as Siger of Brabant (*ca.* 1240–1284), John of Jandun (*ca.* 1295–1323), and Boethius of Dacia (*fl.* thirteenth century). These philosophers adopted some version of Averroes' thesis of the unicity of the material intellect for the human species.[22] While this may appear to some today to be a reasonable Aristotelian position to take, the thesis generated enormous controversy in its day, and Aquinas was faced with opposition from multiple sides. Franciscans such as John Peckham (*ca.* 1230–1292) even publically argued with Aquinas. The Franciscan preference for the plurality of substantial forms thesis became known as the "*Correctoria*" debates, after the *Correctorium fratris Thomae* written by William de la Mare in about 1277. By this stage, there was already a widespread theological rejection of Aquinas' unicity of form argument, primarily due to its undesirable theological implications for core Christian beliefs about Christ's numerical identity (before and after Christ is in the tomb), the Eucharist, the doctrine of original sin, and others.[23] But the most striking blow against the unicity of substantial form thesis came from Robert Kilwardby (*ca.* 1215–1279),[24] who was responsible for generating a list of 217 condemned theses that could not be taught in the universities. This was the well-known collection of "Condemnations of 1277", although the impact they really had on changing the course of intellectual history is a subject of much debate;[25] certainly the topic of the soul's unicity or plurality continued to be discussed and debated.

While debates about the soul and its parts continued through the end of the thirteenth century and into the start of the fourteenth (which marks the end of the period covered in this volume), the influence of Aristotle's *On the Soul* began to wane to a certain degree. According to Bázan (2005, 596), some arts masters continued to teach and comment on Aristotle's treatise, but

> not without feeling oppressed, though, and censored. . . . And perhaps not without also feeling perplexed, may we add, because if there was so much error in Aristotle's texts, why should they be kept in the curriculum? . . . The focus of their attention shifted, then, from the mere exegesis of Aristotle's texts to the analysis of Averroes' interpretation and its philosophical difficulties.

While the many debates and theories about the soul's unicity or plurality are probably the best known part of the thirteenth century's interest in the science of the soul amongst historians of philosophy, it is by far only a fraction of what held the philosophical and theological interests of the many masters working in Paris and Oxford. Some of the many topics are covered in the following chapters: intellectual cognition (Chapter 2), intellectual abstraction (Chapter 3), the will (Chapters 4 and 5), perceptual experience (Chapter 6), emotions (Chapter 7), the relation between the soul and agent intellect (Chapter 8), the soul and its parts (Chapter 9), immortality (Chapter 10), morality (Chapter 11) and the self (Chapter 12).

Notes

1 On Boethius' writings, see Marenbon and Magee 2009. On the agreement between Plato and Aristotle, see Karamanolis 2006, Chiaradonna 2013, and Griffin 2015.
2 *Periphyseon* 770B. For this position Eriugena was very attractive to later mystical thinkers such as Meister Eckhart (*ca.* 1260–*ca.* 1328), as well as idealists such as Friedrich Hegel (1770–1831), not without having been accused on occasion of being pantheistic (and thus heretical).
3 See Gersh 1978 and Perl 2008; on Pseudo-Dionysius' ongoing influence, Rourke 1992.
4 See especially Marenbon 1981 and Marenbon 1983. Marenbon's history of the period from *ca.* 780 to 1100 remains the single best study, although his focus is mainly (though not exclusively) on the impact of logic on theological developments (see also Marenbon 2008). A study that focuses on the history of philosophical anthropology from this period remains to be written, but see Erismann 2011.
5 Translation from Toivanen 2015, 67, from the Latin translation by Dominicus Gundissalinus and Avendauth. On this experiment see Black 2008, Marmura 1986, and Toivanen 2015.
6 Avicenna's arguments for this position are translated in Khalidi 2005, 48–52.
7 According to Adamson and Taylor 2005, 3–4: "Like Kant in the German tradition or Plato and Aristotle in the Greek tradition, Avicenna significantly influenced everything that came after him in the Arabic tradition." See Janssens 1991, Langermann 2010, and Hasse and Bertolacci 2012 for recent scholarship on Avicenna's legacy.
8 There is considerable secondary literature on Averroes' changing theories of the material intellect. See Ivry 2002, Taylor 2000, Taylor 2009, and Cory 2015.
9 For example, on memory see Black 1996; on imagination see Druart 2007.
10 Some scholars prefer to think of this as a period of the study of Boethian logic, since the study of Aristotle's and Porphyry's ideas was mediated by Boethius' commentaries on their works.
11 This was not the case in the earlier half of the twentieth century when interest in these Neoplatonic thinkers was much greater amongst historians of philosophy.
12 To what extent it is correct to speak of a "School of Chartres" has been a matter of debate: see Jeauneau 2009.
13 See Piché 1999 and the bibliography he provides.
14 See Callus 1939, Dales 1995, and Hasse 2000, 13–18.
15 It is generally thought that the first commentary on Aristotle's *On the Soul* was written by Peter of Spain (a different author than the better-known Peter of Spain who wrote the *Summulae logicales* and later became Pope), but see Wood 2001 for the claim that the Franciscan Richard Rufus (d. *ca.* 1260) was the earliest, since he was "the earliest Western teacher of the new Aristotle we know". A chronological list of thirteenth-century commentaries by known and anonymous authors can be found in Bazán 2005, 626.

16 See Minio-Paluello 1972.
17 Denifle and Châtelain 1889–1897, 1, 124. This is the notice in the 1252 Statutes of the English nation at the University of Paris.
18 Aristotle 402a1–11 first calls the study of the soul "more honourable and precious than any other", and then says that "To attain any knowledge about the soul is one of the most difficult things in the world".
19 Quoted in Hasse 2000, 19.
20 For an excellent overview of the commentary tradition on *De Anima* in the late thirteenth and early fourteenth centuries, see De Boer 2013.
21 Aquinas' views are set out in his *Commentary on Aristotle's* De Anima, *Summa theologiae* I, qq. 75–79 and *De unitate intellectus* and have been widely studied. On Averroes' influence on Aquinas, see Taylor 2013, which also provides a translation of Aquinas' *Commentary on Book II of the* Sentences, *Distinction 17, Question 2, Article 1* containing Aquinas' first encounter with Averroes' thought: "Whether there is one soul or intellect for all human beings".
22 The interpretation of Radical Aristotelianism is still controversial, although recent studies present the position in much less radical terms than in the past, when the position on the soul's unicity as well as on the eternity of the world were thought to be part of a "doctrine of double truth". See Bazán 2005 and the bibliography he provides there.
23 Glorieux 1974.
24 On Kilwardby's science of the soul, see Silva 2012.
25 For a recent study of the condemnations that chronicles the lengthy debates over their correct interpretation and intellectual effects, see Piché 1999. According to Silva 2012, 261–262, the idea that many of these condemnations were directed against Aquinas stems from what he calls a "pro-Thomist historiographical bias". Silva follows Wilshire 1964, who presents Kilwardby as "an old man caught off guard without enough knowledge of the newer philosophical discussions of which Aquinas is the leading figure".

Bibliography

Primary sources

Alcuin (1863). "*De animae ratione*," in (ed.) J. P. Migne, *Patrologia Latina* 101, cols. 639–649.
Anselm (1998). "*On Truth*," trans. R. McInerny, in (eds.) B. Davies and G. R. Evans, *Anselm of Canterbury: The Major Works*, Oxford: Oxford University Press, 151–174.
Averroes (2002). *Averroës Middle Commentary on Aristotle's De Anima*, trans. A. Ivry, Provo, UT: Brigham Young University Press.
Averroes (2009). *Averroes (Ibn Rushd) of Cordoba Long Commentary on the De Anima of Aristotle*, New Haven and London: Yale University Press.
Avicenna (1968–72). *Avicenna Latinus, Liber de anima seu Sextus de naturalibus*, ed. S. van Riet, Louvain/Leiden: Peeters/Brill.
Isaac of Stella (1893). "*Liber spiritu et anima*," in (ed.) J. P. Migne, *Patrologia Latina* 190, cols. 1875–1890.
Isaac of Stella (1977). "The Letter of Isaac of Stella on the Soul," trans. B. McGinn, in (ed.) B. McGinn, *Three Treatises on Man: A Cistercian Anthropology*, Kalamazoo, MI: Cistercian Publications, 153–178.
John Scottus Eriugena (1996–2003). *Periphyseon*, ed. E. Jeauneau, Turnhout: Brepols (Corpus Christianorum 161–165).

Richard of St. Victor (1958). "*De Trinitate*," in (ed.) J. Ribaillier, *Richard de Saint-Victor. De Trinitate. Texte critique avec introduction, notes et tables*, Paris: Vrin.
Thomas Aquinas (1882–). "*Summa theologiae*," in *S. Thomae Aquinatis Doctoris Angelici Opera Omnia*, vols. 4–12, Rome: Commisio Leonina.
Thomas Aquinas (1999). *Thomas Aquinas: A Commentary on Aristotle's De Anima*, trans. R. Pasnau, New Haven and London: Yale University Press.
William of Conches (1997). *A Dialogue on Natural Philosophy (Dragmaticon Philosophiae)*, trans. I. Ronca and M. Curr, Notre Dame, IN: University of Notre Dame Press.
William of St. Thierry (1977). "The Nature of Body and Soul (trans. B. Clark)," in (ed.) B. McGinn, *Three Treatises on Man: A Cistercian Anthropology*, Kalamazoo, MI: Cistercian Publications, 101–152.
William of St. Thierry (1988). *De Natura Corporis et Animae*, ed. and trans. M. Lemoine, Paris: Les Belles Lettres.

Secondary sources

Adamson, P. and R. Taylor (2005) *The Cambridge Companion to Arabic Philosophy*, Cambridge: Cambridge University Press.
Bazán, C. (2005). "Radical Aristotelianism in the Faculty of Arts: The Case of Siger of Brabant," in (ed.) L. Honnefelder, *Albert Magnus and the Beginnings of the Medieval Reception of Aristotle in the Latin West: From Richard Rufus to Franciscus de Mayronis*, Münster: Aschendorff Verlag, 585–629.
Black, D. (1996). "Memory, Individuals and the Past in Averroes' Psychology," *Medieval Philosophy and Theology* 5, 161–187.
Black, D. (2008). "Avicenna on Self-Awareness and Knowing that One Knows," in (eds.) S. Rahman, T. Street, and H. Tahiri, *The Unity of Science in the Arabic Tradition*, Dordrecht: Springer, 63–87.
Callus, D. (1939). "Gundalissinus' *De Anima* and the Problem of Substantial Form," *New Scholasticism* 13, 338–355.
Chiaradonna, R. (2013). "Platonist Approaches to Aristotle: From Antiochus of Ascalon to Eudorus of Alexandria (and Beyond)," in (ed.) M. Schofield, *Aristotle, Plato, and Pythagoreanism in the First Century BC*, Cambridge: Cambridge University Press, 28–52.
Constable, G. (1997). *The Reformation of the Twelfth Century*, Cambridge: Cambridge University Press.
Cory, T. S. (2015). "Averroes and Aquinas on the Agent Intellect's Causation of Intelligibles," *Recherches de Théologie et Philosophie mediévales* 82, 1–60.
Dales, R. C. (1995). *The Problem of the Rational Soul in the Thirteenth Century*, Leiden: Brill.
De Boer, S. (2013). *The Science of the Soul: The Commentary Tradition on Aristotle's De Anima, c. 1260–c. 1360*, Leuven: Leuven University Press.
Denifle, H. and Châtelain, A. (eds.) (1889–1897). *Chartularium Universitatis Parisiensis*, Paris: Delelain.
Druart, T.-A. (ed.) (2007). "Imagination and Intellect in Avicenna and Averroes," *Bulletin de Philosophie Médiévale* 49.
Erismann, C. (2011). *L'Homme Commun: la genèse du réalisme ontologique durant le haut Moyen Age*, Paris: Vrin.

Gersh, S. (1978). *From Iamblichus to Eriugena: An Investigation of the Prehistory and Evolution of the Pseudo-Dionysian Tradition*, Leiden: Brill.

Glorieux, P. (1974). "Pro et contra Thomam. Un survol de cinquante années," in (ed.) T. W. Köhler, *Sapientiae procerum amore*, Rome: Editrice Anselmiana, 255–287.

Grabmann, M. (1911). *Die Geschichte der scholastischen Methode, vol. 2, Die scholastische Methode im 12. und beginnenden 13. Jahrhundert*, Germany: Herder; reprint (1988) Berlin: Akademie-Verlag.

Griffin, M. (2015). *Aristotle's Categories in the Early Roman Empire*, Oxford: Oxford University Press.

Gutas, D. (1998). *Greek Thought, Arabic Culture: The Graeco-Arabic Translation Movement in Baghdad and Early 'abbasid Society (2nd–4th/8th–10th Centuries)*, London and New York: Routledge.

Gutas, D. (2010). "Origins in Baghdad," in (ed.) R. Pasnau, (assoc. ed.) C. Van Dyke, *The Cambridge History of Medieval Philosophy*, vol. 1, Cambridge: Cambridge University Press, 11–25.

Harvey, S. (2006). "The Place of the *De Anima* in the Orderly Study of Philosophy," in (eds.) M. Pacheco and J. Meirinhos, *Intellect et imagination dans la philosophie médiévale*, Turnhout: Brepols, 677–688.

Hasse, D. N. (2000). *Avicenna's De Anima in the Latin West: The Formation of a Peripatetic Philosophy of the Soul 1160–1300*, London: The Warburg Institute.

Hasse, D. N. and A. Bertolacci (2012). *The Arabic, Hebrew and Latin Reception of Avicenna's Metaphysics*, Berlin-Boston: De Gruyter.

Hissette, R. (1997). "L'Implication de Thomas d'Aquin dans les censures Parisiennes de 1277," *Recherches de Théologie et Philosophie médiévales* 64/1, 3–31.

Ivry, A. (2002). "Introduction," in *Averroës Middle Commentary on Aristotle's De Anima*, Provo, UT: Brigham Young University Press, xiii–xxix.

Janssens, J. (1991). *An Annotated Bibliography on Ibn Sînâ (1970–1989)*, Leuven: Leuven University Press.

Jeauneau, E. (2009). *Rethinking the School of Chartres*, trans. C. P. Desmarais, Toronto: University of Toronto Press.

Karamanolis, G. E. (2006). *Plato and Aristotle in Agreement?: Platonists on Aristotle From Antiochus to Porphyry*, Oxford: Clarendon Press.

Khalidi, M. A. (2005). *Medieval Islamic Philosophical Writings*, Cambridge: Cambridge University Press.

King, P. (2007). "Why Isn't the Mind-Body Problem Medieval?," in (ed.) H. Lagerlund, *Forming the Mind*, Verlag: Springer, 187–205.

Lagerlund, H. (2007). "Introduction: The Mind/Body Problem and Late Medieval Conceptions of the Soul," in (ed.) H. Lagerlund, *Forming the Mind*, Verlag: Springer, 1–15.

Langermann, Y. T. (ed.) (2009). *Avicenna and His Legacy: A Golden Age of Science and Philosophy*, Turnhout: Brepols.

Marenbon, J. (1981). *From the Circle of Alcuin to the School of Auxerre*, Cambridge: Cambridge University Press.

Marenbon, J. (1983). *Early Medieval Philosophy (480–1150)*, London and New York, Routledge.

Marenbon, J. (2008). "The Latin Tradition of Logic to 1100," in (ed.) D. M. Gabbay and J. Woods, *Handbook to the History of Logic*, vol. II, Amsterdam: North-Holland, 1–63, 65–81.

Marenbon, J. and Magee, J. (2009). "Appendix: Boethius' Works," in (ed.) J. Marenbon, *The Cambridge Companion to Boethius*, Cambridge: Cambridge University Press.

Marmura, M. (1986). "Avicenna's 'Flying Man' in Context," *Monist* 69, 383–395.

McGinn, B. (1977). *Three Treatises on Man: A Cistercian Anthropology*, Kalamazoo, MI: Cistercian Publications.

Minio-Paluello, L. (1972). "Le Texte du '*De anima*' d'Aristote: la traduction latine avant 1500," in *Opuscula: The Latin Aristotle*, Amsterdam: Hakkert.

Pasnau, R. (2007). "The Mind-Soul Problem," in (eds.) P. J. J. M. Bakker and J. M. M. H. Thijssen, *Mind, Cognition and Representation: The Tradition of Commentary on Aristotle's De Anima*, Burlington, VT: Ashgate, 3–20.

Perl, E. (2008). *Theophany: the Neoplatonic Philosophy of Dionysius the Areopagite*, Albany: SUNY Press.

Piché, D. (1999). *La Condamnation Parisienne de 1277*, Paris: Vrin.

Rosemann, P. W. (2004). *Peter Lombard (Great Medieval Thinkers Series)*, Oxford: Oxford University Press.

Silva, J. F. (2012). *Robert Kilwardby on the Human Soul: Plurality of Forms and Censorship in the Thirteenth Century*, Leiden: Brill.

Taylor, R. (2000). "*Cogitatio, Cogitativus* and *Cogitare*: Remarks on the Cogitative Power in Averroes," in (eds.) J. Hammesse and C. Steel, *L'élaboration du vocabulaire philosophique au Moyen Age*, Louvain-la-Neuve: Brepols, 111–146.

Taylor, R. (2009). "Introduction," in Avicenna (2009), xv–cix.

Taylor, R. (2013). "Aquinas and 'the Arabs': Aquinas' First Critical Encounter With the Doctrines of Avicenna and Averroes on the Intellect, *In 2 Sent*. D. 17, Q. 2, A.1," in (eds.) L. X. López-Farjeat and J. A. Tellkamp, *Philosophical Psychology in Arabic Thought and the Latin Aristotelianism of the 13th Century*, Paris: Vrin, 141–184.

Toivanen, J. (2015). "The Fate of the Flying Man: Medieval Reception of Avicenna's Thought Experiment," *Oxford Studies in Medieval Philosophy* 3, 64–98.

Wilshire, L. E. (1964). "Were the Oxford Condemnations of 1277 Directed Against Aquinas?," *The New Scholasticism* 48, 125–132.

Wood, R. (2001). "Richard Rufus' *De anima* Commentary: The Earliest Known, Surviving, Western *De anima* Commentary," *Medieval Philosophy and Theology* 10, 119–156.

1

PETER ABELARD ON MENTAL PERCEPTION

Margaret Cameron

1 Introduction

Peter Abelard (1079–1142) follows Aristotle's view that all understandings are in the first place generated on the basis of sense experience. But he also recognizes that we seem to be able to generate understandings of many things of which we have had no previous or current sense experience whatsoever; indeed, for some things sense experience would be altogether impossible. For example, we have thoughts about fictional characters such as chimeras and centaurs. Understandings about the past and future and about incorporeals such as the soul and God present similar problems. Moreover, as an anti-realist about the ontological status of universals, Abelard noted that nonetheless we seem to be able to make true statements using generic and specific words. How is this possible if we do not sense universals (because they do not exist) and thus lack the corresponding understandings?[1] What, if anything, do we understand in these cases?

In response to this question, Abelard advanced an innovative, proto-phenomenological theory of mind. According to this theory, in addition to the physical capacity to see individual corporeal objects using our sense organs, the mind possesses its own ability to see with the mind's eye. According to Abelard, human understanding, which is the highest cognitive power (beyond reason, memory, imagination and sense experience), is able to attend to mental objects and consider them otherwise than as they appear to us in reality. There are constraints: an object cannot be attended by the mind in any which way whatsoever, as we will see. Once the mind attends something otherwise than as it exists in reality ("seeing as" as an act of mental attention), then reason is able to form a judgement about whether or not what is understood is true. This ingenious twelfth-century theory shares much in common with the phenomenological theories advanced in the nineteenth and twentieth centuries by Brentano and Husserl. Brentano was self-conscious about his theory of intentionality's medieval origins; the theory's core feature was named after the later scholastic term for thought, "*intentio*".[2] But that heritage is wholly distinct from Abelard's theory, which apparently did not gain traction for a number of contingent historical reasons. My primary interest in this chapter is to identify the ancient sources that inspired Abelard's own theory, and more narrowly to investigate the language of mental perception that lies at its foundation. Abelard turned to three well-known ancient writings available to him in the early twelfth century: Boethius' *Commentary on Porphyry's Isagoge* and his *Consolation of Philosophy*, as well as Augustine's *On the Trinity*. King (1982) first emphasized the importance of acts of attention in Abelard's philosophy. The explicit link with Augustine's theory was elaborated by Rosier-Catach (2004). Their interpretations of Abelard on attention differ considerably from one another, and my own differs from both of theirs. Without access to Aristotle's *De Anima*, which was first translated into Latin in the late twelfth century (and even then it took a number of years before it began to be seriously studied), Abelard is left to come up with a theory of mind, ultimately rooted in sense experience, that can account for our true understanding of things that have no correlates or *denotata* in the reality that we presently sense.

2   Boethius on understanding universals

In his presentation of the problem of universals at the start of his commentary on Porphyry's *Isagoge*, Boethius (*ca.* 475–*ca.* 526)[3] encountered a particularly difficult philosophical problem, one that became very well known to his medieval readers, including (among others) Peter Abelard. After setting out Porphyry's famously unanswered questions about the status of universals, that is, of genera and species, Boethius articulates the particular dilemma he faces:

For everything the mind understands, it

- *either* intellectually conceives what exists constituted in the nature of things, and it describes it to itself by reason,
- *or* the mind paints for itself by empty imagination what does not exist.

(Spade 1994, 20)[4]

The problem so articulated is epistemological. If universals are constituted in the nature of things, then we can intellectually conceive them as they are. But if universals are not constituted in the nature of things, which Boethius in fact argues is the case, then what, if anything, is understood with regard to universals? This dilemma crescendos to the following question: "Therefore, the question is, to which kind does the understanding of genus and the other predictables belong?" (160, 6–7). Boethius' answer provides a glimmer of a theory which is then richly developed by Abelard to explain how we can have true understandings of things that present themselves otherwise than as we grasp them by sense experience.

Boethius tries to respond to the questions left wholly unanswered by Porphyry at the very start of his *Isagoge*, namely, whether universals exist or not, whether they are corporeal or incorporeal and, if incorporeal, whether they subsist in connection with bodies or not. "As for genera and species," Porphyry says,

> I shall decline for the present to say (a) whether they subsist or are posited in bare understandings only, (b) whether, if they subsist, they are corporeal or incorporeal, and (c) whether they are separated from sensibles or posited in sensibles and agree with them. For that is a most exalted matter, and requires a longer investigation.
> (Quoted in Spade 1994, 20)[5]

Drawing from what is said in Aristotle's *Categories*, Boethius assumes that for a universal to be common to several things, it must be common in its entirety, at one and the same time, and as the very substance (or, as Spade 1996, 3 put it, "metaphysically constitutive") of the particulars it is in. There have been many analyses of Boethius' answers to these questions, and most scholars agree there are two, if not three, distinct arguments that result in the conclusion that universals do not actually exist in the world.[6] For this reason, Boethius has been characterized as an anti-realist about the ontological status of universals.[7] But this just dissolves the first horn of the dilemma, since universals turn out not to exist as constituted in the nature of things. If genera and species do not exist in reality, then (following the dilemma mentioned earlier) does the mind "paint for itself by empty imagination what does not exist"?

Boethius repeats the dilemma in a different formulation:

> Do we understand species and genera as we do things that exist, from which we take true understanding? Or do we *delude ourselves* when we form for ourselves, *by the vain thought of the mind*, things that do not exist?
> (Spade 1994, 20-21, my emphasis in italics)

Having argued that universals do not exist, then what is happening with our understanding of them? Are we deluded? Are they merely empty or vain thoughts, and so no thoughts at all? Boethius recognizes that thoughts, or understandings (*intellectus*), are generated either by the way something is or by the way it is not (*cum omnis aut ex re fiat subiecta ut sese res habet, aut ut sese res non habet*), to which he adds, "for no understanding can arise from no subject (*nam nullo subiecto fieri intellectus non potest*)." Moreover, according to Boethius, "what is understood otherwise than the thing is is false (*id est enim falsum quod aliter atque res est intellegitur*)" (163, 6–10). How, then, can we have veridical, sound understandings of what we do not have sensory experience of in reality? This is the central question.

Since Boethius has argued that universals do not exist, then it seems to follow that we would have but an empty understanding of them; worse, because it is empty it is entirely false. In what follows in his commentary, Boethius mounts a case for the claim that, while genera and species do not exist in reality, nevertheless our understandings of them are neither empty nor false. To do so, Boethius needs to convince us that we can have true understandings of things otherwise than they are in reality, or otherwise than as we perceive them by sense experience.

In his *Commentary on Isagoge*, Boethius' language is rich with perceptual imagery; there is no doubt that this imagery had a strong influence on Abelard. Despite the imagery, however, Boethius fell short of advancing either a clear argument or a theory of any kind to account for the phenomenon. He simply indicates, using analogies and examples, what seems to be happening in the mind to give rise to a true understanding of universals imperceptible to the senses.[8]

For Boethius, as for Abelard, as we shall see, nature constrains what can and cannot be soundly understood: "If one puts together by the understanding what nature does not allow to be joined, no one fails to recognize that that is false. For example, if someone joins a horse and a man in imagination, and portrays a centaur" (Spade 1994, 23). There is thus something detectable *in nature* – but not detectable by sense experience. It is detectable by means of the mental operation of abstraction which, according to Boethius, can produce understandings that are true and sound. He provides as an example of this process the abstraction of a line from a body: the line cannot exist without the body, yet the mind can abstract it as if it could.

Our focus is narrowly on the way Boethius describes this process of abstraction using the language of mental perception. According to his description, what the senses contribute to understanding is "confused and mixed up" (Spade 1994, 24) but the mind "gazes on and sees the incorporeal nature by itself":

> In this way, when the mind takes on these things all mixed up with bodies, it divides out the incorporeals and gazes (*speculatur*) on them and considers them.
>
> (Spade 1994, 24)

The perceptual verb at work here is *speculari*, meaning "to spy out, watch, observe, examine".[9] But what, exactly, does the mind "see" when it identifies the incorporeal, i.e., the genus, in the corporeal that is sensed? Boethius illustrates his point with an example:

> For example, from single men, dissimilar among themselves, the likeness (*similitudo*) of humanity is gathered. This likeness, thought by the mind and gazed at truly, is the species.
>
> (Spade 1994, 24)

As stated earlier, Boethius' explanation does not rise to the level of being a theory of mental perception, although clearly and consistently Boethius describes the operation of the mind in terms of perceptual language. The mind has its own view:

21

it can see likeness (*similitudo*) among things that present as unlike to visual perception and the other physical senses. This likeness is not produced by the mind. Rather, the mind's gaze is uniquely able to identify likenesses. Mental perception of things' likeness provides the understanding of the universal, otherwise invisible. On this thin metaphor, Abelard begins to build his theory. In the end, however, Boethius is content to rest with the view that we can sometimes generate truths on the basis of a reality that is perceived and experienced otherwise than it is, admitting, "For not every understanding is to be regarded as false that is grasped from subject things otherwise than as they themselves are disposed" (Spade 1994, 24).

3 Cognitive hierarchy in Boethius' *Consolation of Philosophy*

Boethius' *Consolation of Philosophy*, written when the fifth-century author was in prison awaiting his execution, had a surprising and significant impact on Abelard's thought. There are two important points of influence: first, Boethius' description of the differences between the senses, imagination, reason and understanding, outlined in Book V; and second, the introduction of the two cognitive activities of attending and judging. Abelard uses and transforms Boethius' ideas in the following way: he appropriates from Boethius some of the activities of the understanding, which Boethius had ascribed only to God, and assigns them to human understanding.

In *The Consolation*, Boethius (the author) depicts himself as Boethius (the prisoner), who awakes in his prison cell in psychological misery, lamenting his condition and suffering. Appearing before him is Lady Philosophy, a personification of philosophical wisdom in the figure of a woman, and she becomes Boethius' philosophical interlocutor throughout.[10] In Book V, Boethius wrestles with a serious dilemma: God's perfection entails that he is omniscient, and accordingly knows all things past, present and future. But if God knows everything that will happen, in what way can there be human freedom? The problem comes down to this: is God's foreknowledge the cause of the necessity of future things, including everything that humans do and think, or is the necessity of future things the cause of God's foreknowledge? The latter question is dismissed summarily, since it cannot be the case, as Boethius and Lady Philosophy agree, that "the outcome of temporal events is the cause of divine knowledge", an alternative Boethius characterizes as "utterly backwards" (Vp3, 15–16).[11]

To answer this question, Lady Philosophy contends that while there is divine foreknowledge (to hold otherwise would have been simply impious), "it binds no necessity on events" (Vp4, 9). This is true both for things that are currently happening as well as for things that will happen (Vp4, 20). What is the justification for this claim? According to Lady Philosophy, what is known is not known in accordance with the nature of *what is known*, but rather in accordance with the nature of *the knower*. This is known as the "Iamblichean principle". According to Boethius, "Everything that is perceived is grasped not according to its own force but rather according to the capability of those who perceive it" (Vp4, 24). What follows in *The Consolation* is an explanation for this claim, and it is the part that is most relevant for appreciating how Abelard used this work as one of his sources for his own doctrine.

Boethius arranges the types of cognitive activity involved in human understanding hierarchically: beginning with sense, we move to imagination, to reason and, finally, to understanding – the only stage, as we will see, at which human cognition can engage in the activities of attending and judging what things truly are. Here is Boethius on the cognitive hierarchy:

> [S]ense perception, imagination, reason, and understanding, each in its distinct way, view (for example) the same human being. For sense perception judges the shape as it has been constituted in its subject material, while imagination judges the shape alone, without its material.
> (Vp4, 27–28)

It turns out that Abelard doubly disagrees with Boethius on this point. First, here Boethius says that both sense and imagination engage in judgment (*iudicare*). On this point Abelard disagrees: only reason is capable of acts of judgment. Second, for Abelard the only contribution made by imagination to human cognition is the storage of sense perceptions. On this front, rather, he follows Augustine who, among others, describes the imagination as a storehouse – a common trope among ancient authors. But for Boethius, the elements retain their hierarchical arrangement, with reason and understanding following next:

> [R]eason transcends this (i.e., the imagination) as well and from its universal point of view weighs in the balance that very appearance that is present in all individuals. And the eye of understanding exists as something higher yet; for it has passed beyond what is encompassed by universality and views the one simple form itself in the pure vision of the mind (*pura mentis acie*).
> (Vp4, 29–30)

"The eye of understanding": this is the introduction in Boethius' text of the idea of a mind's eye, something Abelard will find again in Augustine. Now, to be clear, Abelard would part company with Boethius on the heavily Platonizing language used here (e.g., "the one simple form itself"), since Abelard did not believe that universals – that is, forms[12] – exist in a pure manner, separated from material composition. To be sure, no philosopher engaged in Abelard's intellectual circles espoused such a radical realist position on universals. But, putting the metaphysics aside, what Abelard is interested in is Boethius' description of the cognitive process in humans.

The following passage, in which Boethius distinguishes the highest cognitive power, namely understanding, from the others, seems to have had the greatest influence on Abelard's own theory of cognition. First, the limitations of the other cognitive powers are listed:

> [T]he higher power of comprehension embraces the lower, but in no way does the lower rise to the level of the higher. For sense perception has no power beyond what is material; imagination does not view universal appearances; reason does not grasp the simple form.
>
> (Vp4, 31–32)

However, reason is the highest cognitive power available to human beings, according to Boethius. Only God is capable of understanding: this is the highest cognitive power, which embraces not only its own objects (the pure forms) but also everything else graspable by the other, lower cognitive activities (Vp5, 4). The uniqueness of understanding, given its special activities, is brought out this way:

> Understanding, however, looking down as it were from on high (*quasi desuper spectans*), grasps the form and then judges separately the things that are beneath it, all of them; but it does so in the way in which it comprehends the form itself, which could not be known to any of the other powers.
>
> (Vp4, 32)

What seems to have attracted Abelard's interest are the two activities of understanding identified by Boethius as its distinguishing acts: the act of seeing or grasping with the mind's eye (*spectans*) and the subsequent act of judging (*diiudicat*) of the form that is grasped. As we will see, these become Abelard's two acts of human reason: attending (*attendere*) and then judging (*deliberare*). It is interesting that these two activities of attending and judging pure form, which are attributed uniquely to God by Boethius, are drawn into the sphere of human cognition by Abelard. Moreover, as we will see, given the ability of an act of attention of otherwise grasping things than as they exist, human understanding turns out to be capable, on Abelard's own account, of grasping pure form, i.e., of cognitively attending something as if it were without matter.

4 Augustine on "seeing as"

Let us now turn to Augustine's influence on Abelard's theory. Augustine's influence on Abelard is unmistakable, but it has been, I argue, overemphasized at the expense of showcasing Abelard's ingenuity: Augustine serves as inspiration, but the theory is richly developed by Abelard. Augustine's *On the Trinity* is a rich philosophical reflection on the nature of the Christian trinity – God the Father, Christ the Son, and the Holy Spirit. This work had a profound impact on Abelard, and Augustine's references to mental intentions were of great importance to the development of Abelard's ideas. While explicitly a theological work of reflection on the Trinity, the theme of explaining how something multiple can be unified was also philosophically very attractive to Abelard (as well as to others). For the Trinity, according to Augustine, is one God ("*Trinitas quae est deus*"), and the triune God (God, Christ, Holy Spirit) is somehow replicated in human beings because humans are made in God's image. Throughout, Augustine utilizes the Neoplatonic language of ascent, borrowed from Plotinus,[13] and in Books VIII through XI, Augustine analogically explicates the Trinity by means of a study of the triadic structure of the human mind. These triads vary somewhat (sometimes it is a triad of memory, intelligence and will, sometimes of objects sensed, perception and attention or will), but the theme is consistent. The activities of human understanding analogically track by endlessly replicating in their actions the structure of the Holy Trinity.[14] Abelard draws on Augustine's *On the Trinity* while developing his own theory of human understanding, as scholars have noticed. But at the same time, Abelard does not wholly agree with Augustine's views, and he modifies them in fundamental ways.

Book XI opens with a distinction between what Augustine calls the "inner man" and the "outer man": humans' interiority is their being endowed with understanding, and their exteriority being endowed with bodily sense (*sensus corporis*). Augustine's guiding question is this:

> Let us endeavour, therefore, to discover, if we can, any trace at all of the Trinity even in this outer man, not that he himself is also in the same way the image of God.
>
> (XI.1.1)[15]

The broad distinction at work is between the realm of the visible, which is perceptible to the senses (Augustine employs vision as the paradigm sense), and the realm of the intelligible, accessible only by the mind.

Augustine repeatedly underscores both the weakness and the familiarity of sense experience. In fact, he remarks that when the rational soul tries to fix its attention on intellectual objects of understanding, there is a tendency to revert to the familiarity of sense experience:

> Yet, as I have said, our familiarity with bodies has become so great, and our thought <*intentio*, i.e. attention>[16] has projected itself outwardly with so wonderful a proclivity towards these bodies, that when it has been withdrawn from the uncertain realm of bodies and fixes its attention on the much more certain and more stable knowledge of the spirit, it again takes refuge in these bodies and seeks rest there from the place where it drew its weakness.
>
> (XI.1.1)

Abelard borrows not only this very same point about the effects on our understanding that arise from the frequency and familiarity of our sense experiences but also Augustine's language of mental intentionality.

Augustine uses the language of vision, here a vision of the mind rather than of the eyes, to explain the role and activity of attention. In acts of attention, the understanding "fixes its gaze" (X.2.3) and perceives with "the eye of the mind" (XI.3.6). Intending is glossed by Augustine as "the will" (*voluntas*) – a clear indication that it is enacted purposively – and identifies it as "proper to the rational soul alone" (XI.2.5).

The primary activity of mental intention for Augustine – primary, that is, in the order of human experience – is to bring together the objects of perception (or any sense experience) with the activity of perceiving, i.e., with vision (or touch, smell, taste, sound). As we will see, in this regard Augustine's theory is different from Abelard's. To explain, Augustine distinguishes between:

(1) the object which we see, whether a stone, or a flame, or anything else that can be seen by the eyes, and this could, of course, exist even before it was seen;
(2) the vision, which was not there before we perceived the object that was presented to the sense;
(3) the power that fixes the sense of sight on the object that is seen as long as it is seen, namely, the intention (*intentio*) of the mind.

(XI.2.2)

An act of intention/attention has the job of uniting the extramental object with vision itself. It brings together two corporeal things – the object and the instrumental corporeal sense – with the result that a unity is made of the three. Specifically, it unifies:

(i) the *form* of the body that is seen;
(ii) its image impressed on the senses, which is vision, or *the sense informed*;
(iii) the will of the soul which directs the sense to the sensible thing and keeps the vision itself fixed on it.

(XI.2.5)

The intentional act is required because the senses, as purely passive instruments whose activity must be directed by the rational soul, cannot on their own, in the presence of an object that is to be sensed, be engaged (XI.2.3). (As they are theorized by Abelard, however, as we will see, acts of attention are *not* required in order to direct the body's instruments, i.e., its eyes, its ears and so on. At the same time, however, Abelard does agree completely with Augustine's point that it is *by means of* the soul's instruments that the rational soul can be said to see or to hear.)

But for Augustine, intentional acts do more than simply direct the focus of the senses. In the absence of sense objects of direct experience, acts of intention depend on what is for Augustine a very important human capacity: the ability to remember. In fact, intention *requires* memory for any understanding that is not prompted by present sense objects:

> But the place of that bodily form, which was perceived from without, is taken by the memory, retaining the form which the soul absorbs into itself through the bodily sense; and the vision that was without, when the sense was formed by a sensible body, is succeeded by a similar vision within, when the eye of the mind is formed from that which the memory retains and absent bodies are conceived; and the will itself, as it moved the sense to be formed to the body that was presented to it from without, and combined both of them when it had been formed, so in the act of remembering it causes the eye of the mind to turn back to the memory, in order that it may be formed by that which the memory retains, and that there may be a similar vision in thought.
>
> (XI.3.6)

Augustine repeats the point that the vividness of sense experiences, even as they are stored in memory, makes it such that intentional acts are often utterly indistinguishable from those sense experiences (XI.4.7).[17] Abelard borrows this very point.

What impresses Abelard most of all about Augustine's ideas about intentionality are what we can call the "as if" power of the rational soul to understand by means of an act of attending something otherwise than as it is in reality. According to Augustine:

> But the mind possesses the great power of forming images, not only of things that it has forgotten, but also of those that it has not felt or experienced, while enlarging, diminishing, changing, or arranging at its pleasure those things which have not slipped away, it often fancies that something is so and so, when it knows either that it is not so, or does not know that it is so.
>
> (XI.5.8)

Augustine mentions but does not dwell on the peculiar danger that this mental activity presents, namely, to be deceived by it and thereby to have understandings that are neither true nor sound. He advises only that we ought to try to guard against being so misled.

To the extent that he does, how does Augustine account for the truth and soundness of understandings derived from attending to the contents of memory? First, as Abelard will also emphasize, all understanding is ultimately rooted in sense experience. Unless we have perceived, we do not have memory (XI.7.11). The point is strongly emphasized:

> For it is impossible to form any concept at all of a colour or of a bodily figure that one has never seen, or of a sound that one has never heard, or

of a flavour that one has never tasted, or of an odour that one has never smelled, or of any touch of a corporeal object that one has never felt.

(XI.8.14)

It is one thing to remember what has previously been sensed, but it is something very different to have an understanding based on an intention that understands something remembered otherwise than it is or was. Augustine's examples include (XI.8.13):

Object sensed	Understanding produced by act of intention
one sun	two or three suns
one sun with specific size and dimension	one sun larger or smaller than the actual sun
one sun running its course	one sun standing still
yellow sun	green sun

However, these understandings produced by intentional acts that depict extramental reality in ways that it is not – e.g., my understanding produced by an act of intention on the basis of having had the sense experience of the regular, yellow sun as green – are simply false, according to Augustine. He explains:

> Since, however, these forms of things are corporeal and apparent to the senses, the mind is certainly in error when it imagines them as being without in the same way as they are conceived within, either when they have already perished without and are still retained in the memory, or when in any other way also, that which we remember is formed, not by the reliability of our memory, but by the changeableness of our thought.
>
> (XI8.13)

These acts of mental intention are not memories: they are imaginative constructs (XI.10.17).

At the end of this book *On the Trinity*, Augustine makes a brief point that was surely influential on Abelard's own thought. By means of an intentional act, Augustine notes, we are able to have some understanding that goes beyond what memory is able to afford, namely, of infinitely large bodies, infinitely divisible bodies, and indeed of infinity itself (XI.10.17). None of these acts are easy to achieve. Abelard follows Augustine's point that acts of intention/attention require effort or exertion (*nisus*) (XI.10.17).

As we will see, Abelard adopts but also adapts Augustine's ideas on intentionality in crucial ways. Firstly, for him intentionality is not required to explain how the senses track their extramental objects. Second, Abelard extends the theory to a very wide range of phenomena that can be understood, including universals, non-existent and no longer existent objects and fictional objects such as chimeras and sirens, as well as immaterial substances such as God and the soul. Finally, and what is most philosophically interesting, Abelard explains not how these acts of intention/attention produce understandings that are not, as Augustine said, certainly erroneous, but can distinguish what is sound and true from what is not.

5 Abelard on mental perception as attention

Let us now turn to Abelard's own theory of mental perception, which for him is a theory of mental attention – seeing, as it were, with the mind's eye. I have suggested that Abelard's theory was motivated, at least in part, by Boethius' question about how we can have understandings that are true of things otherwise than as they exist in reality. In the end, as we have seen, Boethius falls short of providing a robust answer but seems to concede that this is just the way it is in the relationship between understanding and reality. Not so for Abelard. Abelard distinguished two operations of the mind – an act of attention and an act of judgement – to arrive at a truly novel response to Boethius' question.[18]

The activities of attending and judging are intimately related to one another. In short, the mind's eye attends to some nature or property of a thing, which is then held in attention awaiting an act of judgement whereby something is judged to be either true or false, sound or empty. Abelard uses "*attentio*" to signify mental focus, according to which one is able to focus on some aspects of some thing, whether present or absent to the senses, in specific ways. Acts of attention always take as their cognitive objects some nature or property of the thing cognized.

"*Attentio*" is a version of Augustine's "*intentio*" (for whom the intention of the will (*intentio voluntas*) is what joins the form of the corporeal body, which is perceived by the senses, to the image formed in the vision of the perceiver). By drawing "*deliberatio*" and "*attentio*" together, Abelard also means by "*deliberatio*" something like "bringing into mental focus". "To deliberate" carries the connotation in English of a cognitive act in which one takes time, considering its object of thought carefully. The same connotation is meant by Abelard. It also suggests that it is an activity done with intention or will: the deliberator moves objects of thought into focus.[19]

But in fact to deliberate is, for Abelard, more than merely attending some property or nature of something in the sense of having it as a mere object of mental focus. In fact, typically in the *Treatise on Understandings* Abelard modifies "*deliberare*" with adverbs such as "truly", "falsely", or "soundly": what occurs in an act of deliberation is a judgement. Hence, I have chosen to translate "*deliberatio*" as judgement.

The act of attending and then judging the nature or property of some thing is a fundamental component of Abelard's theory of understanding: it explains how we are able to otherwise understand things than as they are in reality, and yet nonetheless distinguish between understandings that are sound and not empty, true and not false.

We cannot run through all the examples of things otherwise understood than as they are listed at the start of this chapter. But let us focus on one example as illustration. Take the phrase, "A chimera is something." This seems to generate an understanding, but since chimeras do not exist it is in fact an empty phrase. Abelard explains this in the *Treatise* in terms of the cognitive act of attention failing to be engaged and, thus, there being nothing about which a judgement can be made:

> For because this understanding of CHIMERA in reality lacks an underlying subject – something which, according to this type of understanding, could be soundly judged such that it would permit this thing to be truly attended *as* a chimera – the understanding is empty.
>
> (II.4, M¶59)[20]

To attend something is to focus one's mental gaze on some nature or property of a thing. Acts of attention are necessarily selective: they attend just one or two of many – indeed very many – properties and characteristics of a thing, and this mental focus is made difficult by myriad presentations of that thing by means of the senses and recorded in imagination (I.4, M¶19). Once something is attended in accordance with one of its properties (e.g., in that it is a substance or in that it has this or that certain quality, etc.), then an act of judgement can ascertain whether or not what is attended is sound, i.e., whether it attends something as it is in reality or not. In the case of the chimera, the understanding of the chimera *as* existent (e.g., "A chimera is something") is judged to be empty. As empty, statements about existing chimeras turn out to be false. (Other types of statements about fictional entities, however, are to be taken as figurative speech as long as they make no reference to their actual existence in reality. See II.4, M¶100.)

Acts of attention, being selective, do not focus on something as it actually exists in reality. This would be, Abelard concedes, utterly impossible given the vast multiplicity of any thing's modes or ways of being. But this does not mean that the act of attention conceives something as *wholly otherwise* than it actually is, but rather in a limited or restricted way, i.e., in accordance with just its nature or one of its various properties. This is clearly stated by Abelard in his *Commentary on Isagoge*:

> If someone understands a thing otherwise than as it is in the sense that he attends it in terms of a nature or characteristic that it does not have, *that* understanding is surely empty.[21]

For example, it is possible to attend to the nature of something insensible and incorporeal, such as a rational soul or even God. This understanding of something incorporeal is possible because an act of attention considers the incorporeal *as if* it were corporeal (I.4, M¶19). This is the lesson Abelard drew from Augustine. However, how can an act of attending an incorporeal as if corporeal *not* be an understanding of something otherwise than it actually is? The answer is simply this: acts of attention focus only on a nature or select property of some thing, not on how the thing is in its entirety. Accordingly, attending an incorporeal as if it were corporeal is focusing on just one characteristic of the thing, and so the modal variance between how the thing actually is and how it is in the understanding is limited. It is still *an understanding of*, e.g., *a rational soul* that is being attended in some limited way otherwise than as it actually is. In this sense, Abelard remarks, we can think of *all* acts of attention – including those generated on the basis of direct sense experience – as attending otherwise than as things are in reality to the extent that they are always so restricted in scope (II.4, M¶75).

Abelard's explanation for the determination of the soundness of understandings goes even further to account for what at first might seem a very wide discrepancy between what is attended and how something actually is in reality. For just as one can rhetorically or performatively utter something in a certain way, e.g., by speaking quickly, but what is said describes, e.g., some person who is moving very slowly, such that there is a mismatch between *how* something is said and *what* is said, so too can there be a mismatch between how something is attended by the rational soul and the thing that is understood (II.4, M¶82).

Is this a good explanation for the phenomenon? Although it might seem somewhat odd, the force of the explanation is to pull apart the symmetry or isomorphism implied by, among other things, Aristotle's scheme of signification between what is in reality, what is in the understanding and what is said.[22] Within the rational soul, humans are able to attend a particular nature or characteristic of some extramental thing that, because of its selective ability, turns out to be otherwise understood than as it actually is. But this is not a problem, since according to Abelard this is true for everything that is understood, including what is understood on the basis of sense experience.

Notes

1 Given the complexity of Abelard's answers to the question of the status and corresponding understandings of universals, this topic will be put to the side in this chapter to focus on the other incorporeals he mentions.
2 Brentano made use of late scholastic terminology and was unlikely to have been aware of Abelard's views. If he did, his resource would have been the first modern publication of *De Intellectibus* by Cousin 1840. Brentano 1995, 67 was, however, deeply influenced by Aristotle, Augustine, the late eleventh century Anselm of Canterbury and thirteenth-century scholastics such as Thomas Aquinas:

> Aristotle himself spoke of this mental in-existence. In his books on the soul he says that the sensed object, as such, is in the sensing subject; that the sense contains the sensed object without its matter; that the object which is thought is in the thinking intellect.... The same is true of the Neoplatonists. St. Augustine in his doctrine of the *Verbum mentis* and of its inner origin touches upon the same fact. St. Anselm does the same in his famous ontological argument; many people have observed that his consideration of mental existence as a true existence is at the basis of his paralogism. Thomas Aquinas teaches that the object which is thought is intentionally in the thinking subject, the object which is loved in the person who loves, the object which is desired in the person desiring, and he uses this for theological purposes.

3 Anicius Manlius Severinus Boethius was a Roman politician who also translated several works from the Aristotelian logical corpus, including Porphyry's *Isagoge*, into Latin. His plan to write commentaries on all of Aristotle and Plato's works was curtailed by his early death. From Boethius the early Latin medieval tradition had access to Porphyry's *Isagoge* and Aristotle's *Categories* and *On Interpretation*, as well has his commentaries on these works, in addition to a collection of other logical writings. Boethius is best known as the author of *The Consolation of Philosophy*, as well as his five theological tracts.
4 All quotations in this section are from Boethius, *In Isagogen*, translated by Spade 1994.
5 Boethius interchangeably uses the verbs "subsist" (*subsistere*) and "exist" (*existere*). For an analysis of their synonymy and interchangeability, see King 2011.
6 Tweedale 1976, 53–88, Spade 1996, Marenbon 2003, King 1982, 31–55, vol. 1, Sirkel 2011, and De Libera 1999.
7 Spade 1994, x, characterizes Boethius as a moderate realist; King 2011 calls him an anti-realist.
8 Boethius states that he is following the view of Alexander of Aphrodisias (*fl.* early third century CE) on universals: "*Haec quidem est ad praesens de propositis quaestio, quam nos Alexandro consentientes hac ratiocinatione soluemus*". Until later in the scholastic tradition, Alexander was considered to be *the* commentator on Aristotle's philosophy. Precisely what opinion Alexander held on universals is a matter of some controversy, although from what is known Boethius is generally in alignment with Alexander's view. But as Sirkel 2011, 310 aptly cautions, "Just how Boethius' solution is related to Alexander's view is a controversial issue, not only because Alexander's view is open to different and conflicting interpretations, but also because Boethius' solution is difficult to interpret." This does not affect the substance of our discussion, although tracing the ultimate source of Abelard's theory back to Alexander would be an interesting exercise.
9 Lewis and Short, *speculor, -atus*.
10 For studies of *The Consolation of Philosophy*, especially Book V, see Gaskin 1995, Marenbon 2003, Sharples 2005, and Donato 2013. I was first alerted to the potential importance of Boethius' *Consolation of Philosophy* for the interpretation of Abelard's views on this topic by an unelaborated citation of Boethius' work made by King 1982 in a passage where he was translating Abelard's *Treatise on Understandings*.
11 All references in this section are to the *Consolation of Philosophy*, translated by Relihan 2001.
12 For Abelard, as for Boethius, forms are universals. Whereas Alexander of Aphrodisias seems to have distinguished between forms and universals, this distinction is obscured by Boethius, and it is thus hidden to his medieval readers. But both Boethius and Abelard recognize that things *have* natures, and these natures function, in part, to constrain how nature is understood by humans. See Sirkel 2011.
13 Plotinus was a third-century philosopher and is commonly considered to be the founder of Neoplatonism. Porphyry was his student.
14 For studies on Augustine's *On the Trinity*, see O'Daly 1987, Clark 2001, and Ayres 2010.
15 All references in this section are to *On the Trinity*, translated by McKenna 2002.
16 For Augustine, the term is "intentio" – intention, not "attentio". There seems to be no real difference, however. Abelard also uses these two terms interchangeably, and I have argued (Cameron 2007) that for Abelard, at least, their meaning is the same.
17 As evidence of this phenomenon, Augustine relates an anecdote of a man who could have an orgasm just by remembering a woman's body.
18 Abelard is the first medieval philosopher to write a treatise on human understanding, the *Tractatus de Intellectibus*. In it, he distinguished various mental operations from one another, in an effort to distinguish them from understanding itself. Abelard's catalogue distinguishes between sense, imagination, estimation, knowledge, reason,

abstraction and its converse substraction, mental impulses and acts of cognitive labour, as well as acts of attention and judgement. Our focus will be on the last two.
19 King 1982 translates "*deliberatio*" as "examination", which carries the unwanted connotation in English of an act of testing or judging in accordance with a standard or rule. There is, however, no standard against which the contents of cognitive acts of judging or attending can be compared (except, perhaps, in the mind of God, but to which humans have no cognitive access).
20 Unless otherwise noted, all quotations are from the *Treatise on Understandings*, my translation.
21 *Glosses on Isagoge* 25.19–22; translated by Spade 1994.
22 See Aristotle, *On Interpretation* 16a3–12.

Bibliography

Primary sources

Aristotle (1961). "*De interpretatione vel Periermeneias, translatio Boethii*," (ed.) L. Minio-Paluello, *Aristoteles Latinus* II, 1–5, Bruges/Paris: Desclée de Brouwer.
Augustine (1968). "*De Trinitate*," (eds.) W. Mountain and F. Glorie, *Corpus Christianorum Series Latina* 1–1A, Turnhout: Brepols.
Augustine (2002). "*On the Trinity Books 8–15*," (ed.) G. Matthews, (trans.) S. McKenna, *Series Latina* 27, 2nd edition, Turnhout: Brepols.
Boethius, A. M. S. (1906). "*Anicii Severini Boethii, In Isagogen Porphyrii Commenta Editionis secundae*," (ed.) S. Brandt, *Corpus Scriptorum Ecclesiasticorum Latinorum* 48, Leipzig: Freytag.
Boethius, A. M. S. (2000). *Opuscula Sacra and De consolatione philosophiae*, ed. C. Moreschini, Munich/Leipzig: K.G. Saur.
Boethius, A. M. S. (2001). *Boethius Consolation of Philosophy*, trans. J. C. Relihan, Indianapolis/Cambridge: Hackett Publishing.
Brentano, F. (1995). *Psychology From an Empirical Standpoint*, 2nd edition, trans. A. C. Rancurello, D. B. Terrell, and L. L. McAlister, London: Routledge.
Peter Abelard (1840). "De Intellectibus," in (ed.) V. Cousins, *Fragmens Philosophiques*, vol. 3, 2nd edition, Paris: Ladrange.
Peter Abelard (1919). *Die Logica 'ingredientibus': die Glossen zu Porphyrius*, ed. B. Geyer (Beiträge zur Geschichte der Philosophie des Mittelalters 21/1), Münster: Aschendorff.

Secondary sources

Ayres, L. (2010). *Augustine and the Trinity*, Cambridge: Cambridge University Press.
Cameron, M. (2007). "Abelard (and Heloise?) on intentions," *American Catholic Philosophical Quarterly* 81/2, pp. 323–339.
Clark, M. T. (2001). "*De Trinitate*," in (eds.) E. Stump and N. Kretzmann, *The Cambridge Companion to Augustine*, Cambridge: Cambridge University Press, pp. 91–102.
De Libera, A. (1999). *L'Art des Généralités. Théories de l'Abstraction*, Paris: Aubier.
Donato, A. (2013). *Boethius' Consolation of Philosophy as a Product of Late Antiquity*, London-New York, Bloomsbury Academic.
Gaskin, R. (1995). *The Sea Battle and the Master Argument*, Berlin: De Gruyter.

Hedwig, K. (1979). "Outlines for the history of a phenomenological concept," *Philosophy and Phenomenological Research* 39/3, pp. 326–340.
King, P. (1982). *Peter Abailard and the Problem of Universals*, 2 vols. PhD thesis, Princeton University.
King, P. (2011). "Boethius' anti-realist arguments," *Oxford Studies in Ancient Philosophy* 40, pp. 381–401.
Marenbon, J. (2003). *Boethius*, New York: Oxford University Press.
O'Daly, G. (1987). *Augustine's Philosophy of Mind*, Berkeley-Los Angeles: University of California Press.
Rosier-Catach, I. (2004). "Les Discussions sur le Signifié des Propositions chez Abélard et ses contemporains," in (eds.) A. Maierù and L. Valente, *Medieval Theories on Assertive and Non-assertive Language* (Acts of the 14th European Symposium on Medieval Logic and Semantics, Rome, June 11–15, 2002), Florence: Leo Olschki, 1–24.
Sharples, R. W. (2005). "Alexander of Aphrodisias on universals: Two problematic texts," *Phronesis* 50, pp. 43–55.
Sirkel, R. (2011). "Alexander of Aphrodisias's account of universals and its problems," *Journal of the History of Philosophy* 49/3, pp. 297–314.
Sorabji, R. (2005). *The Philosophy of the Commentators, 200–600 AD: A Sourcebook*, vol. 3, *Logic and Metaphysics*, Ithaca, NY: Cornell University Press.
Spade, P. (1994). *Five Texts on the Medieval Problem of Universals: Porphyry, Boethius, Abelard, Duns Scotus, Ockham*, trans. P. Spade, Indianapolis/Cambridge: Hackett.
Spade, P. (1996). "Boethius against universals: Arguments in the second commentary on Porphyry," Unpublished PDF.
Tweedale, M. (1976). *Abailard on Universals*, Amsterdam: North-Holland.

2

THE PROBLEM OF INTELLECTUAL COGNITION OF MATERIAL SINGULARS BETWEEN 1250 AND 1310

David Piché

1 Introduction[*]

At the centre of the vast field of enquiry that Latin medieval thinkers carried out on the subject of human cognition, the medievalist philosopher discovers one crucial question: the intellection of singular things. This question, which concerns the object of the intellective act, involves in a way all of the important themes about which theorists of cognition debated in the universities throughout the thirteenth and fourteenth centuries: the extent of the intellect's power of cognition, the cause of the act of intellection, the existence, nature and function of the intelligible species, abstraction, the articulation of sensory and intellectual faculties, and so on. Moreover, such a question reveals itself to be of a great interest to historians of medieval thought, in that the emergence in this period of the thesis that the intellect grasps not merely universals but also and primordially singulars[1] makes for an observation of the lively passage, so to speak, from a traditional Aristotelian paradigm to a resolutely modern scheme of thought. Indeed, to ask whether the intellect can cognize singulars only takes on its full meaning within a critique of an Aristotelian-inspired theoretical model, which apportions distinct cognitive roles between the intellect and the sensory faculties. Cognition of singular things befits the sensory faculties, which are intimately related to corporal organs. The intellect, for its part, which detains the power to abstract away from individualizing material conditions, is the faculty to which it properly falls to grasp universals.[2] In this perspective, the human intellect does not apprehend singular things inasmuch as they are singular, since it grasps them on the mode of abstract universality. Thomas Aquinas was one of the most brilliant promoters of this theoretical paradigm, and we will come back to it later on. According to him, the intellect cognizes universals directly and cognizes singulars only in an indirect fashion, that is, through the mediation of sensible representations (phantasms) that the imagination, one of the internal senses, produces from the data provided by the external senses. In the last quarter of the thirteenth century, however, several thinkers, especially Franciscan theologians whom we will identify in due time, question this repartition of cognitive tasks between the senses and the intellect. They put forth the idea that the intellect can cognize singular things directly, without denying that it also has the capacity to cognize universals.[3]

I would like, in the present study, to guide the reader to the heart of this debate about the intellectual cognition of singulars. The best way to achieve this, I believe, is to follow the account given by a philosopher who personally took part in the debate and who meticulously registered the various defended positions as well as the arguments that supported them. Gerard of Bologna (*ca.* 1240/1250–1317), the first Carmelite to have obtained the title of master in theology at the University of Paris (1295), offers a privileged path for our ends, since, in one of his *Quodlibeta* in all likelihood debated in Paris between 1305 and 1307, he left us what is, in my opinion, the vastest and most precise panorama of the subject to have been produced in the High Middle Ages.[4]

2 The defended positions

The positions that were maintained by medieval philosophers of the years 1250–1310 can be divided, first, according to the answer provided to the question of the very fact of an intellection of singular things and, second, according to the proposed solution to the problem of the modality of the intellect's cognition of singular things, if it is admitted that such cognition indeed occurs. Thus, regarding the *de facto* question, a philosopher such as Albertus Magnus (*ca.* 1200–1280) supposedly maintained that singular things as such are not cognized by our intellect in the state of this life.[5] Although not common at the time, this position, which denies that the intellect has any sort of access whatsoever to singular things, could still claim the authority of a very widespread gnoseological theory of Aristotelian descent, in which a strict parallelism is traced between, on the one hand, the hierarchy of cognitive faculties and, on the other, the degree of abstraction of cognitive representations.[6] This theory relies on the principle that a thing can only be cognized through its resemblance (*similitudo*). Indeed, a thing must in some way be *in* the intellect in order to be cognized. Yet it is obviously not the thing itself which is found in our cognitive faculties, but rather its resemblance or species (*species*), to employ a technical term used by medieval philosophers, following Aristotle's famous phrase: "it is not the stone that is in the soul, but the species of the stone".[7] Thus, on this view, cognition is produced at every level by the reception of species in the cognitive faculties. The mere fact that exterior things exist in virtue of their forms entails that they emit species in their surroundings, that is, that they produce around them formal representations of themselves, which affect anything that is naturally disposed to receive them. From the external senses, through the internal senses, such as memory and imagination, and finally to the intellect, species are gradually abstracted from or deprived of matter. Thus, at the lowest level of the external senses, sight for instance, the received species are divested of the very matter of sensible things, while not being abstracted from the individuating conditions in which those things exist, whereas at the highest level, in the intellect, the received species are not only divested from the matter of sensible things but are also abstracted from the individuating conditions that affect these things.[8] From this one can conclude that the intellect, in virtue of the intelligible species in it, only grasps universals and never singulars.

This last claim, as I mentioned earlier, did not garner much support among scholastic thinkers in the period that interests us.[9] Almost all of them agreed to say that the intellect cognizes singular things in some way. Two sorts of considerations can then support this statement: the first is theoretical, whereas the second draws from ethical considerations. The first makes the point that the faculty that performs syllogistic deductions, the intellect, constructs deductions that yield to conclusions that comprise both a universal and a singular term:[10] thus we have to admit that the intellect, in some way, apprehends singular things. The second counts on the fact that man has, to a certain extent, control over his actions. The faculty that can ensure such a command by directing human actions is the intellect, which, in order to do this, must be capable of apprehending human actions. Since these are particular and bear upon singular realities, it must be acknowledged that the intellect grasps singular things.[11]

Once the fact of the intellection of singulars is acknowledged, the debate then shifts towards the modality according to which the intellect cognizes singular things. The central question is the following: is the intellection of singulars direct and anterior to the intellection of universals, or is it indirect and posterior to it? The views of philosophers of this period can be divided following the two main options proposed by this alternative. The second branch is the most common; the first is much less widespread, although it will induce an important change of paradigm in gnoseology – an epistemic transformation whose repercussions will be felt throughout the fourteenth century and beyond.

Before exploring in turn each of these theoretical options, I should add a few remarks that are important to a proper understanding of the notion of intelligible species (*species intelligibilis*), which has already been mentioned and which will reappear throughout the present study,[12] since it plays a key role in the gnoseological debates of the medieval period. A first remark: although we use, in the wake of medieval philosophers, the vocabulary of cognitive representation to designate the intelligible species invoked by their theories, I do not intend thereby to suggest that a species is a mental object that the soul would have to cognize first in order to have access, through it, to cognition of things in the world. Although this interpretation of the intelligible species as a mental object was indeed at the centre of discussion in the works of thirteenth- and fourteenth-century philosophers, and even though, as we shall later see, Latin scholastics who postulated the existence of species in the human intellect did indeed attribute a representational function to them, most medieval philosophers who subscribe to the idea of intelligible species[13] nonetheless agree that it is not what the intellect cognizes (*id quod cognoscitur*)[14] but rather that through which the intellect cognizes an extramental thing (*id quo res extra cognoscitur*). In short, the intelligible species is a formal medium by means of which a thing is presented to the intellectual faculty, which can apprehend, through this medium, the thing thus represented. The notion of cognitive species thus calls for an adjustment of our theoretical framework so as to accommodate a type of representation that is neither thing-like nor merely iconic, something which is rather a formal vehicle by means of which the cognitive faculties of the human soul are drawn to cognition of realities in the external world. That being settled, what are the functions that medieval thinkers attribute to intelligible species? In other words, for what reason did several Latin philosophers of the thirteenth and fourteenth century postulate the existence of this particular type of mental entities? We can chiefly discern two reasons that they adduce in favor of the intelligible species.[15] The first motive is provided by the necessity of finding the cause of the act of intellection. This is the first function of the intelligible species: being a causal principle with regards to intellection. Since it is plain that an extramental thing cannot itself be found in the intellect so as to cause intellection in it, the intelligible species will take over this role in its stead and assume the causal function. Thus, the intelligible species is postulated as the formal principle in virtue of which an act of intellection occurs in the intellect that receives it.[16] The second motivation that is cited in favor of the intelligible species has to do with representation. For its advocates, this species is necessary in order for universals to be represented to the intellect. Seeing as, on the one hand, the grasp of universals is proper to the intellect, and, on the other, these do not exist as such in the extramental reality, there must be something in the intellect that represents universals, something through which or by means of which the intellect can apprehend universals: this is the part played by the intelligible species, which, according to its proponents, is thus a formal representation of universals[17] that the agent intellect abstracts from phantasms.[18]

3 The direct intellection of the singular

The thesis of the direct and prior intellection of singular things first appeared in the last quarter of the thirteenth century and was put forth by Franciscan thinkers, namely Matthew of Acquasparta (*ca.* 1238–1302), Roger Marston (*ca.* 1235–1303) and Vital du Four (*ca.* 1260–1327).[19] As Gerard of Bologna presents it,[20] it is supported by four paradigmatic arguments, which are well worth presenting here.[21] I will endeavor to make clear, when the case arises, the tacit presuppositions that dictate their premises and to evaluate the arguments by formulating critiques that proponents of the opposite thesis could have expressed.

(1) The first argument relies on the principle of correspondence between intellections and things. It proceeds as follows:

> Major premise: What is in the intellect stands as things do in reality, for our intellections conform to things, not the other way around.[22]
> Minor premise: Yet in reality, singulars exist by themselves and prior to universals, which only exist on account of singulars and are posterior to them.
> Conclusion: Therefore, there is an intellection of singulars themselves on the intellect's own powers,[23] prior to an intellection of universals, which are intellectually apprehended only as a further consequence.

The major premise of this argument presupposes a form of epistemological realism, which, indeed, the vast majority of medieval philosophers endorse, whereas the minor premise affirms the ontological primacy of the singular over the universal. Following this conception, a substantial individual (the first substance of Aristotle's *Categories*) is a self-sustained being, whereas universals, namely genera and species (secondary substances, according to the Stagirite's same treatise),[24] only exist in virtue of the substantial individuals that realize them. This ontological scheme, however, is obviously rejected by the medieval thinkers who endorse the thesis of the ontological primacy of universals over singulars. We may recall the Neoplatonic doctrine of the three states of universals, heralded by Albertus Magnus (*ca.* 1200–1280) in the Latin thirteenth century,[25] according to which universals exist in a self-sustained way, inasmuch as they are intelligible forms emanating from God,[26] before being realized in the singular things of the sensible world whose essence[27] is constituted by these universals. A supporter of this kind of theory thus arrives at the opposite conclusion of argument (1). The latter's cogency thus depends on the type of ontology to which one subscribes.

(2) The second argument draws on the notion of real action. It goes as follows:

> Major premise: What is grasped first and directly by the intellect is what acts first and directly on the intellect.
> Minor premise: Yet only singulars act on their own. Indeed, real actions are only effectuated by universals as a result of something else, namely the action of the singulars that realize them.
> Conclusion: Therefore, singulars are grasped first and directly by the intellect.

Within the intellectual framework of the thirteenth century, this argument had to overcome an objection that maintained that singular material things cannot act directly on the intellect, on account of the latter's immateriality. This objection originates, on the one hand, from an indisputable postulate of the medieval era, according to which what is immaterial is ontologically more perfect than what is material, and, on the other hand, from the Aristotelian principle that what acts is ontologically more perfect than what is passive.[28] Consequently, an immaterial reality – namely the intellect – cannot undergo the action of a singular material thing. According to the proponents of this conception,[29] singular material things can however act directly on the senses, since these are organic faculties, that is, capacities that function by means of bodily organs (the eyes and optic nerves in the case of sight, for instance). The intellect comes into play actively by abstracting the intelligible species from the individuating materiality conveyed by the phantasms that are produced by the imagination (one of the internal senses) on the basis of the sensible species that come to it from the external senses via the common sense. On this view, material singulars do not exert any direct action on the intellect, which by its own powers extracts the intelligible from the sensible so as to generate a universal representation of the essence of singular material things.

Various strategies were deployed, separately or jointly, by scholastic thinkers of the last quarter of the thirteenth century, most of them Franciscans, in order to break the barriers that this theory erects between the intellect and the material concreteness of things in the sensible world, and thereby to make way for the idea of a direct intellection of material singulars: repudiating Aquinas' theory according to which particular matter (*materia signata*) is the principle of individuation; devising a conception of the intellect that characterizes it as an essentially active faculty capable of intentionality directing itself towards things in the world, without necessarily receiving anything from them; bringing modifications to the doctrine of mental representations, so as to allow the existence of singular intelligible species in addition to universal species. Matthew of Acquasparta stands out as pioneer and model in this regard: the key features of his doctrine of the intellection of singulars are thus well worth exhibiting.[30] According to him, singular things are apprehended by singular species,[31] whereas universals are apprehended by universal species. For example, the intellect grasps this particular man through the species of that man, whereas he cognizes any man *qua* man through the universal species of man. Singular things, moreover, are what the intellect first cognizes in act: for it is by actively producing singular species that the intellect can abstract or collect (*colligere*) universal species from them. These singular intelligible species are produced by the intellect on the basis of the sensible species provided by the external and internal senses. Once the intellect has actively produced for itself its own singular species, it can apprehend singular things through them without resorting to the senses or to imagination.[32] However, such an intellectual species, considered alone, is unable to represent a thing as existent or non-existent. It is an abstract representation, not with respect to the singularity of a thing, but rather with respect to its existence.[33] Thus, when a singular thing previously perceived is no longer in the mind's field of view (*conspectus mentis*), what remains in the intellect is a representation detached from the existence of its object, through which the intellect can apprehend this or that singular thing, for instance a man who possesses certain characteristics and is attended by particular circumstances which distinguish him from any other man; yet the intellect cannot cognize, in virtue of this abstract representation, whether this man exists or not. In order to cognize that a singular thing exists in a determinate time and space, the intellect must call upon the senses, through which the species of the singular existing in act will reach the intellect: for it is in this sensible species, coeval with the singular thing apprehended in act by the senses, that the intellect can intuitively grasp a material singular existing in act.[34] And while the singular species in the intellect does not afford such existential cognition, it nonetheless has a crucial function, namely that of enabling the intellect to remember that a singular thing, previously perceived but now absent, was located at such a time and place and had this or that property.

(3) Let us now return to the arguments in favor of the direct intellection of singular materials. While the two arguments I presented earlier pertained to ontology, the third, for its part, is of an epistemological nature. It focuses on the concept of the object of a cognitive faculty.

Major premise: The object of a cognitive faculty is naturally prior[35] to the operation of this faculty.
Minor premise: Yet the singular is naturally prior to the act of intellection, whereas the universal is posterior to this act, since it is produced by it.
Conclusion: Therefore, the singular is the object of the act of intellection and, as a result, cognition of singulars by the intellect is naturally prior to cognition of universals.

The major premise of the argument is not particularly problematic for any of the protagonists of the present debate. Indeed, it goes without saying, in the framework of epistemological realism, that the object of a cognitive faculty is something real that is ontologically prior to the operation of this faculty. The minor premise rests upon a conceptualist doctrine regarding the ontological status of universals. On this view, universals are not something in the extramental reality but rather concepts that are produced by an intellectual act. This doctrine, however, is rejected by a thinker such as John Duns Scotus (*ca.* 1265–1308),[36] who maintains that the abstracting act of the agent intellect provides the potential intellect with an intelligible species that represents the common nature of the singular thing. This intelligible species, just like the common nature of which it is the similitude, is naturally prior to the act of intellection it causes.[37] In this perspective, then, it is the common nature of material singular things, and not these considered individually, which is the proper object of the act of intellection. Hence argument (3) is conclusive only if one manages to demonstrate either that there is no such thing as a common nature in sensible things (extramental reality being composed of only singular things) or that common nature is only potentially or virtually present in material singular things, which alone exist in act or effectively in the external world, seeing as the universality of their nature is only revealed by virtue of an act of abstraction carried out by the agent intellect.

(4) The last argument proceeds by eliminating the alleged obstacles to the intelligibility of material singulars.

For, as a matter of fact, what is it that prevents material singular things from being intellected first and directly? It cannot be the singularity of these things, seeing as medieval philosophers of the time hold that the intellective soul, once separated, apprehends other separate souls as well as angelic substances: yet these are singular entities.[38] Nor can it be the materiality of these things, since the intellect is capable of formulating and understanding definitions of the essences of sensible things, in which matter is included (for instance: the definition of man as 'mortal rational animal' takes into consideration the corporality of man).[39] Nor, again, can it be the accidental properties of these things, such as quantity or sensible quality, for the theories of the mathematician and the physicist, respectively, show that these properties can be intellectually grasped. Therefore, it would appear that nothing prevents material singulars from being cognized first and directly by the intellect.

4   The indirect intellection of the singular

This, however, is not the opinion of the majority of Latin thinkers of the thirteenth century. Indeed, many among them maintain that our intellect cognizes universals directly before cognizing material singulars, which our intellect hence cognizes only indirectly. How should we understand this thesis? First, as regards the claim of a first and direct intellection of universals, it originates from a principle commonly accepted at the time, according to which the degree of abstraction or universality of cognition varies proportionally to the degree of immateriality of the faculty that cognizes: the more immaterial a cognitive faculty is, the more it cognizes abstractly and universally, that is, in a common and indeterminate way. Following the prevailing notion, moreover, the human intellect is entirely immaterial. Indeed, although it is united to the body, either as a faculty of the soul that is the form of the body or as one of the substantial forms that exist in the body,[40] it is devoid of any matter and carries out its proper operation, intellection, without employing any bodily organ. In other words, the intellect is not the act (the perfection or first determination) of a bodily organ, unlike the sense of sight, for instance, which is the act of the eyes and optic nerves. This is the reason why, following this logic, the intellect cognizes in a more abstract fashion than any other sensory faculty;[41] it even cognizes in a radically abstract way. This is tantamount to saying that the intellect cognizes things first and by itself by abstracting them completely from the determinate space and time in which they are found, as well as from the attending contingencies. It cognizes things first and by itself in a universal way, not inasmuch as they are individuals. The human intellect can however apprehend singular things afterwards, namely in a secondary and indirect fashion. But what do the proponents of the thesis mean exactly when they assert that the intellect apprehends singular things indirectly? To answer this question, they call upon the concept of *reflexio*:[42] the intellect cognizes a material singular through a *reflexio* that it operates on what is in it or in the internal senses. But in turn then: how does such a *reflexio* occur?

The most prominent account by a medieval philosopher is the one developed by Thomas Aquinas. Yet, if we look closely at Aquinas' texts on the subject, it appears to me that one finds not one but rather two explanations of the indirect intellection of material singulars. It is worth shedding light on the doctrinal duality that these texts convey, although, as far as I know, it went unnoticed by medieval philosophers.[43]

The first explanation draws on the idea that the intellect's *reflexio* is carried out on the species, forms or images that the sensitive powers receive, produce or preserve in them.[44] Thus, the later version of the first explanation puts forth the idea of the intellect's necessary return to sensible images:[45] in order to cognize material singulars, the intellect must, so to speak, turn towards (*convertere se*) the phantasms that represent them. Given that the intelligible species, through which the intellect cognizes universals, originates from a phantasm[46] by abstraction, and that there is a natural continuity between the intellect and the sensitive faculties, a return to the phantasm, the source of the intelligible species, enables the intellect to cognize, albeit indirectly, the material singular of which the phantasm is a similitude.[47] In fact, Thomas goes even further, since he maintains that here below, on earth, the human intellect by nature functions so as to necessarily require returning to phantasms, not only to apprehend material singulars but also to cognize its proper object.[48] Indeed, since its proper object is a universal essence or one abstracted from material things in so far as it exists in these material things, the human intellect can only cognize its proper object in a true and accomplished way if it cognizes it as existing in singular materials. However, as we well know, according to Aquinas, the senses, not the intellect, directly apprehend material singulars. In order for the intellect to cognize in act its proper object, it is thus necessary that it turns towards phantasms, so as to apprehend the universal essence as existing in material particulars.[49] In sum, according to my reading of the first explanation, the direct intellection of universals and the indirect intellection of singulars would not be two distinct operations but rather the two poles of one same operational dynamic: the act of intellection, in so far as it is necessarily attended by a production of phantasms by the internal sense, would always be both the direct grasp of a universal that exists in a singular and the indirect grasp of the singular that realizes this universal.

As I wrote earlier, it seems to me that there is in the works of Aquinas another explanation to be found regarding the indirect intellection of material singulars, one which distinguishes itself from the first by a different conception of the intellect's *reflexio*. Indeed, the intellectual *reflexio* in this case requires the grasp of noetic entities prior to its reaching the sensible level. What we have here then is a *reflexio* that takes place in several steps, according to a process that goes as follows:⁵⁰ starting from the universal that it grasps directly, the intellect backtracks, so to speak, in order to consider the intellective act whereby it grasps the universal; from the cognition of this act, the intellect backtracks to consider the intelligible species that was the principle of this act; from the cognition of this intelligible species, the intellect backtracks to consider the phantasm from which the intelligible species was extirpated by abstraction; finally, from the cognition of this phantasm, the intellect obtains cognition of the singular material thing that is directly represented by the phantasm. Two points bear mentioning regarding this second explanation: first, this model differs from the first explanation in that it suggests that the indirect intellection of a material singular is an operation clearly distinct from the direct intellection of a universal, although it does originate from the latter; second, and this is a corollary to the previous point, the indirect intellection of a material singular cannot be a common operation, let alone an operation that is concomitant to each direct intellection of a universal. Indeed, nowhere does Aquinas maintain that, each time the intellect apprehends its proper object, it engages *ipso facto* in a reiterated *reflexio* whereby it cognitively revisits its act, its species and a phantasm, in order to attain cognition of a material singular. It would, in any case, be strange and cognitively burdensome for the intellect to have to proceed in this way at every single grasp of a universal! In all likelihood, then, we have two different explanations on our hands. But is that really the case? Are there one or two explanations? If there are two, what is their relationship?

In my opinion, there are three possible answers to these questions.

(I) The second explanation presents in a detailed way what the first only briefly describes or, what amounts to the same, the first is a succinct or abridged version of the second.[51]
(II) Between the first and the last text that Thomas dedicated to our question of interest, his thought evolved towards a simplified understanding of the matter: thus, Thomas would have abandoned the more complex second explanation in favor of the first. To support this interpretation, one could point out that the second explanation no longer appears in the final works where Thomas discusses the question of the intellection of material singulars, namely, the *Commentary on the De Anima* (1267–68) and the *prima pars* of the *Summa theologiae* (1267–68 for the relevant questions).[52] In works prior to these, Thomas still wavers between the two explanations.
(III) The two explanations are complementary and not equivalent; both explanations are indeed distinct, and Thomas would have jointly maintained both. The first accounts for the implicit cognition of material singulars, so to speak, which the intellect spontaneously obtains during the common exercise of its proper operation. As for the second, it accounts for the way in which the intellect can obtain cognition of a material singular when it occasionally undertakes to retrospectively examine and render fully explicit the cognitive process that runs from the singular thing to the universal object.

To recapitulate: the two explanations (I) could be equivalent in substance without being identical in their formulation, (II) could constitute two versions of one same theory between which Thomas hesitated before ultimately opting for the simpler one or (III) could have been conceived of by Thomas as distinct, albeit complementary, theoretical models. Which of these interpretations should we opt for? I believe the first must be rejected on the basis of the significant differences we have already highlighted, in light of which it does not seem possible to take the two explanations as equivalent. Moreover, the third interpretation ascribes to Aquinas ideas that he never presented himself. Indeed, from one text to the other Thomas will answer the same question formulated in similar ways without ever indicating that he understands the two theoretical models to be distinct. This he certainly could have mentioned explicitly.[53] Consequently, if we abandon the third interpretation because it attributes to Thomas sentences he did not write, only the second remains: at the end of his intellectual career, Thomas discarded the more complex explanation. This interpretation, however, is not fully satisfactory. Indeed, the second explanation is not merely more complex or more developed than the first: it appears that it purports to explain something quite different. For it seeks to account not only for the way in which our intellect grasps material singulars but also for the modality according to which our intellect cognizes explicitly the various links of the causal chain that runs from the sensible singular to the abstract universal. Yet this is another question altogether, principally regarding cognitive psychology, as to how (and if) the intellect can cognize the mental entities of which it is the subject, namely universal objects, acts of intellections and intelligible species. Could Thomas have confused, except in his last works, these two clearly distinct theoretical motivations? I leave the question unanswered and invite the reader to examine Aquinas' texts, if she so wishes, in order to ascertain for herself which of the three proposed interpretations seems most plausible to her.

Another model that explains the indirect intellection of material singulars by the notion of *reflexio* is presented by the secular theologian Henry of Ghent (*ca.* 1217–1293).[54] His explanation is distinct from the one offered by Thomas Aquinas in part because it avails itself of a different ontology of universals but also in that it eliminates the notion of intelligible species.[55] Indeed, according to Henry or, at least, according to how a contemporary like Gerard of Bologna understood him, a same thing is both universal and singular: the universal and the singular are not two distinct things but rather two real aspects of one and the same thing that are fit to be distinguished by the cognitive operations whereby we apprehend this thing. Consequently, there is no need for two distinct representations, namely the phantasm and the intelligible species, in order for cognition of a thing under these two aspects to be possible: a single one suffices, and that is the phantasm. Thus, the agent intellect lays bare, or unveils, the universal aspect of the thing represented by the phantasm, which, at that point only, is apt to conduct the potential or passive intellect towards an intellection of the universal. In other words, the phantasm is apt to produce an act of intellection in the passive intellect once the agent intellect has divested or abstracted it from its individuating features so as to transform it into a universal representation. This process brings it about that the passive intellect initially apprehends the thing directly as a universal. It is as if there is a straight line running from the mover – the universalized phantasm – to the moved – the passive intellect that cognizes the thing under its universal aspect. Only after having covered this trajectory does the intellect engage in a *reflexio*, that is, does it return to the phantasm and thereby apprehends the same thing, now under the aspect of singularity. The trajectory here is followed in the opposite direction of the previous one: cognition of the universal is the starting point, and the process culminates in the singular, or the phantasm that represents it.

A possible objection to this explanatory model – which is notably put forth by John Duns Scotus[56] – consists in pointing out that it is not possible that a representation whose intrinsic function is to represent a singular could also represent a universal, for these are opposites. One concludes from this that there must be, in addition to phantasms, representations that possess in and of themselves the function of representing universals; this, as we have seen, is one of the reasons why several medieval philosophers, including Duns Scotus, postulate the existence of intelligible species. Alongside his vigorous defense of the necessity of intelligible species, the subtle Doctor makes way for the idea of a properly intellectual intuition of material singulars.[57] This idea, still discreet and uncertain in Duns Scotus, will become the cornerstone on which William of Ockham builds his gnoseology, thereby beginning a new chapter in the history of theories of cognition.

5 Conclusion

This chapter, which must shortly come to an end, does not make the slightest claim of being exhaustive, even regarding only the period that has been considered (1250–1310). Such an undertaking would have required an in-depth analysis, most notably, of a Franciscan theologian and philosopher whose radicalism is matched only by his originality: Peter John Olivi (*ca.* 1248–1298).[58] Some key elements of his theory of our cognition of the external world are worth mentioning. Olivi is, without doubt, the only philosopher of his century who wholeheartedly rejects the Aristotelian theoretical devices that all his contemporaries employ, to various degrees, in conceptualizing human cognition: active and passive intellects, intelligible and sensible species, all of which he deems unfit to account for that alone which is true and compatible with the Christian doctrine, namely, the free and vital activity characteristic of the human soul. According to Olivi, the cognitive grasp of an object takes place when the soul actively turns towards a thing upon which it concentrates its attention. The soul thus first and directly apprehends the material and singular thing (or an aspect of it); it is only as a further result that the soul produces universal cognitions about the material singular initially apprehended. Olivi thus emphasizes the efficient causality of the soul at all levels of human cognition: our soul does not arrive at cognition by undergoing the pressures of extramental things on its cognitive faculties (which would contravene to the dignity of the human soul, whose nature is purely spiritual), but rather by virtually or intentionally extending itself to things in the world so as to grasp them.[59] The object cognized is only a cause of cognition in the sense of a final cause, that is, in so far as it completes and marks the end of the cognitive act that aims at it. As for the species, whether sensible or intelligible, it is neither necessary as a cause of the cognitive act, since the soul actively produces its acts of cognition, whether sensitive or intellective, nor as a representation, since every cognitive act is in and of itself a similitude of the cognized object. It goes without saying that the thought of Peter John Olivi marks the dawn of a new paradigm (albeit finding its roots in a certain gnoseological Augustinianism) in the philosophy of mind and cognition.

One last crucial question, which on its own could be the topic of an entire article, was not discussed as part of the present chapter but deserves at least to be touched upon before we conclude. To my knowledge, this question did not appear in its full acuteness or even explicitly before the end of the thirteenth century – in Vital du Four, for instance. It can be formulated as such: when we say that the intellect cognizes singulars, what exactly is designated by the term 'singular'? The existence of the singular or the very singularity of the singular? Vital du Four implements a clear distinction between the two terms of this alternative.[60] In the first sense, according to him, 'singular' designates the existence in act of a thing or, to put it otherwise, a thing as existing in act. In the second sense, the term designates the natural modality according to which an individual pertains to its species, a modality that is distinct from that of any other individual of the same species. Can we come to cognize both these aspects of a singular thing? As a general rule, the medieval philosophers of the period we have considered believe that our cognitive faculties, in the state of this life, are unable to cognize the very singularity of a singular but that they can apprehend (directly or indirectly) the existence in act of a singular.

Ultimately, the debate whose essential theses and arguments I have attempted to restore, beyond its obvious relevance for whoever is interested in the question "What can I know?" is embedded in the question to which, according to Kant, any genuinely philosophical enquiry leads: "What is man?" Indeed, the debate about intellectual cognition of material singulars points towards two antagonistic anthropologies. On the one side, one finds Aquinas' conception, which insists on the unity of the concrete composite of body and soul that each human being is; this strong unity is guaranteed by the thesis of the uniqueness of the substantial form. From this perspective, it is not, strictly speaking, the intellect, the imagination or the senses that cognize, but rather the entire human being, body and soul, by means of his faculties of cognition[61] whose collaboration ensures the unity of the cognitive dynamics that the human being experiences. We can wonder whether the endorsement of an anthropology along the lines of the one Aquinas propounds does not allow one to withhold attributing direct cognition of material singulars to the intellect, to the extent that its focal point is the human subject considered as a whole, who, as we have seen, cognizes both universals and singulars, albeit according to different modalities. In any case, it seems undeniable that if we consider the thought of Aquinas in all its dimensions there is no way to separate the thesis of the indirect intellection of material singulars from the anthropology that underlies and justifies it. On the other hand, we also find proponents of the doctrine of the plurality of substantial forms in each human being, which include the Franciscan philosophers we have come across in this study. According to them, a human being is defined first and foremost by his intellective soul, which is a substantial form distinct in reality from the other forms (animal, vegetative, corporal) with which it constitutes the concrete composite we call human being. An anthropology of this type aims at securing perfect sovereignty for the intellective soul relatively to the body, as well as its autonomy in principle with regards to the bodily faculties.[62] For the followers of this doctrine, only such an anthropology is in a position to provide a basis for one of the central theses of Christian thought: the human soul is a subsisting reality whose existence goes beyond physical death. Putting aside the resolution of this problem, which is absolutely crucial for medieval philosophers, I think it is rather evident that the thesis of the direct intellection of material singulars is intimately related[63] to the anthropological paradigm that conceives of the intellect as a power of cognizing autonomous with regards to the sensory powers as well as superior to them. Such a paradigm cannot deny, on pain of tarnishing the intellective soul's intrinsic dignity, which lies notably in its cognitive capacity, that the intellect has a direct apprehension of singular material things, whereas all the protagonists of the present debate attribute this apprehension to the senses. That being said, can Aquinas' anthropology, without contradicting itself, confer upon the intellective soul both the status of subsisting reality – necessary to ensure its immortality – and that of the unique substantial form of the human body? Conversely, if the proponents of the doctrine of the plurality of substantial forms provide better conceptual grounds for the justification of the immortality of the intellective soul, do they really manage to preserve the inalienable ontological unity that each human being constitutes? These are important questions, but ones that belong to another study.

Notes

* Translated from the French by Samuel Dishaw. I wish to thank the Canadian Social Science and Humanities Research Council (SSRHC) for the financial support granted to the research which led to this chapter.
1 The opposition between universal and singular that will be at issue throughout this study is typically exemplified, in Aristotelian vocabulary, by the opposition between a genus or species of the category of substance and the individuals that are classified under this genus or species, for instances 'animal' or 'man' in opposition to 'this horse' or 'Socrates'. It is also exemplified by the opposition between a genus or species of an accidental category (the category of quality, for instance) and the individuals that are classified under this genus or species; for example, 'colour' or 'whiteness' in opposition to 'this colour' or 'this shade of white'. Throughout this study, I will use the terms 'individual', 'particular' and 'singular' as synonyms.

2 Cf. notably Aristotle, *De anima*, II, 5 (417b22–25) and *Physics*, I, 5 (189a2–9).
3 There are strictly philosophical reasons (pertaining to ontology, epistemology, theory of cognition, ethics, etc.) in support of the thesis of the direct intellection of material singulars: these will be the focal point of the present study. We should, however, not forget that the proponents of this thesis were also drawn to it for motivations of a religious nature (for instance, by the assertions of biblical texts, or their belief in beatific vision, etc.).
4 Cf. Gerard of Bologna, *Quodlibet* III, q. 15 (Piché 2014, 229–248).
5 Cf. Albertus Magnus, *De intellectu et intelligibili*, lib. I, tract. 2, cap. 1, 490a–492a.
6 Thomas Aquinas clearly expounds this theory, even though he does not in the end endorse the thesis of the radical unknowability of singulars for the intellect. Cf. especially *De veritate*, q. 2, a. 5, co. Since the works of Thomas Aquinas are all available on the internet and access to printed versions is the most convenient there is in the bibliographic field of philosophical medievalism, I have not considered it necessary to refer to any particular printed edition (the reader may easily find the passage she wishes to read on the internet website www.corpusthomisticum.org/).
7 Aristotle, *De anima*, III, 8, 431b29–432a1.
8 In the peripatetic tradition, the function of abstracting species from individuating material conditions is assigned to the 'agent' or 'active' intellect, whereas the intellect that receives the intelligible species thus abstracted is called 'possible', 'potential' or 'material'.
9 To reiterate: the view that the intellect apprehends only universals and no singulars at all is a rare one; however, the gnoseological paradigm I have just presented, along with its notions of a hierarchy of faculties, of species and of abstraction, is commonly endorsed by medieval thinkers of the years 1250–1310.
10 To take a simple example: all men are mortal; Socrates is a man; hence Socrates is mortal.
11 It should be noted that, in the present debate, the singular things in questions are sensible things, that is, following the Aristotelian ontology, concrete composites of matter and form. In other words, they are sensible substances (a particular horse, for instance) or even determinations of those substances, namely accidents (such as the colour of a particular horse). The case of intellectual cognition of immaterial singular things (namely, separate souls, angels, divine realities) causes problems of a different sort than the one that occupies us here. For this reason I will not consider them in this chapter.
12 Seeing as the notion of intelligible species is the significant one for the topic of the present study, I shall leave aside the notions of sensible species and species *in medio*, which would call for considerably different explanations than those I will shortly provide and would divert us from our central topic.
13 Besides Albertus Magnus and Thomas Aquinas, whom we have already cited, and certain Franciscan theologians who will be considered later on, we should mention Giles of Rome, Hervaeus Natalis and John Duns Scotus. Among university thinkers of the years 1250–1310 who argued that it is not necessary to postulate intelligible species that are distinct from, and causally prior to, acts of intellection, the main proponents are Godfrey of Fontaines, Henry of Ghent, Peter John Olivi, Durandus of Saint-Pourçain and Gerard of Bologna. For a complete historical panorama on the topic of intelligible species, see Spruit 1994.
14 This claim only covers cases of direct cognitive operations, that is, non-reflexive ones. Indeed, if the intellect reflects upon itself or upon the other powers of the soul, it could then obtain cognition of the species that are in it or in the other powers of the soul.
15 One of the most eloquent medieval witnesses of the debate over intelligible species, which comprises a substantial summary of the *pro et contra* arguments, is the *Quodlibet* I, q. 17 of Gerard of Bologna: cf. Piché 2014, 136–147.

16 Critics of the notion of intelligible species argue that a phantasm – a sensible representation produced by the imagination – suffices, once illuminated-universalised by the agent intellect, to cause an act of intellection in the possible or potential intellect.

17 As we shall see later on, the end of the thirteenth century will bear witness to the novel and non-Aristotelian notion of an intelligible species that represents a singular thing. This idea notwithstanding, what I present here constitutes the standard or common version of the doctrine of the intelligible species in the thirteenth century.

18 Opponents of the notion of intelligible species argue that if an intelligible species is to represent anything, then it must be cognized prior to what it represents – at least according to a priority by nature – since a representation can only afford cognition of what it represents on the condition that it is first apprehended in itself. Yet, as we have already emphasized, proponents of the intelligible species maintain that it is not cognized before the thing it represents. Their opponents thus conclude that it cannot represent what it is supposed to represent. According to them, the function of representing an extramental thing to the human soul is carried out by phantasms: although it is a singular representation when considered in itself, a phantasm can nonetheless afford cognition of the universal traits of a thing by virtue of the illuminating-abstractive action exercised upon it by the agent intellect.

19 Cf. Matthew of Acquasparta, *Quaestiones disputatae de cognitione*, q. 4, resp., 304–311; Roger Marston, *Quaestiones disputatae de anima*, q. 2, resp., 231–240; Vital du Four, *Quaestiones disputatae de cognitione*, q. I, a. 2 et 3, 163–185. The reader can find recent biographical sketches for these authors in Pasnau 2010, 924, 965 and 983–984.

20 Cf. Gerard of Bologna, *Quodlibet* III, q. 15 (ed. Piché 2014, §§32–38, 234–236).

21 I should mention that these four arguments, which Gerard grouped together, do not constitute a unified argumentative sequence that could be found in one and the same text, nor even in one philosopher of that time. Each of them, rather, forms an autonomous argumentative structure that could have been called upon in debates, with or without the support of other arguments.

22 The claim of this major premise can be understood either as regarding simple intellection – the apprehension of the essence of things – or complex intellection – the formation of propositions that bear a truth-value: in both cases, it is because reality is as it is that intellections are as they are, not the other way around.

23 The intellection of singulars themselves on the intellect's own powers is contrasted with the intellection by accident or as a consequence. In the first case, which obtains according to the argument's conclusion, singulars are themselves set as objects before the intellectual faculty, which can then grasp them on its own. The opposite thesis asserts that singulars are the direct object of another faculty of the soul, for instance the cogitative faculty, which is an internal sense that grasps singulars by its own powers, whereas it is only by accident or as a consequence of the initial grasp that the intellect apprehends singulars. In the present context, the opposition between intellection on the intellect's own powers and intellection by accident overlaps with the opposition between direct and indirect intellection.

24 Cf. Aristotle, *Categories*, c. 5.

25 Cf. M. Führer 2014.

26 These are the universals *ante rem*, which are both outside of God, out of whom they emanate, and outside the sensible world towards which they emanate.

27 These are the universals *in re*, which are incarnated, so to speak, in material singular things.

28 Cf. Aristotle, *De Anima*, III, 5 (430a18–19).

29 Of which there are many. Most notably, we can mention Thomas Aquinas, whom we will consider more thoroughly later in this chapter.

30 Cf. Matthew of Acquasparta, *Quaestiones disputatae de cognitione*, q. 4, resp., 304–311. These *Disputed Questions* were most probably held in Paris in 1278–79. For the life and work of Matthew of Acquasparta, as well as the salient features of his theory of cognition and references to important secondary literature, see Putallaz 1991a, 13–33.

31 The notion of singular intelligible species is also a key component of the distinct theories that Roger Marston and Vital du Four developed in trying to account for the direct intellection of material singulars. Alongside these developments, a new question became central to gnoseology starting from the years 1280: is the substance of a thing cognized by a proper species or through some kind of inference from the species of the accidents? Regarding this topic, see Robert 2007, 363–393 (especially 382–389).

32 We thus have to distinguish between the direct intellection – or by the intellect itself – of singulars, on the one hand, and the immediate intellection of singulars, on the other. The first, which Matthew defends, is an intellection that, although mediated by an intelligible species, is carried out without reflecting upon the species produced in the other powers of the human soul, namely the phantasms of imagination, which are sensible representations; the second, whose model was to be championed by William of Ockham (see the references to this author in the subsequent notes), is an intellection that is not only direct in the previous sense, but which, moreover, takes place without the representational mediation of any sort of intelligible species, whose necessity for cognitive processes Ockham denies.

33 Abstraction with respect to existence, inasmuch as it is differentiated from universalization-abstraction, plays a crucial role in Ockham's gnoseology. Cf. McCord Adams 1987, vol. I, 495–550, Panaccio 2004, 5–20, Piché 2005.

34 From Matthew of Acquasparta to William of Ockham, including John Duns Scotus, the thesis of the intellectual intuition of singulars, outlandish from the point of view of Aristotelian gnoseology, was progressively strengthened and eventually deemed important by theories of cognition. On this subject, see Bérubé 1964, Day 1947.

35 Regarding this notion of priority, cf. Aristotle, *Categories*, c. 12.

36 For the gnoseological theory of this major thinker, of which I only bring out some central features here, see Pasnau 2003, Williams 2015.

37 To be precise, according to Scotus' theory, the object (common nature) represented by the intelligible species and the intellect are the two partial causes that concur in producing an act of intellection.

38 One could object here that the human intellect loses this capacity to cognize singular things when it is united to the body and immersed in the material world. One could then conclude that, while the human intellect can cognize singulars in principle, it cannot do so as a matter of fact in the present life. However, in addition to the fact that this argument is an examination of hypothetical obstacles to intelligibility that could be found on the side of extramental things, not on the side of the human intellect's powers of cognition, a rejoinder to such an objection would point out that, for anthropological and theological reasons that could be eventually exposed, the human intellect cannot radically change in nature and power when it passes from life on earth to life after death (if such a passage takes place, which is an entirely different question that does not concern me in the present chapter).

39 To which a philosopher such as Thomas Aquinas would retort that common matter, which is part of the definitions of the essences of sensible things, is not an obstacle to the intelligibility of the latter; this obstacle comes from the particular or designated matter (*materia signata*), which is the principle of individuation of sensible things. That is why, according to Aquinas, the human intellect in the state of the present life must abstract from particular matter in order to apprehend the intelligible. Cf. Thomas Aquinas, *Summa theologiae*, I^a, q. 85, a. 1, ad 2; ibid., q. 86, a. 1, co.

40 The first branch of this alternative corresponds to the thesis of the unity of the substantial form of man, whereas the second refers to the plurality of substantial forms in the human composite. I will not consider this topic in itself, which, for that matter, was hotly debated by Latin scholastics of the thirteenth century, but I will touch upon it again in the conclusion of this chapter.

41 From this perspective, there is thus no insurmountable cognitive gap between the intellect and the sensory powers. From the external senses all the way to the intellect, including internal senses such as common sense, imagination, cogitative power and sensible memory (following the Averroist model), there is rather a progressive universalization-abstraction. That being said, it remains true that this theoretical model acknowledges the intellect's prerogative to cognize universals as universals, or even universals *tout court* in the strict sense of the term, i.e. all that pertains to genera and species, as well as the various categories (substance, quality, quantity, etc.) among which the latter are distributed, and even what is beyond the categories, namely that which historiography calls "transcendentals" (being and its related notions, such as one, true and good).

42 I keep the original Latin '*reflexio*' instead of using the translated 'reflection' so as to avoid any confusion between our topic in this context and what ordinary language refers to by 'reflection'. It is also important to note that *reflexio* in our context is *not* the operation whereby the intellect reflects upon its own acts in order to cognize itself. Regarding this distinction, see Putallaz 1991b, 117–123. On the various meanings of the term '*reflexio*', see Wébert 1930.

43 The only recent commentators I know of who mention the duality of doctrines present in the works of Thomas Aquinas, besides J. Wébert in the study cited in the previous note, are Klubertanz 1952, Lonergan 1967, chapter 4, sections 4–5. The most exhaustive study on the subject, that of C. Bérubé, discerns, throughout all the texts where Aquinas considers the indirect intellection of material singulars, only one doctrine which, according to the author, does not vary either in the substance of its problem or in the explanation of the mechanism whereby this indirect intellection takes place. Cf. Bérubé 1964, 42–64 (in particular p. 55 for his claim of the unity and stability of Aquinas' doctrine).

44 Cf. Thomas Aquinas, *De veritate*, q. 19, a. 2, co.; *Quodlibet* VII, q. 1, a. 3, co.; *Scriptum super Sententiis*, lib. 2, d. 3, q. 3, a. 3, ad 1; *Sentencia libri De anima*, lib. 3, l. 8, n. 13–14; *Summa theologiae*, I^a, q. 86, a. 1, co.

45 Cf. Thomas Aquinas, *Summa theologiae*, I^a, q. 86, a. 1, co.

46 In the strict sense, within the context of Aquinas' thought, phantasms are sensible representations produced by the imagination. Yet nothing forbids us from taking 'phantasm' in the broader sense that designates a sensible representation produced by any of the internal senses, be it imagination, memory or the cogitative faculty. In any case, a complete study should be devoted to the role that the cogitative faculty plays in cognition of singular things, especially cognition of particular substances, according to Aquinas but also other thinkers of the thirteenth and fourteenth century.

47 This theory of a 'conversion' towards phantasms raises an important difficulty that Thomas Aquinas did not apparently notice: if the intellect cannot directly grasp the material singular that is outside the soul, how can it directly apprehend the phantasm, which, as it is inherent to a corporeal faculty (an internal sense), is also a singular and material reality?

48 Cf. Thomas Aquinas, *Summa theologiae*, I^a, q. 84, a. 7, co.; ibid., q. 85, a. 1, ad 5.

49 Pasnau 2002, 443n22 and 448n17 maintains that the *conversio ad phantasmata* is something altogether different from the *reflexio* and that we must not conflate the two. In his opinion, Thomas only mentions the first in order to explain the way in which the proper operation of the human intellect takes place, which is to grasp universal natures inasmuch as they exist in singular things of the sensible world, whereas he uses the second precisely to explain the mode according to which our intellect cognizes material

singulars indirectly. In my opinion, this interpretation clashes with what Thomas himself asserts in his *Summa theologiae*, I^a, q. 86, a. 1, co. Indeed, not only does Thomas appeal in this passage to the *conversio ad phantasmata* in order to explain the concept of *reflexio* in an answer whereby he explicitly defends the thesis of the indirect intellection of material singulars, but he also refers to his previous discussion of this *conversio*, essentially *Summa theologiae*, I^a, q. 84, a. 7, co., in which he asserts the necessity for our intellect to turn towards (*convertere se*) the phantasms of material things if it is to apprehend in act the essence of these things, even after having acquired their intelligible species. In other words, Aquinas establishes himself the explanatory conceptual link between the *conversio ad phantasmata* and the *reflexio* regarding the indirect intellection of singular material things.

50 Cf. Thomas Aquinas, *De veritate*, q. 10, a. 5, co.; *Quaestio disputata de anima*, a. 20, ad 1 s.c.; *Scriptum super Sententiis*, lib. 4, d. 50, q. 1, a. 3, co.
51 One can find support for this first interpretation in a relatively early text in Thomas' career, the *De veritate*, q.2, a.6, in which the two explanations appear together in one and the same answer to the question asked. But it is just as plausible to read this text as bearing witness to the fact that at the time Thomas was still hesitating between two different explanations. In this sense, it does not enable us to resolve the issue in favor of the first interpretation.
52 We could also quote the *Quodlibet* XII, q. 8 (held between 1268 and 1272), but we have to be cautious when using this document since it is a *reportatio* that Thomas did not revise. Moreover, the second interpretation would be undermined if we recalled that Thomas's *modus operandi* in the *Summa theologiae* consists in addressing in a succinct way the topics he has more amply developed in his previous works. If we bear this in mind, we might be tempted to eschew the second interpretation and embrace the first. This, however, would be to overlook the *Commentary on the De anima*, a text contemporaneous with questions 75–119 of the *prima pars*, which expounds the first explanation despite its being a literal commentary. This type of text certainly allowed for a more detailed explanation. For the chronology of the works of Thomas Aquinas, see Torrell 1993 (2nd ed. 2002; trans. Royal 1996, rev. 2005).
53 He does so, for instance, in the answer he provides to the question of the self-cognition that the intellect can acquire through its own acts, which of course is a question not without affinities to the one we are considering here. To the question "does the intellective soul cognize itself by its essence" (*Summa theologiae*, I^a, q. 87, a. 1), Thomas answers:

> Our intellect does not cognize itself by its essence, but by its act. And this in two ways. In a <first> way, in a particular manner, when Socrates or Plato perceives that he possesses an intellective soul, because he perceives that he thinks (*intelligere*). In another way, in a universal manner, when we consider the nature of the human mind on the basis of the act of the intellect. (. . .) Yet, there is a difference between these two cognitions. Indeed, the mere presence of the mind suffices for the possession of the first cognition about the mind, which is the principle of the act whereby it perceives itself. That is why we say that it cognizes itself by its presence. However, the presence of the mind does not suffice for the possession of the second cognition about the mind, for which a conscientious and penetrating examination is required.

In this answer, we can see that Thomas clearly distinguishes between two modes of self-cognition for the intellective soul. He could have proceeded in the very same fashion for the case of the intellection of material singulars, but he did not do so. Why? If Thomas had in mind two distinct theoretical models when explaining the intellection of material singulars, why did he not acknowledge it explicitly?
54 Cf. Henry of Ghent, *Quodlibet* IV, q. 21, resp., Parisiis, 1518, fol. 137rL–138rN.

55 I should mention that Henry of Ghent is one of the thinkers of the thirteenth century who argued against the existence of a species that is printed upon the intellect. Henry thus considers that such a species is superfluous not only as regards the indirect intellection of material singulars but more generally for any human intellection on earth.
56 Cf. John Duns Scotus, *Ordinatio* I, d. 3, p. 3, q. 1, resp., 211–212, §352; Idem, *Reportatio Parisiensis* I-A, d. 3, q. 4, II, (ed. King), 4, l. 19 – 5, l. 5.
57 The doctrine of Duns Scotus regarding intellectual cognition of material singulars is complex and ambiguous: considering it here would lead us well beyond the limits allotted to the present chapter. Aside from the references I have already mentioned, I refer the reader to Bérubé 1964, 134–224.
58 On Olivi's theory of cognition, see, among others, Pasnau and Toivanen 2013, Pasnau 1997, Perler 2003, 33–75.
59 This 'extension' is called virtual or intentional because it is not, obviously, a real movement whereby the soul would cover the space that separates it from the object and take hold of it in the way our hands do. This is just another way of saying that the cognitive acts of the human soul are immanent to it.
60 Cf. Vital du Four, *Quaestiones disputatae de cognitione*, q. I, a. 2, 163–164.
61 Cf. Thomas Aquinas, *De veritate*, q. 2, a. 6, ad 3; ibid., q. 10, a. 5, co.; Ibid., *Scriptum super Sententiis*, lib. 4, d. 50, q. 1, a. 3, ad 3 s.c. .
62 An autonomy in principle, not in fact, since the fallen condition of man on earth makes it necessary for him to resort to the senses in order to acquire cognition.
63 Intimately, but not necessarily, as we can see with Henry of Ghent, who maintains both the plurality of substantial forms and the indirect intellection of material singulars.

Bibliography

Primary sources

Albertus Magnus (1890). "*De intellectu et intelligibili*," in (ed.) A. E. Borgnet, *Opera Omnia*, Paris, Vivès.

Gerard of Bologna (2014). "*Quodlibet* III, q. 15," in (ed.) D. Piché, *La théorie de la connaissance intellectuelle de Gérard de Bologne (ca. 1240/50–1317). Édition critique et étude doctrinale de quatorze Quodlibeta*, Louvain-la-Neuve, Peeters (Philosophes médiévaux, 61), 229–248.

John Duns Scotus, *Reportatio Parisiensis* I-A, d. 3, q. 4, II, ed. P. King, <http://individual.utoronto.ca/pking/editions_and_translations.html>.

John Duns Scotus (1954). "*Ordinatio* I, dist. 3," in *Opera omnia*, Vol. 3, (eds.) C. Balic et al., Vatican City, Typis Polyglottis Vaticanis.

Matthew of Acquasparta (1903). *Quaestiones disputatae de cognitione*, Quaracchi, Florentiae.

Roger Marston (1932). "*Quaestiones disputatae de anima*," in *Quaestiones disputatae de emanatione aeterna, de statu naturae lapsae et de anima*, Quaracchi, Florentiae.

Vital du Four (1927). "*Quaestiones disputatae de cognitione*, (ed.) F. Delorme in Delorme, F., 'Le Cardinal Vital du Four: huit questions disputées sur le problème de la connaissance'," *Archives d'histoire doctrinale et littéraire du Moyen Âge* 2, 151–337.

Secondary sources

Bérubé, C. (1964). *La connaissance de l'individuel au Moyen Âge*, Montréal/Paris, Presses de l'Université de Montréal/Presses universitaires de France.

Day, S. J. (1947). *Intuitive Cognition: A Key to the Significance of the Later Scholastics*, St. Bonaventure, NY, The Franciscan Institute.
Führer, M. (2014). "Albert the Great," in (ed.) E. N. Zalta, *The Stanford Encyclopedia of Philosophy* (Winter 2014 Edition), <http://plato.stanford.edu/archives/win2014/entries/albert-great/>.
Klubertanz, G. P. (1952). "St. Thomas and the Knowledge of the Singular," *The New Scholasticism* 26, 135–166.
Lonergan, B. (1967). *Verbum: Word and Idea in Aquinas*, Notre Dame, IN, University of Notre Dame Press.
McCord Adams, M. (1987). *William Ockham*, Vol. 1, Notre Dame, IN, University of Notre Dame Press.
Panaccio, C. (2004). *Ockham on Concepts*, Aldershot, Ashgate.
Pasnau, R. (2002). *Thomas Aquinas on Human Nature*, Cambridge, Cambridge University Press.
Pasnau, R. (2003). "Cognition," in (ed.) T. Williams, *The Cambridge Companion to Duns Scotus*, Cambridge, Cambridge University Press, 285–311.
Pasnau, R. (1997). *Theories of Cognition in the Later Middle Ages*, Cambridge, Cambridge University Press.
Pasnau, R. (ed.) (2010). *The Cambridge History of Medieval Philosophy*, Vol. II Cambridge, Cambridge University Press.
Pasnau, R. and Toivanen, J. (2013). "Peter John Olivi," (ed.) E. N. Zalta, *The Stanford Encyclopedia of Philosophy* (Summer 2013 Edition), <http://plato.stanford.edu/archives/sum2013/entries/olivi/>.
Perler, D. (2003). *Théories de l'intentionnalité au Moyen Âge*, Paris, Vrin.
Piché, D. (2005). *Guillaume d'Ockham. Intuition et abstraction*, Paris, Vrin.
Piché, D. (2014). *La théorie de la connaissance intellectuelle de Gérard de Bologne (ca. 1240/50–1317). Édition critique et étude doctrinale de quatorze Quodlibeta*, Louvain-la-Neuve, Peeters.
Putallaz, F.-X. (1991a). *La connaissance de soi au XIIIe siècle. De Matthieu d'Aquasparta à Thierry de Freiberg*, Paris, Vrin.
Putallaz, F.-X. (1991b). *Le sens de la réflexion chez Thomas d'Aquin*, Paris, Vrin.
Robert, A. (2007). "L'universalité réduite au discours. Sur quelques théories franciscaines de l'abstraction à la fin du XIIIe siècle," *Documenti e studi sulla tradizione filosofica medievale* 18, 363–393.
Spruit, L. (1994). *Species Intelligibilis: From Perception to Knowledge. Volume 1: Classical Roots and Medieval Discussions*, Leiden, Brill.
Torrell, J.-P. (1993; 2nd ed. 2002). *Initiation à saint Thomas d'Aquin. Sa personne et son œuvre*, Paris/Fribourg, Cerf/Éditions Universitaires (translated into English by R. Royal (1996, rev. 2005), *Saint Thomas Aquinas. Volume 1: The Person and His Work*, Baltimore, MD, The Catholic University of America Press).
Wébert, J. (1930). "'Reflexio'. Étude sur les opérations réflexives dans la psychologie de saint Thomas d'Aquin," in *Mélanges Mandonnet. Études d'histoire littéraire et doctrinale du Moyen Âge*, t. I, Paris, Vrin, 285–325.
Williams, T. (2015). "John Duns Scotus," (ed.) E. N. Zalta, *The Stanford Encyclopedia of Philosophy* (Summer 2015 Edition), <http://plato.stanford.edu/archives/sum2015/entries/duns-scotus/>.

3

AVICENNA AND THE ISSUE OF THE INTELLECTUAL ABSTRACTION OF INTELLIGIBLES

Richard C. Taylor

1 The Aristotelian context

Al-Farabi (d. 980 CE), Avicenna (Ibn Sina, d. 1037) and Averroes (Ibn Rushd d. 1198), widely known classical rationalists in the Arabic/Islamic philosophical tradition and strongly influential sources for Latin philosophy in the High Middle Ages, all thought themselves to be following Aristotle's lead regarding the intellectual abstraction of intelligibles in the formation of necessary and unchanging scientific knowledge. For Aristotle it is clear that sensation is a potentiality for apprehending or coming to be individual sensed objects found in the world exterior to the human soul. This takes place by way of a separation of the forms of sensibles from matter and a reception of them as an actualization of the senses of the soul.[1] In an analogous fashion, intellectual knowing is a potentiality for apprehending or coming to be in act non-individuated intellectual forms (*noeta*) that are somehow in individuated particular sensible things. Although Aristotle says that "the objects of thought are in the sensible forms" (*De Anima* 3.8, 432a5), the analogy with sensation breaks down when it comes to the objects intellectually known. The reason for this is that the non-individuated or universal forms of human knowledge are not in the sensibles *in act* as they must be in the intellect.[2] Again following Aristotle *De Anima* 3.4 and 3.5, these thinkers hold for a part of intellect that is passive (*ginesthai*) or receptive of all things and another part that is active in making (*poiein*) all things, this latter described as a disposition like light (*hōs hexis tis, hoion to phōs*), this as well describing the active agent as acting like light. This second part, which the Arabic tradition called the Agent Intellect (*al-'aql al-fa"āl*), sometimes describing it also as Active Intellect, *al-'aql al-fā'il*, was understood *per Aristotelem* to be an eternal (*aidion*) cause of the intellectual forms in the human intellect. It was accepted that, without a grounding in separate eternal intellect, there may well be generalization or abstraction – in some sense of the term – but scientific knowledge understood as true, necessary and unchanging will not be achieved.³ Of course, in *Posterior Analytics* 2.19 Aristotle writes of sensory experience and provides the image of a retreat gradually coming to a halt, saying, "The soul is so constituted that it is capable of the same sort of process" (*Posterior Analytics* 100a14, Aristotle, 1956). This process somehow establishes the universal in the soul even though perception is of the particular. He describes this as taking place by induction, writing, "Clearly then it must be by induction (*epagōgē*) that we acquire knowledge of the primary principles, because this is also the way in which general concepts are conveyed to us by sense-perception." These are "first things" (*ta prōta*) or primary principles or premises required by demonstration. And the Arabic tradition understood Aristotle to hold for the necessity of demonstration in the formation of scientific knowledge, something that stringently requires not only proper syllogistic form but also first premises that are known to be true, not just supposed or simply generalized on the basis of experience.⁴ For the Arabic tradition, Aristotle's doctrine of intellectual understanding required the involvement of that separate Agent Intellect to provide a solid foundation for human scientific knowledge by way of intellectual abstraction.

2   What is meant by abstraction in the Arabic tradition

Yet no clear account or definitive statement of *intellectual* abstraction is found in Aristotle's own writings.⁵ The teachings of these three philosophers on intellectual abstraction, rather, came not directly and solely from the study of Aristotle but rather through an interpretive framework set out in works on intellect and intelligibles by Alexander of Aphrodisias (*fl.* 200 CE). He explicitly writes of the intellect separating (*chōrizōn/yufridu-hā/faṣala-hā*) forms from matter and producing the intelligible requisite for science by abstraction (*aphraisesei/ifrād*).⁶ For Alexander in his *On the Intellect*, the First Cause and Unmoved Mover or God is also the Productive or Agent Intellect which provides a receptive disposition to the individual perishable human being and assists in intellectual abstraction (see Cerami 2016). His account of abstraction was well known by our three major figures of the Arabic tradition. The *Paraphrase of the De Anima* by Themistius,⁷ itself influenced by Alexander and Plotinus on the issue, was also available in Arabic and may have been a source for Avicenna, and certainly it was a key source for Averroes (see Taylor 2013; Taylor 2009).

Al-Farabi, while not identifying the Agent Intellect with God, was surely influenced in a significant way by the account of human intellect and abstraction in Alexander, even to the point that Marc Geoffroy has contended that he may never have read the *De Anima* of Aristotle but instead derived much of his thought from the work of Alexander (see Geoffroy 2002). In his *Letter on the*

Intellect, he explains that the Agent Intellect (*al-'aql al-fa"āl*)[8] provides to the particular human soul a power of receptivity. This power enables that individual human being to separate or abstract (*intaza'a*) the form from its original mode of being as a sensible to a new mode of being as an intelligible in act. Prior to that it was an intelligible in potency, i.e., able to be an object of intellect and thought, while now it is in actuality as a intelligible in the human intellect. That is, it existed as a determinate particular entity in the world and then as a sensed particular in the perceiver. By intellectual abstraction it ultimately comes to exist in a distinctively different mode of being. Now it is an intelligible in act in the human power of intellect that allows for the formation of a universal predicable of many individual instances in the world. He says that "it abstracts (*tantazi'u*) the essences (*māhiyāt*) and forms (*ṣuwar-hā*) of all the beings without their matters such that it makes all of them a form or forms for it" (al-Farabi 1983, 12.7–9, my translation; see Taylor 2006). Insofar as this power is natural to all human beings, in forming intelligibles in act that constitute the basis for scientific universals, the agent is the individual human being's actual intellect. In other works such as his *Perfect State,* for example, a more simple and general account is given of the Agent Intellect as needed as an intermediary between God and human beings for the sake of revelation.[9] But even there abstraction is discussed and described as a transferring (with the verb *naqala*) of an intelligible in potency to a new mode of actuality, with the separately existing Agent Intellect providing to the human soul something like light for the abstraction to take place.[10]

For Averroes, who sets out in his mature *Long Commentary on the De Anima* a new and complex theory in which the human individual requires the use of the powers of the separate Agent and Material Intellects shared by all human beings, the content of scientific knowledge comes from the world.[11] The Agent Intellect, though a separate substance in its own right with no knowledge of things in the natural world, plays an explanatory role in intellectual abstraction by being available for use by individuals in the garnering of knowledge from sensory experience through a transfer of content from particularity to immaterial intelligibility. The light of the Agent Intellect illumines images formed by the external and internal sense powers and abstracts or separates the intelligible in potency and impresses it on the receptive Material Intellect. Averroes writes that this is through the willing agency of the individual human being, and so these activities are in the soul:

> It was necessary to ascribe these two activities to the soul in us, namely, to receive the intelligible and to make it, although the agent and the recipient are eternal substances, on account of the fact that these two activities are reduced to our will, namely, to abstract intelligibles and to understand them (Averroes 1953, 439; 2009, 351).

In this way he follows al-Farabi in insisting that the content of human understanding must come from experience by way of an abstractive intellectual process which involves the individual imagined form apprehended through sensation, in the words of Averroes so reminiscent of those of al-Farabi, being "transferred in its being from one order into another" (Averroes 1953, 439; 2009, 351), that is, from the mode of being of a particular to the mode of being of an intelligible in act. For Averroes the consequent set of intelligibles in act must be contained in a single shared intellect, the Material Intellect, for the sake of common knowledge and science, something based on the account of Themistius (see Taylor 2013).

Both al-Farabi and Averroes maintained that the content of natural human knowing comes from the forms of things in the world, that is, the content of natural knowledge does not come directly from the Agent Intellect. Al-Farabi, as we have seen, provided two accounts. The Agent Intellect provides the human individual with a power of receptivity by which the individual by personal effort may strive to realize itself through intellectual understanding to attain existence as an immaterial substance; or the Agent Intellect provides the power of abstraction through its light. Al-Farabi's other account allows for the abstractive light of the Agent Intellect to do the abstraction and at the same time allows for the content of religious teachings to come from God through the Agent Intellect to an individual prophet. For both of these thinkers three conditions must obtain for abstractive knowledge of the world: (i) the activity of intellectual abstraction is carried out by a particular human being acting intentionally and by will; (ii) the intelligible content of the generated intelligible in act should come from sense experience of the natural world; and (iii) the knowledge garnered must be of real scientific knowledge of intelligibles as the human apprehension of essential definitions or necessary essences. For Avicenna, the concerns are whether and, if so, how his thought on intellectual abstraction is to be understood regarding criteria (ii) and (iii).

In the case of Avicenna, scholars of his thought have given widely divergent accounts. The traditional understanding held by some is largely in accord with thinkers of the medieval Latin theological and philosophical tradition who were influenced by translations from Arabic. On this view, for Avicenna the content of intellectually apprehended intelligibles in act comes to be in the human soul by way of an emanation (*fayḍ*) or by a conjoining (*ittiṣāl*) with the separately existing Agent Intellect. The Agent Intellect houses all the intellectual forms of things of the world, with human sensation playing a prompting role but not alone providing the content of intellectual understanding (see Rahman 1958; Davidson 1992; Black 2005; Taylor and Herrera 2005; Taylor 1996). Others have contended vigorously and valuably that the content of knowing does come from sensation through a naturalistic process involving discursive reasoning, with the Agent Intellect playing little role concerning the content of intellectual understanding.[12]

In another approach which will not be considered in detail here, Jon McGinnis (McGinnis 2006; McGinnis 2008; McGinnis 2010) has suggested that forms of things arising in the human soul through sense perception and the activities of the internal senses are changed from particularity by receiving, by emanation from the Agent Intellect, the accident of universality. McGinnis proposes that the forms emanated are the forms which are intelligible accidents such as universality itself. For him, when the human rational power is suitably prepared through the levels of material abstractions carried out by the external senses and internal sense powers of the brain, the Active Intellect then emanates upon the abstracted essence the accident of universality and other accidents consequent upon the existence of the essence or intelligible in act in the human intellect. This approach to the issue, however, is predicated on a category mistake. In the physical world of hylomorphic entities particularity is a logical characterization that follows immediately upon the realization of a determinate form in matter. Particularization is not something separate and prior but rather a descriptive logical term that follows upon a prior real actuality of a form in matter to yield a determinate particular entity as a substance or an accident. No essence can be particularized in the absence of a subject. To put it in more general terms, an essence or form is classified as particular only subsequent to its realization in a subject. Much the same is the case for universality. It is, rather, a descriptive logical term to characterize something that can be predicated. There is no such thing as universality as such, as a real accident emanated upon and received by an essence. The essence horse can exist either in the world or in the mind. In the latter, it is described as having existence in human knowing in such a way that it can be predicated. Intelligible "accidents" such as universality and particularity, as well as others, are not prior but instead posterior to and consequent upon the nature of the essence or form in relation to the subject in which the essence or form exists. But, more to the point, particularity and universality are logical second intentions, not realities that can be emanated.

More recently some espousing a naturalistic process have attempted to reconcile the various accounts by way of a distinction between the epistemic and the ontological sources of intelligibles in act. A more recent contribution by another author provides a valuable rethinking of the issue of intellectual abstraction yet is insufficiently clear in accounting for the integration of Avicenna's denial of individual human intellectual memory. However, consideration of the *Paraphrase of the De Anima* by Themistius[13] – a work known to Avicenna – offers novel considerations that may permit new conciliating insights into our understanding of the teachings of Avicenna on intellectual abstraction.

In what follows here, I examine the accounts of Avicenna on intellectual understanding as found in writings by Dag Nikolaus Hasse and Dimitri Gutas. I next highlight the analyses by Tommaso Alpina and consider the problem of intellectual memory as posed by him. I then recount the teaching of Themistius on intellectual abstraction in his *Paraphrase of the De Anima* and argue that the account of Avicenna can be best understood as inspired substantially, albeit not wholly, by that of Themistius, something not previously proposed, to my knowledge. Then I conclude with some final remarks on the issue of intellectual abstraction in Avicenna.

3 Dag Nikolaus Hasse and Dimitri Gutas: critique of the traditional view and promotion of a naturalistic account

3.1 Dag Nikolaus Hasse (2000, 2001)

In his book *Avicenna's De anima in the Latin West*, published in 2000, and in his 2001 article, "Avicenna on Abstraction," Dag Hasse marshals impressive arguments from a wide array of texts from the corpus of Avicenna in favor of a doctrine of intellectual abstraction. In his book, critique of the traditional view is incidental; in the article, it is the central focus of his attention. He writes, "I think this interpretation cannot stand as it is. One of its unpleasant consequences is that Avicenna would not have achieved what he is thought to have achieved, namely the development of a theory of abstraction," that is, a theory of the "transformation of sense-data into intelligibles" (Hasse 2001, 40). He also takes the opportunity to examine the thought of one of Avicenna's chief sources of inspiration in philosophy, al-Farabi, and concludes that in this case the results yielded are not consequential, since "al-Farabi's remarks about abstraction remain sketchy and are in danger of being overinterpreted" (Hasse 2001, 43, but see Taylor 2006).

In his study of the texts of Avicenna on this issue, Hasse looks at writings from three periods of the life of Avicenna. He explains that in the *Compendium of the Soul* (*ca.* 996–7), written when Avicenna was young, the human power or faculty which forms intelligible intentions "acquires intelligible forms from sense-perception by force of an inborn disposition." The imaginative and estimative faculties then process the forms in the common sense and memory into singular intelligible intentions, thanks to "the assistance of the universal intellect . . . and with the mediation of necessary, intellectual axioms that naturally exist in it" (Hasse 2001, 44).[14] In this work Avicenna writes,

> Just as the faculties of sense-perception perceive only through imitation of the object of sense-perception, likewise the intellectual faculties perceive (*tudriku*) only through imitation of the object of intellection. This imitation is the abstraction (*tajrid*) of the form from matter and the union with [the form]. The sensible form, however, does not come about when the faculty of sensation wishes to move or act, but when the essence of the object of sensation reaches the faculty either by accident or through the mediation of the moving faculty; the abstraction (*tajarrud*) of the form [occurs] to the faculty because of the assistance of the media which make the forms reach the faculty. The case is different with the intellectual faculty, because its essence performs the abstraction of forms from matter by itself whenever it wishes, and then it unites with [the form]. For this reason one says that the faculty of sense-perception has a somehow passive role in conceiving [forms], whereas the intellectual faculty is active, or rather one says that the

faculty of sense-perception cannot dispense with the organs and does not reach actualization through itself, while it would be wrong to apply this statement to the intellectual faculty.
(Hasse 2001, 44–45)[15]

Here it is the individual human rational soul[16] by its own natural intellectual faculty carrying out the activity of abstraction or separation of the form from matter. Avicenna uses other standard terms indicating abstraction, as Hasse points out: *istafāda* : acquire, *wajada* : find, *istanbata* : derive, *jarrada* : abstract. Hence, there is no real doubt about the words of Avicenna or about his extensive emphasis on the efforts of individual human work and effort by use of a natural power in the process of abstraction. Hasse rightly characterizes this early account of Avicenna as one that appears to entail that "both the senses and the universal intellect are necessary accompanying conditions rather than powers active in the process" (Hasse 2001, 46). Nevertheless, Avicenna finds that reference to a universal intellect, the Agent Intellect, is somehow indispensable for abstraction, even if its precise activity is not spelled out; the efforts of the individual rational soul are not sufficient alone for this.

In works which Hasse characterizes as "mature works of his middle period" (Hasse 2001, 46), *The State of the Human Soul* or *The Destination*, the *De anima* of the *Shifā'*, the *al-Najāt*, and the *Mashriqiyyun*, "The Easterners," Avicenna gives a consistent account of four stages of abstraction: (i) sense perception abstracts or separates a thing's form from matter; (ii) retentive imagination abstracts or separates insofar as it receives the still particular form of the thing; and (iii) estimation abstracts or separates non-sensible intentions and also, functioning as the human cogitative power, denudes the particular of the extraneous. Finally, (iv) the rational power frees it of all material considerations and particularity, abstracting (*intaza'*) it completely

> both from matter and from their material attachments and grasps them in the way of abstraction; hence in the case of "man" which is predicated of many, this faculty takes the unitary nature of the many, divests *(afraza)* it of all material quantity, quality, place, and position. If [the faculty] did not abstract *(jarrada)* it from all these, it could not be truly predicated of all.
> (Hasse 2001, 48, trans. Avicenna 1952b, 40, slightly modified by Hasse)[17]

Predication, which involves the assertion of an intelligible universal of one or more particulars, requires that all materiality and particularity be absent from the predicated intelligible. In this middle period, Avicenna holds that the first three sorts of abstraction or separation are in the power of human beings, while the fourth, which brings about the intelligible in act in the rational soul, requires the assistance of the Agent Intellect. He states, "there emanates from the Agent Intellect a power and proceeds to the imaginable things that are potentially intelligible, in order to make them intelligible in actuality and to make the intellect in potentiality an intellect in actuality" (Hasse 2001, 52, trans. Avicenna 1952b, 69.) Here the Agent Intellect makes the human soul to be in the very act of intellectual understanding. It does so by making particular images of things which are intelligible in potency in the image-forming power and memory of the soul into the intelligibles in act in the human intellect. Yet Avicenna stresses that this is not an issue of "the particulars themselves ... transferred (*tantaqilu*)[18] from imagination to our intellect." Rather, this preparation of the rational soul is properly explained in this way: "looking at the particulars disposes the soul for something abstracted (*al-mujarrad*) to flow upon it from the active intellect," in the translation of Hasse (Hasse 2001, 54, trans. Avicenna 1959, 235).[19] The referent of *al-mujarrad* here is suspect since in context it seems it must refer to unblemished or uncontaminated (*mujarradāt*) forms as intelligibles in act received into the rational soul. Here the unexplained notion of a need for assistance from a universal intellect (scil., the Agent Intellect) in the earlier works characterized by Hasse as a necessary accompanying condition is spelled out more fully. In this work there is willed and intentional human activity directed toward the attainment of knowledge, but the source content of the intelligibles in act is in the Agent Intellect.

For the late period writings of Avicenna, Hasse finds some of reflections of teachings of the middle period but notes the importance of a new development in the *Isharāt*. He notes that through the earlier periods Avicenna moved from a model of the Agent Intellect as somehow assisting the rational soul to one of it mediating in the apprehension of intellectual knowledge. Now Avicenna abandons use of the analogy of light and the teaching on mediation. In the *Isharāt* Hasse finds that the role of the Agent Intellect appears to recede completely from Avicenna's account of abstraction: the process of the abstractive formation of the intelligible seems to be given over to the human intellect acting alone (Hasse 2001, 62–63).

Having clearly set out many of the key texts on abstraction in Avicenna, Hasse then draws his conclusion.

> Since abstraction is a complex phenomenon and since Avicenna developed his position gradually, one can find passages relevant to the topic in many different contexts of Avicenna's oeuvre. Combining these passages does not yet give us a clear picture of the theory: the increasing complexity of his philosophy makes it difficult to decide which pieces of doctrine are interrelated and which are not. This is why it seems advisable to attempt a developmental interpretation by describing the gradual transformation of groups of doctrines.
>
> (Hasse 2001, 64)

The implication of Hasse's analyses is that Avicenna began with a naturalistic understanding of intellectual abstraction without a clearly defined role for the Agent Intellect. Then in his middle period he found it necessary that the Agent Intellect be an essential factor in the abstraction of intelligibles in accounts where he employed the famous metaphors of emanation from and conjoining with the

Agent Intellect. Finally, the later works of Avicenna appear to have in some way moved back toward a naturalistic account without the involvement of the Agent Intellect for human intellectual abstraction.

In sum, in *Avicenna's De Anima in the Latin West. The Formation of a Peripatetic Philosophy of Soul 1160–1300* (2000) and in "Avicenna on Abstraction" (2001) Hasse clearly establishes in his text studies that the doctrine of the intellectual abstraction is not a mere *façon de parler* for emanation from the Agent Intellect. (i) Avicenna was seriously seeking to work out the details of sensory and intellectual abstraction on the part of individual human rational agents using logic and discursive and intuitive reason. (ii) Avicenna consistently indicates that the content of human knowing comes from sensory experience and the employment of intellectual powers on the part of the human rational soul, though in the middle period he clearly seeks to ground human attainment of intelligibles in act somehow in the Agent Intellect by way of the metaphors of emanation (*fayḍ*) and conjoining (*ittiṣāl*). And (iii) in the early and middle works, there is a role played by the Agent Intellect, as there is in the thought of al-Farabi and Averroes, but for Avicenna this recedes in later works.

3.2 Dimitri Gutas (2001, 2012)

In his "Intuition and Thinking: The Evolving Structure of Avicenna's Epistemology," Dimitri Gutas provides a meticulous study of the texts of Avicenna on the nature of intuition and the role it plays in his discussion of the apprehension of intelligibles. As he describes it, Avicenna developed a theory of intuition (*ḥads*) according to which "[a]ll intelligible knowledge, that is, all non-a priori knowledge of universals that depends on syllogistic reasoning, is accomplished by the discovery of the middle term in a syllogism" (Gutas 2001, 3). When that discovery comes about instantly it is by acumen (*dhakā'*), with intuition either directly or through a teacher's intuition by a movement of intellect. In a later revised version, intuition is identified as that instantaneous grasp of the middle term and thinking (*fikr*) "is now defined as a movement of the soul in search of the middle term" (Gutas 2001, 4). Gutas highlights the views of Avicenna on *ḥads*, an intuitive power for apprehending the middle term for use in syllogisms, which is developed through his key works. The search for the middle term with ordinary thinking (*fikr*) "paves the way" for the reception of "Middle terms [which] come only from the divine effluence" (Gutas 2001, 27). This "effluence" from the Agent Intellect is intuition (*ḥads*) in the human knower. For Avicenna, according to Gutas, the Agent Intellect is not an immediately and actively involved efficient causal agent in the activity of human intellectual abstraction, though it plays an important role in connecting human endeavors at intellectual understanding with the locus of intelligibles in the Agent Intellect. Regarding the Agent Intellect, Gutas writes,

> Avicenna fully subscribed to the reality of the active intellect as the eternal substance, ontologically prior to us, which makes our potential

powers of thinking actual by being itself incessantly an actual thinker and hence the real "locus" of all intelligibles, or all thoughts actually being thought. The principle behind this idea is that for something to exist potentially in something it must exist actually in something else – a principle which Avicenna uses in connection with prophecy in the *Proof of Prophecies* – and it is analogous to his core conception of necessary and contingent being: just as we are contingent beings because there is a necessary being – and in *that* sense being emanates to us therefrom so also are we potential thinkers because there is an actual thinker – and in *that* sense thoughts emanate to us therefrom.

(Gutas 2001, 29–30)

What Gutas has in mind here appears to be that the Agent Intellect functions as a necessary condition making human thinking and intellectual abstraction possible, not as a distinct efficient cause pouring forth intelligibles to be received passively by adequately prepared human minds, the traditional view referred to earlier. The precise meaning of Gutas here is worthy of further analysis. But for present purposes it suffices to note that he holds an understanding of abstraction whereby human beings by their own natural and intrinsic powers are responsible for the formation of intelligibles in act in the soul. For Gutas, as the Necessary Being is required to ground the existence of contingent beings in Avicenna, similarly the Agent Intellect grounds the apprehension of intelligibles in act that constitute scientific knowledge. What is more, since for Avicenna the rational soul does not have intellectual memory for the storage of intelligibles, the soul must connect with the Agent Intellect where those intelligibles primarily exist in its actuality (Gutas 2001, 13).[20]

In "The Empiricism of Avicenna" Gutas 2012 provides the most comprehensive account of Avicenna on experience and the development of human intellectual thought. He emphasizes all the more a naturalistic account of Avicenna on abstraction and provides an exemplary account of texts on forms of abstraction from across the corpus of Avicenna's writings.

As Gutas recounts, Avicenna's account of human knowing is based on concept formation (*taṣawwur*) and propositional truth (*taṣdīq*), the former to be verified by the latter. For the issue of intellectual abstraction which interests us here, truth is attained through sense perception and rational reflection, with confirmation through experience or repeated instances of the same events or information (Gutas 2012, 395–396). Regarding sense perception according to Avicenna,

the perceptive faculties in humans are essentially two, the five external senses of the animal soul and the intellect of the rational (human) soul. Raw data from the five external senses are processed at a level of secondary elaboration by three of the five internal senses of the animal soul – common sense, estimation, and imagination – while the other two, imagery and memory, are merely storage areas. The internal common sense, located in the front part of the brain, processes and renders meaningful the raw data of the external senses; as Avicenna says, the sense that really does the perceiving is the common sense. The internal sense of estimation, located in the middle part of the brain, judges what the non-sensible implications of the sensory data are. The internal sense of imagination, also located in the middle part of the brain, combines and separates forms and images received from sensory data.

(Gutas 2012, 398)

The internal sense of imagination has the task of manipulating received images, and in the case of human beings it has what Gutas calls a "procedural" task "in combining and separating intellective data provided to it by the intellect" (Gutas 2012, 402). Reflection on the part of the rational soul also plays a role in the preparation for intellectual abstraction.

After recounting senses or stages of intellect (receptive material intellect, dispositional intellect or actual intellect possessing primary principles of understanding), Gutas cites Avicenna's remarks in the *Najāt*:

In forming concepts, sense perception and imagination (*takhayyul*) assist the intellect because sense perception presents to the [internal sense of] imagery (*khayāl*) things in a mixture, and imagery [presents them] to the intellect. The intellect then discriminates among them, breaks them down into parts [i.e., categories], takes up each one of the concepts individually, and arranges [in order] the most particular and the most general, the essential and the accidental. Thereupon there are impressed on the intellect, in [a process of] concept formation, the primary notions (*al-maʿānī al-ūlā*), and then definitions are composed out of them.

(Gutas 2012, 406)

In this way sensation is the foundation for the formation of concepts. Intellect here Gutas describes as being "procedural" in that sense that it does not of itself contribute any content to what comes to be in the receptive material intellect. Even the primary principles of understanding and thought emerge from experience of the world and are not emanations from the Agent Intellect (Gutas 2012, 407). Hence, rather than asserting that intelligibles in act come to the rational soul in an emanation from the Agent Intellect, as the traditional account of Avicenna would have it, Gutas finds in Avicenna that the individual rational soul has responsibility for the content of intelligibles. He quotes Avicenna,

The animal faculties [i.e. the external and internal senses] assist the rational soul in various ways, one of them being that sensation brings to it particulars from which result four [processes]: Firstly, the [rational] soul extracts (*intizāʿ*) single universals from particulars by way of abstracting (*tajrīd*) their concepts from matter. . . . Secondly, the [rational] soul brings about relations, like those of negation and affirmation, among these separate universals. Where this combination by negation and affirmation is self-evident, it simply accepts it; but where this is not the case it leaves it till the discovery of the middle term. Thirdly, it acquires premises based on testing and proving (*tajribiyya*). . . . In the fourth category are the reports whose truth is acknowledged because of their sequential and multiple transmission (*tawātur*).

(Gutas 2012, 410. Avicenna 1959, 221–222; trans. adapted, with slight modifications, from that of Avicenna 1952b)

The formation of the syllogism and the apprehension of the middle term is the grasp of the truth of the intelligible in act, the grasp of the connection that yields the essential definition. This is done by the intellect of the rational soul and results in the apprehension of "secondary intelligibles, which are acquired by the intellect upon its demand and after search by hitting on the middle term in a process which Avicenna describes also as coming in contact with the active intellect" (Gutas 2012, 414).

On this explanation the Agent Intellect ("active intellect" in the translation of Gutas) plays little of a role. With a more substantial explanation than that found in his 2001 article, Gutas here relegates the Agent Intellect to the role of being the locus of intelligibles, since Avicenna holds that the individual rational soul does not have its own intellectual memory. As he sees it, the Agent Intellect as well as the intellects of the spheres are eternally active in thinking all the intelligibles. This Intellect, Gutas explains, even when described as something providing a divine emanation, being in contact with the human soul, and illuminating the rational soul's procedures of formation of intelligibles in act,

has no bearing on the entire epistemological process of the human intellect as it is aided by the external and internal senses in ways described in great detail and rigor by Avicenna. This process is squarely and exclusively based on empirical data, processed, as need may be, by reason.

(Gutas 2012, 412)

The writings of Hasse and Gutas discussed here go far in putting away the traditional notion that for Avicenna the content of intellectual abstraction comes into the soul as an emanation of forms from the separate Agent Intellect. Yet difficulties remain. The traditional account holds the Agent Intellect is replete with forms and uses that notion to ground human intellectual abstraction in the eternity of the Agent Intellect and its forms. The first analysis of Gutas 2001 reviewed seems to relegate the Agent Intellect to the status of some necessary condition for the existence of science among human beings without an explicit account of its causality in the process of intellectual abstraction. His second article seems to push the Agent Intellect out of the picture with the claim that it "has no bearing on the entire epistemological process of the human intellect," as cited earlier. Further, the notion that the intelligibles in act, purportedly abstracted solely by the natural powers of the human soul, must be stored in the separate Agent Intellect which is "eternally thinking them," is severely problematic. Since the Agent Intellect is pure actuality, it has no potency for receiving abstracted intelligibles. It would seem then that this notion of *storage* cannot be taken literally. Further, for those stored intelligibles in act to be accessible to the human intellect through time, there must be some sort of real, not metaphorical, causal connection between the Agent Intellect and the human rational soul. As we have seen, however, Hasse recounts the many times Avicenna finds the Agent Intellect essential in the human formation of intelligibles in act in the course of reviewing works of the various periods of Avicenna's writings.

Before taking up consideration of Avicenna, I earlier set out three conditions that must be met in an account of intellectual abstraction. The first was that the activity of intellectual abstraction be carried out primarily by a particular human being who acts intentionally and by will. This condition is clearly met by Avicenna. The second condition was that the intelligible content of the generated intelligible in act should come solely from sense experience of the natural world. On the basis of the accounts of Hasse and Gutas, this condition also is met by Avicenna. The third condition is that the knowledge garnered by intellectual abstraction not be tentative or conditional but rather must be of real scientific knowledge of intelligibles as the human apprehension of essential definitions or necessary essences. This condition was met by al-Farabi and Averroes in their accounts of intellectual abstraction but is not satisfied in the account of Gutas and in one of the versions set out by Hasse.

Hence, two problems remain, both of which concern the issue of a real connection with the Agent Intellect: (i) How can the necessity and eternality of knowledge be properly grounded without an appeal to a causal connection with the eternal Agent Intellect; and (ii) How can the Agent Intellect – which is pure act without potency – become the storehouse for intelligibles in act abstracted by the individual rational soul?

3.3 *Dag Nikolaus Hasse (2013)*[21]

In revisiting the issue of human intellectual abstraction and the role of the Agent Intellect in 2013, Hasse proposes "a way out of the antagonism of interpretation by arguing that the opposition between abstraction and emanation is foreign to Avicenna's philosophy and also problematic in itself" (2013, 110). After examining two other recent accounts, Hasse – in agreement with Gutas – proposes to split into two the issue of whether the content of intellectual abstraction comes from experience of the world or from an emanation of forms from the Agent Intellect. Hasse, as he puts it, "suspects that the difficulties of interpretation arise because the question is improperly asked" (2013, 114). The proposal, which is also found in Gutas 2012, 411, is that abstraction is a solution to an epistemological problem and emanation is a solution to an ontological problem. As he analyzes the texts of

Avicenna, he finds emanation to be a response to Avicenna's denial of intellectual memory to the rational soul. Abstracted intelligibles in act cannot be stored in the brain's physical power of memory without being particularized, and they cannot be held in the individual rational soul, so they must be in the Agent Intellect and somehow accessible to the human rational soul when it wishes. As he puts it, to solve the problem of intellectual memory,

> Avicenna thus opts for the emanation of forms from the active intellect whenever the soul wishes. The forms disappear from the intellectual soul when they are not thought in actuality, but the disposition to think the form remains, which explains why we do not have to learn everything again from the beginning.
> (Hasse 2013, 116–117)

This is meant to be a clever solution to the persisting philosophical problem in the interpretation of the texts of Avicenna on the rational soul's power of intellectual abstraction and emanation of intelligibles in act to the soul from the Agent Intellect. Yet the proposed solution seems rather to dig a deeper hole and exacerbate the problem. Proposing a disconnection of the Agent Intellect from the rational soul's initial grasp of the intelligible in act robs human science of its grounding in eternality and necessity by leaving the abstraction of essences to the human soul's natural powers of the external and internal senses and of reflection. As with Gutas, the question of the causality of the Agent Intellect and its role in the formation of the intelligible in act is not sufficiently addressed. The intellectual abstraction that first generates the intelligible in act is not merely the result of imperfect human powers in relation to sensible particulars, if it is truly to be the attainment of the universal requisite for eternal scientific knowledge and discourse. The necessity for the veracity of the universal is not entailed in the sensory apprehension on the part of the individual human being. Further, if abstraction on the basis of sensation is not needed after its first instance, what sense does it make to say that the soul is left with an ability to recollect intelligibles through a connection to the Agent Intellect? The soul cannot store abstracted intelligibles in the Agent Intellect, which is pure actuality and is already replete with all the intelligibles of things of the sublunar realm. Even if there is to be such a connection, there needs to be an explanation of how a causal connection is made to the ontologically distinct intelligibles existing in the Agent Intellect.

Hasse is certainly on track when he writes that,

> Avicenna is not metaphorical when saying about abstraction that particulars "are transformed (*istaḥala*) into something abstracted from matter" and that "the imaginable things, which are intelligible in potentiality, become (*ṣāra*) intelligible in actuality, though not themselves, but that which is collected (*iltaqaṭa*) from them." And, likewise, he is serious about emanation when saying that "abstracted forms flow upon the soul from the active intellect" (De Anima v. 5) (Hasse 2013, 117).

Even if the meaning of the last sentence's quotation of Avicenna may be problematic, still the solution is not found in disjunction of the epistemology of the attainment of intelligibles in act by the rational soul from the ontological status of intelligibles eternally present in actuality in the Agent Intellect. Rather, the solution has to involve an account that brings these together. What is more, it is clear that in some significant sense, this attempt to solve the problem in fact revivifies the rejected traditional account. This is clear when Hasse writes, "We get to know the universal form by looking at the sublunar world and engaging in abstraction, but we do not separate the form ontologically from the world but receive it from above" (Hasse 2013, 117).[22] This seems simply to mean that the content of the intelligible in act, the abstraction, comes from the Agent Intellect above and is not garnered from the rational soul's activities using the external and internal senses.

4 Tommaso Alpina (2014)

In his article "Intellectual Knowledge, Active Intellect and Intellectual Memory in Avicenna's *Kitāb al-Nafs* and Its Aristotelian Background,"[23] Tommaso Alpina reviews the teachings of Aristotle in the *De Anima* and reexamines the texts of Avicenna on the roles of the Agent Intellect and the human rational soul in the formation of intellectual knowledge. Quite opposite to the solution of Hasse, Alpina instead rightly emphasizes the complementary nature of the epistemological problem and the ontological problem and unifies them into a single account.

Through reconsideration of Avicenna's conception of the Agent Intellect providing its light in the process of human intellectual abstraction in Avicenna's *De Anima* 5.5, Alpina's analysis allows for human agency in intellectual abstraction in a collaboration with the separate Agent Intellect that avoids the problematic traditional account. He writes,

> Avicenna claims that, in order for actual intellection to occur, the light of the Active Intellect must radiate upon the imaginative particulars and mingle – so to speak – with their potential intelligibility. The Active Intellect's shining light points metaphorically at the Active Intellect's proper activity of perpetually intelligizing the principles of intellectual forms, i.e. the essences themselves. This illumination is accordingly the cause (*sabab* , V, 5, p. 234, 15, 17) of the bestowal of intellectual forms on the human intellect: the light of its perpetual intellection of intellectual forms shines upon the imaginative particulars, which are potentially intelligible, makes them actually intelligible to the human intellect, and, consequently, establishes a connection between them and the human intellect, which results in intellection. Therefore, the Active Intellect acts in no way upon the human intellect; rather, it acts on the imaginative particulars and brings their potential intelligibility into actuality.
>
> (2014, 168)

Without the entrance of this illuminating light *into the soul to shine on the images of particulars garnered through the external and internal senses*, a human being's knowledge would remain at the level of particulars and generalizations. Instead, what is required is something external to enlighten the intelligibles in potency found in the images for the abstractive formation of intelligibles in act by the personal efforts of the individual rational soul. This was the chief problem addressed by Aristotle in *De Anima* 3.5, the fundamental source for the issue Avicenna confronts. The attainment of the intelligible in act is the attainment of the knowledge of an essence or scientific real definition in the human soul. For Avicenna there is a correspondence between the forms in the particulars and the forms as apprehended intelligibles in act. Alpina describes this, saying,

> The correspondence between imaginative particulars and intellectual forms, and the continuity between internal senses (imagery, in particular) and intellect are crucial to explain how intellection takes place and to put the entire process in the right perspective. At the first stage of the intellective process, the soul is not only provided with a mere disposition to acquire intellectual forms, but it is also somehow, i.e. potentially, acquainted with the very object of thought. For, when Avicenna claims that intelligible is what is collected from the imaginative particulars, namely the common nature shared by both imaginative particulars and intellectual forms, which the intellect succeeds in freeing from material appurtenances, *he certifies the aforementioned correspondence*. Ultimately, imaginative particulars and intellectual forms can be said to be the same with respect to their essence, namely with respect to the formal core they share, while they differ according to their way of existence, which is connected with particularity in one case and with universality in the other.
>
> (Alpina 2014, 165, my emphasis)[24]

Alpina's account recognizes the Aristotelian problematic and provides a more clear and integrated account of human rational powers and the Agent Intellect to meet the issue of the eternality and necessity of scientific knowledge of essences.[25] Yet on the issue of the lack of a personal intellectual memory in Avicenna, he considers the issue in a fashion seemingly somewhat similar to that of Hasse and Gutas. As Alpina describes it, the Agent Intellect solves the issue by being a "*collector* of the intellectual forms already acquired, it is an immaterial entity and, consequently, can preserve immaterial forms" (Alpina 2014, 173). Nevertheless, the problem with this interpretation, raised earlier in the interpretations of Hasse and Gutas, would seem to remain in Alpina's account: the Agent Intellect is a fully actual intellect without potentiality and receptivity, so it cannot literally "collect" intellectual forms abstracted by the individual human rational soul. However, if one may substitute language from the previous long quotation and say that the Agent Intellect "certifies" the "correspondence" of the particulars in the imagination with the "intellectual forms" by way of their having a common nature, the account of Alpina would seem to be on the mark as a clear account of Avicenna.[26]

5   Themistius's *Paraphrase of the De Anima of Aristotle*[27]

In his *Paraphrase of the De Anima of Aristotle*, the Greek commentator Themistius provides his own detailed account of the reasoning of Aristotle in *De Anima* 3.5, a key text in the discussion of intellectual abstraction. As indicated earlier, while Aristotle neither in *De Anima* 3.4–5 nor elsewhere in that work or others provides a clear account of intellectual abstraction, the Arabic tradition knew the abstractionist accounts of Alexander and read them back into Aristotle. In his *Paraphrase of the De Anima* Themistius does the same thing, though his account does not conceive of the Agent Intellect as God, as had Alexander. Rather, for Themistius the Productive or Agent Intellect "has all the forms all together and presents all of them to itself at the same time" (Themistius 1899, 100.9–10; Themistius 1973, 181; Themistius 1996, 124),[28] and yet plays a literally intrinsic role in the formation of intelligibles in act in individual human knowers.

According to Themistius in this paraphrastic work providing an explication of Aristotle, the human soul has a potential intellect and an actual intellect. The latter is the potential intellect in a completed state of actuality in which it has knowledge of universals. Yet this

> potential intellect must be perfected by some other intellect that is already perfect, i.e. actual, not potential. [This intellect] moves the potential intellect analogously to the craft [moving matter], and it perfects the soul's natural disposition for thinking, and fully constitutes its *hexis* "And this intellect is separate, unaffected, and unmixed" (430a17–18).
> (Themistius 1899, 98; Themistius 1973, 177; Themistius 1996, 123)[29]

This separate actual intellect, here the Agent Intellect,

> advances the potential intellect, and not only makes it an actual intellect, but also constitutes its potential objects of thought as actual objects of thought. These are the enmattered forms, i.e. the universal thoughts assembled from particular objects of perception.
> (Themistius 1899, 98; Themistius 1973, 179; Themistius 1996, 123)

Here what Themistius calls the potential intellect is not an intellect as such (in contrast to Avicenna), but rather it is his denomination of the human soul as containing a collection of images from the external and internal senses. It is a potency which the Agent Intellect takes over to make its collection of thoughts, thereby enabling the human soul "able to make transitions, and to combine and divide thoughts" (Themistius 1899, 98; Themistius 1973, 179; Themistius 1996, 123). Here the Agent Intellect, though itself full with forms, does not emanate from its forms upon the individual's potential intellect but instead assists the potential intellect in actualizing itself as knower of intelligibles in act, that is, as an intellect in act or actual intellect. Though not stated explicitly, the implication is that the Agent Intellect will not mislead the human potential intellect but rather will function as a positive guide for the human intellect, assisting it to a knowledge of forms that corresponds to the eternal forms it possesses in itself.

In this realization of human intellectual knowledge, the potential intellect:

> becomes all things, while the former [productive intellect, scil. the Agent Intellect] produces all things. That is why it is also in our power to think whenever we wish, for <(the productive intellect) is not outside <the potential intellect as> the craft <is outside> its matter (as [for example] the craft of forging is with bronze, or carpentry with wood), but the productive intellect settles into the whole of the potential intellect, as though the carpenter and the smith did not control their wood and bronze externally but were able to pervade it totally. For this is how the actual intellect too is added to the potential intellect and becomes one with it. For [the compound] consisting of matter and form is one, and also has the two definitions of matter and creativity (*démiourgia*) by in one way becoming, and in another producing, all things. For in a way it becomes the actual objects [that it thinks] by being active in its thinking; and the one [aspect] of it, in which there is a plurality of its thoughts, resembles matter, the other [sc. its thinking] a craftsman. For it is in its power, when it wishes, to comprehend and structure its thoughts, since it is productive, and thus the founder (*arkhégos*), of these thoughts. (Themistius 1996, 123; Themistius 1899, 99.)

The corresponding Arabic translation of the Greek has the following.

> The relation of art to matter is [the same as] the relation of the Active Intellect to the intellect in potency. In this way the intellect becomes everything and the intellect knows everything. On the basis of this it comes about for us that we know whenever we wish by the fact that the Agent Intellect is not external to the intellect in potency in the way the art is external to the matter as, for example, the art of the bronze forger is external to the bronze and the carpenter is external to the wood. Rather, the Agent Intellect enters into the intellect in potency entirely, as if one were to imagine the carpenter not only as approaching the wood from outside and the smith [likewise] the bronze but rather he has the power so that it penetrates it completely. For in this way the intellect in act [scil. the Agent Intellect], when united to the intellect in potency becomes one with it, since the composite [of the two] is one. And there are in it two notions, I mean the notion of matter

and the notion of art. For in a way it becomes everything and in a way it makes everything. For in a way it comes to be the things themselves by its act according to intelligible forming (*taṣawwur*) by intellect and there appears from it a thing like a certain matter, I mean as all the intelligibles, and a thing from it like the maker. So this is so for it insofar as it possesses and brings about any intelligible it wishes. For it is the maker (*fa"āl*) and the commander (*qā'id*) of the intelligibles. (Themistius 1973, 179–180; my translation of the Arabic)

Although its known that Avicenna read the *Paraphrase* by Themistius (see Gutas 2013, 54, 58, 172, 326, 354–355), none of the discussants of Avicenna's theory of intellectual abstraction considered here have cited this work. As we have seen, the problems in understanding Avicenna have been with (i) how individual human beings can be gatherers of intelligibles in potency and also participants in the intellectual abstraction that brings about intelligibles in act in the human being, (ii) how the Agent Intellect can be involved with that without directly emanating – by efficient causality – the intelligibles in act into the human material intellect, and (iii) how, given Avicenna's denial of intellectual memory to the human soul, there can be a connection of the actualized human intellect with the separate Agent Intellect to allow human access to the ontologically distinct intelligibles in the Agent Intellect to permit the individual human soul the ability to recall abstracted intelligibles at will.

Regarding (i), for the account in this work by Themistius the human souls gather the images that constitute the intelligibles in potency via external and internal sense powers drawing from encounters with the world,[30] just as we have seen in Avicenna. Further, human beings act as willing participants in the activity of intellectual abstraction that results in their becoming actual intellects. This much is in accord with what we have seen in the interpretations of Hasse, Gutas, and Alpina. As well, (ii) the Agent Intellect does not directly emanate upon the human soul the intelligibles in act, all of which are already contained in the Agent Intellect. Rather, the individual thinker already has the intelligible in potency in the imagination and memory subsequent to sense perception, and it is on the basis of this that the Agent Intellect supervenes on and penetrates the human rational soul, assisting it to come to have the intelligible in act, with the potential intellect now becoming an actual intellect. The content clearly is from the world and not emanated from the Agent Intellect. This explanation, completely contrary to the traditional view, is in accord with the explanation of Alpina and seems to satisfy the concerns raised by Hasse and Gutas. Finally, (iii) Agent Intellect can be said to guide the human intellect in its organization of images toward a sound abstraction of the intelligible in accord with the corresponding intelligibles in act present in the Agent Intellect itself. This assures that all abstracted intelligibles are correlated with those in the Agent Intellect and that science is universal, veridical, and eternal for all. In this way there is a perfect identity of the form or essence of the intelligibles in the human actual intellect with the form or essence of the intelligibles in the Agent Intellect, with the intelligibles in each remaining ontologically distinct in distinct subjects. In this, Themistius is not in accord with Avicenna in denying intellectual memory to the rational soul. But the Avicennian notion of a connecting with the Agent Intellect for the understanding of intelligibles in act which had previously been abstracted can be explained using the Themistian notion of the collaboration and correspondence of the human intellect and the Agent Intellect in forming the intelligibles in act in the human. As Alpina indicates, for Avicenna the correspondence can be said to be established through the assistance the Agent Intellect provides to the individual human material (potential) intellect. While for Themistius there is no need to store the rational soul's abstracted intelligibles in the Agent Intellect, since Its own intelligibles are the same in essence as those in the human soul, this teaching could be easily adapted to Avicenna's denial of intellectual memory to the rational soul and his affirmation of a connection (*ittiṣāl*) with the Agent Intellect for the retrieval of the essences abstracted earlier by the human rational soul in collaboration with the Agent Intellect.

6 Conclusion

The controversy over Avicenna's conception of intellectual abstraction in recent years has been energetic and hearty, with valuable advances made on several fronts. The contributions of Hasse and Gutas on the experiential foundations of Avicenna's account in apprehension of the world through the human external and internal senses have been decisive in setting to the side the traditional view of Avicenna that intelligibles are emanated directly into the human soul by the Agent Intellect. Alpina's reasoning that the Agent Intellect works collaboratively with the human rational soul on the intelligibles in potency, raising them to the level of intelligibles in act, accords well with the view of Themistius available to Avicenna. The Agent Intellect penetrates the potential intellect, which for Themistius is the place of the images intelligibles in potency derived from sensation. This is analogous to the explanation that the light of the Agent Intellect shines on the images in the rational soul's imagination or memory for Avicenna. Further, the problematic issue of the storage of abstracted intelligibles in the Agent Intellect according to Avicenna is resolved by recognizing that the intelligible essence is the same in the individual rational soul as it is in the Agent Intellect. To connect with the Agent Intellect is to connect to something the same in essence as that which was abstracted, though the original abstracted essence was ontologically received into a subject distinct from that of the Agent Intellect. On this account there is no problem of the Agent Intellect literally storing, collecting, or saving of an essence abstracted by the rational soul, something ontologically impossible given the lack of potency for receiving essences on the part of the Agent Intellect.

The issue of intellectual abstraction in the Arabic philosophical tradition has its grounding in Alexander of Aphrodisias's interpretive accounts of Aristotle's own underdetermined texts on the issue of human scientific knowledge. It is clear that al-Farabi drew on the work of Alexander and that the *Paraphrase of the De Anima* of Themistius drew much from Alexander. It is confirmed that it was studied in detail by Averroes concerning abstraction. As for Avicenna, while it is generally held that he knew this work by Themistius, there are no known direct quotations of the *Paraphrase* by Avicenna. Still, as scholars of Avicenna know well, it is not at all Avicenna's custom to cite sources and to quote their texts. Hence, we are left to reason on internal doctrinal evidence regarding his sources. In the present case it seems highly likely that knew the text of Themistius and may have taken much from his study of the *Paraphrase* for the formation of his own teachings on intellectual abstraction. The recognition of the likelihood of this contributes valuably to the clarification of the teachings of Avicenna, perhaps to the point of solving key questions on the nature of intellectual abstraction in Avicenna.

Notes

1. For Aristotle, human beings are naturally constituted with the ability or potentiality for sensory apprehension of the forms of external sensible things. In sensing, this is actualized, with the sensory characteristics of the external thing that come to exist in the perceiver now characterized as being "in act."
2. *De Anima* 2.4, 415b24–25 (Aristotle 1984): "Sensation is held to be a qualitative alteration, and nothing except what has soul in it is capable of sensation." *De Anima* 2.5, 416b32–33 emphasis added: "Sensation depends, as we have said, on a process of movement or affection *from without*, for it is held to be some sort of change of quality." *De Anima* 2.5 417b17–27:

    > In the case of what is to possess sense, the first transition is due to the action of the male parent and takes place before birth so that at birth the living thing is, in respect of sensation, at the stage which corresponds to the possession of knowledge. Actual sensation corresponds to the stage of the exercise of knowledge. But between the two cases compared there is a difference; the objects that excite the sensory powers to activity, the seen, the heard, &c., are outside. The ground of this difference is that what actual sensation apprehends is individuals, while what knowledge apprehends is universals, and these are in a sense within the soul itself. That is why a man can think when he wants to but his sensation does not depend upon himself – a sensible object must be there. A similar statement must be made about our knowledge of what is sensible – on the same ground, viz. that the sensible objects are individual and external.

    While there are some passages in Aristotle's *De Anima* what might sustain an abstractionist interpretation (see *De Anima* 3.5; 3.4, 3.7 and 3.9 as discussed in Cleary 1985), there is no clearly developed doctrine of the intellectual abstraction of intelligible content from sensory experience. For a recent account that ignores any notion of a transference of intelligible content from the world, see Burnyeat 2008.

3. The criteria of *Posterior Analytics* 1.4 were firmly kept in mind.
4. Aristotle, *Posterior Analytics* 1.2, 71a14–24 (Aristotle 1956):

    > By demonstration I mean a scientific deduction; and by scientific I mean one in virtue of which, by having it, we understand something. If, then,

understanding is as we posited, it is necessary for demonstrative understanding in particular to depend on things which are true and primitive and immediate and more familiar than and prior to and explanatory of the conclusion (for in this way the principles will also be appropriate to what is being proved). For there will be deduction even without these conditions, but there will not be demonstration; for it will not produce understanding.

5 The Arabic tradition seems largely to have taken the Agent Intellect of *De Anima* 3.5 as an efficient cause. The Greek *aitios*, however, can also be read as a reason or explanation. See, for example, Tuominen 2006 and Tuominen 2010. For a brief account of intellectual abstraction in the Arabic tradition, see Taylor 2015.
6 The following texts are from Alexander's *De Intellectu / Peri nou*, a work well known in Arabic.

> [E]nmattered forms are made intelligible by the intellect, being intelligible potentially. The intellect separates them (*chōrizōn/yufridu-hā*) from the matter with which they have their being, and itself makes them intelligible in actuality, and each of them, when it is thought, then comes to be intelligible in actuality and intellect; [but] they are not like this previously or by their own nature.
> (Alexander of Aphrodisias, *De Anima Liber Cum Mantissa*, 108.4–7, trans. Sharples 2004, 28; Arabic text Badawi 1971, 34.3–7)

> For intellect, apprehending the form of the thing that is thought and separating it (*chōrizōn/faṣala-hā*) from the matter, both makes it intelligible in actuality and itself comes to be intellect in actuality.
> (Alexander, 108.14–15; trans. Sharples 2004, 29, Arabic text Badawi 1971, 34.10–11)

> First it [the intellect] produces by abstraction (*aphairesei/ifrād*) [something] intelligible, and then in this way it apprehends some one of these things which it thinks and defines as a this-something. Even if it separates and apprehends at the same time, nevertheless the separating is conceptually prior; for this is what it is for it to be able to apprehend the form.
> (Alexander, 108.14–16, trans. Sharples 2004, 36, Arabic text Badawi 1971, 38.16–18. These texts are also cited in Taylor 2015.)

7 Themistius 1899, Arabic Lyons 1973, trans. from Greek Todd 1996. The Arabic text, based on an incomplete manuscript, is missing Greek pp. 2–22 and some other passages.
8 The poietic intellect of the Greek tradition is generally characterized as *al-'aql al-fa''āl*, Agent Intellect, in the Arabic tradition. Since this is an intellect in full actuality it is also "the intellect which is in act" and "the Actual Intellect." In the Greek tradition (e.g., Themistius) it is sometimes characterized as *ho nous . . . ho energeia* or *hoi kat'energeian nous* (Themistius 1899, 99) intellect in act or actual intellect, which the Arabic tradition also follows precisely with *al-'aql alladhi bi-l-fi'l* and *al-'aql al-fā'il* (Themistius 1973, 179). The term "intellect in act" or "actual intellect" can be used to refer to any intellect in act, be it human or supra-human.
9 In this work he describes the descent of the Agent Intellect (or in Walzer's translation, the Active Intellect) on a human being in writing, "When this occurs in both parts of his rational faculty, namely the theoretical and the practical rational faculties, and also

in his representative faculty, then it is this man who receives Divine Revelation, and God Almighty grants him Revelation through the mediation of the Active Intellect, so that the emanation from God Almighty to the Active Intellect is passed on to his Passive Intellect through the mediation of the Acquired Intellect, and then to the faculty of representation. Thus, he is, through the emanation from the Active Intellect to his Passive Intellect, a wise man and a philosopher and an accomplished thinker who employs an intellect of divine quality and through the emanation from the Active Intellect to his faculty of representation a visionary prophet: who warns of things to come and tells of particular things which exist at present." al-Farabi 1985, 244. Also see pp. 220 and 223–224. On the notion of there being four emanations in al-Farabi, see Taylor 2006, 165 n. 30.

10 See al-Farabi 1985, 198–200. For the somewhat different but related account of *The Political Regime*, see Taylor 2006, 165, n. 30.

11 Averroes 1974, 88 explains in his *Commentary on the Republic* that. "The purpose of man, inasmuch as he is a natural being, is that he ascend to . . . the intelligibles of the theoretical sciences." Averroes 1974, 86: "This [intellectual understanding of the theoretical sciences] is man's ultimate perfection and ultimate happiness."

12 Among the most important are the following which are considered in this chapter: Hasse 2000, Hasse 2001, Hasse 2013, Gutas 2001, Gutas 2013, Alpina 2014.

13 For references, see note 7.

14 The reference to intellectual axioms is to primary axioms of thought such as "The whole is greater than the part" and others. These are called by al-Farabi and Averroes principles which are such that we do not know how and whence they have arisen. Still, these thinkers do occasionally attribute these to the Agent Intellect. In general these are considered primary intelligibles, and they are used in the generation of secondary intelligibles or universal concepts with quidditative content for knowing, such as the universal horse. For Avicenna they arise in the rational soul's encounter with the world and are not a separate emanation from the Agent Intellect.

15 Hasse's references for his translation of the text of Avicenna: Avicenna 1875, 362.16, Avicenna 1952a, 169.10, Avicenna 1956/1969, 23v. Throughout this chapter I have modified Hasse's emphatic capitalization of the term 'ABSTRACTION' and others to lower case. For a discussion of the parallel passage in the *Najāt* of Avicenna, see Alpina 2014, 153–155.

16 Hasse 2001, 45, my emphasis: "Avicenna plainly states that in contrast to sense-perception, the rational faculty is an active faculty which can perform (*fa'ala*) the abstraction of a form *at will*. The power to form concepts is innate." See also p. 48. It should be kept in mind that for Avicenna a human being is primarily a rational soul using the body as a tool for its intellectual development. For Avicenna all rational souls are naturally incorruptible. For al-Farabi the human soul is capable of developing itself into a separate incorruptible intellectual substance, something not universally attained by all human beings.

17 Multiple senses of abstraction in Avicenna are spelled out and distinguished by Herrera 2010, 86ff.

18 I add this Arabic to Hasse's translation. As indicated earlier, al-Farabi 1985 uses this term to explain how the Agent Intellect empowers the individual rational soul *to transfer* intelligibles in potency into actuality in the human intellect. See note 10, this chapter.

19 The key text for this is unclear and can be understood in different ways. Hasse renders it,

> when the rational soul looks at these imaginable forms and [when] the light of the active intellect makes contact with them in some way, [the rational soul] is disposed to have appear in it, due to the light of the active intellect, uncontaminated abstractions (*mujarradat*) from these forms.

Since *mujarradat* refers to unblemished or uncontaminated forms, the text can quite naturally be taken as asserting that forms flow from the Agent Intellect.

20 Also Gutas 2001, 35 n. 27, where he cites the *Ishārāt*'s teaching that the necessity of intelligibles existing outside the human soul indicates the need for the Agent Intellect.

21 In publications in 2013, Gutas emphasizes the empiricism of Avicenna and rejects any sort of mystical account of the flow of intelligibles from the Agent Intellect. He seems to want to allow that the content of abstraction is garnered empirically and yet writes that emanation or flow

> just means that the intelligibles are permanently available to human intellects who seek a middle term or other intelligibles at the end of a thinking process by means of abstraction and syllogisms. Avicenna is quite explicit about the need for the human intellect to be prepared and demand to hit upon a middle term or actively seek an intelligible in order to receive it: "The active principle [i.e. the active intellect] lets flow upon the [human rational] soul form after form in accordance with the demand by the soul; and when the soul turns away from it [the active intellect], then the effluence is broken off."
>
> (Gutas 2013, 41 and Gutas 2014, 377)

I hesitate to impose an interpretation on these comments, but taken at face value they seem not to be coherent with his earlier accounts.

22 The apprehension of intelligibles in act in the Avicennian context of Aristotelian science involves the attainment of eternal essential or real definitions. The Arabic tradition understood Aristotle to have posited the assistance from an immortal and eternal separate entity in *De Anima* for what the human soul could not do alone. *Pace* Gutas 2012, 423 ff., the intellectual abstraction set out here is very different from Locke's empirical conception of abstraction and scientific knowledge which eschews real definitions of the essences of things. See, for example, Ayers 1981, Jones 2014, Kochiras 2016.

23 Alpina 2014, 141 ff. provides an analysis of Hasse 2013. He remarks regarding that account that

> his interpretation fails to bridge the gap between abstraction and emanation, that are no longer two well-integrated moments of one and the same process, as Avicenna intended to show; they appear rather as two juxtaposed processes, completely unrelated, aimed at solving two distinct problems. For, in spite of the ontological correspondence between universal forms in the Active Intellect and particular forms in the sublunar world, which Hasse rightly points out, his interpretation is not able to explain the way in which Avicenna combines these two processes on the other level, i.e. the epistemological one.

24 Though acknowledging that Avicenna never explicitly connected his cosmological teaching on the emanation of forms to the world by a Giver of Forms with his use of Agent Intellect, Alpina 2014, 170 writes,

> Nevertheless, the identification of these two entities is crucial for Avicenna's theory of intellectual knowledge because it entails the identification of the forms that the *Dator formarum* infuses in the sublunar matter with the forms whose actual intelligibility is guaranteed by the Active Intellect's perpetually intelligizing their principles. If the relation of the epistemological level of the Active Intellect to the onto-cosmological level of the *Dator formarum* is assumed, the sense in which the Active Intellect provides the condition

of possibility for the imaginative particulars' actual intelligibility becomes clearer: the Active Intellect's shining light guarantees that the human intellect has correctly abstracted from matter the very forms that the *Dator formarum* has previously infused in it.

25 Alpina 2014, 174 writes,

at the epistemological level, the Active Intellect acts as the source of intelligibility of any intellectual form in the sublunar realm: its active presence throughout the intellective process provides the condition of possibility for the actualization of the human intellect's potentiality to conceive intellectual forms, and the validation of the entire process, and can be considered the pinnacle of the human intellect's act of inspecting imaginative particulars.

26 Regarding the issue of the Agent Intellect as a store for abstracted intelligibles in act according to Gutas and Hasse, Alpina shared with me in personal correspondence that his use of "collector" may be easily misunderstood. He added that he did not mean the Agent Intellect to be a literal collector of intelligibles abstracted by the human power of intellect. Let me express here my thanks for this clarification and for some other valuable comments and suggestions he provided on a draft of this chapter. In a direct reply to Hasse 2001, Black concedes the important of some form of abstraction but maintains the necessity of form emanated "as long as the ordinary human soul remains in the body." See Black 2014, 142. Her account which differs from that of Alpina is not examined here.
27 I will provide a more extensive study of Themistius and Avicenna on abstraction and intellection elsewhere. In the present context my purpose is to give an initial account indicating how Avicenna's doctrine may be inspired by key teachings of Themistius.
28 Although Themistius oftentimes is considered a strong Aristotelian in his commentaries, in this case his teachings on the intellect betray a foundational Neoplatonic influence.
29 Note that this is a form of efficient causality on the part of the Agent Intellect.
30 Themistius 1899, 99, Themistius 1973, 179, Themistius 1996, 123:

But when the productive intellect encounters it and takes over this "matter" of thoughts, the potential intellect becomes one with it, and becomes able to make transitions, and to combine and divide thoughts, and to observe thoughts from [the perspective of] one another.

Bibliography

Primary sources

Alexander of Aphrodisias, Greek: *De Anima Liber Cum Mantissa*, ed. I. Bruns, Berlin: George Reimer (Commentaria in Aristotelem Graeca, Suppl. II, pt. 1), 1887, p. 108.4–7; English: *Alexander of Aphrodisias: Supplement to On the Soul*, trans. R. W. Sharples, London: Duckworth, 2004; Arabic Finnegan: J. Finnegan (ed.), "Texte arabe du *Peri nou* d'Alexandre d'Aphrodise," *Mélanges de l'Université Saint-Joseph* 33: 185.1–6; Arabic Badawi: *Commentaires sur Aristote perdus en grec et autres épîtres*, ed. A. Badawi, Beirut: Dâr el-Mashriq, 1971, p. 34.4–7.
Al-Farabi (1983). *Risalah fi al- 'aql*, ed. M. Bouyges, Beyrouth: Dar el-Machreq Sari, 2nd edition.
Al-Farabi (1985). *Al-Farabi on the Perfect State: Abū Naṣr al-Fārābī's Mabādi' Ārā' al-Madīna al-Fāḍila*, trans. R. Walzer, Oxford: Clarendon Press.
Aristotle (1956). *Aristotle, Posterior Analytics*, trans. H. Tredennick, London: William Heinemann Ltd, Cambridge, MA: Harvard University Press.

Aristotle (1984). *The Complete Works of Aristotle*, ed. J. Barnes, Princeton: Princeton University Press.
Averroes (1953). *Averrois Cordubensis Commentarium Magnum in Aristotelis De Anima Libros*, Cambridge, MA: The Mediaeval Academy of America.
Averroes (1974). *On Plato's Republic*, trans. R. Lerner, Ithaca and London: Cornell University Press.
Averroes (2009). *Averroes (Ibn Rushd) of Cordoba: Long Commentary on the De Anima of Aristotle*, trans. and introduction R. C. Taylor, subeditor T.-A. Druart, New Haven: Yale University Press.
Avicenna (1875). "*Compendium on the Soul*, (ed.) in S. Landauer, 'Die Psychologie des Ibn Sina'," *Zeitschrift der deutschen morgenlandischen Gesellschaft* 29.
Avicenna (1952a). "*Compendium on the Soul*," in (ed.) A. F. al-Ahwānī, *Ahwal al-nafs*, Cairo: el-Halaby and Co.
Avicenna (1952b). *Avicenna's Psychology: An English Translation of Kitāb al-Najāt*, trans. F. Rahman, London: Oxford University Press.
Avicenna (1959). *al-Shifā', al-Tabi'iyyāt, Kitāb al-nafs*, ed. F. Rahman, London: Oxford University Press.
Avicenna (1546/1969). *Compendium de anima*, Latin trans. A. Alpago, Venice: Giunta; repr. Farnborough: Gregg International.
Themistius (1899). *In Libros Aristotelis De Anima Paraphrasis*, ed. R. Heinze, Berlin: G. Reimeri.
Themistius (1973). *An Arabic Translation of Themistius' Commentary on Aristotle's De Anima*, ed. M. C. Lyons, Columbia, SC: University of South Carolina Press, and Oxford, UK: Bruno Cassiere Publishers Ltd.
Themistius (1996). *On Aristotle's On the Soul*, trans. R. B. Todd, Ithaca, NY: Cornell University Press.

Secondary sources

Alpina, T. (2014). "Intellectual Knowledge, Active Intellect and Intellectual Memory in Avicenna's *Kitāb al-Nafs* and Its Aristotelian Background," *Documenti e studi sulla tradizione filosofica medievale* 25, 131–183.
Ayers, M. R. (1981). "Locke Versus Aristotle on Natural Kinds," *The Journal of Philosophy* 78, 247–272.
Black, D. (2005). "Psychology: Soul and Intellect," in (eds.) P. Adamson and R. C. Taylor, *The Cambridge Companion to Arabic Philosophy*, Cambridge: Cambridge University Press, 308–326.
Black, D. (2014). "How Do We Acquire Concepts? Avicenna on Abstraction and Emanation," in (ed.) J. Hause, *Debates in Medieval Philosophy. Essential Readings and Contemporary Responses*, New York: Routledge, 126–144.
Burnyeat, M. (2008). *Aristotle's Divine Mind*, Milwaukee: Marquette University Press.
Cerami, C. (2016). "Alexander of Aphrodisias," in (ed.) A. Falcon, *Brill's Companion to the Reception of Aristotle in Antiquity*, Leiden/Boston: Brill, 160–179.
Cleary, J. J. (1985). "On the Terminology of 'Abstraction' in Aristotle," *Phronesis* 30, 13–45.
Davidson, H. A. (1992). *Alfarabi, Avicenna, and Averroes on Intellect*, Oxford: Oxford University Press.
Geoffroy, M. (2002). "La tradition arabe du *Peri nou* d'Alexandre d'Aphrodise et les origines de la théorie farabienne des quatre degrés de l'intellect," in (eds.) C. D'Ancona and

G. Serra, *Aristotele e Alessandro di Afrodisia nella Tradizione Araba*, Padova: Il Poligrafo casa editrice, 119–231.
Gutas, D. (2001). "Intuition and Thinking: The Evolving Structure of Avicenna's Epistemology," *Princeton Papers. Interdisciplinary Journal of Middle Eastern Studies* 9, 1–38, repr. in R. Wisnovsky (ed.), *Aspects of Avicenna*, Princeton: Markus Wiener, 1–38.
Gutas, D. (2012). "The Empiricism of Avicenna," *Oriens* 40, 391–436.
Gutas, D. (2013). "Avicenna's Philosophical Project," in (ed.) P. Adamson, *Interpreting Avicenna: Critical Essays*, Cambridge: Cambridge University Press, 28–47.
Gutas, D. (2014). *Avicenna and the Aristotelian Tradition, Second, Revised and Enlarged Edition*, Leiden/Boston: Brill.
Hasse, D. N. (2000). *Avicenna's De anima in the Latin West: The Formation of a Peripatetic Philosophy of the Soul 1160–1300*, London: The Warburg Institute; Turin: Nino Aragno Editore.
Hasse, D. N. (2001). "Avicenna on Abstraction," in (ed.) R. Wisnovsky, *Aspects of Avicenna*, Princeton: Markus Wiener Publishers, 39–72.
Hasse, D. N. (2013). "Avicenna's Epistemological Optimism," in (ed.) P. Adamson, *Interpreting Avicenna: Critical Essays*, Cambridge: Cambridge University Press, 109–119.
Herrera, M. (2010). *Arabic Influences in Aquinas's Doctrine of Intelligible Species*, doctoral dissertation, Marquette University, Milwaukee, Wisconsin.
Jones, J.-E. (2014). "Locke on Real Essence," in (ed.) E. N. Zalta, *The Stanford Encyclopedia of Philosophy*, <http://plato.stanford.edu/archives/fall2014/entries/real-essence/>.
Kochiras, H. (2016). "Locke's Philosophy of Science," in (ed.) E. N. Zalta, *The Stanford Encyclopedia of Philosophy* (Winter 2016 edition), <https://plato.stanford.edu/archives/win2016/entries/locke-philosophy-science/>.
McGinnis, J. (2006). "Making Abstraction Less Abstract: The Logical, Psychological, and Metaphysical Dimensions of Avicenna's Theory of Abstraction," *Proceedings of the American Catholic Philosophical Association* 80, 169–183.
McGinnis, J. (2008). "Avicenna's Naturalized Epistemology and Scientific Method," in (ed.) S. Rahman et al., *The Unity of Science in the Arabic Tradition*, Dordrecht: Springer, 129–152.
McGinnis, J. (2010). *Avicenna*, Oxford: Oxford University Press.
Rahman, F. (1958). "Essence and Existence in Avicenna," *Mediaeval Studies* 4, 1–16.
Taylor, R. C. (1996). "Davidson on al-Farabi, Avicenna and Averroes. A Critical Review," *Journal of Neoplatonic Studies* 5, 89–105.
Taylor, R. C. (2006). "Abstraction in al-Fârâbî," *Proceedings of the American Catholic Philosophical Association* 80, 151–168.
Taylor, R. C. (2013). "Themistius and the Development of Averroes' Noetics," in (eds.) R. L. Friedman and J.-M. Counet, *Medieval Perspectives on Aristotle's De Anima*, Louvain-la-Neuve/Louvain, Paris, Walpole, MA: Editions de l'Institut Supérieur de Philosophie/Peeters, 1–38.
Taylor, R. C. (2015). "The Epistemology of Abstraction," in (eds.) R. C. Taylor and L. X. López-Farjeat, *Routledge Companion to Islamic Philosophy*, London/New York: Routledge, 273–284.
Taylor, R. C. and Herrera, M. (2005). "Aquinas's Naturalized Epistemology," *Proceedings of the American Catholic Philosophical Association* 79, 83–102.
Tuominen, M. (2006). "Aristotle and Alexander of Aphrodisias on the Active Intellect," in (eds.) V. Hirvonen, T. Holopainen and M. Tuominen, *Mind and Modality: Studies in the History of Philosophy in Honour of Simo Knuuttila*, Leiden: Brill, 55–70.
Tuominen, M. (2010). "Receptive Reason: Alexander of Aphrodisias on Material Intellect," *Phronesis* 55, 170–190.

4

DUNS SCOTUS ON FREEDOM AS A PURE PERFECTION

Necessity and contingency[1]

Cruz González-Ayesta

1 Introduction

The question of free will is, of course, a central topic in medieval philosophy, standing at the vertex of many different discussions that touch on the distinction between theoretical and practical philosophy. On the one hand, the question of freedom involves a clear definition (by opposition) of nature and natural processes, a key point for natural sciences. 'Free actions' and processes must be clearly or at least sufficiently distinct from natural processes, so both natural theology and human agency are highlighted by the very definition of the free. Still, as we shall see, it would be incorrect to simply equate 'contingent' actions or processes with 'free' and 'necessary' with 'natural'. Precisely, on the other hand, the definition of freedom has a pivotal role in determining the complex and foundational issues of agency and ethics. From the point of view of the philosophy of mind, freedom has to do with a constitutive mode of our very form of being (or at least with the way we perceive it), having thus an enormous impact on the way we 'own' and 'deal with' ourselves (what Stoics called *oikeiosis*). Furthermore, medieval philosophy takes freedom into account within the much larger horizon of theology, for the Godhead is free.

John Duns Scotus (*ca.* 1266–1308) occupies a central position in this universe of questions. On one hand, he is a direct successor of the greatest scholastic minds, including Anselm (*ca.* 1033–1109), Thomas Aquinas (1225–1274), and Henry of Ghent (*ca.* 1217–1293), among many others. On the other hand, Scotus also lives in a conflictive time, facing disputes both within and outside his order (the problem of *usus pauper*, the conflict between conventuals and spiritualists, including the condemnation of forty-four propositions from Peter John Olivi (1248–1298) in 1282, the problematic relations of mendicant and secular clerics, the disputes between Pope Boniface VIII and King Philip IV of France which got Scotus exiled, etc.). While some of these issues may appear inconsequential for philosophy, as a matter of fact, Scotus's treatment of them requires a precise philosophical analysis. The question of *usus pauper*, for example, explores the kind of use mendicant friars can have of material beings and thus demands a very precise delineation of the notions of use, possession (*dominium*), and usufruct. Possession, in turn, has to do first with self-possession, and then with external possession (*habitus*), and thus relates directly to the problem of the free will.

Special attention must be given to the condemnations of the Bishop of Paris in 1277.[2] With the introduction of Aristotle's philosophy and that of his Arab commentators (among other works recovered from Arabic sources), certain church officials were worried of contamination by paganism. There was actually a first condemnation in 1210 by a synod of bishops in Sens, which ultimately prohibited the public reading of Aristotle's natural philosophy in the Faculty of Arts at Paris (the Faculty of Theology was exempted). By 1270 this condemnation was not respected anymore, and thus Étienne Tempier, Bishop of Paris, condemned the teaching of Averroist Aristotelianism in Paris, declaring thirteen propositions as heretical. One of the condemned propositions, e.g., stated: 'That human acts are not ruled by the providence of God'. Some years later, he issued an even bigger list of 229 articles declared as errors. (That same year, Robert Kilwardby issued a similar condemnation in Oxford.)[3] According to a recent overview of the condemnations,

> [a] very helpful summary of the condemned propositions has been provided by John F. Wippel. The first seven of the philosophical propositions bear on the nature and excellence of philosophy. Propositions 8 through 12 (in the numbering of Mandonnet) have a bearing on the knowability and nature of God. Propositions 13–15 concern divine knowledge, and 16 through 26 divine omnipotence. Many of the articles, notably 34–61 regard the separate intelligences (angels). [. . .] By condemning these articles, Tempier endorsed God's absolute power to do whatever he wills.[4]

When speaking about free will, Scotus had thus to tread lightly, for there were many connected issues to keep in mind. As we shall see later, his analytical acumen would serve him greatly when dealing with issues that often supersede each other. I will now give a general overview of the matter.

As I have mentioned, there are two main frameworks for the question of contingency and necessity, both in Greek and medieval philosophy (whether Arab or Christian): one refers to the domain of being and the other to the domain of action. A contingent being (a being for which non-being is possible) is more imperfect than a necessary being. However, when referring to operation, an active principle that may not act even if all conditions for a certain operation are given (*passo approximate*, as medievals would say) is more perfect than one that is compelled to act. The former case describes a peculiar kind of contingency that surpasses the mere fact that an action may be impeded and suggests a different kind of possession or self-determination by the active principle. In the latter case, none of this is the case, and we may thus speak of a kind of necessity.

Ever since Duns Scotus, the first kind of principle is established to be the will in a clear way, and its self-determination constitutes freedom. The second kind of active principle is referred to as nature. The application of these modalities (necessary-contingent) to action was in effect developed with particular insight by Duns Scotus, who contributed at least three key notions:

a) He distinguished between potency and act as referring to being in an absolute sense, and as referring to the principles of action (*Quaestiones super libros Metaphysicorum Aristotelis* IX, q. 2, n. 14). Potency and act are incompatible only in the first case (*Ibid.* q. 14, n. 85). This means that an active potency is a certain kind of act, and thus he employs the terms 'first act', 'virtual act', etc. When speaking about the will, Scotus will defend that it is an active potency (distinct from other potencies, which are put into action by the presence of their respective objects). This establishes a distance between the will as a cause or as an active potency (which was Scotus's view) and the will as an appetite.[5]

b) Scotus provided a systematic account of his predecessors' work – especially of Peter John Olivi – regarding the kind of contingency that corresponds to the act of the will,[6] namely, that the will that wants something in a certain instant can not-will it at that same instant. This entails no contradiction, for the proper modality must be applied *in sensu diviso* and not *in sensu composito*. Scotus also distinguishes 'instants of nature'. We can talk in this sense of a contingency of the present (following Normore), or a synchronic contingency (in Knuuttila's terminology), which implies a great novelty in the use of modalities applied to moral psychology.[7]

c) Scotus formulated a distinction between rational and irrational active principles following Aristotle's guidelines in *Metaphysics* 9.2, radically opposing the two ways in which these principles act by having them conform to a transcendental disjunction: an active principle is nature or will, the latter being free.[8] This opens a question with which I've dealt elsewhere, regarding the meaning of the expression *voluntas ut natura* and its relation to the more natural inclination of the will to desire the advantageous (*affection commodi*).[9] In turn, Scotus defends the idea that the *affection iustitiae* or the capacity to will that which is just must refer to a kind of self-determination by which the will can direct itself to the just good, thus overcoming the inclination to the advantageous. In all these cases, the will acts without being forced to do so *passo approximate*, i.e. in a spontaneous way, like an appetite would.

However, if freedom is, as Scotus seems to admit, a pure perfection, his texts and doctrine seem to contain a paradox:[10] while the notion of freedom as intrinsic to the will belongs to contingency when referred to the created will (i.e. to the will of a man or an angel), or to the relation of the absolute will referred to creation (God's will *ad extra*), this is not the case when he speaks about God's love for

Himself, or in the case of the spiration of the Holy Spirit. In these cases, the opposite is true: Scotus speaks here of necessity, and even defends that this necessity is compatible with freedom (*Quodlibetum* 16; *Ordinatio* I, d. 10, and corresponding passages). This seems to work against a univocal concept of freedom as defined by contingency. Does it also mean that freedom cannot be a pure perfection? In the following pages I will hold that what is proper to freedom is self-determination, and that this does not of itself imply contingency; in fact, some free acts are both self-determined and necessary.

2 Situation of the problem

As is well known, whether Duns Scotus's account of freedom of the will is libertarian or compatibilist is a subject of much debate. Although it is not my aim to discuss these views in depth, this chapter seeks to clarify some underlying metaphysical points, namely: the relationship between the will as a faculty, its act, and its freedom. This clarification allows one to give a definition of freedom as a pure perfection valid for a finite will, an infinite will operating *ad extra*, and an infinite will operating *ad intra*.

My thesis is that freedom belongs to an active principle in as much as it is naturally prior to its act and, consequently, freedom is compatible with both a necessary act and one that is contingent. In other words: while freedom of the will as such involves self-determination, it does not involve synchronic contingency in all cases. Nonetheless, this assertion does not commit my interpretation of Scotus's theory to some form of compatibilism or determinism.[11]

Duns Scotus explains the metaphysical distinction between nature and will in his *Questions on Aristotle's Metaphysics*, Lib. IX, q. 15. This is a well-known text that has been frequently translated and analyzed in the secondary literature.[12] Scotus distinguishes therein two kinds of active principles, namely nature and will. A natural principle is of itself determined to act, and, so as far as it is concerned, it cannot fail. On the other hand, the will is not of itself so determined; on the contrary, it can will or nill, as well as will or not-will.[13]

Nature and will differ in the way in which they respectively elicit their acts: by 'naturalness' (*naturalitas*) and freedom (*libertas*). Nature is not capable of controlling its own act when the subject it acts upon is present; so a natural agent acts according to the fullest extent of its power (*secundum ultimum potentiae suae*). The will, on the contrary, possesses self-determination; it can control its own act and is not determined by its object.[14] Thus, when the will wills something, it can still not-will or will otherwise in the very instant that it is willing.[15] This is its so-called synchronic contingency. Scotus explains the created will's structure and its contingent mode of acting in *Lectura* I, 39 (nn. 45–52)[16] and the parallel texts (*Reportatio* IA, d. 39–40).

Although natural active principles are sometimes open to opposite effects (e.g. the sun dries the mud and melts the ice, or the intellect can affirm or deny the same judgment unless it is evident), a natural action occurs necessarily if the circumstances are favorable. Nevertheless, natural actions can be impeded if some requisite condition fails. On these occasions one can say that these actions are 'contingent', even though they have not been caused 'contingently'. Acting 'contingently' involves the ability to do otherwise in the same instant in which the principle is acting. This mode of action is proper to the will. However, Scotus says that it is possible for a free agent to act with necessity 'for a similar reason' to that in light of which it is possible for a natural agent to act contingently.[17]

It is clear that natural agents are characterized by a kind of 'other-determination' which results in a special kind of necessity in the causation of the act. The will, on the other hand, is characterized by its freedom. The passages quoted have indicated that freedom involves self-determination. Must freedom also involve acting contingently? This is the crucial question.

Not infrequently, scholars read Scotus's texts as supporting just such an identification between freedom of the will and synchronic contingency, or at least as holding that synchronic contingency accompanies every act elicited freely by the will. Freedom would then be a kind of self-determination which involves the ability to do otherwise in such a way that when the will wills 'a' it can not-will 'a'. This view finds support in several passages of Scotus's work, especially the texts wherein he analyzes the created will.[18] Libertarian interpretations of Scotus on freedom hold this view and take these texts into account above all others.[19]

Of greater interest is the identification between contingency and freedom implicitly present in some studies of Scotus's doctrine on the will and freedom.[20] This analysis is not necessarily committed to the libertarian position. For example, in chapter 4 of *Duns Scotus on God* ('Knowledge and Volition of a First Being'), Richard Cross comments on *De Primo Principio*, 4, n. 5, using some passages from *Questions on Aristotle's Metaphysics*, Lib. IX, q. 15 (nn. 22, 31 and 32) as parallel texts.[21] He argues rightly that 'contingency entails will'. This means that contingency involves indetermination in the cause and consequently a free cause or principle. He also reads Scotus as stating in the *De Primo Principio* that natural causes involve determinism and exclude contingency. Since will and nature are opposites, the will involves indeterminism and contingency. He thus concludes that 'on this understanding *freedom entails contingency*', and since contingency is to be understood synchronically, for Scotus 'a free power is one that has more than one outcome under its scope'.[22] Cross's argument and conclusions can be summarized in eight propositions:

(1) *Contingency entails will*
(2) *Will is a free principle*
(3) *Contingency entails freedom* (1) + (2)
(4) *Will is opposed to nature*
(5) *Nature entails no contingency*
(6) *Will entails what is opposed to nature, that is, contingency* (4) + (5)
(7) *Freedom entails contingency* (2) + (6)
(8) *Contingency entails freedom and freedom entails contingency* (3) + (7)

The problem with this argument is the conclusion of (6) from (4) and (5). Cross draws this conclusion from his interpretation of the text from the *De Primo Principio* in light of the passages from *Questions on Aristotle's Metaphysics* on the distinction between nature and will. The text from the *De Primo Principio* states: 'there is no principle of acting contingently other than the will [. . .] for everything else acts by the necessity of nature' (*De Primo Principio*, 4, n. 5). How does Cross move from the proposition that 'only the will acts contingently' to the one that 'it is essential to the will to act contingently'? He does so by identifying necessity with nature and contingency with will. But such an identification would require further support. So Cross concludes to (7) and (8) without sufficient evidence. He concludes that freedom and contingency are interchangeable notions.

Yet Scotus clearly states that in God's immanent activity (*in divinis ad intra*) there is a free and necessary act of will (*Ordinatio* I, d. 10, q. 2 and *Quodlibetum*, q. 16, a. 1). Scotus also holds that the distinction between nature and will transcends the finite order. Nature and will must be considered as disjunctive properties (*passiones disiunctae*) because they belong to the transcendental realm: every single principle of action is either a nature or a will. Even in God's immanent activity, the processions of the Son and Holy Spirit take place according to these two principles, namely, intellect (nature) and will.[23]

I will now show that, for Scotus, contingency accompanies freedom of the will when finitude is involved, but contingency has no part in the freedom of an infinite will regarding an infinite object. Thus, it will be clear that contingency does not pertain to the definition of the will's freedom as such, nor to the metaphysical distinction between nature and will as active principles.

Therefore, although in most cases free will produces its act contingently (provided that finitude is present in the active principle, in the object willed, or in both), it is not impossible for a free principle to produce its act necessarily. I will thus argue that contingency does not essentially belong to freedom of the will.

3   Freedom is in the will itself

Certain passages found in *Ordinatio*, distinctions 12 and 13, support this thesis, namely: 'freedom is in the will itself rather than in its act'. The first question of distinction 12 discusses how the Father and the Son can jointly spirate the Holy Spirit. The question of how two subjects can share one same will is raised. Scotus gives five reasons in opposition to Henry of Ghent's view. I will focus on the first reason presented in nn. 14–23. Scotus explains that Henry understands a concordant will (*voluntas concors*) as the will which wills, and, consequently, for him the will in itself as a power or first act (*ut actus primus*) would be prior to the Holy Spirit (n. 15). On the contrary, Scotus states that the will spirates the Holy Spirit as a will (*ut voluntas*) and not as an act of willing (*ut actus volendi*) (n. 16). He gives two explanations in confirmation of these assertions. The first is as follows (n. 17):

> Regarding the first point, I argue thus: the will, since it is a first act in us, is free to make an act of willing, but the very act of willing is not free,

unless as a principle of producing something freely, for the act of willing is a certain natural quality; and if it is the principle of some act, it seems to be its natural principle, and not a free principle. (Thus, if from such an act [of will] there were generated an appetitive habit, it would be generated naturally, because the generation of such a habit is not in the power of the [will's] act, as seems to be the case.) Therefore it seems that the Holy Spirit's being freely produced is better preserved if It is produced by the will insofar as it is a first act, than if It is produced by the will as it is willing in act, which is what is understood by 'second act'.[24]

Scotus rejects Henry's idea that the Father and the Son have a *voluntas concors* if *voluntas* is understood as the will's operation (*actus secundus*), but he accepts this expression (which comes from Richard of St. Victor (d. 1173)) if *voluntas* means the will itself (*actus primus*).[25]

In doing so, he indirectly indicates that freedom belongs to the will and not to the act of willing. This is the statement that interests us. Scotus is not denying that the will produces free acts, on the contrary he asserts this. Yet he explains that freedom has to do with a certain feature of the principle which posits the act rather than with a feature of the act of willing. Freedom is the way in which the power produces the act: 'the will . . . is free to make an act of willing, but the very act of willing is not free, unless as a principle of producing something freely'.

Nevertheless, Scotus points out that freedom and naturalness are not active principles but two modes of 'a relation of aptness' (*habitudo aptitudinalis*) between the principle and the produced act. The expression *habitudo aptitudinalis* occurs in *Ordinatio* I, d. 13 (q. un., nn. 45–62). This single question discusses whether generation and spiration are the same or differ in as much as they are productions. To defend their distinction, Scotus rejects the objection which argues that both productions stem immediately from the divine essence. However, Scotus does not say that their difference is on the part of the thing (*a parte rei*). To make clear his view of this difference, he explains how freedom and naturalness should be understood:

> If this argument concluded, it would conclude that there is necessarily a distinction of intellect and will in the creature, and by this a distinction of what is absolute on the part of the thing, which seems unnecessary. Whence I reply that the same principle can have different relations to two products and to two productions. Moreover, in the present case *freedom and naturalness do not essentially imply an active principle but a relation of aptness of a principle to its product, and a relation of non-aptness*; e.g. naturalness implies the determination in itself of a first act to a second and third, but freedom implies such a non-determination.[26]

The key point herein is the statement: 'freedom and naturalness do not essentially imply an active principle but a relation of aptness of a principle to its product, and a relation of non-aptness'. Thus it can be said that freedom has to do with the ability to establish a certain kind of relationship between the first act (the will itself) and the second act (volition taken as a quality which remains in the will as in its subject).

Since there are no powers and acts different from their terms in God, it could be objected that to speak of first and second act is not valid for the infinite will. However, Scotus uses this terminology to explain the Trinitarian processions when distinguishing in God (*in divinis*) between intellect and will, the processions as coming from these 'principles', and the Son and the Holy Spirit themselves.[27] Once this point has been clarified, we will return to the argument.

The relation of aptness (*habitudo aptitudinalis*) of the will itself to volition is the particular aptness of the power (*actus primus*) for establishing a relationship (other than naturalness) to its operation (*actus secundus*). The texts specify that the first act (the will) is indeterminate regarding its second act (its volition).

Scotus describes the nature of the will as a potency in several texts. Summarizing his doctrine, one can say that the will (in as much as it is free):

(i) Is a potency in the sense of an active principle (not in the sense of a mode of being).[28]
(ii) Consequently, it is not a potency in the sense of what is opposed to an 'act'.[29] The will as an active potency is a 'virtual act';[30] that is, a 'formal potency' or '*actus primus*'.
(iii) As an active principle, the will is an equivocal cause (versus a univocal one).[31] In contrast, natural active principles (or causes) can be univocal or equivocal causes.
(iv) While nature is an equivocal cause in producing opposite effects, the will is an equivocal cause not only in producing opposite effects but in operating by opposite acts.[32]
(v) Consequently, the indetermination of the will itself is an indetermination beyond mere illimitation (proper to the indetermination of natural equivocal causes) and beyond the indetermination of matter.[33] It is an indetermination of superabundant sufficiency[34] (as is found exclusively in free causes).
(vi) Therefore the will is not a mere intellectual appetite, and generally it is not an appetite at all (in the sense that is not moved by its object to act).

If we consider (i)–(vi) together we can conclude that the difference between naturalness and liberty lies in the different interplay between indetermination and determination in the production of the act or effect. In *Ordinatio* I, 13, Scotus gives a definition of a free power (*potentia libera*), with emphasis on the elements that explain this specific interplay:

> A free power is a sufficiently active power that is not determined from itself (*ex se*) to operation regarding any object that is not finally perfective.
> It is 'active', by an action of the genus [or category] 'action' and from the consequent operation; neither is the expression 'operative

active' sufficient, because thus the intellect would be active, although it is passive.

It is so 'sufficiently', in its order of acting, therefore it receives no act from another, by which it acts in its order, because if that were so it would be insufficiently active.

It is 'not determined from itself', i.e. from its first act; and this in its own order of causation (as follows from the corollary 'sufficiently'); and it is due to this that it determines itself to act. Indeed, it does not determine an action of the genus of action by some preceding determination, but it determines itself, i.e. it is indeterminate in its first act; yet it acts determinately, with nothing else determining it to act.[35]

'A free power is sufficiently active' and 'not determined from itself' (*ex se*, as distinct from 'by itself' [*a se*], as explained later). So what is freedom after all? It is the indetermination of a certain kind of active potency that has the ability to determine itself to operate without being determined by its own form (*ex se*) or by any exterior agent (e.g. by the object). Freedom belongs to an active principle which is a virtual act or a formal potency, namely, a potency which can move itself. As I have said earlier, freedom lies in the aptness of the power to establish by itself a kind of relationship to its second act, namely self-determination or self-movement: an indeterminate power can determine itself to act.

Indetermination belongs to the power and is manifested in its capacity for self-determination. In speaking of the finite will, Scotus states that the will itself is naturally prior to its act, and that it causes not inasmuch as it is indifferent but inasmuch as it is (self-) determined:

> In reply to the argument that there is no effect from some cause that is indifferently related to non-being and to being, it is true when it is from a cause that is so related when the effect is produced. *Whence the indifferent will does not produce [something], but determines itself.* Yet *nature is indifferent to being and non-being before an effect is produced*, and that nature is determined to an effect is for the effect to be. Whence one ought not imagine that the cause is determined and moved to determinate existence before the effect is produced; for then it would be necessary to posit that a cause would be changed and moved before it caused, which is not true; but the cause's being determined to produce the effect is the effect's being produced.[36]

Consequently, a power acting in a way that is always determined (self-determined, in this case) does not constitute the difference between nature and will. The difference lies first in the kind of indetermination prior to the act and second in whether or not the power has been determined by itself.

In addition, when Scotus compares will and nature, he keeps in mind the relationship between the will and the intellect. The intellect is a natural and equivocal cause. Yet it does not possess the same kind of indetermination as the will but rather an indetermination similar to other natural agents such as the sun: it can produce different effects if it concurs with other natural causes. On the other hand, it is not self-sufficiently active (*sufficienter activum*). It requires the will in order to finish deliberation (in the case of the practical intellect), and it is moved by the evidence of the object in the case of grasping concepts or judgments.[37] It is moved 'by another'. For these two reasons, it acts naturally. Its mode of action is *naturalitas*. The comparison with the intellect is a good counterpoint for understanding freedom as a mode of action. It requires that the active power possess indetermination of superabundant sufficiency and the ability to move by itself.

4 Self-determination

Thus far, Scotus has said that freedom is in the will itself, but also that it is not identical with that power. Freedom is a kind of relationship between the power and the act, more concretely, self-determination (i.e. it is not determined by its form but rather by itself, *non determinata ex se sed determinata a se*) and not necessarily the ability to do otherwise.

Just after giving the definition of a free power in *Ordinatio* I, d. 13, Scotus faces the question of the relationship between power and object. He points out the compatibility between freedom and necessity in line with the assertions of *Ordinatio* I, d. 10 (n. 57). Accordingly, he states that 'It belongs to perfection to be determined to the perfective object' (*Perfectionis est determinari ad obiectum perfectivum*; n. 59). It is crucial to notice that, for Scotus, perfection is compatible with being determined 'towards' the perfective object (*ad*), yet he never says that perfection could be compatible with being determined 'from' (*ex*) the perfective object. Furthermore, being determined need not involve being other-determined but can be interpreted as self-determination.

With these observations in mind, we find in n. 60 the distinction between three modes of determination and their classification according to two criteria (free or natural; more or less perfect):

> To determine oneself naturally to anything [be it to the perfective or the non-perfective] is more imperfect than to not determine oneself freely to a non-perfective object, because the determination to some non-perfective object pertains to imperfection; the intellect is determined to either of the two kinds of object necessarily, because it is so determined naturally. And thus I reply to the objection that It belongs to perfection to be determined to a perfective object: it is true, in this way, regarding only that [free mode of self-determination], and consequently not naturally; therefore it is more fitting for the more perfect is true uniformly, because it holds for the divine will and for no intellect.[38]

The passage describes three kinds of relationship between indetermination and determination:

(i) natural determination to diverse effects (e.g. the case of intellect);
(ii) free indetermination to a non-perfective object (e.g. the case of the finite will);
(iii) free determination to a perfective object (e.g. the case of God's will toward Himself).

Scotus explains that determination to a unique perfective object does not imply any imperfection when it is free. On the other hand, while natural determination to opposite effects involves imperfection, free indetermination to a non-perfective object is rather perfection.

Scotus infers (n. 61) that natural determination to opposite effects is incompatible with freedom. It requires other-determination. Free determination to a perfective object is compatible with will but is not the way in which the created will is undetermined. So he concludes that the indetermination of 'our' will is free indetermination to either of two objects (*ad utrumlibet*).

Scotus explains this kind of indetermination in *Lectura* I, d. 39 and *Reportatio* I A, d. 39–40. In such a case, the will's free indetermination entails its self-determination towards an act in such a way that this act can be not-willed at the moment that it is willed. The will acts freely, and the act is contingent (so-called 'synchronic contingency').

5 Necessity and contingency of free action

Hence, in certain cases freedom does not require indetermination to one of two objects. Scotus asserts that freedom is compatible with determination to an object which is essentially perfective: 'It is consistent with freedom that it be determined to operation regarding [an essentially perfective object]' (*[S]tat autem cum libertate quod sit determinata ad operandum circa illud [obiectum essentialiter perfectivum]*).[39]

Precisely because freedom lies in the indetermination of superabundant sufficiency and in self-determination even in the case wherein the will moves itself to a unique object (e.g. God loving himself or spirating the Holy Spirit), it *acts freely*. The will, which is of itself undetermined, is naturally prior to its act. When the will determines itself in such a way that it cannot act otherwise, *its act is necessary* rather than contingent. Scotus sometimes refers to this particular kind of *self-determination* towards the essentially perfective object as steadfastness (*firmitas*), as we will see later (*Quodlibetum*, q. 16, n. 37 [8]).

So the act is free because there is self-determination of an undetermined principle but is necessary because there is not the alternative to act otherwise or to suspend the act. To deny this alternative does not entail the denial of freedom.

For freedom not to exist, the object would have to move the power to act. Only in the case of other-determination would the act be necessary in a natural way and opposed to freedom.

The compatibility between freedom and necessity is the main topic of *Quodlibetum*, q. 16. In the second of three articles, Scotus provides two *propter quid* arguments to the reasoned fact showing the compatibility between necessity and freedom. The first argument is as follows:

> Action that has to do with the ultimate end is the most perfect. But steadfastness (*firmitas*)[40] pertains to the perfection of such an action. Therefore, the necessity to be found there does not do away with but rather demands what is needed for perfection, namely, freedom.[41]

If we formalize the argument we find something like the following:

P is M: (1) Steadfastness (P) *belongs to* the perfection (M) of the action.
S is M: (2) [Necessary] action regarding the last end (S) *is* perfect (M).
S is P': (3) [Necessary] action regarding the last end (S) requires what is needed for perfection, namely, freedom (P').

This syllogism fails because the conclusion includes a new term (P) instead of the major term (P). To be valid the syllogism should conclude:

S is P [Necessary] action regarding the last end requires what is needed for perfection, namely, steadfastness (P) [=freedom (P')]).

Scotus's argument is only conclusive if he intends to make 'steadfastness' and 'freedom' synonymous. In this argument, Scotus predicates 'what is needed for perfection' of both 'freedom' and 'steadfastness'. This equation is important: the self-determination which characterizes free as opposed to natural action is expressed in the divine will *ad intra* through steadfastness (*firmitas*) or the ability to maintain the act with constancy. Thus, Scotus seems to say that steadfastness is the way in which self-determination takes place in immanent divine actions.

In contrast, in *Commentary on the Sentences* I, d. 39 he states that synchronic contingency is the way in which self-determination occurs when the divine will faces a finite object or when one is speaking of a finite will.

It is not by chance that after exposing the second *propter quid* argument (which I need not analyze here), Scotus clearly states that the difference between acting necessarily and contingently does not parallel the difference between acting by way of nature or freely (as noted in the beginning of this chapter):

> The division of agents into those which act naturally and those which act freely is not the same as the division of agents into those acting necessarily and those acting contingently. For some natural agents act

contingently, because their action can be impeded. For like reasons, then, it is possible that some free agent act necessarily without detriment to its freedom.[42]

Scotus's idea is that acting contingently is not a property (*proprium*) of the will but that both modes – necessity and contingency – can be found in the will; thus, they are accidental differences.[43]

I have shown how a free active principle can act necessarily. So Scotus's doctrine in *Commentary on the Sentences* I, d. 10 and *Quodlibetum*, q. 16 is consistent with the account of freedom given in the *Questions on Aristotle's Metaphysics* (Lib. IX, q. 15) and in the *Lectura* (Lib. I, d. 39).[44]

6 Freedom as a pure perfection

Based on *Commentary on the Sentences* I, d. 10[45] and *Quodlibetum*, q. 16, one can state that:

(i) Scotus does not identify freedom and contingency, on the one hand, and naturalness and necessity, on the other; on the contrary, he defends the compatibility between necessity and freedom in some cases.
(ii) Scotus holds that freedom of the will is compatible with acting necessarily in the case of an infinite will that loves an infinite object.

Consequently, one can conclude from these texts that the contingency of the will's act is not a necessary condition for freedom of the will. The 'compatibilist' interpretation of Scotus tends to appeal to the aforementioned passages for support.

While it cannot be denied that Scotus tends to link self-determination and synchronic contingency when he describes the distinction between nature and will as active principles of the finite realm, this is because synchronic contingency is a characteristic feature of the free act produced by a created will. There is another set of texts which provides the basis for this: *Commentary on the Sentences* I, d. 39,[46] *Ordinatio* II, d. 7, *Ordinatio* IV, d. 49, q. 6, and *Questions on Aristotle's Metaphysics*, Lib. IX, q. 15. Libertarian theories account for his views on freedom mainly from these texts.

The arguments developed in sections 2–4 of this chapter do not intend to support compatibilism against libertarianism. The arguments presented seek to support a definition of freedom as a pure perfection. Neither compatibilism nor libertarianism seem capable of giving such a definition. However, Scotus considers freedom to be a pure perfection.[47]

Scotus takes the definition of pure perfection from Anselm as a perfection 'which, in whatever has it, it is better for it to have it than not to have it' (*quae, in quolibet habente ipsam, melius est ipsum habere quam non ipsum habere*).[48] Consequently pure perfections exclude by definition any form of limitation. This statement does not entail that they must be unlimited or infinite: a pure perfection is compatible with a finite or an infinite mode. Thus, pure perfections can be predicated of both God and creatures. On the other hand, as logical concepts, pure perfections belong to the group of concepts that are simply simple (*simpliciter simplex*).[49] These concepts are those grasped simply (by a simple act) and whose content is also simple (i. e., not analyzable into other elements).[50] It is a consequence of Scotus's doctrine that whether they are predicated of the infinite or the finite, they are predicated univocally.

To summarize, something is a pure perfection if it fulfills the following conditions:

(i) For a subject to possess such a perfection is better than its absolute negation (contradictory opposition).
(ii) The subject is capable of possessing such a perfection.
(iii) Such a perfection is not incompatible with any other pure perfection.
(iv) Such a perfection is understood by a simple act of understanding (without composition).
(v) The conceptual content of such a perfection is simple.
(vi) The meaning of the concept of a pure perfection is univocal when predicated of infinite or finite beings.

According to Scotus's teaching, being and transcendental properties qualify as pure perfections. It is also well known that Scotus considers not only 'good', 'true', 'one', and so on as transcendentals but also certain disjunctions such as 'finite-infinite', 'necessary-contingent', 'free-natural', and so on. He calls them disjunctive (*disiunctae*) transcendentals. In this chapter, we have focused on the pair 'freedom-nature', and more precisely on freedom.

One can now give a definition of freedom that fulfills the six aforementioned conditions. One can state the following:

(1) If freedom is defined in terms of synchronic contingency, it cannot be a pure perfection (at least for Scotus) because conditions (i) and (iii) do not obtain. An infinite being loves himself freely and necessarily, which is better than if he loved himself freely and contingently. This is contrary to libertarianism.
(2) Neither can freedom be a pure perfection if it is defined in terms of determination, steadfastness, or some kind necessary inclination (equal to the Aristotelian voluntary). Both an infinite being who wills a finite being and a willing finite being make an act of will freely and contingently (when they will *a*, they can not-will *a* at the very instant). Again conditions (i) and (iii) do not obtain. This is contrary to compatibilism.
(3) On the contrary, if freedom defined as self-determination (*indeterminata ex se, se determinat*) is compatible with finite and infinite modes and with contingent and free modes of action, it can be considered a pure perfection. In this case, all conditions obtain.

To conclude, I will elaborate a more complete definition of freedom as a pure perfection. Prior to doing so, it is best to recapitulate four previously established points. First: freedom does not belong to the will's operation inasmuch as it is already produced; rather, it is a relation of aptness of the first act to the second act ('*habitudo aptitudinalis actus primi ad actum secundum*'). Second: this relation of aptness should be described as *determinatio a se*: self-determination (in contrast to mere other-determination). Third: 'necessity' and 'contingency' should not be predicated of the free act as properties (*propria*) but rather as logical accidents. The reason being that, while a will may act necessarily or contingently, in every case it acts freely (it is not moved *by* its object). Fourth: freedom includes as essential elements a certain illimitation of the active principle (indetermination of superabundant sufficiency) and a certain ability to act (self-determination).

At this point, one can posit a definition of freedom as pure perfection. Such a definition should be based on all the available texts. Hence, if there is a univocal concept of freedom to be predicated of the will as such – disregarding its finite or infinite mode – it should express both the first act's indetermination and its self-determination towards a second act, but not the contingency of the elicited act of will.

I think that Scotus would accept the following definition of freedom: Freedom of the will in general is a *relationship of aptness of a first act to a second act*, by which the will, which is indeterminate of itself as a first act, determines itself to operation (i.e. to second act).

On the other hand, the definition of freedom in immanent divine activity (*in divinis ad intra*) would be: the freedom of an infinite will regarding an infinite object is a relationship of aptness of a first act to a second act, by which the will, which is indeterminate of itself as a first act, determines itself (necessarily) to a second act (namely, to loving an object that is finally perfective).

Finally, the definition of freedom of the will when finitude is present would be: the freedom of a finite or infinite will regarding a finite object is a relationship of aptness of a first act to a second act, by which what is indeterminate of itself as a first act determines itself (contingently) to a second act, namely, to volition (*velle*), non-volition (*non-velle*), or nolition (*nolle*).

7 Concluding remarks

Scotus was not, of course, the only medieval philosopher to deal with the issue of the will. He did, however, as we have seen, examine these issues critically and in great detail. We thus cannot sufficiently underscore his idea of the will as a self-determining active principle, as it can help in defining both the created and the Absolute will. As theologians, Scotus and other scholastics may have an interest in drawing further conclusions in the realm of angelology and demonology, the will of the Blessed, and even in theological Mariology.

But the implications of the will as a self-determining principle are, of course, also evident in topics much more relevant for philosophy. While Scotus's writings and teachings have historically laid in a very complex state, nevertheless, his clear emphasis on the difference between self- and hetero-determination were decisive, for example, in early modern investigations of juridical and political philosophy. The self-determination of the will entails self-possession, and this in turn is the principle of external *dominium*, which is the foundation for property and even contracts. Scotus thus paved the way for later explorations into human rights, international law, political and juridical philosophy, etc., among many late scholastic and early modern philosophers (many of whom were Scotists or at least readers of Scotus).[51]

Still, many questions remain open in Scotus. For example, the relation between a self-determinating will and habits, the idea of the contingent (which now may seem more attuned to the object and its corresponding act than to the active principle), the open discussion between libertarianism and compatibilism, and, of course, the issue of voluntarism.[52] While labels like 'voluntarist' should always be used carefully, I believe a careful reading should prevent us from reading Scotus as a voluntarist, i.e. a philosopher who believes God can do anything and whatsoever at all, even beyond the boundaries of the principle of contradiction (a full voluntarism), or at least a philosopher who believes God can will something without reasons (moderate voluntarism). Scotus's ideas on the will and freedom, as read, expanded and criticized by William of Ockham (*ca.* 1287–1347), would of course play a central role in the nominalist tradition.

The necessity of having reasons and the role they play in our choices, along with the will's power, can easily change the general framework of ethics. In this sense, Scotus's influence in late scholastic and baroque philosophy can hardly be denied, even if the specific connections have not yet been fully mapped.[53] Scotus's influence on Suárez is at least well known,[54] and through Suárez and other Scotists like Bartolomeo Mastri and John Punch, and even Scotus's indirect influence on nominalists, it is not surprising that we find the ideas of will as self-determination and nature as hetero-determination, to quote Fernando Inciarte, as 'the twin pillars of Kantism'.[55]

Notes

1 Thanks to D. González-Ginnochio for his valuable suggestions during the last revision of this chapter and to M. J. Barker for his help in editing it.
2 Among many others, see Aertsen, Emery and Speer 2001.
3 Larsen 2011.
4 Thijssen 2013.
5 I have dealt with this issue elsewhere: cf. González-Ayesta 2014.
6 On Olivi's relevance for the current topic, see Dumont 1995.
7 For a more thorough analysis on this matter, see González-Ayesta 2010.
8 On Scotus's dependency and novelty in this matter regarding Aristotle, cf. González-Ayesta 2007.
9 Cf. González-Ayesta 2012.
10 Cf. González-Ayesta 2009.
11 Besides some references to the classical texts (*Quaestiones super libros Metaphysicorum Aristotelis* IX, q. 15, *Ordinatio* I, d. 10, *Lectura* I, d. 39, and *Quodlibet* q. 16), I base my arguments mainly on texts from *Ordinatio* I, d. 12–13 which deal with the Trinitarian generation of the Son and spiration of the Holy Spirit.

12 Cf. Johannes Duns Scotus 2012, J. Duns Escoto 2007, Pich 2008.
13 Cf. John Duns Scotus, *Quaestiones super libros Metaphysicorum Aristotelis*, IX, q. 15, n. 22. For Scotus the will can reject an object (nill it) but can also refrain from acting in the presence of an object (not will). This distinction is important for example to explain that finite will does not love the beatitude necessary, because although it cannot nill it it can not will it (cf. John Duns Scotus, *Reportata Parisiensia*, IV, d. 49, q. 10, n. 10).
14 Cf. Ibid., q. 15, n. 43.
15 Cf. John Duns Scotus, *Opera Philosophica*, v. 4: *Quaestiones super libros Metaphysicorum Aristotelis*, IX, q. 15, n. 59.
16 A. Vos and his research group provide a translation and detailed commentary of this text focused on the explanation of synchronic contingency. Cf. John Duns Scotus 1994.
17 Cf. John Duns Scotus, *Quodlibet*, q. 16, n. 40. The last number corresponds to the critical edition of this text by Noone and Roberts 2007. I have used this edition.
18 Cf. John Duns Scotus, *Quaestiones super libros Metaphysicorum Aristotelis*, IX, q. 15; *Lectura* I, d. 39, q. 1–5; *Reportatio* I A, d. 39–40, q. 1–3.
19 Cf. Williams 2003 and Williams 1998. Although Williams focuses on human freedom, when he addresses freedom as a pure perfection, he considers synchronically contingent action to be an attribute of both created and divine freedom.
20 Cf. Honnefelder 2012, 73–88, Cross 2005, 49–54, Vos et al. 2003, 208–222.
21 '[A] free power is "not determined of itself, but can cause this act or the opposite act, and act or not act" [*Quaestiones super libros Metaphysicorum Aristotelis*, IX, q. 15, n. 22] – presumably in the self-same circumstances, since the feature of a natural power is that the circumstances determine whether or not it actually causes an effect. These features entail, for Scotus, that a free power can "determine itself" in both ways [Cf. Ibid. 32][. . .], and this on the basis of "its unlimited actuality" [ibid. 31][. . .]. In line with these sorts of consideration, the second part of 2 [a text quoted earlier] is devoted to showing that *contingency entails will*. He does not believe, for example, that things could arise just randomly and he believes – plausibly enough – that all material processes are determined' (Cross 2005, 56).
22 Cross 2005, 57.
23 Cf. John Duns Scotus, *Quaestiones super libros Metaphysicorum Aristotelis*, IX, q. 15, n. 36.
24 Ioannis Duns Scoti, *Opera Omnia*, v. 5, *Ordinatio*, I, d. 12, q. 1, n. 17, p. 34. Translations from the Latin are thanks to Mark J. Barker unless otherwise indicated.
25 Cf. John Duns Scotus, *Ordinatio* I, d. 12, q. 1, n. 37.
26 John Duns Scotus, *Ordinatio*, I, d. 13, q. un., n. 47; Vatican, v. 5: p. 90 (emphasis is mine).
27 Cf. John Duns Scotus, *Lectura* I, d. 13, q. un., n. 22.
28 Cf. John Duns Scotus, *Quaestiones super libros Metaphysicorum Aristotelis* IX, q. 1–2, n. 14 and *Ordinatio* I, d. 7, nn. 28–29.
29 Cf. John Duns Scotus, *Quaestiones super libros Metaphysicorum Aristotelis* IX, q. 13, n. 11; q. 11, n. 12 and q. 15, n. 22.
30 Cf. John Duns Scotus, *Quaestiones super libros Metaphysicorum Aristotelis* IX, q. 14, n. 62, 76 and 88–94.
31 Cf. John Duns Scotus, *Quaestiones super libros Metaphysicorum Aristotelis* IX, q. 11, n. 16 and *Ordinatio* I, d. 20, n. 10.
32 Cf. John Duns Scotus, *Quaestiones super libros Metaphysicorum Aristotelis* IX, q. 14, n. 126 and q. 15, n. 11.
33 Cf. John Duns Scotus, *Ordinatio* I, d. 3, p. 3, q. 2, n. 545.
34 Cf. John Duns Scotus, *Quaestiones super libros Metaphysicorum Aristotelis* IX, q. 15, n. 31.
35 John Duns Scotus, *Ordinatio*, I, d. 13, q. un, n. 56; Vatican, v. 5: p. 94.

36 Ioannis Duns Scoti, *Opera Omnia*, v. 19, *Lectura*, II, d. 25, q. un, n. 95, 261–262 (emphasis is mine).
37 Cf. John Duns Scotus, *Ordinatio*, I, d. 13, q. un, n. 62.
38 John Duns Scotus, *Ordinatio*, I, d. 13, q. un, n. 60; Vatican, v. 5: p. 96.
39 John Duns Scotus, *Ordinatio*, I, d. 13, q. un, n. 58; Vatican, v. 5: p. 96.
40 The Wadding-Vivès edition reads '*libertas*' instead of '*firmitas*'. The critical edition of this paragraph by Frank 1982 made clear that it should be read '*firmitas*', so this is the word that appears in Noone's critical edition of the question. I have corrected the translation (Alluntis and Wolter 1975, 378) since it follows the text of the Wadding-Vivès edition.
41 John Duns Scotus, *Quodlibet*, q. 16, n. 8 [37] (Alluntis and Wolter 1975, 378). The number in brackets corresponds to Noone's edition.
42 John Duns Scotus, *Quodlibet*, q. 16, n. 9 [40] (Alluntis and Wolter 1975, 379).
43 Cf. John Duns Scotus, *The Examined Report of the Paris Lecture. Reportatio I A*, v. 1, d. 10, q. 3, n. 53, 402–403. Hoeres 1976, 81–95 has argued this point convincingly. Although I have developed my own arguments, I remain indebted to his insights.
44 In a previous article, I held a different position (Cf. González-Ayesta 2009). I had argued that simultaneously holding the doctrines expressed in these two sets of texts presented a difficulty for the definition of freedom as a pure perfection. Hence I had concluded that Scotus's doctrine and texts contained a true paradox. Herein I have clarified that indetermination (in the sense of self-determination) does not always involve contingency. This resolves the apparent paradox in Scotus's texts.
45 Cf. John Duns Scotus, *Lectura* I, d. 10, q. un; *Ordinatio* I, d. 10, q. un; *Reportatio* IA, d. 10, q. 1–2.
46 See note 16.
47 I will partially follow the explanation by Hoeres 1976, 17–43 of what a pure perfection is. As noted earlier, I have kept in mind many of his insights to develop the idea that the core of freedom is self-determination. He develops his own explanation of the 'essence of the will as pure perfection' (Hoeres 1976, 81–195). Although this book is still valuable, one should keep in mind that its textual basis is somewhat outdated due to advances in the critical edition of Scotus's work.
48 Anselm of Canterbury, *Monologion*, chapter 15. Cf. John Duns Scotus, *Quodlibet*, q. 5, n. 13 (cited in Hoeres 1976, 22).
49 Cf. John Duns Scotus, *Quodlibet*, q. 1, n. 4.
50 Cf. John Duns Scotus, *Ordinatio* I, d. 8, q. 3.
51 Cf. for example, Brett 2003.
52 For a discussion on a voluntaristic reading of Scotus cf.: Ingham 2001, Wolter 2003, and the web-only reply: Williams (online).
53 Cf. Pink 2004.
54 Cf. González-Ayesta 2011.
55 Inciarte 1987 (rpt. 2005).

Bibliography

Primary sources

Anselm of Canterbury (1984). *Opera Omnia, v. 1: Monologion et al.*, Stuttgart Bad Cannstatt: Frommann.
John Duns Scotus (1894). *Opera Omnia, v. 24: Reportata Parisiensia. Liber quartus a distinctione septima usque ad quadragesimam nonam*, Parisis: Apud Ludovicus Vivès.

John Duns Scotus (1959). *Opera Omnia, v. 5: Ordinatio. Liber primus. A distinctione undecima ad vigesimam quintam*, ed. by C. Balic et al., Civitas Vaticana: Typis Poliglottis Vaticanis.
John Duns Scotus (1975). *God and Creatures: The Quodlibetal Questions*, translation with an introduction, notes and glossary by F. Alluntis and A. B. Wolter, Princeton: Princeton University Press.
John Duns Scotus (1993). *Opera Omnia, v. 19: Lectura in secundum librum Sententiarum. A distinctione septima ad quadragesimam quartam*, Comissionis Scotisticae editio, Civitas Vaticana: Typis Vaticanis.
John Duns Scotus (1994). *Contingency and Freedom: Lectura I 39*, introduction, translation and commentary by A. Vos et al., Dordrecht/Boston/London: Kluwer Academic Publishers.
John Duns Scotus (1997). *Opera Philosophica, v. 4: Quaestiones super libros Metaphysicorum Aristotelis VI–IX*, ed. by R. Etzkorn et al., St Bonaventure, NY: The Franciscan Institute-St Bonaventure University.
John Duns Scotus (2004). *The Examined Report of the Paris Lecture: Reportatio I A, v. 1*, trans. by A. B. Wolter and O. V. Bychkov, St Bonaventure, NY: Franciscan Institute Publications.
John Duns Scotus (2007). "*John Duns Scotus' Quodlibet A Brief Study of the Manuscripts and an Edition of Question 16 by* T. B. Noone and F. Roberts," in (ed.) C. Schabel, *Theological Quodlibeta in the Middle Ages*: *The Fourteenth Century*, Leiden/Boston: E. J. Brill.
Juan Duns Escoto (2007). *Naturaleza y Voluntad. Quaestiones super libros Metaphysicorum Aristotelis*, IX, q. 15, Introducción, traducción y notas de C. González-Ayesta, Pamplona: Servicio de Publicaciones de la Universidad de Navarra (Cuadernos de Anuario Filosófico, 199).
Johannes Duns Scotus (2012). *Freiheit, Tugenden und Naturgesetz*, Übersetzt, eingeleitet und mit Anmarkungen versehen von T. Hofmann, Freiburg/Basel/Wien: Herder.

Secondary sources

Aertsen, J. A., Emery Jr., K. and Speer, A. (eds.) (2001). *Nach der Verurteilung von 1277. Philosophie und Theologie an der Universität von Paris im letzen Viertel des 13. Jahrhunderts*. Studien und Texte, Berlin/New York: De Gruyter (Miscelanea Mediaevalia, 28).
Brett, A. S. (2003). *Liberty, Right, and Nature: Individual Rights in Later Scholastic Thought*, Cambridge: Cambridge University Press.
Cross, R. (2005). *Duns Scotus on God*, Aldershot: Ashgate.
Dumont, S. (1995). "The Origin of Scotus's Theory of Synchronic Contingency," *Modern Schoolman* 72, 149–167.
Frank, W. (1982). "Duns Scotus' Concept of Willing Freely: What Divine Choice Teaches Us," *Franciscan Studies* 42, 68–90.
González-Ayesta, C. (2007). "Scotus's Interpretation of *Metaphysics* 9.2: On the Distinction Between Nature and Will," *Proceedings of the American Catholic Philosophical Association* 81, 39–52.
González-Ayesta, C. (2009). "A Paradox In Scotus's Account of Freedom of the Will," *Itinerarium* 55, 257–279.

González-Ayesta, C. (2010). "Duns Scotus on Synchronic Contingency and Free Will: The Originality and Importance of His Contribution," in (ed.) M. B. Ingham and O. Bychkov, *John Duns Scotus Philosopher: Proceedings of the Quadruple Congress on John Duns Scotus*, v. 1, Munster/St Bonaventure, NY: Aschendorff Verlag/Franciscan Institute Publications, 157–174.
González-Ayesta, C. (2011). "Duns Scotus's Influence on Disputation XIX," in (ed.) J. Meirinhos and P. Silva, *As Disputaçoes Metafísicas de Francisco Suárez. Estudios e antologia de textos*, Porto: Fac. de Letras da Universidade do Porto-Humus, 257–291.
González-Ayesta, C. (2012). "Duns Scotus on the Natural Will," *Vivarium* 50, 33–52.
González-Ayesta, C. (2014). "¿Es la voluntad un apetito o un poder? La perspectiva de Duns Escoto," *Anuario Filosófico* 47, 77–102.
Hoeres, W. (1976). *La volontà come perfezione pura in Duns Scoto*, Padova: Liviana Editrice.
Honnefelder, L. (2012). "John Duns Scotus on God's Intellect and Will," in (ed.) R. Cross, *The Opera Theologica of Duns Scotus: Proceedings of the Quadruple Congress on John Duns Scotus*, v. 2, Munster/St. Bonaventure, NY: Aschendorff Verlag/Franciscan Institute Publications, 73–88.
Inciarte, F. (1987). "Natura ad unum – Ratio ad opposita. Zur Transformation des Aristotelismus bei Duns Scotus," in (eds.) P. Beckmann, L. Honnefelder, G. Scrimpf, and G. Wieland, *Philosophie im Mittelalter. Entwicklungslinien und Paradigmen*, Hamburg: Meiner, 259–273. (Repr. Flamarique, L. (ed.) (2005). *First Principles, Substance and Action: Studies in Aristotle and Aristotelianism*, Hildesheim/New York: Olms Verlag).
Ingham, M. B. (2001). "Letting Scotus Speak for Himself," *Mediaeval Philosophy and Theology* 10, 173–216.
Larsen, A. E. (2011). *The School of Heretics: Academic Condemnation at the Universitz of Oxford, 1277–1409*, Leiden: Brill, 25–41.
Pich, R. H. (2008). "Introduçào, estrutura e traduçào A questâo 15 do Livro IX das *Quaestiones Super Libros Metaphysicorum Aristotelis* de Duns Scotus," *Veritas: revista de filosofia*, 118–157.
Pink, T. (2004). "Suárez, Hobbes, and the Scholastic Tradition in Action Theory," in (eds.) T. Pink and M. Stone, *The Will and Human Action: From Antiquity to the Present Day*, London: Routledge, 127–153.
Thijssen, H. (2013). "Condemnation of 1277," in (ed.) E. N. Zalta, *The Stanford Encyclopedia of Philosophy* (Winter 2013 Edition), <http://plato.stanford.edu/archives/win2013/entries/condemnation/>.
Vos, A. et al. (2003). *Duns Scotus on Divine Love: Texts and Commentary on Goodness and Freedom, God and Humans*, Aldershot: Ashgate.
Williams, T. (1998). "The Libertarian Foundations of Scotus's Moral Philosophy," *The Thomist* 62, 193–215.
Williams, T. (2003). "From Metaethics to Action Theory," in (ed.) T. Williams, *The Cambridge Companion to Duns Scotus*, Cambridge/New York: Cambridge University Press, 332–351.
Williams, T. (online). "The Divine Nature and Scotus's Libertarianism. A Reply to Mary Beth Ingham," <http://shell.cas.usf.edu/~thomasw/The%20Divine%20Nature%20and%20Scotus%27s%20Libertarianism.pdf>.
Wolter, A. (2003). "The Unshredded Scotus: A Response to Thomas Williams," *American Catholic Philosophical Quarterly* 77, 315–356.

5

SOUL, WILL, AND CHOICE IN ISLAMIC AND JEWISH CONTEXTS

Sarah Pessin

1 Introduction

In this chapter, I explore a variety of "will threads" across medieval Islamic and Jewish thought,[1] including Aristotelian and Neoplatonic trajectories, philosophical and theological topics in psychology, epistemology, metaphysics, and ethics, and considerations of theories of Divine Will and their impact on theories of human freedom and genuine choice.

I begin with an overview of some of the resonances of Greek ideas about desire, deliberation, and choice within a number of Neoplatonic and [Neoplatonized] Aristotelian texts. Next, in recognition of how broader contexts can often provide important cues for understanding philosophical texts, I embark on a series of theological excursions, including a consideration of three leading Islamic schools of thought on the question of genuine human choice and a further consideration of theological points on inclination, capacity, and power. I then go on to consider how various conceptions of Divine Will lead to and correlate with various conceptions of human agency and deliberation, including explorations of (1) two notions of divine grace in Islamic and Jewish texts, (2) Plotinian-inspired Islamic and Jewish "theologies of will" where freedom is related to God's goodness, and (3) Aristotle-inspired Maimonidean and Averroean contexts in which divine and human freedom are rooted in the order of God's Wisdom-as-manifest-in-Will.

But before getting started, let's turn to some of the conceptual and terminological shifts from an Aristotelian theory of rational decision to the more varied (and in many cases, more robust) ideas of will, deliberation, and choice at play in our thinkers.

2 A starting word on Aristotle(s)

While not all the thinkers in this chapter operate under Aristotelian influence, even among those who do, we must keep in mind that they are writing under a number of additional influences, including a range of religious and philosophical traditions which either interpret Aristotle (often in arguably non-Aristotelian ways) or simply provide non-Aristotelian insights on which our thinkers draw alongside drawing on Aristotle (and/or commentaries on Aristotle), sometimes resulting in hybrid views which are never simply "Aristotelian." This is arguably the case for the notions of *al-irāda* (will – we might even say free will) and *al-ikhtiyār* (choice, or decision) in a number of the thinkers in this chapter. Mindful of the complexity and debates around interpreting Aristotle theory of *boulesis + prohairesis*, we will draw in the following brief sections on Frede (2011) and Nielsen (2011) to highlight the contrast between Aristotle and the (arguably) more Stoic-inflected version of Aristotle that makes its way into the Aristotelian thinkers whom we address in this chapter. We start, though, with ways in which our thinkers are indeed genuinely Aristotelian.

2.1 When reason grounds morality

Speaking here again only of those thinkers in this chapter who uphold Aristotelian ideas (in whatever hybrid way), we find a deeply Aristotelian appreciation for the strength of intellect, along with the sense that good actions follow from intellects which are indeed strong: The more well-honed one's faculty of reason is, the more it can be host to the kind of rational goal-settings, deliberations, and decisions that lead to virtuous – as well as flourishing – living. Within such a context, we ought not be surprised to find more of a focus in our thinkers on cognitive details. In other words, in looking for a theory to ground moral agency and responsibility, our thinkers are able to turn, with Aristotle, to a theory of intellect. And while, as such, neither Aristotle nor our Aristotelians spend a great deal of time on *boulesis* and *prohairesis* as compared with the details of intellection (and while both Aristotle and our Aristotelians ultimately view even what limited amount they do have to say about *boulesis* and *prohairesis* as ultimately subcategories of a study of intellect), whereas Aristotle's "theory of will" (as Frede rightly warns us not to call it) is not really about "will" at all (in any number of ways many of us understand the term), our later Aristotelians' theories of will arguably are.

2.2 A brief overview of Aristotelian boulesis-prohairesis *(and why it's not really about will)*

We start by emphasizing, with Frede and Nielsen, that – contrary to many later notions of will – there is nothing in the actual Aristotelian account of rational deliberation and decision that implies a freedom to choose between alternatives. Following from what we have seen to be a strong regard for the cognitive, we begin, for starters, in an overall context in which reason (not some separate faculty of will) is the site of deliberation and decision (a joint *bouleusis* [deliberation] and *prohairesis* [decision] rooted first of all in *boulesis* [a wish, in the particular sense of the kind of goal-setting involved in wanting a given object or outcome]). Helping emphasize that it is not "weighing options" or "choosing between alternatives" that is the engine of Aristotelian *boulesis-prohairesis*, Nielsen (2011, 399) explains that for Aristotle, even when we "identify only *one* way to promote our end" this still very much counts as (and as such, highlights what is really the main distinguishing factor of) "having deliberated successfully." Indeed, helping emphasize this point, Nielsen draws our attention to the judiciary undertones of *bouleusis* (not *boulesis*, but rather the deliberation which leads to *prohairesis*) in relation to the *boulē* (the legislative body) primarily working to "determine what steps should be taken to achieve the city's aim"; as Nielsen (2011, 397) puts it, this is a "how" question and not at all a "choice between alternatives" sort of deliberation.

2.3 Alexander and Plotinus: two registers of freedom?

Following Frede, we might here point to the development, first in the hands of Stoics, of "more robust" conceptions of will – including emphases on assent, *eleutheria* (freedom), and *exousia autopragias* (the power to act independently). Integrating these sorts of elements into his own thinking – including into his own interpretations of Aristotle – we find in Alexander of Aphrodisias a robust sense of *boulesis* as a power of assent and deliberation, with *prohairesis* emerging expressly – and in direct contrast to what we've seen earlier in Aristotle – as freedom to choose between alternatives in the sense of being free to choose otherwise than we do.

That said, we must also consider the influence of Neoplatonism and the presence within that tradition of a very different – indeed, we might say opposite – sense of *boulesis* and freedom; in particular, we find within Neoplatonic contexts that God Himself – in his unity and goodness – is often the paradigm of both will and freedom; but of course, within such a context, "choosing between alternatives" is certainly not what is meant. On the contrary, in such a context, true will and true freedom are found (as we will see in our discussion of Neoplatonic approaches to Divine Will later) in a strong internal relationship to goodness.

2.4 Jewish and Islamic Aristotelians on al-irāda *and* al-ikhtiyār

Turning to Islamic and Jewish medieval contexts, we find textual connections between *boulesis* and *al-irāda* (as will – and even sometimes translated as free will) and *prohairesis* and *al-ikhtiyār* (as decision/choice – though sometimes also translated as free choice, or even as free will – as we will see, for example, in the case of Maimonides below).[2] We might additionally note that while *al-irāda* and *al-ikhtiyār* are sometimes treated together (in contrast – or sometimes in the case of God, in confluence – with one another), we might also speak of a stronger focus on *al-ikhtiyār* (Hebrew, *beḥira*) as a crowning human proprium,[3] with *al-irāda* emerging as a way of referring to the souls' (including animals' souls') many appetites.[4]

In approaching *al-irāda* and *al-ikhtiyār* we are well-served to emphasize, even among our Aristotelians – and a fortiori for our more heavily Neoplatonic, pietistic, and theological thinkers – the importance of keeping an open mind about whether the kind of genuine choice being heralded (from one thinker to the next, and even from case to case within a given thinker) is the kind of choice that involves choosing between alternatives.

In this spirit, we are well-served on the one hand to consider the influence of Alexander. In this sense, we can approach any number of our thinkers as operating with senses of *al-irāda* (will) in Alexander's more deliberative spirit of *boulesis* as assent, and as operating with senses of *al-ikhtiyar* (decision, choice) in line with Alexander's sense of *prohairesis* in terms of a freedom to choose otherwise.[5] But, on the other hand, we are also well-served to supplement this insight with its reverse, for indeed, many of our thinkers additionally use the terms *al-irāda* (alongside *al-mashī'a*, another term for "will") and/or *al-ikhtiyār* to describe God's pure unity – precisely not a choosing between alternatives in the sense highlighted in Alexander. Not only does ascribing these terms to God create a second register of meanings and associations, but thinking – as many of our thinkers do – within the further context of religious and Neoplatonic calls to *imitatio dei*, many of our thinkers might well hear an invitation to apply some of the elements at play in the divine uses of these terms to the human cases as well.

2.5 On translating al-ikhtiyār: *"free will/free choice" v. "decision/choice"*

In an attempt to remain neutral about the precise philosophical implications of *al-ikhtiyār* in a given thinker (in this way remaining open to both of the aforementioned – and other – registers in an overview chapter of this sort), when I address *al-ikhtiyār* I will forgo the terms "free will" and "free choice," speaking instead of "decision" or "choice" (sometimes with the modifier "genuine"), and I will connect these to ideas of human agency, deliberation, and freedom.

For a sense of the tendency to translate *al-ikhtiyār* as "free will" or "free choice" (as well as for a sense of the additional challenges that arise in working with translations where sometimes, for a host of reasons, more than one translation is used for a single term in the original language, even within a single text translation – and certainly across texts translated by different scholars), consider Shlomo Pines' translation of Maimonides' *Guide of the Perplexed* (henceforth, *Guide*) 2.48 and Isadore Twersky's translation of section 8 of Maimonides' "Eight Chapters" as compared with Maimonides' Arabic use of *al-ikhtiyār* in these two texts:

Pines, *Guide* 2.48, said of God[6]	Arabic for *Guide* 2.48 on God[7]	Pines, *Guide* 2.48 said of humans[8]	Arabic for *Guide* 2.48 on humans[9]	Twersky on "Eight Chapters" (section 8), said of humans[10]	Arabic for "Eight Chapters" (section 8) on humans[11]
will + free choice	*al-mashī'a* + *al-ikhtiyār*	voluntary + free choice	adj. form of *al-ikhtiyār* + *al-ikhtiyār*	free will	*al-ikhtiyār*

In light not only of these sorts of translation complexities but in light too of the intersections of Aristotelian ideas with a range of different "will traditions," including religious sources, Stoic theories of assent and freedom, Alexander's reading of Aristotle in terms of choosing between alternatives, and Neoplatonic emphases on freedom in one's simple connection to goodness itself, this chapter can at best provide some initial openings in which to think about *al-irāda* (*boulesis*/will) and *al-ikhtiyār* (*prohairesis*/decision) in some Islamic and Jewish contexts.

3 Greek *boulesis-prohairesis* in Islamic and Jewish contexts

One way to highlight the importance of will in Islamic and Jewish medieval philosophy is to consider the dual pull of Greek and religious insights about the importance of refining one's virtue and wisdom, and (as such) choosing to live one's life deliberately. In addressing these themes (often in terms of *al-ikhtiyār* ["decision"]), many medieval Islamic and Jewish philosophers (1) reflect Aristotle's division of ethical and intellectual virtues, (2) engage his sense that ethical virtues (viz. virtuous character traits) can only be perfected in the context of the perfection of the particular intellectual virtue of practical wisdom or prudence (*phronesis*), and (3) carry out Aristotelian reflections on *phronesis* alongside deliberation (*bouleusis* in Aristotle, but transmuted to *boulesis* – in the sense of an assenting, deliberative act of will – by the time we get to Alexander), decision (*prohairesis*), and "weakness of will" or incontinence (*akrasia*, literally "lack of mastery"), with roots too in Plato's tripart analysis of the soul in the *Republic* and *Phaedrus*.

Following on the Aristotelian idea that

> to deliberate well (τὸ εὖ βουλεύεσθαι) is the most characteristic function of the prudent man
> (Aristotle, *Nicomachean Ethics*; Rackham, 345)

and that prudence is

> a truth-attaining rational quality, concerned with action in relation to things that are good and bad for human beings,
> (Aristotle, *Nicomachean Ethics* (1140b6–7); Rackham, 337)

al-Fārābī (*ca.* 872–*ca.* 951) enumerates a scale of deliberative virtues, each aimed at uncovering the good for different categories and subcategories of people: On the one end of this scale is the *political* deliberative virtue of being able to discern what is good for a number of nations or a single nation or city; in the middle of the scale is the *economic* deliberative virtue of being able to discern what is good for citizens of a city or members of a household; on the far end of this scale is the deliberative virtue of being able to discern what is good for oneself or for another (*Attainment of Happiness*; Mahdi, 28–29).

Looking at al-Fārābī a bit further, we might note his description of the appetitive faculty as desiring (*yashtāqu*) or disliking (*yakruhu*) things, and, as such, as the faculty that "makes the will (*al-irāda*) arise" (*Perfect State* 4.10.1, 4.10.6; Walzer, 164–5, 170–1). He goes on to note that will (*al-irāda*) is "an 'inclination' (*an yuzra'*) in the appetitive faculty toward that which has been apprehended" (*Perfect State* 4.13.17; Walzer, 208–9); it is:

> an appetite (*nuzū'*, longing, desire, inclination) towards or away from what has been apprehended either by sense-perception or by representation or by the faculty of reason, and a decision (*ḥukm*) [about it] whether it ought either to be accepted or rejected.
> (*Perfect State* 4.10.6; Walzer, 170–1)

Al-Fārābī elaborates that in cases where there is an appetite (*nuzū'*) to know something that must be apprehended by the senses, that appetite will be satisfied by an act of body and soul (e.g. we will raise our eyelids and direct our gaze to something, walk towards it, etc.), whereas in cases where there is an appetite (*nuzū'*) to know something that must be apprehended by the rational faculty, that appetite will be satisfied by an act of practical reasoning (e.g. we will form a thought of some sort, or enter into some deliberation) (*Perfect State* 4.10.8; Walzer, 172–3). More generally, he describes the rational faculty as that by which a human "distinguishes (*yumayyizu*) good and evil" and is drawn to objects of reasoning (*Perfect State* 4.10.1; Walzer, 164–5). He goes on to distinguish will (*al-irāda*) from choice (*al-ikhtiyār*) by describing the former as the appetite/inclination (*nuzū'*) for an item apprehended by sensing or imagining (available to all animals) and the latter as "the outcome of deliberation (*al-rawīya*) or rational thought" (available only to humans) (*Perfect State* 4.13.4; Walzer, 204–5).[12] Indeed, in his commentary on Aristotle's *De Interpretatione*, he highlights the importance of *al-ikhtiyār* for moral responsibility (highlighted there as a condition for divine reward and punishment) (*Commentary on De Interpretatione*; Zimmerman 93).[13]

Following in an Aristotelian tradition with many of his own interpretive-innovative elements, Avicenna (*ca.* 980–1037) speaks of the active, motive (*mukhraka*) (*Kitāb al-Najāt*; Fakhry, 197) faculty in the animal soul and the practical faculty of the rational soul. While the impulsive (*bā'itha*) aspect of the animal soul's motive faculty involves the subject in a kind of automatic (or at least, sub-volitional) process of attraction (via the faculty of desire) or repulsion (via the faculty of anger) vis-a-vis various stimuli, the *active* aspect of the motive faculty is the power to move one's body (through relaxing or contracting muscles and nerves). Beyond this very basic active element, it is through the practical faculty or power (*al-'āmila quwwa*) of her rational soul that an agent governs her desires and bodily faculties so as to help enable the cultivation of morality as well as the soul's turn towards theoretical knowing. In these respects, Avicenna describes this practical faculty as "the principle of movement of the human body, towards individual actions characterized by deliberation (*al-rawīya*)."[14]

Working too through the details of Aristotelian psychology, Averroes (1126–1198), commenting on *De Anima* 433a26–30, notes that:

> Every activity of intellectual understanding is correct, while activities which come about from appetite and imagination are sometimes correct and sometimes not. For this reason the appetitive part always causes motion, because it causes motion toward what is correct and toward what is not correct. Intellectual understanding, however, causes motion only toward what is correct alone, and for this reason it does not always cause motion.
> (*Long Commentary on the De Anima of Aristotle*, 3.51; Taylor, 417)

We might here add that for Averroes, although humans share an active and material intellect, they do not share a will – a point he sees (perhaps not ultimately successfully) as allowing him to uphold human responsibility in spite of his "shared intellects" theory (which would appear to place the blame for human decisions outside of individuals).[15]

In considering Maimonides (1135/8–1204), we find an analysis of human choice through a commentary on "turning." In the context of reflecting on Adam's turn away from intellect as a turn to imagination and desire that results in his being turned away from the Garden of Eden, Maimonides quickly draws on a passage from Job in which a human "change of face" is itself described as leading to a divine act of turning away. Reflecting on the passage, "He changes his face and You send him forth" (Job 14:20), Maimonides notes that:

> the interpretation and explanation of the verse are as follows: when the direction toward which man tended changed, he was driven forth. For *panim* [the Hebrew word for "face"] is a term deriving from the verb *panoh* [to turn], since man turns his face toward the thing he wishes to take as his objective. The verse states accordingly that when man changed the direction toward which he tended and took as his objective the very thing a previous commandment had bidden him not to aim at, he was driven out of the *Garden of Eden*.
> (*Guide* 1.2; Pines, 26)

Focusing on this unrestrained human capacity to "tend" towards or "face" (or "decide on") one object or another, Maimonides sees "being driven out of the Garden" as an allegorical reference to the human turn away from intellectual virtues. As such, for Maimonides the point of this verse is not that God exiles humans, but that humans choose to turn themselves away (to exile themselves) from their own intellectual perfection (here allegorized as the Garden of Eden).[16] We might add that this human turn away from intellectual aims, for Maimonides, can also – at the level of practical intellect – thwart one's moral choices: Absent a truth-ward intellectual orientation (a grounding of morality, as we've seen in Aristotle, in the intellectual virtue of *phronēsis*), there is not only no hope for perfected intellectual virtue, but there is also (and as such) no hope for perfected moral virtue. It is in this spirit that Maimonides understands the Biblical claim that God hardened Pharaoh's heart (*Exodus* 9:12): Interpreted allegorically by Maimonides as part of his Aristotelian theory of human decision-making, the claim is taken as reminding us that after a certain amount of bad living – related, we might say, to a cultivated viciousness of character – it is no longer really "up to us" to choose what a good version of ourselves would have known to be the actions most likely to yield *eudaimonea*.[17] In this spirit, and with Platonic as well as Aristotelian overtones, Maimonides speaks of this state of being "turned away from intellect" as one in which Adam (allegorically referencing human nature) "followed his pleasures and his imaginings" (*Guide* 1.2; Pines, 26).[18]

Drawing on the "turning" image in Maimonides – in direct relation to the Hebrew term "face" – we might also consider Avicenna's emphasis on the "dual facings" of practical and theoretical intellect:

> The human soul, though one substance, has a relation and reference to two sides, one below it and one above it, and for each side there is a faculty through which the connection between it and that side is ordered. The practical faculty, then, is the one that the soul possesses for the side below it, that is, the body and its maintenance. The theoretical faculty is the one that the soul possesses for the connection to the side above it, to be affected by it, learn from it, and receive from it. So, it is as though our soul has two faces.
> (*Psychology*, I.5, 47.8ff; McGinnis 2010, 211–212)

Unlike the negative implication of the "downward facing" in the aforementioned Maimonides context, Avicenna here – and Maimonides too, in other parts of the *Guide* – goes on to explain the "downward facing" in terms of practical intellect's most important engagement with the sensory world as a condition for the production of moral dispositions.

Turning to *al-ikhtiyār*, in his "Eight Chapters" – an introduction to his *Commentary on Avot* – Maimonides emphasizes this genuine choice as the distinctive mark of humans. This is, of course, not only consistent with the idea that intellectual perfection is key (an idea one finds throughout the *Guide of the Perplexed*) but also helps emphasize that it is through a human's proper deliberation and choice that she is able to arrive at (or at least work toward) said intellectual perfection. Emphasizing the uniqueness of the human creature in this regard, Maimonides draws attention to God's own Will (*mashī'a ilāhī*)[19] and notes that it was God's will that:

> man should move or rest of his own accord, and that his actions should be [based on his own decision (*al-ikhtiyār*)] without any outside influence or restraint, which fact God clearly states in the truthful Law, which elucidates this problem when it says, "Behold, the man is become as one

of us to know good and evil" (Gen. 3:22). The Targum, in paraphrasing this passage, explains the meaning of the words *mimmennu ladaat tov vara* [viz. as one of us to know good and evil]. Man has become the only being in the world who possesses a characteristic which no other being has in common with him. What is this characteristic? It is that by and of himself man can distinguish between good and evil and do that which he pleases with absolutely no restraint.

("Eight Chapters"; Twersky, 383)[20]

Emphasizing this "absolute lack of restraint" at the core of the human agent, Maimonides goes on:

Since this is so, it would have even been possible for him to have stretched out his hand and, taking of the tree of life, to have eaten of its fruit, and thus live forever.

("Eight Chapters"; Twersky, 383; Pocock 88)

Directly connecting to the theme of intellectual perfection in his *Guide*, and arguably influenced by traditions of readings of *De Anima* 3.5 on the immortality of human intellect, here Maimonides envisions (as he does too in the *Guide*) the Genesis "tree of life" as an allegorical reference to intellectual perfection – the state in which one has most fully actualized the aspect of oneself that "lives forever." In place of the Biblical story of a fruit wrongly chosen, Maimonides here envisions the counter-story of rightly chosen fruit – it is in our hands, as it were, to choose our way to virtue and knowledge culminating in knowledge of God (to whatever extent such knowledge is ultimately possible for Maimonides).

Emphasis on this human "lack of constraint" can also be seen, for example, in Solomon Ibn Gabirol's (1021/2–1050/70) *On the Improvement of the Moral Qualities*. Faced with the Biblical verse "The steps of a good man are ordered by the Lord" (Psalms 37:23; a verse similar in spirit to the Exodus verse about God's hardening Pharaoh's heart that we've seen earlier), Ibn Gabirol notes that properly read, this verse does not entail compulsion (*jabr*) when it comes to obedience (*ṭā'a*) or disobedience (*ma'ṣiya*).[21] Ibn Gabirol instead reads the verse as describing the divine approval that comes to the human who "inclines" (*māla*) her soul towards virtue (and thus, we may say, orders herself toward the divine order).

Turning to al-Kindi (*ca.* 801–873), we find an emphasis instead on human action as "constrained yet free." Holding in balance the idea that human actions are causally determined along with the idea that humans are free agents,[22] he places emphasis on a person's need to reorient herself, as seen in his likening the human tendency to prevent her own return to her divine source with a homeward-bound ship traveler who gets hopelessly distracted with – and burdened down by – the excursions and souvenirs at every port (see al-Kindi, *On Dispelling Sorrows*, section 9 and 10; Adamson and Pormann, 262–263). In his *On Dispelling Sorrows*, Al-Kindi also emphasizes that we must "improve our souls by firmly resolving to adhere to whatever can better us ... by accustoming the soul to the right behaviours," namely, in part, ways of living that make us less attached to worldly possessions and less engaged in wordly distractions (*On Dispelling Sorrows*, section 4; Adamson and Pormann, 253). In this spirit, and drawing too on the thematic of *imitatio dei*, he notes that

> those in whom the power of the intellectual soul is most dominant, and who are most accustomed to thinking, discerning, knowing the true natures of things, and investigating the difficult points of science, are virtuous men, close to being similar to the Creator.
> (*Discourse on the Soul*; Adamson and Pormann, 114)

On the soul's role in choosing a correct path home, we might also consider the *Theology of Aristotle*. Marking a more robustly Neoplatonic tradition in Islamic medieval philosophy than the more Aristotelianized versions of Neoplatonism found in al-Fārābī, Maimonides, and others, and advancing the Plotinian vision of an eternally emanating God denied by al-Kindi, al-Ghazālī (*ca.* 1058–1111), Judah Halevi (*ca.* 1075–1141), and other Islamic and Jewish thinkers, the *Theology of Aristotle* follows a Neoplatonic thematic of downward-directed emanation alongside upward-directed return. In the spirit of Plotinus' own complex sense that this descent is at once (1) an act of rebelliousness on the part of the souls descending, but also (2) the manifestation of an infinitely gracious divine outpouring of goodness (a theme rooted in the *Timaeus*' claim that God produces "without jealousy," about which we will say more later), the *Theology of Aristotle* (engaging in what I have elsewhere [see Pessin 2014a] described as a dual rhetoric of "rebellion/fall" and "salvation/rescue") describes the condition of soul as at once fallen and depleted but as also holding a special place in the cosmos. Relating to the ideas of deliberation and decision-making that we have been exploring, soul has the special gift of being able to bring the truths of Intellect into the world:

> We say that, although the noble lordly soul has left her high world and descended to this low world, she did that by an aspect of her high ability and power, in order to give form to and to administer the essence that is after her.
> (*Theology of Aristotle*, chapter 7, trans. Lewis: 243;
> Arabic at Badawi 1955, 84, ll. 1–3)

Following this line of thought, soul is described as that which

> expend[s] her powers on it [viz. this world] and manifest[s] her resident [or, latent; Ar. *al-sākina*] noble deeds and acts that were within her when she was in the world of Intellect.
> (*Theology of Aristotle*, trans. Lewis: 243 with my revisions;
> Arabic at Badawi 1955, 84, ll. 5–6)

We may, of course, identify the soul's unique function here with the capacity to choose wisely (her ability, that is, to manifest her original root in Intellect). Soul, we may say, occupies the role of chooser as a precise outgrowth of on the one hand being born of the truths of Intellect but on the other hand being at a distance from those truths. In this respect, one might certainly include the entire Neoplatonic tradition of "soul return" – and here, the related tradition of the soul's enacting noble deeds – as part of the Islamic and Jewish tradition of decision-making. We will turn to the further Neoplatonic implications of God as Divine *Irāda* (Divine Will) below.

In this very regard, we might consider too Isaac Israeli, who, after outlining rational soul's emanated origin in intellect, speaks of perfect and imperfect actions, with the latter emerging as "desires of the rational soul":

> Perfect actions pass beyond the sphere, i.e. the everlasting sphere.[23] These perfect actions are those which are in accordance with the demands of the intellect, while the imperfect are those which are in accordance with the demands of the animal soul. The proof is from the passage in Scripture: "What profit hath man of all his labour wherein he laboureth under the sun?" (Eccles. 1.3). By "under the sun" are meant the works of ignorance . . . which are the desires of the animal soul. . . . The noble works are the desires of the rational soul, such as worship, purity, and sanctity.
> (*The Book of Spirit and Soul*, section 11; Altmann and Stern, 111–112)

In his *Book of Definitions*, Israeli (*ca.* 872–*ca.* 932) (drawing on elements of Ibn Ḥasday's Neoplatonist throughout, and here directly engaging al-Kindi)[24] identifies estimation (*ẓann*) as judging based only on appearances, not based on truth (*The Book of Definitions*; Altmann and Stern, 63), and as the way that animals, not humans, "make choices" that are not really the kind of choices that we speak about when we speak of human responsibility and of the related notion of reward and punishment in the human context:

> A proof of the fact that animals have estimation, but no faculty of discernment is the behaviour of the ass, which, if it is very thirsty and comes near water and sees its own form or another form in it, is frightened and flees, regardless of the fact that water gives it its life and constitution. If, on the other hand, it sees a lion, it goes towards it, though it will be killed by it. For this reason animals do not receive reward or punishment, since they have no faculty of discernment and do not know for what action they should be rewarded, or, on the other hand, punished. The reason is that they are deprived of the faculty of inquiry and discernment and of perceiving the truth of things.
> (*The Book of Definitions*; Altmann and Stern, 41–2)

4 Theological inflections 1: the Islamic theological debate on human agency

While religious and theological elements within an Islamic or Jewish philosophical text do not on their own necessarily entail a conceptual departure from Greek philosophy, reading Islamic and Jewish philosophy with a sense of some of the choice-related ideas and debates theologically at play in their respective traditions and/or in their socio-political backgrounds can allow us to better discern possible inflections within their texts. Familiarizing ourselves with the theological context in this way can either help us reveal theological points of influence on philosophical writing, or (equally plausibly) can help us reveal moments within philosophical writing aimed at overturning (either reworking or criticizing) a particular theological claim. It is in this spirit that we turn to three competing theological approaches to human choice – rooted in three competing ways to understand God and the Islamic doctrine of "*al-Qaḍā' Wa'l-Qadar*" [The Divine Decree])[25] operating in the background of medieval Islamic and Jewish philosophy.[26]

4.1 Human compulsion

With its strong emphasis on *jabr* (compulsion), the "Jabrite" theological tradition denies human agency of any kind. On this view, God is the only true agent, and humans are said to act in only a metaphorical sense – similar to saying of the sun that "it sets" (see Watt 2012).

For this "extreme determinism,"[27] consider Jahm ibn Ṣafwān's (d. 746) claim that "man is compelled (*majbūr*) in his actions, having no power (*qudra*) and no will and no choice,"[28] reflected further in the following Jahmī account of human action:

> No one acts in reality except God alone. He is the agent, and men have the acts ascribed to them only by way of metaphor. Thus it is said that the stone moves, the sphere revolves, and the sun sets; and yet it is God Who does that with the stone and the sphere and the sun.[29]

4.2 Human "acquisition"

Associated with the Ash'arite school of theology, this view is often categorized as a "middle position" between the Jabrite view of compulsion and the Mu'tazilite view of agency (see section 4.3), though is lambasted by Averroes as simply sliding back into the Jabrite position outlined in section 4.1 (*Kashf* (233); Najjar, 114–115). In their focus on God *qua* Divine Will, the Ash'arites can be seen as taking up an extreme voluntarist approach to God according to which God's actions appear arbitrary from the human point of view: Related to the strong emphasis on Will (here in the sense of absolute omnipotence to do as He wishes), this position denies any laws of nature and upholds a doctrine of occasionalism.

The Ash'arites further uphold a rather robust sense of predeterminism in the idea of *al-Qaḍā' Wa'l-Qadar* (The Divine Decree), seeing *qaḍā'* (lit. "judgment") and *qadar* (lit. "measure") as aspects of the eternal Divine Will (itself theorized as a divine "attribute of essence"), with *qaḍā'* as a divine "attribute of essence" that signifies the divine decree from pre-eternity and with *qadar* as a divine "attribute of action" that signifies the manifesting of that pre-eternal decree into the world here and now at this moment (itself theorized by al-Djurdjānī as the actualization or coming to be of possible beings from non-being).[30] The eternal and essential Command of God (*amr ilāhī*), *qaḍā'* is enacted in the world "between *qadar*, the attribute of action which determines every contingent thing, and *maqdūr*, the enacted object."[31]

On this picture, any autonomous sense of human agency seems to fall by the wayside: Seemingly identical to the falling of a stone, human acts are manifestations of God's Will manifesting His own sovereign, eternal decree. That said, Ash'arites do make a point to distinguish the human from the stone, emphasizing, as they do, what they take to be a genuine sense of human agency and responsibility: Unlike stones, humans serve as a receptacle (*maḥall*) for the divine decree through the special relation of "*kasb*" (acquisition; also sometimes as "*iktisāb*"). The human in this way is said to "acquire" the act that God manifests, and is in this sense identified as a genuine agent. As described by al-Ash'arī (attributed by him to Ḍirār b. 'Amr), the view holds that:

> the acts of men are created, and that one act comes from two agents (*fā'ilān*), one of whom creates it, namely God, while the other acquires it, namely man; and that God is the agent of the acts of men in reality, and that men are the agents of them in reality.[32]

It is through a focus on this doctrine of *kasb* that the Ash'arites uphold the responsibility of the human being and, as such, can be seen as a middle position (described by Watt [1946, 143] as "moderate determinism") between compulsion and genuine agency.

4.3 Human agency

Among the various Islamic theological traditions, it is the Mu'tazilites who uphold the strongest sense of human agency, as seen in their inter-related senses of *al-ikhtiyār* (though with different implications from the Aristotelian ideas we've seen earlier) and responsibility. They can be categorized in this respect as holding a Qadarite perspective, here emphasizing not the divine *qadar* in the sense of predestination, but the human *qadar* (here in the sense of "power" or "ability"),[33] theorized as itself arisen from a special human *qudra* (understood as an effective power) created by God. Referred to also as a human capacity (*istiṭā'a*) from God, this *qudra* is seen by some as a power with which humans are born, and by others (here arguably drifting closer to an Ash'arite sensibility) as a power instilled by God each time a human acts.[34]

Emphasizing human agency and responsibility, the Mu'tazilites not only describe the human being as "agent" and "innovator," but as the "creator" (*khāliq*) of her actions – a point which directly opposes the Ash'arite claim (section 4.2) that God alone *creates* actions.[35] In this regard, consider Shahrastānī's (1086–1153) description of the Mu'tazilites:

> they are in agreement that man is a possessor of power (*qādir*) and creator (*khāliq*) of his actions, good and bad.[36]

In their theology, they emphasize God's Justice (describing themselves as "Proponents of [Divine] Unity and [Divine] Justice"). In emphasizing Divine Justice, the Mu'tazilites are precisely highlighting the sense in which a just God would not hold people responsible (or, as such, reward or punish them) for actions unless they were genuinely able to choose those actions.

5 Theological inflections 2: inclinations, capacity, power, and choice

> "There is no caliph who does not have two courtiers, one ordering and inciting him to good, and one to bad; and the protected is he whom God protects."
>
> – (Islamic *Ḥadīth*)[37]

In Islamic and Jewish theology, one additionally finds talk of "inclinations," and in particular, two competing inclinations – one towards good and one towards bad – within the human heart or soul. Found in Islamic traditions in the notion of "*khāṭirānī*" (a dual form meaning "two inclinations")[38] and in Jewish traditions in the idea of "*yeẓarīm*" (lit. creations, meant in the sense of two competing inclinations: *yeẓer ha-ra* is the "evil inclination" and *yeẓer ha-tōv* is the "good inclination"), there is ambiguity (and difference of opinion) on the precise origin and nature of these inclinations, including whether these are both from God or whether only the inclination for good is.

Emphasizing that choice (*al-ikhtiyār*) emerges from these competing inclinations, Ibrāhīm al-Naẓẓām (*ca.* 775–*ca.* 845) notes:[39]

> There must needs be *khāṭirāni* [two inclinations], of which one bids advancing (*al-iqdām*) and the other bids desisting (*al-kaff*), so that one's choice between them may be a genuine choice.

And,

> [M]an has no power [of genuine choice][40] over that for which he has no *khāṭirāni* (*lā yukhṭar*) in his heart.

In his study of Kalām, Wolfson (1976, 631) notes that Al-Naẓẓām himself views these inclinations as created by God in man's heart, whereas other Mu'tazilites attribute to Satan the inclination towards disobedience (Wolfson 1976, 634). Wolfson (1976, 633) also considers possible connections between *khāṭirāni* and (1) Plato's distinction (Republic 4, 439c-d) between the rational (*logistikon*) and irrational (*alogistikon*) or concupiscent (*epithumētikon*) parts of the soul, with the former playing the role of *to kōluon* (restrainer) from harm and the latter playing the role of *to keleoun* (prompter), and (2) Aristotle's *De Anima* 3.10 (433a9–30) notion of desire (*oreksis*) which can operate with reason to generate *boulēsis* or with imagination to generate concupiscence (*epithumia*).

6 Theological inflections 3: from divine will to human soul

In the remainder of the chapter, we consider implications of three senses of Divine Will for three approaches to the human soul. As we will see, more fully appreciating the philosophical-theology at play in a given context can help deepen our understanding of possible motivations behind and (as such) details of differing perspectives on human agency and choice. We can view senses of Divine Will trickling down to (or serving as conceptual grounds for) emerging views of human souls; at the very least, we can view the two pictures as correlative. Either way, considering theological alongside psychological-epistemological details can allow us a fuller appreciation of a given thinker's understanding of human being.

6.1 Divine Will as "gift-giving God" and as "God, I know not what": grace and attenuated human agency in the Theology of Aristotle, *Ibn Pequda*, and *al-Ghazālī*

While divine grace is often tacitly read through particular traditions and thinkers, it is useful to step back and think of grace as describing a God who enters into relation with human beings in a way that in some sense exceeds the bounds of economical thinking. To be sure, this depiction of God has historically been associated, in at least some traditions, with a God of bountiful love who is able to bestow gifts on subjects regardless of their works or merits, in this way exceeding the narrow bounds of justice. Of course, the flip side of this particular theological coin is that a God who exceeds economies does not rely on order, and so need not Himself be seen as even creating or maintaining order, a point which at once opens the door to radical occasionalism and to radical injustice, at least from the mere human perspective (i.e. if God does not operate according to laws of nature, then we have occasionalism; and if God does not operate according to laws of justice, then we have what to the human perspective can appear to be a lot of injustice). We might call the first approach to a free willing God of grace the "gift-giving God" version and the second approach to a free willing God of grace the

"God, I know not what [He's doing]" version. Individual thinkers can hold both, and each can be seen as coming along with particular implications for human souls.

An example of the "gift-giving" version of grace can be found in many Islamic and Jewish thinkers, including the *Theology of Aristotle* and Baḥya Ibn Peqūda (*ca.* 1020). This view of a God who generously shares forward beyond what is merited comes along with a correlative sense of the human's receptivity to unmerited divine gifts – generally seen in terms of a supra-rational capacity to receive, itself either theorized as a non-discursive noetic moment in intellect or as an experience taking place in a faculty outside of intellect altogether (e.g. Halevi's and al-Ghazālī's joint senses of revelation by way of an "inner eye" more akin to imagination than to intellect).

We find this version of grace in the *Theology of Aristotle*'s description of soul's receiving an unmerited gift from Intellect (itself arisen from God):

> [W]hen the soul is filled with light and power and the other virtues, she cannot stand still in herself, because those virtues in her are the awakening of her desire [*al-tashwiq*] for action. So she travels down, not travelling up because Intellect does not need any of her virtues, for it is the cause of her virtues. Since she cannot travel up she travels down and pours forth of her light and her other virtues on whatever is beneath her, and fills this world with light and beauty and splendor.
> (*Theology of Aristotle*, chapter 7, trans. Lewis with my revisions: 249; Arabic at Badawi 1955, 89, 11.12–16)

At other points in the text called upon to deliver virtue into the world, soul here occupies a complex position: On the one hand, she is the agent called upon to act virtuously; on the other hand, she is the passive recipient of virtues that overflow into her from Intellect (itself created by God).

Looking for similar themes in Jewish philosophy, we might turn to Baḥya ibn Pequda. In his *Duties of the Heart*, Baḥya notes that while a human is responsible for choosing the right path, it is God who first puts this ability into the human heart, emphasizing that one can only love and serve God if one's heart is opened to God (*Duties of the Heart*, 8.3.14; Mansoor, 374–6). Further emphasizing the dual roles of human choice and divine love, Baḥya highlights the human responsibility to proper intention and action, while also noting that it is God who guides us by opening our hearts to his love via His gifts of Torah and intellect. Furthermore, one finds the final stage of human love for God described on the one hand as an aligning of one's will with God's Will and on the other hand as a nullification of personal will to the Will of God (*Duties of the Heart*, 10.2; Mansoor, 429–431).

An example of the "God, I know not what [He's doing]" version of divine grace focuses so strongly on the radically free aspect of God's activities as to nullify theodicy: Because God acts completely freely, we do not know anything about His sense of justice. Because God acts completely freely, we can also talk in occasionalist terms of "laws of nature as mere illusion." For this version of

Divine Will, we might revisit the Islamic Ash'arite view that we've seen earlier (section 6.2). As we have seen, in their "doctrine of acquisition," the Ash'arites can be seen as holding a middle position between the Jabrite view that humans are compelled by divine decree and the Mu'tazilite view that humans are free to create their own actions.

This Ash'arite view can be seen in al-Ghazālī. In detailed descriptions of what might, absent his theological view of Divine Will, appear to be robust causal mechanisms for human agency,[41] al-Ghazālī speaks of the perceptive and motive faculties of the human soul and follows Avicenna in dividing the motive power (or inclination) into the faculties of (1) will (*irāda*) which incites (*ba'ath*) desire and pursuit, irascibility and avoidance, and (2) power (*qudra*) which produces motion in the limbs, muscles, nerves.[42] Al-Ghazālī speaks too of the soul's inclinations (*khawāṭir*).[43] And yet, alongside these ideas we find an emphasis on acquisition (*iktisāb*). Distinguishing between the power to move and the movements themselves, al-Ghazālī describes two divine creations:

> The power is an attribute (*waṣf*) of man and a creation of God but is not an acquisition (*kasb*) of man, whereas the movement is a creation of God and an attribute (*waṣf*) of man but is also an acquisition of man, for it is created as an object of power by [another] power [namely, the power to choose]; which is to him [also] an attribute. The movement thus has a relationship to another attribute which is to be called power, and it is with reference to this relationship that movement is called acquisition.
> (*Iḥyā'*, Book 2, section 3, principle 3, ll. 13–14;
> as cited in Wolfson 1976, 700)

Reflecting on the poles of compulsion and independent agency, al-Ghazālī concludes that neither of these correctly describes the situation; rather

> the movement is determined by the power of God by way of creation and by the power of man by way of another kind of relationship, that which is designated by the term acquisition (*iktisāb*).
> (*Iḥyā'*, Book 2, section 3, principle 3,
> ll. 19–20; as cited in Wolfson 1976, 701)

6.2 Divine Will as pure goodness: Neoplatonism and the status of the soul in the Theology of Aristotle, *Avicenna, and Ibn Gabirol*

For our second sense of Divine Will, we turn to God as pure emanating unity and goodness in the Islamic and Jewish Neoplatonisms of the *Theology of Aristotle*, Avicenna, and Ibn Gabirol. Exceeding Aristotle's sense that God's goodness enables Him to function as object of desire and, as such, as final cause of motion (*Metaphysics* Lambda 7 [1072b]), the Neoplatonic Islamic and Jewish

God emerges as a pure unity and goodness that (*qua* goodness) emanates, a concept itself rooted in the idea of Plato's Form of the Good above Being, and in the *Timaeus*' description of God's goodness being such that He is "without jealousy" (*Timaeus* 29d) traced through into Plotinus' sense of a God who shares His Goodness forward (*Enneads* 5.4.7), and Proclus' sense of a God who is not simply a final cause but an efficient cause of existence.[44]

It is this sense of God-as-Good that grounds Plotinus' own sense of God as pure freedom and pure *boulesis*, often translated in this context as pure Will (see *Enneads* 6.8; Armstrong, 223–297): For Plotinus and traditions of Neoplatonists after him, true freedom – and, in the human case, genuinely good deliberation (*boulesis*) – consist in being able to enact goodness and (relatedly) in not being forced to act – contrary to goodness – by outside forces. It is in this sense that we can see the *Theology of Aristotle*'s description of God as the Pure Good (*al-khayr al-maḥḍ*) who creates "by the mere fact of His being" (*Theology of Aristotle* 1.52; Lewis 231; Badawi, p. 27, line 6).[45] This notion of God's creating by virtue of His being, itself identified as "emanation" (the term used in that context to describe what happens in virtue of the fact that the Good "should not be alone"),[46] can also be seen in the *Theology of Aristotle*'s description of God's creating without reflection:

> the First Creator (*al-bāri' al-awwal*) originated (*abda'a*) all things without reflection or thought (*bi-ghair rawīya wa-lā fikra*) . . . the First Creator originated the upper world, containing all the forms, complete and perfect, without reflection.
> (*Theology of Aristotle*, Chapter 10; English at Lewis 1959, 453; Arabic at Badawi 1955, 147, ll. 12–15)

Emphasizing a Neoplatonic idea of goodness that is so good that it shares itself forward by its very nature (which is to say, as we have seen earlier, "without jealousy"), the *Theology of Aristotle* is part of a Plotinian tradition that measures freedom not in terms of the ability to have chosen otherwise but in terms of the absence of obstacles to fulfilling one's ownmost goodness. It is precisely this idea that the *Theology of Aristotle* has in mind when it emphasizes God's creative act as involving no choice or mental activity at all. Since God is always pure Goodness, and since nothing prevents Him from enacting that Goodness (which in part manifests as a sharing forward of that Goodness), God – precisely in not choosing between alternatives – is the paradigm of freedom, agency, and choice.

It is in this precise spirit that we must understand both Avicenna's idea of Divine Necessity and Ibn Gabirol's idea of Divine Will. Describing God's unity and goodness in terms of pure intellect (as opposed to emphasizing God's lack of reflection, as we've seen in the *Theology of Aristotle*, though arguably with very similar meaning), Avicenna and Ibn Gabirol join the *Theology of Aristotle* in their Neoplatonic sense of God's goodness as the mark of pure freedom and agency. It is a mistake, in other words, to read Avicenna's description of God as "the Necessary of Existence" as suggesting that God is unfree: For Avicenna, God is Necessary by way of Himself inasmuch as His essence is pure existence, which entails that He is neither subject to any external causes nor ever prevented from enacting His own pure existence (or, as such, the existence of all other beings). Avicenna's God is radically free along precisely the same lines as the Absolutely Free God of Pure Goodness that we've seen.

Similarly, in spite of a long tradition of scholars reading Ibn Gabirol's Divine Will as opposing the Greek and Islamic Neoplatonic notion of eternal divine emanation, properly read Ibn Gabirol's Divine *Irāda* is (as I have argued elsewhere)[47] a way of describing the very downward flow of Plotinian divine emanation itself. Tacitly or overtly inspired, I have argued, by the Augustinian ring of the term "*voluntas*" in the Latin translation of Ibn Gabirol's Arabic text, readers have attempted to "save" Ibn Gabirol from what they perceive as Plotinus' own diminished God-bound-by-necessity-and-compulsion, where arguably, Ibn Gabirol's very notion of Divine Freedom arises precisely in conceptual kinship with Plotinus' notion of God as a pure goodness that shares his Goodness forward "without jealousy." Divine emanation in Plotinus, Avicenna, *Theology of Aristotle* and Ibn Gabirol is precisely the sign of God's pure goodness – and it is that pure goodness which is the marker of His absolute freedom; as such, one precisely *robs* Ibn Gabirol's God of pure freedom when she insists (wrongly) that his notion of Divine Will opposes divine emanation.

It is precisely in the spirit of recognizing that pure freedom is marked by the unimpeded actualization – and hence overflowing – of pure goodness that Avicenna goes so far as to describe the eternally emanating God in terms of *al-ikhtiyār*,[48] the term used by opponents within the Islamic tradition (e.g. al-Ghazālī) to describe the freedom to choose between alternatives (and, as such, an idea often used by opponents to argue that the Neoplatonic God is entirely unfree). While opponents lacking a Neoplatonic conception of freedom maintain that God's not choosing between alternatives shows His lack of freedom, Neoplatonists maintain that it is precisely in not so choosing that God's freedom is shown; indeed, put in Avicenna's language of *al-ikhtiyār*, we may say that it is precisely in His purity and oneness beyond "choosing between alternatives" that God is Pure Choice itself.

Turning to the implications for genuine human choice, we can find a rather straightforward parallel between the divine and human cases (in other words, following in proper Neoplatonic form, the microcosm mirrors the macrocosm): From the Neoplatonic sense of absolutely free Divine Will (*boulesis*) going hand-in-hand with goodness, we arrive at a sense of human deliberation, choice, and freedom which itself goes hand-in-hand with goodness. Just as for God, so too for the human soul, one is most free when one is manifesting goodness. In such a context, true human freedom and choice are found in one's ability to align oneself with goodness (and, relatedly, truth). Perhaps more popularly known in Augustine's Plotinus-inspired teaching that true human freedom is freedom *from* sin, not freedom *to* sin, the Neoplatonic teaching of a human freedom-in-goodness (not in "ability to choose between alternatives") reverberates throughout Islamic and

Jewish traditions, conceptually linked too to the Neoplatonic notion of "Double Selfhood"[49] – the idea that we are each at once in *and* away from our home in Intellect (an idea mirrored earlier in different senses in each of Maimonides' and Avicenna's "dual facing" insights, and in the *Theology of Aristotle*'s image of the intermediation of Soul between upper and lower realms): Mirroring Soul's own boundary position between her home in Intellect and her home-away-from-home in Nature, the human soul is constantly challenged to "Return to Intellect" (which is to say, to turn towards wisdom and goodness). As part of this struggle, Intellect reorients soul "upward" while matter – itself theorized in terms of privation – disorients the soul "downward." In her struggle to align with her higher self, soul is primarily found in choosing the good and the true. (We might in this regard consider compatibilist theories on which free agents need not have been able to do otherwise, including theories that emphasize free will as choice for the good and true [see Wolf 1980, 1987, and 1990]).[50]

This dynamic of soul's choice – in which one comes closer to God's own freedom to the extent that one is more aligned with reason and goodness – relates to Neoplatonic notions of soul's partial descent, as for example can be seen in the *Theology of Aristotle*:

> If the soul can reject sense and the transient sensory things and does not hold fast to them, she then controls this body with the slightest effort, with no fatigue of toil, and assimilates herself to the universal soul and become like her in conduct and control, with no difference or variation between them.
> (*Theology of Aristotle* 7.34; Lewis, 251; Badawi, 91)

And, in contrast to God who "does his deed by the mere fact of his being without any attribute," we learn of the state of soul:

> The deficient agent is the one who does his deed not by the mere fact of his being but by one of his attributes. Therefore he does not do a perfect complete deed, for he is not capable of doing his deed and its end simultaneously, for he is deficient, not perfect.
> (*Theology of Aristotle* 5.41; Lewis 437; Badawi, 71)

And so while, to be sure, genuine human choice structurally mirrors the Divine Will in its excellence being found in its relation to Goodness, the human soul – caught in the embodied sway of materiality, space, and time – must struggle to enact goodness in a way that God Himself must never struggle: human *boulesis* involves struggle;[51] divine *boulesis* does not.

Focusing specifically on this Neoplatonic sense of struggle, Frede contrasts an Aristotelian paragon who acts virtuously "without any difficulty or conflict whatsoever."[52] When turning to Islamic and Jewish thinkers who engage Aristotelianized versions of Neoplatonism, it is instructive to ask whether and to what extent they tend more towards Plotinus or more towards Aristotle on this issue – or whether their sense of deliberation and choice is – under the weight of some one or more theological or other considerations – different from either of these pictures.

6.3 Divine Will as expression of pure wisdom: from God's Wisdom to natural law and human choice in Maimonides and Averroes

In their respective writings, Maimonides and Averroes both emphasize God's Will in His ordering of the world through laws of nature. We may in this respect discern in their philosophies a joint appreciation for the order of the Divine Wisdom itself manifest in the order of nature – with "Divine Wisdom" signaling the fullness of God's knowledge per se, and "Divine Will" signaling the manifesting of that wisdom into the world:[53] Not unrelated to the Neoplatonic idea explored earlier (though in Averroes absent the notion of divine emanation), God's freedom is not seen here in His range of choices but in the manifesting of aspects of his order within the structure and laws of nature.

Turning to Maimonides' own frequent reference to Divine Will, we are advised in his *Commentary on the Mishnah* to avoid reading "Divine Will" in any way that dishonors the unchanging essential reality of God as a pure intellect filled with truths that are manifest in the orderly laws of nature (in contrast to Ash'arite – and other – voluntaristic occasionalist readings of God's operating without laws of nature):

> The theory generally accepted by people and found in rabbinical and prophetical writings, that man's sitting and rising and all of his movements are governed by the will (*al-mashī'a*) and desire (*al-irāda*) of God,[54] is true only in one respect. For instance, when a stone is thrown into the air and falls to the ground, it is correct to say that the stone fell in accordance with the will of God, for it is true that God decreed that the earth and all its elements should be the center of attraction, so that when any part of it is thrown into the air, it is attracted back to the center. . . . The Mutakallimun[55] are, however, of a different opinion in this regard, for I have heard them say that the Divine Will is constantly at work, decreeing everything from time to time. We do not agree with them, but believe that the Divine Will ordained everything at creation and that all things, at all times, are regulated by the laws of nature.
>
> ("*Eight Chapters*," Chapter. 8; Twersky, 38; Pocock, 87, 23ff)

Here reflecting on God's reality, *qua* Divine Will, as manifest in the order of nature – and not as a force that contravenes or obviates nature – Maimonides goes on to emphasize (*pace* the Ash'arites) that human free will is part of the divinely willed order of nature. Far from something incompatible with Divine Will (here understood as the force of God as manifest in laws of nature, not in their absence or abrogation, as we find in Ash'arism), human deliberation and decision are themselves ordained by God as part of the order of reality; they are, in this sense, a manifestation of Divine Will.

Consider in like spirit Averroes' emphasis on God's ordaining laws of nature in direct opposition to the Ash'arite view:

> it appears that, but for the powers that God [Almighty] implanted in our bodies, with respect to nourishment and sensation, our bodies would have perished, as we find Galen and all other philosophers admit, saying that without these powers that God implanted in the bodies of animals for their survival, it would not have been possible for the bodies of these animals to last for a single hour following their coming into being. We hold that, but for the powers that inhere in the bodies of animals and plants, and for the forces diffused throughout the universe due to the movements of the heavenly bodies, [existing things] could not have lasted for a single moment. How marvelous is God the Subtle and the Well informed!
>
> (*Kashf*; Najjar, 112)

Averroes goes on, though, to creatively repurpose (by way of naturalizing) the Islamic notion of predetermination, decree, and the Preserved Tablet (*lawḥ maḥfūẓ*);[56] whereas these are precisely the ideas that lead Ash'arites to do away with nature and to qualify human agency, Averroes instead interprets the *lawḥ* – as well as *al-qaḍā' wa'l-qadar* – to refer to the laws of nature:

> every effect that results from specific and determinate causes must necessarily be specific and determinate. This connection is not found between our actions and their external causes only, but also between [our actions] and the causes that God Almighty has created within our bodies. The determinate order of the internal and external causes (those that do not fail) is the decree and foreordination (*al-qaḍā' wa'l-qadar*) that God has prescribed for His creatures; that is the Preserved Tablet (*al-lawḥ al-maḥfūẓ*). God's knowledge of these causes and of what results from them is the cause of the existence of these causes.
>
> (*Kashf* 226–227; Najjar, 108–109)

In Maimonides and Averroes, Divine Will – itself correlated with Divine Decree by Averroes in these quotes, and by Maimonides at various points in his *Guide* – is the order of God's Wisdom as manifest in the order of nature, which itself includes the human capacity for genuine choice, agency, and responsibility. As it relates to Divine Will, Maimonides and Averroes reject occasionalist rejections of laws of nature, maintaining instead that it is precisely in the laws of nature that key aspects of God's knowledge and order are most fully revealed. Relatedly, Maimonides and Averroes reject Ash'arite attenuations of human agency, upholding instead the idea that genuine human deliberation and decision making is part of the divine order of nature itself.

Notes

1 For an overview of and further resources on connections between Islamic and Jewish Philosophy, see Harvey 2005; on the Islamic influences in Maimonides, see Pines 1963; see too Pessin 2014b; on the Islamic-Jewish resonances and influences across Islamic and Jewish Neoplatonism, see Altmann and Stern 1958/2009; see too Pessin 2014a. For recent resources in Islamic and Jewish philosophy, including bibliographies for further study, consider, for example: Frank and Leaman 2003, Adamson and Taylor 2005, Leaman and Nasr 2001, Taylor and López-Farjeat 2015, Nadler and Rudavsky 2008.
2 For textual details in the Arabic translation of Aristotle's *Nicomachean Ethics*, see Akasoy and Fidora 2005; for a discussion and analysis of the terminologies in these translations, as well as in al-Fārābī and Avicenna, see Phillipson 2017, 63–82.
3 Efros emphasizes the distinction in Maimonides' Hebrew translation between *beḥira* (for *al-ikhtiyār*) as the rational choice reserved for humans in contrast to *ratzon* or *ḥefetz* for *al-irāda* as a will (or desire) shared by animals; see Efros 1966, 110–111.
4 Deborah Black notes:

> in the Arabic tradition "will" (*irāda*) is a generic term for all appetites, having roughly the same extension as Aristotle's conception of the voluntary, which applies to animals and children as well as to adult humans. The peculiar appetitive faculty associated with the intellect in Arabic philosophy is not will but "choice" (*ikhtiyār*, equivalent to the Greek prohairêsis), that is, the ability to decide between alternative courses of action and to base one's choices on a process of rational deliberation.
>
> (Black 2005, 323)

As we will see, we also find Ibn Gabirol and others using the term "*al-irāda*" to describe the Divine Will.
5 For a strong presentation of this point – as well as a detailed textual analysis of this trajectory in al-Farabi, Avicenna, and Averroes (as well as Aquinas, Augustine, and others) – see Phillipson 2017; I am thankful to Traci Phillipson for sharing a copy of her recently completed dissertation with me.
6 Maimonides, *Guide* 2.48; Pines, 409.
7 Maimonides, *Guide* 2.48; Munk, 292.
8 Maimonides, *Guide* 2.48; Pines, 410.
9 Maimonides, *Guide* 2.48; Munk, 292.
10 Maimonides, "Eight Chapters"; Twersky, 383.
11 Maimonides, "Eight Chapters"; Kafiḥ; Pocock, 88; Hebrew "*beḥira*" at Gorfinkle, 46.
12 See through p. 211 for further details on voluntary (*irādiyya*) actions and on the relation between theoretical reasoning and proper deliberations of practical reasoning on the path to attaining happiness.
13 I am thankful to Nicholas Oschman for this reference.
14 Avicenna, *Kitāb al-Najāt*; my translation (see too Rahman, 32 for emphasis on "urging"); for Arabic, see Fakhry 1984, 202.
15 In the context of her assessment of the disconnect between Aquinas' critique of Averroes and Averroes' own actual view (though ultimately noting that, for reasons not

addressed by Aquinas, Averroes' view might not ultimately allow for human responsibility), Phillipson notes:

> Averroes believes he can maintain that human beings have moral responsibility despite the fact that they share not only the Agent Intellect but also the Material Intellect; this is possible because of his insistence that the will is a cogitative power – a brain power – which is not shared among individuals.
>
> (Phillipson 2017, 84)

16 Based on our consideration of Frede in the last section of this chapter, one might challenge whether there is here any real choice; on Frede's account of Aristotle at any rate, *akrasia* is never properly understood as "choosing" to do bad (or "choosing" against reason) but rather as having lived in such a way as to preclude reason from choosing what is good to do in the case at hand. That said, Maimonides clearly emphasizes the notion of free will as a core human gift; it is in that spirit that I talk here of "choice".

17 See Maimonides' discussion in *Hilḥōt Teshūvah (The Laws of Repentance)*, 6:3 in his *Mishneh Torah*.

18 In this respect, we might consider Frede's sense that in the matter of whether my rational desire or a lower desire wins out in a given deliberation, often the deciding factor is something about my character, including "what happened in the past, perhaps the distant past" (Frede 2011, 24).

19 See, for example, Pocock, 88, line 2; see too *Guide* 1.66 and 1.98 for God's will as First Will, *mashī'a awwala* [sic].

20 Square brackets are my additions: I have replaced Twersky's phrase "his actions should be such as his own free will dictates to him without any outside influence or restraint" with my edited version: "his actions should be [based on his own decision (*al-ikhtiyār*)] without any outside influence or restraint"; as noted earlier in the chapter, I am working in this way to help free up multiple possible resonances in the Arabic term "*al-ikhtiyār*"; Pocock, 88.

21 Ibn Gabirol, *Improvement of the Moral Qualities*; see Arabic in Wise, Arabic section 14; 72a.

22 For development and defense of a compatibilist reading of al-Kindi – in contrast with Muʿtazilite incompatibilism – see Adamson 2003.

23 In the idea that perfect actions "pass beyond the sphere," we can hear al-Kindi's sense that evil souls, once released from their bodies, can get trapped in the planetary spheres for a long time, whereas only purified souls can return beyond the celestial spheres to sojourn with God; see al-Kindi, *Discourse on the Soul*; Adamson and Pormann, 116.

24 For elaboration on elements from both sources, see Altmann and Stern, 42–45.

25 Lit. "the judgment/decision and the measure/evaluation"; in Islamic theological contexts, where the phrase refers to the "Decree of God," these terms take on the sense of destiny or fate; "*al-qaḍā'*" has the sense of God's "eternal decree" and "*al-qadar*" has the sense of the divine decree in relation to temporal existence. On the definition and overview of the Islamic doctrine of *al-Qaḍā' Wa'l-Qadar*, see: Gardet 2012 and Káldy-Nagy 2012.

26 For my discussion of these theological views, I am drawing on: Gardet 2012, Káldy-Nagy 2012, Watt 1946, 1948, Wolfson 1976, Goldziher 1981, Wensinck [1932] 2007, López-Farjeat 2008.

27 See Watt's description; Watt also takes care to distinguish this kind of theological pre-deterministic view from pre-Islamic versions of atheistic fatalism (see Watt 1946, 145); on this latter point, there are texts that emphasize a pre-deterministic fate in relation to time (*dahr*). To add: Within expressly theological contexts, one finds both an emphasis

on God's role in predetermining events, as well as on the role of such divine items as God's Pen and the Preserved Tablet.

28 As cited in Wolfson 1976, 606; reference to *Milal*, p. 60, ll. 19–20.
29 As cited in Watt 1946, 144; reference to *Maq*. 279 (to which Watt adds "accepting Ritter's conjecture"). Complicating this picture, Watt goes on to cite the remainder of the passage in way of suggesting elements that lead into (and for Watt, are a source of influence on) the Ash'arite *kasb* view (to be addressed later):

> God has, however, created for man a power by which the act takes place, and the will for it and the choice of it, whereby he wills it, just as He has created for man height by which he is tall and colour by which he is coloured.

30 As cited in Gardet 2012; reference to *Ta'rīfāt*, 181.
31 As described by Gardet 2012.
32 As cited in Watt 1946, 145.
33 While Goldziher describes the term "Qadarite" as a misnomer for a group who clearly reject the kind of "Divine *Qadar*" doctrine that emphasizes God's sheer power (and as such, the absence of human free will), Wolfson and Watt both see the title as appropriate since they simply see "*qadar*," in the case of these defenders of human agency, as referring to the "human power." One might of course add that outside of any historical association with Islamic defenders of divine predestination, the term "*qadar*" on its own simply means "power" or "ability" – a term which, applied to God or to humans, can in and of itself mean any number of things. See Goldziher 1981, 82, Wolfson 1976, 619, Watt 1946, 136.
34 See Wolfson 1976, 622. Wolfson points also to debates about whether the human only has power to do wicked acts, and whether ultimately all noble and good acts are ascribed to God; Wolfson notes the vagueness of this view, and connects it with possible elements of grace in Islamic theology, including in aspects of al-Ghazālī's views (Wolfson 1976, 623–624).
35 See Wolfson 621; he notes that most, but not all, Mu'tazilite traditions are open to using the term "creator" in this way.
36 As cited in Wolfson 1976, 622; reference to Shahrastānī, *Milal*, p. 30. ll. 16–17.
37 Al-Bukhārī, *Qadr*, b. 8; as cited in Watt 1946, 132.
38 Wolfson translates "motive forces" (Wolfson 1976, 628), or one might say "desires."
39 As recounted by al-Ash'arī, as cited in Wolfson 1976, 628. While an early follower of Mu'tazilite teachings, and while himself emphasizing free will, al-Naẓẓam broke away from Mu'tazilism to form his own school; see s.v. "Ibrāhīm an-Naẓẓām" in *Encyclopedia Britannica*; see too Ess 2012.
40 Wolfson adds the bracketed addition "free choice" which I have here modified to "genuine choice"; see note 34.
41 Though see Griffel 2010 for consideration of a more robust status to secondary causes in al-Ghazālī.
42 See Wolfson 1976, 640. On the faculty of will, sometimes al-Ghazālī speaks in terms of impulse (*nuzū'*) and sometimes in terms of wills (*al-irādāt*) being moved by inclinations (*khawāṭir*) (Wolfson 1976, 642).
43 Al-Ghazālī roots these inclinations (*khawāṭir*) in the perceptive faculty of soul as the impressions of memories (*al-adhkār*) and cogitation (*al-afkār*); see Wolfson 1976, 640. Wolfson ties this to Islamic, and possibly Jewish and other, traditions of "two inclinations" (*khāṭirāni*) (in the Jewish tradition, *yetzarim*).
44 See Proclus 2001; see McGinnis 2010, 157–158 on this Proclean idea marking a key change in the idea of efficient causation from Aristotle to Avicenna.
45 See: 5.40, Lewis 437; 10.88, Lewis p. 453; 10.175, 179, 186, Lewis p. 391, 393; 10.191, Lewis p. 395.

46 On the idea that *qua* goodness, God "should not be alone," together with the relation between emanation and lack of jealousy (here, though, in reference to Intellect), see Theology 7.8–16; Lewis 243, 245.
47 See Pessin 2013 (and also Pessin 2010 and Pessin 2017). To avoid Augustinian resonances, I have opted to either leave the term untranslated as "Divine *Irāda*" or to translate as "Divine Desire" (itself as part of what I call a Theology of Desire in Islamic and Jewish Neoplatonism).
48 I am thankful to Jon Hoover for bringing this to my attention; for the relevant passage in Avicenna's *al-Ta'aliqāt*, see Hoover 2007, 71:

> In the choice (*al-ikhtiyār*) of the First, no motive motivates It to [exercise] that [choice] other than Its essence and Its goodness. It does not have choice potentially and then become one who chooses actually. Rather, It has been eternally choosing in actuality. Its meaning is that It does not choose other than what It does.

We might note earlier in the chapter Maimonides' also using this term for God; if one reads Maimonides as upholding eternal divine emanation (in the spirit of Avicenna and Plotinus), then this is just as notable in his text; if, however, one reads Maimonides as upholding a non-emanationist metaphysics of creation whereby God "chooses between alternatives," then the description of God in terms of *al-ikhtiyār* is more straightforward and less notable.

49 For example, in his notes to the first volume of Plotinus' *Enneads*, Armstrong speaks of Plotinus' "double-self psychology"; see Armstrong (1966–88, vol. 1, 195 n. 1).
50 We might also consider the implications in this regard of accounts of freely willed action in terms of responsiveness to appropriate reasons; see, for example, MacIntyre 1957, Dennett 1984a, 1984b, Fischer 1987, 1994, Fischer and Ravizza 1998; for overview, see McKenna and Coates 2015. (Note too Nielsen's aligning Aristotle with Pereboom's "deliberation compatibilism" [Nielsen 2011]).
51 In this regard, Frede describes Plotinus' view of the virtuous soul as "challenged":

> the soul's freedom is rather tenuous and qualified. Given the needs and desires of the body and all the more complex desires they draw in their train, the soul constantly becomes perturbed. It may come to be in a bad way, even if it is virtuous, and have to straighten itself out to maintain its virtue and freedom. Hence Plotinus's virtuous soul is not unchallenged in its freedom in the way the Stoic wise man is. Nor, it seems, does his virtuous person fit the image of Plato's or Aristotle's paragon, who has no source of motivation, no inclination left to act other than virtuously without any difficulty or conflict whatsoever. For Plotinus, it seems, the soul's union with the body inevitably presents a threat ([*Enneads*] 5.27ff) to its virtue and hence its freedom.
>
> (Frede 2011, 139)

52 Ibid.
53 Averroes describes Divine Will in relation to the "acts which proceed from [God]" in contrast to Divine Wisdom which he describes as the fullness of all knowledge – including the compresence of opposites. Averroes, *Tahafut*, Eleventh Discussion, 438; Van Den Bergh, 264. For discussion, see Ivry 1979; Ivry also develops a structural analogy in Averroes between God's Will and Wisdom on the one hand and the relationship between human practical and theoretical intellect on the other.
54 We might here consider Alexander of Aphrodisias; in arguing that human action is not bound by necessity, he references as proofs the fact that a human who is seated can stand up and the fact that a man speaking can remain silent (*De Fato* IX). In discussing

this point, Wolfson points to similar statements in Saadya: "As for the argument from sense perception, I find that a human being feels conscious of his own power either to speak or to remain silent" (*Emunot* 4.4, p. 152, ll. 10–11), and in Halevi: "For thou perceives that thou has power over either speaking of remaining silent" (*Kuzari* 5.20; p. 340 ll. 10–11; p. 341, ll. 5–7); see Wolfson 1976, 618.
55 This is a reference to practitioners of Kalām, Islamic speculative theology; arguably he is here referring to the views of the Ash'arites that we have seen in section 4.2.
56 The Preserved Tablet (see Quran LXXXV, 22) is often understood as the repository of divinely pre-ordained decrees; for overview, see Wensinck and Bosworth 2012.

Bibliography

Primary sources

Alexander of Aphrodisias (1983). *Alexander of Aphrodisias on Fate* (text, translation and commentary), ed., trans. R. W. Sharples, London: Duckworth.

al-Fārābī (1949). *Iḥṣā' al-'Ulūm li-al-Fārābī*, ed. U. Amin, Cairo.

al-Fārābī (1953). *Iḥṣā' al-'Ulūm (Católogo de las Ciencias)*, Arabic text with Spanish translation (together with Gundissalinus' medieval Latin translation), ed., trans. G. A. Palencia, Madrid: Imprenta y Editorial Maestre, 1953. (= *Iḥṣā' al-'Ulūm* (The Enumeration of the Sciences)).

al-Fārābī (1963). "The Attainment of Happiness," in (eds.) R. Lerner and M. Mahdi, trans. M. Mahdi, *Medieval Political Philosophy: A Sourcebook*, New York: The Free Press of Glencoe/Collier – MacMillan Ltd., 58–82. (= *The Attainment of Happiness* (Taḥṣīl al-sa'ādah)).

al-Fārābī (1985). *Al-Farabi on The Perfect State, Abū Naṣr al-Fārābī's Mabādi' Ārā' Ahl al-Madīna al-Faḍila* (revised Arabic text with translation and commentary), ed., trans. R. Walzer, Oxford: Clarendon Press. (= *Perfect State* (Mabādi' Ārā' Ahl al-Madīna al-Faḍila)).

al-Fārābī (2001). "Enumeration of the Sciences," in (ed.) C. Butterworth, *Alfarabi, The Political Writings*, Ithaca: Cornell University Press, 71–84.

al-Ghazālī (1927). *Algazel, Tahafot Al-Falasifat*, ed. M. Bouyges, Beirut (= *Incoherence of the Philosophers*, Arabic text).

al-Ghazālī (1995). *Al-Ghazali on Disciplining the Soul, Breaking the Two Desires, Books XXII and XXIII of the Revival of the Religious Sciences*, trans. T. J. Winter, Cambridge: The Islamic Texts Society. (= *Iḥyā' 'Ulūm al-Dīn* (Revival of the Religious Sciences), partial translation).

al-Ghazālī (1997). *al-Ghazālī, The Incoherence of the Philosophers*, trans. M. E. Marmura, Provo, UT: Brigham Young University.

al-Kindi (2012). *The Philosophical Works of al-Kindi*, eds., trans. P. Adamson and P. E. Pormann, Karachi: Oxford University Press.

Aristotle (1926). *Nicomachean Ethics*, trans. H. Rackham, Cambridge: Harvard University Press (Loeb Classical Library No. 73).

Aristotle (1933). *Aristotle: Metaphysics, Books I–IX*, trans. H. Tredennick, Cambridge: Harvard University Press (Loeb Classical Library No. 271).

Aristotle (1935). *Aristotle: Metaphysics, Books 10–14, Oeconomica, Magna Moralia*, trans. H. Tredennick and G. C. Armstrong, Cambridge: Harvard University Press (Loeb Classical Library No. 287).

Aristotle (1957). *Aristotle: On the Soul. Parva Naturalia. On Breath*, trans. W. S. Hett, Cambridge: Harvard University Press (Loeb Classical Library No. 288).
Averroes (1930). *Tahafot at-Tahafot*, ed. M. Bouyges, Beirut. (= *The Incoherence of the Incoherence*, Arabic text).
Averroes (1969). *Averroes' Tahafut Al-Tahafut (The Incoherence of the Philosophers)*, trans. S. Van Den Bergh, London: Oxbow Books. (= English translation).
Averroes (1998). *al-Kashf 'an manahij al-'adla fi 'aqaid al-mila*, ed. M. A. al-Jabari, Beirut. (= *al-Kashf 'an manahij al-'adla fi 'aqaid al-mila* (Clarifying the systems of proof in the beliefs of the nation [of Muslims], Arabic text).
Averroes (2001). *Faith and Reason in Islam [al-Kashf]*, trans. I. Najjar, Oxford: Oneworld.
Averroes (2009). *Averroes, Long Commentary on the De Anima of Aristotle*, trans. R. C. Taylor with T.-A. Druart, New Haven: Yale University Press.
Avicenna (1952). *Avicenna's Psychology: An English Translation of Kitab al-Najat, Book II, Chapter VI*, trans. F. Rahman, London: Oxford University Press.
Avicenna (1960). *Ibn Sīnā, Al-Shifā', al-Ilāhiyyāt*, eds. G. C. Anawati and S. Zayed, Cairo: Organisation Générale des Imprimeries Gouvernementales.
Avicenna (1973). "*Kitāb al-Ta'līqāt*," in (ed.) A. Badawi, *Maktabah al-'Arabīyah*.
Avicenna (1984). *Kitāb an-Najāt*, ed. M. Fakhry, Beirut. (= *Kitāb an-Najāt* (Book of Safety)).
Avicenna (2005). *Avicenna, The Metaphysics of the Healing: A Parallel English-Arabic Text (Al-Shifā': Al-Illāhiyāt)*, trans. M. Marmura, Provo: Brigham Young University Press.
Halevi, Judah (1946). *Book of Kuzari*, trans. H. Hirschfeld, New York: Schocken Books.
Ibn Gabirol (1892). "Avencebrolis (Ibn Gebirol) Fons Vitae, ex Arabico in Latinum Translatus ab Johanne Hispano et Dominico Gundissalino," in (ed.) C. Baeumker, *Beiträge zur Geschichte der Philosophie des Mittelalters, Texte und Untersuchungen*, Münster: Aschendorff'sche Buchhandlung. (= 12th century Latin text translated from the original Arabic).
Ibn Gabirol (1958). "*Fons Vitae*, Fragments in Pines, S. '*Sefer 'Arūgat ha-Bōsem: ha-Qeta'im mi-tōkh Sēfer "Meqōr Ḥayyīm"*,'" *Tarbiẓ* 27, 218–233. [Reprinted – with a renumbering of notes from note 22 ff. – in Shlomo Pines, *Bēyn Maḥshevet Yisrael le-Maḥshevet ha-'Amīm: Meḥqarīm be-Tōldōt ha-Fīlōsōfiya ha-Yehūdit* (Bialik: Jerusalem, 1977), 44–60].
Ibn Gabirol (1966). *The Improvement of the Moral Qualities*, trans. S. S. Wise, Columbia University Oriental Studies, Vol. I. New York: AMS Press. (= *Improvement of the Moral Qualities of the Soul*, Arabic and English text).
Ibn Gabirol (1976). "*Fons Vitae*, Fragments in Fenton, P. 'Gleanings From Mōseh Ibn 'Ezra's *Maqālat al-Hadīqa'*,'" *Sefarad* 36, 285–298.
Ibn Paqūda, Baḥya (1912). *Al-hidāja 'ilā farā'iḍ al-qulūb des Bachja ibn Jōsēf ibn Paqūda, aus Andalusien*, ed., trans. A. S. Yahuda, Leiden: Brill. (= *Duties of the Heart*).
Ibn Paqūda, Baḥya (1973). *The Book of Direction to the Duties of the Heart*, trans. M. Mansoor, with S. Arenson and S. Dannhauser, London: The Littman Library of Jewish Civilization in association with Liverpool University Press.
Israeli, Isaac (1958). "*Book of Substances*," in (ed.) F. W. Zimmerman, in *S. M. Stern, Medieval Arabic and Hebrew Thought*, London: Variorum Reprints. (= Judeo-Arabic).
Israeli, Isaac (1958). "*The Book of Substances, The Book of Spirit and Soul* and *The Book of Definitions*," in (eds.) A. Altmann and S. M. Stern, *Isaac Israeli*, Oxford: Oxford University Press.

Maimonides, Moses (1740). "Eight Chapters (*Porta Mosis*)," in *Theological Works of Dr. Pocock*, 68–93. Nabu Public Domain Reprint. (= Judeo-Arabic text).
Maimonides, Moses (1931). *Dalālat al-Ḥā'irīn*, ed. S. Munk, Jerusalem. (= Judeo-Arabic text).
Maimonides, Moses (1963). *Moses Maimonides, The Guide of the Perplexed*, Volumes I and II, trans. S. Pines, Chicago: University of Chicago Press.
Maimonides, Moses (1972). "Eight Chapters," in (ed.) I. Twersky, *A Maimonides Reader*, Springfield, NJ: Behrman House, Inc., 362–386.
Maimonides, Moses (2000). "*Mishneh Torah*," in (ed.) S. Frankel, *Mishneh Torah*, 12 vols. Jerusalem: Hotzaat Shabse Frankel.
Plato (1929). "*Timaeus*," in (trans.) R. G. Bury, *Plato: Timaeus, Critias, Cleitophon, Menexenus, Epistles*, Cambridge: Harvard University Press (Loeb Classical Library No. 234).
Plato (1930). *Plato: The Republic, Books 1–5*, trans. P. Shorey, Cambridge: Harvard University Press (Loeb Classical Library No. 237).
Plato (2013). *Plato: The Republic, Books 6–10*, trans. C. Emlyn-Jones and W. Preddy, Cambridge: Harvard University Press (Loeb Classical Library No. 276).
Plotinus (1955). *Plotinus Apud Arabes, Theologia Aristotelis et fragmenta quae supersunt*, ed. A. Badawi, Cairo. (= *Theology of Aristotle*).
Plotinus (1959). "*Plotiniana Arabica* (including the *Theology of Aristotle*), trans. G. L. Lewis," in (eds.) P. Henry and H.-R. Schwyzer, *Plotini Opera*, Vol. II, Paris and Bruxelles: Éditions Universelles.
Plotinus (1966–1988). *The Enneads*, trans. A. H. Armstrong, Cambridge: Harvard University Press (Loeb Classical Library).
Proclus (2001). *Proclus: On the Eternity of the World (de Aeternitate mundi)*, eds. H. S. Lang, A. D. Macro, and J. McGinnis, Berkeley/Los Angeles/London: University of California Press.
Saadia Gaon (1880). *Kitāb al-amānāt wa-'l-i'tiqādāt*, ed. S. Landauer, Leiden. (= *Book of Beliefs and Opinions*).
Saadia Gaon (1948). *The Book of Beliefs and Opinions*, trans. S. Rosenblatt, New Haven: Yale University Press.
Shahrastānī (1842–1846). *Kitāb al-Milal wa'l-Niḥal*, ed. W. Cureton, London. (= *Book of Religious and Philosophical Sects*).

Secondary works

Adamson, P. (2003). "Al-Kindī and the Muʿtazila: Divine Attributes, Creation and Freedom," *Arabic Sciences and Philosophy* 13, 45–77.
Adamson, P. and Taylor, R. C. (eds.) (2005). *The Cambridge Companion to Arabic Philosophy*, Cambridge: Cambridge University Press.
Akasoy, Anna A. and Fidora, Alexander (eds.) (2005). *The Arabic Version of the Nicomachean Ethics*. Leiden: Brill.
Altmann, A. and Stern, S. M. (1958/2009). *Isaac Israel*, Oxford: Oxford University Press. (Reprinted with introduction by Alfred Ivry; Chicago: University of Chicago Press, 2009).
Black, D. L. (2005). "Psychology: Soul and Intellect," in (eds.) P. Adamson and R. C. Taylor, *The Cambridge Companion to Islamic Philosophy*, Cambridge: Cambridge University Press, 308–326.
Dennett, D. (1984a). *Elbow Room: The Varieties of Free Will Worth Wanting*, Cambridge: MIT Press.

Dennett, D. (1984b.) "I Could Not Have Done Otherwise – So What?" *The Journal of Philosophy*, LXXXI (10), 553–567.

Efros, Israel. 1966. *Philosophical Terms in the Moreh Nebukim*. New York: AMS Press.

Ess, J. van. (2012). "al-Naẓẓām," in (eds.) P. Bearman, Th. Bianquis, C. E. Bosworth, E. van Donzel, W. P. Heinrichs, *Encyclopaedia of Islam*, 2nd Edition, Brill Online: http://referenceworks.brillonline.com/browse/encyclopaedia-of-islam-2.

Fakhry, M. (1958/2008). *Islamic Occasionalism, and Its Critique by Averroes and Aquinas*, Abingdon, Oxon: Routledge.

Fischer, J. M. (1987). "Responsiveness and Moral Responsibility," in (ed.) F. Schoeman, *Responsibility, Character, and the Emotions: New Essays in Moral Psychology*, Cambridge: Cambridge University Press, 81–106.

Fischer, J. M. (1994). *The Metaphysics of Free Will*, Oxford: Blackwell Publishers.

Fischer, J. M. and Ravizza, M. (1998). *Responsibility and Control: An Essay on Moral Responsibility*, Cambridge: Cambridge University Press.

Frank, D. and Leaman, O. (eds.) (2003). *The Cambridge Companion to Medieval Jewish Philosophy*, Cambridge: Cambridge University Press.

Frede, M. (2011). *A Free Will: Origins of the Notion in Ancient Thought*, Berkeley: University of California Press.

Gardet, L. (2012). "al-Ḳaḍā' Wa 'l-Ḳadar," in (eds.) P. Bearman, Th. Bianquis, C. E. Bosworth, E. van Donzel, W. P. Heinrichs, *Encyclopaedia of Islam*, 2nd Edition, Brill Online: http://referenceworks.brillonline.com/browse/encyclopaedia-of-islam-2.

Goldziher, I. (1981). *Introduction to Islamic Theology and Law*, trans. A. and R. Hamori, Princeton: Princeton University Press.

Griffel, F. (2010). *Al-Ghazali's Philosophical Theology*, Oxford: Oxford University Press.

Harvey, S. (2005). "Islamic Philosophy and Jewish Philosophy," in (eds.) P. Adamson and R. C. Taylor, *The Cambridge Companion to Islamic Philosophy*, Cambridge: Cambridge University Press, 349–369.

Hoover, J. (2007). *Ibn Taymiyya's Theodicy of Perpetual Optimism*, Leiden: Brill.

"Ibrāhīm an-Naẓẓām," s.v. in *Encyclopedia Britannica*. <www.britannica.com/EBchecked/topic/407277/Ibrahim-an-Nazzam>.

Ivry, A. L. (1979). "The Will of God and Practical Intellect of Man in Averroes' Philosophy," *Israel Oriental Studies* IX, 377–391.

Káldy-Nagy, G. (2012). "Ḳaḍā'," in (eds.) P. Bearman, Th. Bianquis, C. E. Bosworth, E. van Donzel, W. P. Heinrichs, *Encyclopaedia of Islam*, 2nd Edition, Brill Online: http://referenceworks.brillonline.com/browse/encyclopaedia-of-islam-2.

Leaman, O. and Nasr, S. H. (eds.) (2001). *History of Islamic Philosophy*, New York: Routledge.

López-Farjeat, Luis Xavier. (2008). "Determinism and Free Will in Alexander of Aphrodisias and the Arabic Tradition," *Proceedings of the ACPA* 81, 161–177.

MacDonald, S. (1998). "Aquinas's Libertarian Account of Free Choice," *Revue Internationale de Philosophie* 52 (204; 2), 309–328.

MacIntyre, A. (1957). "Determinism," *Mind* 66, 28–41.

McGinnis, Jon. (2010). *Avicenna*. Oxford, New York: Oxford University Press.

McKenna, M. and Coates, D. J. (2015). "Compatibilism," in (ed.) E. N. Zalta, *The Stanford Encyclopedia of Philosophy* (Summer 2015 Edition), <http://plato.stanford.edu/archives/sum2015/entries/compatibilism/>.

Nadler, S. and Rudavsky, T. M. (eds.) (2008). *The Cambridge History of Jewish Philosophy: From Antiquity Through the Seventeenth Century*, Cambridge: Cambridge University Press.

Nielsen, K. M. (2011). "Deliberation as Inquiry: Aristotle's Alternative to the Presumption of Open Alternatives," *The Philosophical Review* 120/3, 383–421.

Pessin, S. (2010). "Solomon Ibn Gabirol [Avicebron]," in (ed.) E. N. Zalta, *The Stanford Encyclopedia of Philosophy* (Spring 2013 Edition), <http://plato.stanford.edu/archives/spr2013/entries/ibn-gabirol/>.

Pessin, S. (2013). *Ibn Gabirol's Theology of Desire: Matter and Method in Jewish Medieval Neoplatonism*, Cambridge: Cambridge University Press.

Pessin, S. (2014a). "Islamic and Jewish Neoplatonisms," in (eds.) P. Remes and S. Slaveva-Griffin, *Handbook of Neoplatonism*, Durham, UK: Acumen Press/Routledge, 541–558.

Pessin, S. (2014b). "The Influence of Islamic Thought on Maimonides," in (ed.) E. N. Zalta, *The Stanford Encyclopedia of Philosophy* (Summer 2014 Edition), <http://plato.stanford.edu/archives/sum2014/entries/maimonides-islamic/>.

Pessin, S. (2017). "Ibn Gabirol's Emanationism: On the Plotinian (v. Augustinian) Theology of "Divine *Irāda*","" in *Appropriation, Interpretation and Criticism: Philosophical and Theological Exchanges Between the Arabic, Hebrew, and Latin Intellectual Traditions*, edited by Nicola Polloni and Alexander Fidora, 1–18. Barcelona and Rome: Federation Internationale des Instituts D'Études Medievales / Textes et Études du Moyen Âge.

Phillipson, T. (2017). *Aquinas, Averroes, and the Human Will. Dissertation*, Milwaukee: Marquette University.

Pines, S. (1963). "Translator's Introduction: The Philosophical Sources of The Guide of the Perplexed," in (trans.) S. Pines, *Moses Maimonides, The Guide of the Perplexed*, Chicago: The University of Chicago Press, lvii–cxxxiv.

Taylor, R. C. (2012). "'Averroes on the Ontology of the Human Soul,' The Muslim World ((ed.) A. Shihadh, Special Issue: The Ontology of the Soul in Medieval Arabic Thought)," *The Muslim World* 102 (3–4), 580–596.

Taylor, R. C. and López-Farjeat, L. X. (eds). (2015). *The Routledge Companion to Islamic Philosophy*, New York: Routledge.

Watt, W. M. (1946). "Free Will and Predestination in Early Islam," *The Muslim World* 36 (2), 124–152.

Watt, W. M. (1948). *Free Will and Predestination in Early Islam*, London: Luzac and Company.

Watt, W. M. (2012). "Djahmiyya," in (eds.) P. Bearman, Th. Bianquis, C. E. Bosworth, E. van Donzel, W. P. Heinrichs, *Encyclopaedia of Islam*, 2nd Edition, Brill Online: http://referenceworks.brillonline.com/browse/encyclopaedia-of-islam-2.

Wensinck, A. J. (1932/2007). *The Muslim Creed*, New York: Routledge.

Wensinck, A. J. and Bosworth, C. E. (2012). "*Lawḥ*," in (eds.) P. Bearman, Th. Bianquis, C. E. Bosworth, E. van Donzel and W. P. Heinrichs, *Encyclopaedia of Islam*, 2nd Edition, Brill Online: http://referenceworks.brillonline.com/browse/encyclopaedia-of-islam-2.

Wolf, S. (1980). "Asymmetrical Freedom," *Journal of Philosophy* 77, 157–166.

Wolf, S. (1987). "Sanity and the Metaphysics of Responsibility," in (ed.) F. Shoeman, *Responsibility, Character, and the Emotions: New Essays in Moral Psychology*, Cambridge: Cambridge University Press, 45–64.

Wolf, S. (1990). *Freedom Within Reason*, Oxford: Oxford University Press.

Wolfson, H. A. (1976). *The Philosophy of the Kalam*, Cambridge: Harvard University Press.

6

PERCEPTUAL EXPERIENCE
Assembling a medieval puzzle

Juhana Toivanen

1 Introduction

A simple explanation of sense perception might go as follows: perception is conscious reception of perceptual qualities of an external object. When I see a duck or hear a chime of a bell, the color and shape of the duck – or the vibration of air that the bell causes – act upon my senses, and I become aware of these qualities. However, sense perception is rarely such a simple process, since we do not perceive isolated qualities. Sounds that we hear and colors that we see are moving or at rest, and they have certain intensity or size and a location in relation to us and to other objects. Moreover, our perceptions require that we pay attention to our surroundings, and often we make various kinds of judgments and react emotionally to things that we perceive, and so forth.

Medieval philosophers acknowledged both aspects of perceptual process. They analyzed the reception of perceptual qualities and the more complex psychological processes that are related to perception, and they did so by using a theoretical framework which is commonly referred to as 'faculty psychology.' The core of this approach was to make fine-grained distinctions between various faculties (or powers) of the soul and attribute different elements of the complex perceptual process to them. This way of doing cognitive psychology can be compared to a jigsaw puzzle. A detailed and philosophically rigorous explanation of psychological operations was reached by dividing them into simpler sub-processes – just like a picture can be divided into small pieces – and concentrating on analyzing these sub-processes one by one.

This method was analytical, and it enabled a systematic analysis of the details of limited and well-defined processes that form a part of human (and animal) psychology. On the downside, this method leads to a kind of modular picture, in which perception appears to be a distinct process from, say, memory, estimation, and intellectual operations. Due to this, modern scholars tend to discuss medieval theories of perception in isolation from medieval theories of higher cognitive functions. Of course there is nothing wrong in dividing the subject matter along the medieval divisions, but this approach obscures the fact that we can understand medieval psychology of perception in a wide sense only by considering also the higher cognitive activities of the soul – the functions of the so-called internal senses and perhaps even intellectual powers – insofar as they contribute to perception. In other words, we need to assemble the whole puzzle in order to see the picture, which represents what may be called *perceptual experience*: the experience that the complex perceptual process, involving all the relevant cognitive powers of the soul, yields for the percipient.

The aim of the present chapter is to propose a new perspective in which the complete picture is as important as the individual pieces. I shall begin by presenting the pieces of the medieval jigsaw puzzle of faculty psychology and their basic functions. Then I shall assemble the pieces back together, thereby showing what medieval philosophers had in mind when they undertook the task of explaining human (and animal) cognitive psychology. The main emphasis will be on psychological issues, and I shall leave physiological and metaphysical questions largely aside – although it is clear that in order to say anything intelligible about medieval psychology, we need to know quite a bit of metaphysical aspects as well.

Thus, my central claim is that the starting point of medieval discussions was a complex and holistic perceptual experience and that we may appreciate the sophisticated elements that were included in this experience, if only we realize that *all* the pieces of the psychological jigsaw puzzle contribute to it. A historically rigorous study would of course need to analyze medieval authors and their views concerning perceptual experience one by one and point out the differences and similarities between their different theories, but this kind of detailed presentation cannot be accomplished in a short chapter for the obvious reasons.[1]

2   The pieces and their functions

Medieval theories of perception were heavily influenced by Aristotle's psychological works after they were translated into Latin in the twelfth and thirteenth centuries, but two other traditions were in many respects equally important. Arabic natural philosophy and early Latin discussions on the soul and its functions, both of which were deeply rooted in Ancient Greek philosophy, contributed to medieval theories and in many cases affected the way Aristotle's ideas were understood and adapted.[2] Especially important was the idea that psychological processes can be analyzed as functions of more or less independent powers of the soul. Just as the apprehension of different sensory qualities (color, sound, etc.) was attributed to the five external senses, more complex psychological operations were associated with distinct powers of the soul.

Medieval philosophers used several criteria to divide and organize these pieces of the psychological puzzle. One of the most fundamental divisions was made between rational and irrational powers of the soul. The rationale for this division was the idea that rational powers enable thinking of universal concepts and understanding the essences of things, whereas irrational powers can comprehend only particular objects and qualities. From a practical perspective, however, the rational powers of the soul were thought to differ from the sensory ones for the simple reason that some cognitive subjects have only the latter whereas others have both. Human beings and other animals have the sensory powers, which give them the ability to move and perceive, but only human beings are endowed with the intellect, which enables psychological processes that go beyond individual and particular objects.

This view was calcified in Aristotle's influential division into three different kinds of souls – the vegetative, the sensory, and the rational. Due to their rationality, human beings are capable of understanding the definitions of things and to place them into a systematic taxonomy of species and genera. Thirteenth-century authors usually thought that the sensory powers are necessary for intellectual understanding, because abstracting universal essences from particular objects rests upon sense perception. However, sometimes the influence was thought to go also to the other direction. Some medieval authors claim that human rationality changes the way in which some of the sensory powers operate – for instance, we are capable of actively searching from our memory things that we have forgotten, whereas irrational animals are more passive with respect to their memories.[3] Due to this overflow from the rational soul, the intellectual operations may have an effect on our perceptual experience, at least in some cases.[4] This means that the perceptual experience may be different in the case of human beings and in the case of non-human animals even when the circumstances are otherwise similar, just because the psychological puzzle contains more pieces in the first case. The human ability to use language, for example, may change the way external particular objects appear in our experience: one might say that when I see a duck, I never see it without having some kind of semantic content that qualifies my perception. It is important to note, however, that it is not clear to what extent medieval philosophers accepted the idea that the rational powers permeate the lower cognitive functions. It is quite obvious that there were different opinions, and therefore all kinds of generalizations should be avoided.

Moving downward on the scale of cognitive powers, we encounter the sensory powers of the soul. These powers are divided into two groups. First there are the five familiar external senses – sight, hearing, smell, taste, and touch. The primary function of the senses is the apprehension of various perceptual qualities of external objects. The other group of sensory powers includes the so-called 'internal senses.' Medieval philosophers disagreed on the number of these powers and the details of their functions, and sometimes they used different names for them; therefore there was no single theory of the internal senses. Yet, there were certain generally accepted ideas, especially concerning the criteria by which internal senses were distinguished from each other. One criterion was that powers that pertain to different kinds of objects are distinct; the second distinguished receptive powers from retentive ones. By using these two criteria, medieval philosophers arrived at a well-known fourfold division: the common sense receives the sensible species, and imagination retains them; the estimative power receives the so-called intentions (*intentiones*), and the memory retains them. Intentions were considered as either insensible properties that enter the soul of the percipient together with sensible species or else as relations between the percipient and the object. The main function of intentions and the estimative power was to explain how the percipient is able to make evaluative judgments that lead to an emotional reaction. The famous Avicennian remark that a sheep flees a wolf is a prime example of this process.[5] When a sheep perceives a wolf, its estimative power enables it to apprehend the wolf as dangerous and harmful, and this kind of estimative perception causes the emotion of fear and the flight. Some authors added a third criterion by which active imagination was separated from the other powers, which were considered to be passive, but this addition was not generally accepted.[6]

These five powers were thought to explain various complex elements of cognitive processes. Some of their functions are related directly to external objects during perception, while some of them are post-sensory, which means that they enable processes that do not involve perceiving an external object at the moment (for instance imagination and memory). With this general framework, medieval philosophers were able to analyze both the simple reception of a perceptual quality and the more complex aspects of sense perception as functions of these powers.

The pieces of the psychological jigsaw puzzle can be systematized in a diagram as follows (Figure 6.1):

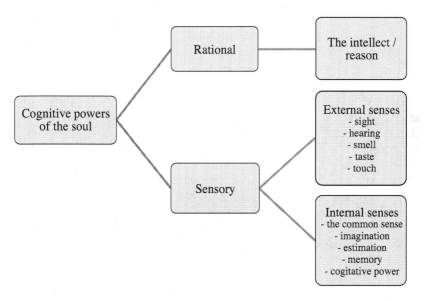

Figure 6.1 The Psychological Puzzle.

Animal species differ from each other with respect to the number of pieces their psychological puzzle contains.[7] Simple animals, such as worms, have only the sense of touch and perhaps the common sense. Higher animals have all the external and internal senses, and on top of that, human beings have the intellectual powers. This difference between various species brings a further complication to our endeavor to assemble the medieval puzzle: the complete perceptual experience is different in the case of simple animals, higher animals, and human beings. I shall leave the simple animals aside for brevity's sake, but it is good to remember that the following discussion applies to human beings and higher animals. If we want to know how worms and the like perceive their environment, we need to leave out the more complex psychological functions, that will be discussed below.

A great deal of medieval psychology is related to these psychological powers. Philosophers discussed their physiological aspects and their relation to the bodily organs, the metaphysics and the functions of the pieces, the "mechanics" of the functions, and so forth. Questions were raised, for instance, on the mutual relations of the powers of the soul (Are senses distinct powers or functions of one sensory power? What are the criteria for distinguishing various powers from each other?), the mechanism of sense perception (How do perceptual qualities actualize the senses? What does it mean that the sight is the most spiritual of the external senses?), and the anatomical location of the powers, as well as the relation between cognitive acts and physiological changes. All these aspects are important if we want to understand the details of any medieval theory of perception, but I shall provide here only a general outline of the most important aspects of the discussions, because mostly they are not relevant for our purposes – the metaphysical and other similar details of theories of perception are but a foundation which sets the stage for analyzing their psychological aspects.

Philosophical discussions concerning the mechanics of perception were important in the natural philosophy of the thirteenth century. As I already mentioned, medieval Latin authors combined elements from Aristotle's philosophy and the Arabic tradition. Moreover, they interpreted Aristotle's texts in light of the new innovations that Arabic philosophers had made. Two of these innovations are especially important. First, the so-called perspectivist theories of perception that focus on analyzing the rectilinear propagation of light and vision led medieval Latin authors such as Roger Bacon (*ca.* 1214–*ca.* 1292), Vitello (*ca.* 1230–*ca.* before 1314), and John Peckham (*ca.* 1230–1292) into detailed discussions concerning the nature of sensible species and optics.[8] Second, Avicenna's theory of the internal senses, which incorporated elements from Galenic anatomy and physiology, played a crucial role in the development of Latin cognitive psychology, including theories of perception. Within the framework set by these two traditions, scholastic authors presented an array of theories that differed in many details.

Generally the process of perception was explained by using a technical term *species*, which accounted for the connection between a perceived object and the perceiving subject or, to be more precise, her perceptual powers. There was no consensus, however, how exactly the perceptual species are supposed to bridge the gap between the percipient and the object. In fact, medieval authors did not even agree upon the exact nature of sensible species. Some authors understood them as forms – as spiritual actualizations of the medium and the organs of sense (Thomas Aquinas (1225–1274), for instance) – while others argued that they are material or physical entities, which explain natural changes in general (Roger Bacon). Yet, despite these differences, the general approach was to consider perception as a complex process that begins from the material object and turns into an immaterial or spiritual reception of the intentional object of perception.[9] The reception of the species in the medium is the first step, and in the next stage the species is received by the external senses. Most authors agreed that the species is abstracted from its materiality in the sense powers, if not before, but not of its particularity, as the sensory powers cannot grasp universal objects.

Another distinction that can be used to classify medieval theories of perception is related to the direction of influence. Many authors accepted Aristotle's position that external objects cause changes in the organs and/or in the powers of the soul and bring about perceptual acts by actualizing the potency to perceive that is in the senses.[10] In contrast, there were authors who were inspired by Augustine's Neoplatonist ideas concerning the ontological superiority of the soul with respect to material objects. Although Augustine's suggestions that seem to defend a visual ray theory were not usually regarded true, many medieval authors tended to emphasize the active elements in perceptual process – for instance, some of them built on the fact that we perceive only those things to which we pay attention. On this basis, they argued that perception is not passive reception of external stimuli but an active process.[11] Of course the difference between active and passive theories of perception is gradual, and many authors combined both elements; there were also several different strategies to emphasize the active nature of the soul. Some authors accepted the Augustinian formulation that the soul pays attention to the changes in the body, while others argued for a more radical version according to which the soul pays attention directly to the external objects.[12] As Aristotle's natural philosophy was an important source of philosophical vocabulary and insights into the process of perception, even those who accepted the most radical versions of the ontological superiority of the soul and rejected Aristotle's theory of perception on this basis usually expressed their own views in Aristotelian terminology.

Despite their differences, all these theories shared a common feature. Medieval authors were unanimous that the action of the external senses alone does not account for complete perceptual experience. We do not have a full account of sense perception when the connection between an external object and the external senses is explained, since some elements of perception can be explained only by the activity of the internal senses. Thus, Alexander of Hales (*ca.* 1185–1245) argues that:

> a particular sense is perfected by the common sense. Because the organs of the particular senses are bipartite [. . .], as is the case in two eyes and two ears, and still the sensible object does not appear to be two but one, it is necessary that it is conveyed to one internal organ. Because the species is thus simultaneously in the external and internal organs, the perfection of a particular sense is done by the common sense, when it is perfected in the internal organ. This applies to all the senses.[13]

Alexander expresses here a common view that perception is completed only with the common sense. The simple reception of perceptual qualities by the external senses is imperfect, and the common sense makes various kinds of additions to it. The core of Alexander's argument is that the object *appears* to the percipient as one, even though it is received via two different channels and two acts (in the case of seeing, the two eyes and their acts). In other words, he thinks that perceptual experience comes about as a collaboration of the external senses and the common sense: without the eyes and the power of sight, the object could not be seen in the first place, but in order to explain the experiential fact that we see one object and not two images of it, we have to appeal to the common sense.[14] All three acts – two acts in two eyes and one in the common sense – are necessary for the complete perceptual experience of the external object.

The general twist of Alexander's argument suggests that a unified perceptual experience results from the co-operation of various powers of the soul – not only from the external senses and the common sense, but from all powers that function together. Even though medieval philosophers discussed the functions of the powers of the soul one by one, it seems that their understanding of psychological activity was holistic. The division into separate powers was a result of an analytical process of dividing complex mental operations into narrower sub-processes, and when medieval philosophers made fine-grained divisions between various psychological functions that are related to sensory cognition, they were in fact analyzing different components of a complex but singular perceptual process.

A strong support for this kind of reading comes from the fact that they often tried to explain how experiential unity comes about. Avicenna addresses this problem by pointing out that we experience different kinds of acts of the soul in such a way that they belong to one and the same subject: "Moreover, we sometimes say 'When I perceived such-and-such, I became angry.' Since this is a true statement, it is one thing that perceived and then became angry."[15] This experience is either due to the fact that various powers belong to one soul or because one of the powers of the soul somehow brings about the unitary experience (for instance by apprehending the acts of other powers),[16] but for our purposes the details of the explanations that various medieval authors gave for this experience are less important than the fact that they felt the need to address it in the first place. They took the experiential unity as granted, and the central philosophical problem was to explain it. It was a problem precisely because faculty psychology distinguishes the powers of the soul and attributes precise functions to them. When the pieces of the psychological puzzle are taken apart and considered separately, it is far from clear where the unitary experience comes.[17]

Before expounding on the various kinds of additions that the powers of the soul make to perception, there is one difficulty that needs to be dealt with. Namely, a typical way of understanding medieval theories of internal senses is to see them as information processing models.[18] According to this model, the external senses receive information from the object, which is then gathered and compiled by the common sense. This information then proceeds to the next power in the hierarchy of the internal senses (usually the estimative power), which processes the information further before handing it over to the next power, and so forth. A new psychological operation takes place in each of these successive stages, and there may even be a temporal order between the acts (in addition to the rather obvious logical order). The rudimentary physiological models that medieval philosophers used to locate the internal senses in the chambers of the brain support this interpretation, since one reason for localizing the powers was that a damage in a certain area of the brain destroys some functions but leaves others intact. If two processes are really distinct from each other and take place in different places, it makes sense to think that they are separate from each other. One might argue that if this is the correct description of medieval views, their starting point was not a holistic perceptual experience.

However, there are reasons to believe that at least some medieval authors understood the cognitive operation of the soul more as a complex but unified process, in which the subject is not necessarily aware of the process itself but only of the result of the combined action of several of the powers of the soul. Take Avicenna for example. Even though he locates the estimative power into the back of the middle ventricle of the brain,[19] he occasionally argues that functionally it resides in the entire brain and that one of its tasks is to govern the whole cognitive process of the sensory soul, from the initial sense perception to various kinds of judgments that are related to the process of perception.[20] On this basis it may be justified to say that the result of the complex mental process is primary, and the analytical division into various powers and sub-processes is but a way of trying to understand and explain it.

At the outset it is difficult to say whether medieval authors considered these as two incompatible models – and if they did, which one they accepted. For our purposes it suffices to note, however, that these models are not necessarily different when it comes to the psychological experience that the internal senses were meant to explain. The information processing model may also be understood as resulting in a unified experience that includes the various additions, caused by the whole process that unfolds through the action of successive powers, and the subject need not be aware of the processing of the information. To repeat the Avicennian example, a sheep does not first perceive a wolf and then have a separate experience of judging that the wolf is dangerous. Rather, it has an instantaneous and complex experience of seeing the wolf *as* dangerous. Similarly, when I see a red object and recognize it as an apple, I do not experience seeing the color and recognizing it as an apple as two distinct steps in a process. Even less do I feel them as two distinct acts. I just have a complex experience of seeing a red apple. After having this experience, I may analyze it into more basic elements (an act of seeing a color and an act of judging that this instantiation of red is an apple), but the experience is primary and the analysis comes only after that. Even though medieval philosophers attributed these two acts to two distinct powers and often discussed them in separation from each other, it can be argued that their idea was to analyze a complex experience without claiming that these elements would be distinguished in our experience.

This experiential unity was sometimes used to make a metaphysical claim that the internal senses are not distinct from each other. Peter Olivi (*ca.* 1248–1298), for instance, points out that:

> Certainly, when we do this [viz. exercise different psychological functions], we do not perceive ourselves as operating now with one power and then with another. Rather, we perceive that the act and the attention (*aspectus*) of one and the same power vary in many ways.[21]

Olivi argues that there is no need to suppose that we have more than one internal sense, the common sense. If we had, our phenomenological experience would be different. Most medieval authors did not make such metaphysical claims, but they seem to have accepted the experience.

If this is on the right track, then we may think that a typical case of sense perception involves the whole psychological apparatus, ranging from the external senses all the way to the highest cognitive powers of the sensory soul, and possibly even to the intellectual powers in the case of human beings. Of course, some of the functions that were attributed to the internal senses are not directly related to perception. For instance, the contents of the mental acts of imagining an absent object or remembering a thing that happened in the past do not come from sense perception, and it is possible to see an instance of red color without reacting emotionally to it. Yet all the internal senses affect the perceptual contents in some cases. When a person perceives an object that she has seen before and recognizes it as familiar, the recognition is an addition made by the memory, but it is an addition to the perception. Even imagination may alter the perceptual experience, at least in the case of a person who suffers from a mental disorder and sees fictional objects created by his imagination around him.[22] When the powers act simultaneously or their acts are part of one unified process, the resulting perceptual experience is affected by all of them. Thus, even though perception proper closes with the common sense, the acts of other powers of the soul are nevertheless part of perceptual experience in a wide sense, and their results cannot be distinguished from perception in the phenomenal experience of the subject.

The approach of looking at medieval discussions on cognitive psychology from the viewpoint of perceptual experience is neutral with respect to the metaphysical views concerning the relations of the powers of the soul. Even if they are considered distinct from each other – as distinct forms that together constitute the soul or, more typically, as distinct properties or potencies of the soul[23] – they still function together and are causally connected to each other. And if the powers are considered to be identical in such a way that they are only different functions of one cognitive power,[24] then it is obvious that they come together to form a unified experience. In both cases the complex experience is, in principle, the same.

3 Assembling the puzzle: perceptual experience

Even though the functions of the powers of the soul were analyzed separately, it is clear that the powers were thought to operate together. As I already mentioned, the principle that two powers can be considered distinct from each other if one of them can act without the other (or if we find animals that can do one thing but not the other) means that the powers are in some sense distinct from each other and do not necessarily and always work together. However, many operations of the internal senses can be understood as adding new cognitive elements to the mere perception of proper sensibles, and by looking at cases in which they *do* work together, we can see what kind of contents perceptual experience may yield.

Let us begin with the first power in the ascending hierarchy of the internal senses, the common sense. One of the fundamental additions to the perception of a single property is related to the idea that I mentioned above, namely that the common sense accounts for the unity of perception. We see through two eyes, and if perceptual experience were a result of the acts of the power of vision that is divided into two eyes, we should see two objects instead of one. In addition to this kind of unity, medieval philosophers discussed intersensory unity: the proper objects of the five external senses are united in our experience when they belong to one object. When I see a duck and hear its quacking, I am aware that these two qualities (the color and the sound) are different from each other and yet belong to the same external object, the duck. The fact that we have both of these abilities – we can distinguish the sensory qualities perceived via two external senses and apprehend them as belonging to the same object – was one of the main arguments that were used to prove the very existence of the common sense as the unifying power behind all the external senses. As Averroes puts it:

> If the final percipient were in the eyes, or in the case of taste in the tongue, then it would be necessary to judge by two different [powers] when we judge sweet to be different from white. [...] For if it were possible to judge these two to be different through two different powers, each of which individually apprehends one of those two, then it would be necessary that when I would sense that a thing is sweet and you that

it is white, and I did not sense what you sensed nor you what I sensed, that I apprehend my sensible to be different from yours, although I do not sense yours. [. . .] This is clearly impossible.[25]

We are aware of both sweetness and whiteness because both of these qualities are transmitted from the external senses to the common sense. There must be one power that apprehends both of them, because otherwise they cannot be compared to each other, as one external sense is incapable of cognizing the objects of the other senses. Thus, the common sense functions as a 'first percipient,' the task of which is to unify the information coming from various senses. Averroes, like many of the medieval Latin philosophers, concentrates on explaining how the common sense is required for distinguishing sensible qualities from each other, but it was commonly agreed that this ability rests on the unity that the common sense provides. When it receives different sensory qualities that happen to belong to one object, it combines them and thereby allows us to perceive them as such. Albertus Magnus (*ca.* 1200–1280) presents this side of the idea with particular clarity:

> The proper sensibles are united in the common sense. For, if there was nothing in us where whiteness and sound were united, we would not know that the thing, the sound of which we hear, is white. The unity of whiteness and sound is apprehended neither by the eyes nor by the ears, but by the common sense.[26]

Again, the starting point seems to have been a unitary experience of a perceived object, and the philosophical problem was to explain how the unity and the distinctions between various aspects of the experience come about, given the framework of faculty psychology.

In addition to the proper sensibles of the external senses, medieval authors acknowledged the perception of the so-called common sensibles, which are properties that can be apprehended by several senses. Upon seeing a color, hearing a sound, or perceiving any of the proper sensibles of an object, we simultaneously perceive its location, magnitude, figure, unity, and movement. Different lists of the common sensibles were presented – Roger Bacon argues that there are a total of twenty-nine of them[27] – and there was a controversy whether they are perceived by the external senses or by the common sense. Some authors even seem to reject that the common sensibles form a unified group of perceptual properties, pointing out that the common sensibles that are related to an object of one of the external senses are numerically distinct from those of another sense. Thus, the magnitude of a color and that of a sound are not the same magnitude, and therefore they are not common in the relevant sense. Without going into detail, we may note that apprehending common sensibles was considered an integral part of the perceptual process. We cannot perceive external objects without perceiving them in a certain place, as having a certain magnitude, and so forth. In our perceptual experience all these elements are united and appear in connection to the perception of an external object, regardless of the number of powers of the soul that are involved in the complex process of perception. Thus, when I perceive a quacking duck, I perceive it as one thing which is in a certain place and distance in relation to myself, as stationary, as having a certain size, and so forth.

Further, if I were a fox, I would perceive the duck as delicious. A fox does not even need to taste the duck in order to apprehend its flavor, because of an ability that medieval philosophers called, following Aristotle, 'accidental perception':

> Note, therefore that there are *per se* sensible and accidentally sensible things. The accidentally sensible things are when an object of one sense is said to be perceived by another, as when it is said that sweetness of an apple is seen. This is accidental perception, because the sweetness is an object of the sense of taste. It is said to be seen accidentally, that is, through another (namely, through the red color of the apple); the sweetness is perceived *per se* and properly only by the sense of taste.[28]

Accidental perception can be thought of as a way of becoming aware of a perceptual quality that is not actually perceived at the moment. When a fox sees a duck from a distance, it does not sense the flavor of its flesh, but it is still aware that the duck is tasty. It is clear that in some cases the ability to perceive an accidental quality is acquired through learning and experience, but the crucial point is that accidental perception forms an integral part of the perceptual experience after it has been acquired. Thus, when Dominicus Gundissalinus (flourished *ca.* 1150) argues that:

> if these [qualities] were not connected in the imagination of animals (which lack the intellectual power), they would not desire to eat a thing which has a certain shape and is sweet when they see it, although they are inclined by their own desire to sweetness,[29]

his central point is that the taste of an object figures in its perception, and that the shape and sweetness are apprehended as properties of the same object. If animals just imagined sweetness without perceiving it as a property of the object they are seeing, they would not know to eat that object when they desire sweet food. Now, regardless of the philosophical problems that may lie behind this view, one thing should be clear: the visible qualities of the sweet object and its sweetness are connected in the perceptual experience of the animal.

A closely related addition that the estimative piece of the psychological jigsaw puzzle makes to perceptual experience is the apprehension of intentions (*intentiones*). I already mentioned that these were considered either as relations or as insensible qualities that enter the soul of the percipient together with the sensible species and affect the estimative power directly. The main reason to argue that the external senses or the common sense cannot perceive intentions was that they cannot be reduced to sensory qualities. A sheep does not run away from a wolf because the wolf is ugly (or gray, big, furry, moving etc.) but because it is dangerous and harmful, and harmfulness as such cannot be seen. An important presumption behind this line of reasoning is that the same sheep does not fear dogs even when they appear similar to wolves. To use another example, which Latin philosophers took from Avicenna's *De anima*, a sheep cares about its own offspring not because it looks different from all other lambs but because the sheep recognizes it by apprehending a special intention in it.[30]

Certain medieval philosophers thought that estimative judgment requires that the substance of the perceived object affects the estimative power. After explaining how estimation takes place, Roger Bacon concludes that:

> the claim that substances are not perceived by sense is to be understood with reference to a particular sense and the common sense and imagination; but it can easily be perceived by the estimation, which, although it is not called a sense, belongs none the less to the sensitive soul.[31]

Bacon's idea is that the sheep has to be aware of the wolf as a harmful substance in addition to perceiving its sensory qualities, because the perception of the sensory qualities alone does not explain the reaction of the sheep. Interestingly, he seems to think that animals perceive things around them as certain kinds of substances and that perception conveys information that goes way beyond the proper objects of the senses. He does not say it explicitly in this connection, but it seems that animals already perceive the world as divided into distinct substances to which the sensory qualities belong.

Later this kind of conception of the estimative function was criticized by John Duns Scotus (*ca.* 1266–1308), who famously argues that intentions can be ditched completely, because learned or instinctual reactions to certain constellations of sensory qualities sufficiently explain the behavior of animals. If a sheep miraculously has all the perceptual qualities of a wolf, other sheep flee from it.[32] Before Scotus it was commonly agreed that the act of the estimative power is not a part of perception proper. However, by claiming that an intention enters the soul *with* a sense perception, medieval authors wanted to say that it is not possible to apprehend an intention without perceiving an external object to which the intention belongs.[33] Thus, the estimative judgment "X is harmful" or "X is something that I need to take care of" presupposes the perception of X. The estimative judgment was not considered to be a part of the elementary perception of an external object, but when the percipient does receive the intention alongside the perceived object, it clearly forms an integral part of the perceptual experience: the wolf is perceived *as* harmful, and the only way to distinguish the awareness of harmfulness from the perception of the wolf is by a philosophical analysis of the complex experience. Human beings are rational and can therefore apprehend harmfulness as an abstract property, whereas irrational animals only perceive material objects as harmful. According to Alexander of Hales, "rational estimation apprehends also intentions that are abstracted from matter, but the sensory estimation apprehends them in connection to sensible forms, which is not beyond matter."[34]

In many cases estimative perception is innate, but medieval authors acknowledged that animals may also learn to perceive external objects as harmful or useful. John of la Rochelle (*ca.* 1200–1245) expresses a typical idea when he argues that there are three kinds of estimative judgments, one of which

> is through experience, as happens when an animal suffers pain from or takes pleasure in a thing, the form of which is registered in the formative power or imagination, and the intention of usefulness or harmfulness is registered in the memory. Immediately when that thing appears outside, the wickedness or harmfulness is in the estimation. This the reason why dogs fear sticks and stones, because they estimate that they are harmful, and they are attracted by bones, because they estimate them pleasurably.[35]

It is easy to see the connections between this type of estimative judgment and accidental perception that was mentioned above. A dog learns that sticks and stones cause pain through experience, and afterwards it becomes afraid upon seeing a stick or a stone.

One interesting aspect of this idea is that it seems to require that dogs are capable of making generalizations. A dog that has been beaten with a stick will fear any stick, not only the one that was used in the first beating. This phenomenon was not often discussed, perhaps because medieval authors do not seem to notice any philosophical problem in it. This is somewhat puzzling, as they were so adamant that only rational beings are capable of apprehending universal concepts and that sensory powers deal only with particular individuals. One might think that this division of labor between the powers of the soul would rule out the possibility that animals are able to generalize, but there are reasons to think that this was not the case. The idea that irrational animals can make generalizations appears every now and then, without ever (to the best of my knowledge) turning into a detailed philosophical analysis of how this takes place.[36] One of the most striking defenses of this idea is the following passage from Roger Bacon's *Perspectiva*:

> But it is clear that a dog recognizes a man, whom it has seen before, and that apes and many other animals also do this. And they distinguish between things they have seen of which they have memories, and they recognize one universal from another – as man from dog or wood – and they distinguish different individuals of the same species. Thus, this cognition [. . .] belongs to brute animals as well as to humans, and therefore it happens by a power of the sensory soul.[37]

It has been argued that for Bacon, recognizing that the thing perceived is a human being rather than a dog would be an intellectual process,[38] but on the basis of this passage it seems clear that animals are capable of distinguishing one universal from another. Moreover, he attributes this ability to the sensory powers of the soul also in another place.[39] It is nevertheless quite obvious that even though he uses the term *universale*, he does not mean that animals would be capable of cognizing a real universal concept. Rather, his idea seems to be that animals perceive natural kinds. If two objects belong to the same species, animals perceive their mutual similarity as well as their difference to the members of any other species without understanding the definitions or essences of these things.[40]

One might think that this kind of ability to perceive natural kinds is a necessary precondition for forming a universal concept that applies to all members of the species, because that would neatly explain why universals are abstracted from a certain group of individuals or individual properties. Medieval philosophers did not think (not before the fourteenth century at any rate) that concept formation is an arbitrary process. It reflects the objective hierarchical structure of the world, which is divided into a descending order of genera and species. Human beings are capable of grasping this hierarchy and placing each species to its proper place – in other words, humans are capable of scientific understanding – but as all knowledge is abstracted from sense perceptions,[41] it seems that there has to be a mechanism that explains the ability to recognize which particular objects are similar to each other before the universal concept is formed. Bacon and other medieval authors may think that the ability to perceive natural kinds is meant to be such a mechanism, but unfortunately he does not provide any explicit consideration of the matter.

Yet, even if this manner of recognizing natural kinds were an intellectual process – and it is likely that for most medieval authors it was – it would play a crucial role in modifying at least the way human beings perceive external objects. If the classification and comparison are done by intellectual powers, they still are part of our perceptual experience. The direct consequence of this remark is that if we want to understand medieval conceptions of perceptual experience, we must be prepared to take into consideration the operations that lie beyond the initial stages of the complex cognitive process that is related to the objects around us. It is not obvious that this necessarily leads us all the way to the intellectual powers, but when it does, we must take also them into account and accept that there are two kinds of perceptual experience, one for irrational animals and other for rational human beings.[42]

Until now we have considered various aspects of perceptual experience that originate in the perceived object, but the cognitive powers of the soul also add contents that are not really there. Even if we leave out imaginary visions caused by mental disorders, medieval philosophers recognized several cases in which we see things that do not exist in reality. Sensory illusions and other similar appearances are good examples of these kinds of additions to perceptual experience. The general idea was that the internal senses participate in the process and alter the way objects appear to us. Peter Olivi summarizes his view as follows:

> Moreover, the common sense perceives so intimately the objects of the external senses in their places that many acts of the common sense appear as acts of the external senses. This is clear because it seems to us that the pictures of diverse clothes and members in a painting have different thicknesses and are placed over each other, as if the colors of the painting were solid bodies. They appear to us in this way because the estimation of the interior sense has shown this to be the case in human beings who are depicted in the paintings. Likewise, when a burning branch is whirled in a circle, it appears as if we were seeing a kind of a circle of fire. And yet [the power of] vision does not see the circle in any instant – neither when it is made nor after it has been made – but it sees only one part of it after another and never the two at the same time. But the interior sense apprehends the circle through the memory which preserves past things and offers things that have recently been done or seen as if they took place now and were seen now. There are numerous other things that are apprehended or estimated only by the interior sense, and yet they are ascribed to the external senses because of the intimacy of the interior sense with the external senses.[43]

One the most important ideas that this passage conveys is that all the various additions that the common sense makes to perception appear as if they were acts of the external senses. This confirms that the complex perceptual experience is a result of the collaboration of several powers of the soul. We see the flat surface of a painting as a three-dimensional image and this *is* the content of our perceptual experience regardless of the fact that it is brought about by several acts that belong to different powers. Even those powers that do not contribute directly to the simple perception of an external quality may have a crucial role in forming the overall experience.

The idea that the common sense accounts for those aspects of perception that are not instantaneous shows that unitary perceptual experience may have an extension in time. The temporal sequence of instantaneous images of a whirling torch appears in our experience as a circle of fire. Another similar example that medieval philosophers repeated is a falling raindrop. The sense of sight sees single static images one after another, but the common sense adds a temporal dimension to our perceptual experience, and it appears to us as if we were *seeing* a line.[44] The content of our perception is constituted of acts that take place over time. This temporal flexibility may have an important consequence for the information processing model of the internal senses, because it opens up the possibility to overcome a temporal order between the functions of the internal senses. For instance, when we perceive a thing that we have seen before and recognize it almost immediately and without difficulty, there may be a short interval between the perception and the recognition, but we are not necessarily aware of it.[45]

Finally, certain functions of the internal senses are related to the perceiving subject instead of the perceived object. One of these functions, the perception of perception, was discussed extensively in medieval philosophical psychology: when someone perceives an external object, she is immediately aware that she perceives that object. The second-order awareness was considered as an integral part of all sensory acts, and the only disagreement concerned the metaphysical and psychological explanations that were given to it.[46] This inherent reflexivity enables the percipient to be aware of the way in which the object is perceived. Upon hearing a sound or seeing a color, we are aware that we are *hearing* the sound or *seeing* the color. It is obvious that we do not normally confuse sense modalities and have an experience of, say, seeing a sound. However, the fact that we distinguish things that we see from things that we imagine seeing calls for an explanation, and second-order perception was used as such. Mentally ill and sleeping persons lose the ability to distinguish whether the content of their minds comes from without or from the imagination, but ordinarily the common sense apprehends whether the senses are functioning or not and thereby provides awareness of the modality of perception.[47] Thus, one of the additions that the common sense brings to perception is a kind of awareness of the activity of one's own senses.

What about the percipient herself? Is it possible that perceptual experience involves some kind of self-awareness, in the sense that in every act of perception the perceiving subject is somehow present as a part of the experience? This question is philosophically difficult and highly controversial, but there are reasons to think that at least some medieval philosophers answer in the affirmative. They claim that every cognitive act is necessarily accompanied by what might be called 'implicit self-awareness,' in distinction to 'explicit self-awareness' where one's cognitive activity is directed to oneself as an object. An example of explicit self-awareness is when someone thinks about herself as a subject who is seeing an external object. By contrast, implicit self-awareness does not require that the cognitive act of the subject is directed at herself. Rather, the subject is explicitly aware of the external object and nothing else, but she nevertheless experiences the seeing as something that happens to her: there is a kind of feeling of ownness involved in the act of seeing.[48] It is possible to argue that implicit self-awareness is a necessary condition for being able to refocus one's attention and cognize oneself in the explicit manner, but we can leave this aspect of medieval discussions aside and concentrate on the implicit self-awareness as a part of all perceptual activity.

One of the most striking texts that convey the idea that we are necessarily aware of ourselves when we perceive things around us is presented by Peter Olivi:

> For, I never apprehend my acts (namely, the acts of seeing, speaking, and so forth) in any other way than by apprehending myself seeing, hearing, cognizing, and so forth. And this apprehension seems to be naturally preceded by an apprehension of the subject (*suppositum*). [. . .] We apprehend our acts only as being predicated or attributed to us – also when we apprehend our acts by an internal sense, and when we, as it were, experientially distinguish the substance from which they are derived and in which they exist from the acts themselves. This is why we sensibly perceive that these acts are derived from, and dependent on, the substance

and not the other way around, and that the substance is fixed and permanent in itself, whereas the acts are continuously in the making.[49]

The core of Olivi's argument is that in order to apprehend a cognitive act as one's own, the subject must be aware of herself prior to being aware of the cognitive act, at least logically if not temporarily. The subject figures in every cognitive act as the necessary subject-pole and as the experiential owner of the cognitive act. Olivi seems to suggest that the ability to apprehend our acts, and distinguish between the subject and the act, belongs to the internal sense (that is, to the common sense), and this indicates that this kind of implicit self-awareness may be attributed also to non-human animals.[50] However, even if self-awareness turns out to be an intellectual addition to perceptual experience – medieval philosophers often thought that only intellectual powers of the soul are genuinely self-reflexive – it does not change the fact that it *is* such an addition in the case of human beings. We simply must be open to the possibility that the perceptual experience of human beings differs from that of irrational animals in this respect and that the additional intellectual piece of the puzzle changes the overall picture.

Even so, it is important to remember that it is not clear to what extent the picture is altered by the addition of the intellectual piece. Some medieval authors argue that all the pieces of the human puzzle differ from their counterparts in animals, because the intellectual piece transforms them.[51] However, at least in some cases the intellectual level falls short of being able to alter the perceptual experience completely:

> We say, therefore, that the estimation is the more excellent judge in animals. It judges according to the invention of the imagination when it is not certain, just like when a human being thinks that honey is foul because it is similar to excrement. For, the estimation judges that it is so, and the soul follows the estimation even though the intellect disapproves.[52]

In this case we cannot help but have an aversion to eating honey, even though we *know* that it is honey and tastes sweet. Sometimes our perceptual experience goes against the better judgment of the intellectual piece of our psychological puzzle.

4 Conclusion

When I see a red apple, my sense of sight is mainly responsible of conveying the color red to my mind. However, if we consider all the additions that the various pieces of my psychological puzzle provide, we may formulate a rough description of my complex perceptual experience as follows: "I am seeing there this one red, sweet and silent object, which is stationary and an apple, and I want to have it, as it is good for me." All the elements in this description may be emphasized, depending on which part of my complex experience I turn my attention to. I may underline that *I* am the one who sees, or that I am *seeing* instead of imagining the apple. Then again, my perception conveys additional information of the *taste* or the lack of *movement* of the apple, and even that I perceive the similarity between this apple and other apples. And so forth for all the elements in the description.

It is important to note that understanding this description requires the ability to use conceptual language and make analytical divisions with respect to the contents of perceptual experience. Human beings are rational and thus capable of this kind of processing of the raw experience and of understanding the various elements in the description in an abstract manner. We can think about harmfulness as such and make a distinction between a substance and its qualities. By contrast, irrational animals can only perceive a harmful object with its qualities, without being able to distinguish these elements from each other. Moreover, some of the elements in the description of the complex perceptual experience may be different for a rational being. For instance, the experience of oneself as a perceiving subject may be richer for a human being, who is aware of herself in a more explicit manner than animals. Moreover, the evaluative element "is good for me" involves normative aspects in the case of rational beings. The most important difference, however, is that humans are able to distinguish the various elements within the unified perceptual experience, the pieces that constitute the puzzle.

By adopting a wider perspective that involves the whole psychological apparatus, medieval theories of perception may be seen in a new light, which also opens up the way for investigating the influence of rational powers on perceptual experience. The picture that I have presented here is but a scratch on the surface, and it is built from pieces that are taken from various authors who were not in complete agreement about the psychological pieces and their functions. The description of the complex perceptual experience may not represent the view of any medieval philosopher faithfully, but the aim of this essay has not been to offer a detailed view of any single medieval jigsaw puzzle but rather to argue that assembling medieval puzzles is a profitable hobby. One finds interesting pictures by adopting this approach to medieval theories of perception.[53]

Notes

1 There is a great deal of common ground in medieval views, but at the same time, the most sophisticated psychological elements were also contested and opinions vary. To continue with the simile, medieval philosophers disagreed on the exact forms and sizes of the pieces of the puzzle, on their mutual relations, and even on the existence of some of them. In the present essay, I shall take various ideas and philosophically interesting positions from different medieval authors without claiming that these ideas would have been accepted by all or even most of them. In doing this, my aim is to suggest a novel perspective from which medieval theories of perception and cognitive psychology in general may be approached.
2 For a general overview of medieval theories of perception, see Knuuttila 2008; Smith 2010.
3 See, e.g., Thomas Aquinas, *Summa Theologiae* (hereafter *ST*) 1.78.4; see Bloch 2007.
4 See, e.g., Albertus Magnus, *De anima* 3.1.3, 318–319.
5 See Knuuttila 2004, 218–226; Perler 2012.

6 Avicenna uses this criterion in his taxonomy. Many Latin authors thought that active imagination is superfluous, because the passive imagination can combine several images when it is guided by the intellect. See, e.g., *ST* 1.78.4.
7 On medieval conceptions of animals, see De Leemans and Klemm 2007, 153–177.
8 For a discussion, see Lindberg 1976.
9 Although it is not completely clear what medieval authors meant by the concept of 'spirituality' in this connection, they thought that acts of perception take place in material organs. For a controversial interpretation of Aquinas' view, see Burnyeat 2001.
10 Knuuttila 2008.
11 See Silva and Yrjönsuuri 2014.
12 Silva and Toivanen 2010.
13 Alexander of Hales, *Summa Theologica* II-1.4, tract. 1, sect. 2, q. 2.1.2, c. 4, 437.
14 The common sense was not always considered necessary for the unity of the sense of sight, as many authors argued that the power of vision is primarily located behind the eyes, where the visual nerves coming from the two eyes meet.
15 See Avicenna, *Avicenna's Psychology*, Rahman 1952, 65–66; Avicenna, *Avicenna latinus: Liber de anima seu Sextus de naturalibus* (hereafter *De anima*), 5.7, 158–160.
16 Avicenna's stance is ambiguous because sometimes he attributes the unifying function to one of the powers of the soul, namely, to the estimative power (Avicenna, *De anima* 4.1, 11 and 4.3, 35). See Black 2000, 60–61. Albertus Magnus thinks that it belongs to *phantasia* (see *De anima* 2.4.7, 303–304).
17 Averroes' formulation goes as follows:

> He [Aristotle] meant this when he said: 'Hence it is necessary that, as we speak, so we act and we sense. That is, hence it is necessary that as the one who says this to be different from that is the same person, so too that which senses and understands this to be different from that is the same power.
> (Averroes, *Long Commentary on the* De anima *of Aristotle*, 2.146, 268; I have amended the translation slightly)

Peter Olivi explains that in the case of human beings, the unity comes from the intellect:

> I concede that there is one power by which we say within ourselves that: 'The same I who understands, also wills and sees,' namely, the intellectual power. It can say this as it apprehends its own subject (*suppositum*) and its own acts, as well as the acts of other powers.
> (Peter Olivi, *Quaestiones in secundum librum Sententiarum*, (hereafter *Summa* II), q. 54, 280)

18 E.g., Kemp and Fletcher 1993, 568.
19 Avicenna, *De anima* 1.5.
20 Kaukua 2014, 236. For Avicenna, see *De anima* 5.8; 1.5; 4.2; 4.3–4. Albertus Magnus suggests that phantasy plays a similar role (*De anima* 3.1.3, 318).
21 Peter Olivi, *Summa* II q. 66, 614. For a discussion, see Toivanen 2013, 258–265.
22 *ST* 1.111.3. The same happens in dreams and under the influence of emotions (see, e.g., Albertus Magnus, *De somno et vigilia*, 2.1.7, 167a–b).
23 Respectively, Peter Olivi, *Summa* II q. 54, 253, and Thomas Aquinas, *Quaestiones disputatae de anima*, q. 12.
24 William of Auvergne, *De anima*, in *Opera omnia*, vol. 2, 3.6, 91–93.
25 Averroes, *Long Commentary on the Soul* 2.146, 267–268; I have amended the translation slightly.
26 Albertus Magnus, *De homine*, q. 35, a. 2, 310.
27 Roger Bacon, *Perspectiva*, 1.1.3, p. 9–10. See Wood 2007, 35–36.
28 John of la Rochelle, *Summa de anima*, 2.94, 237.
29 Dominicus Gundissalinus, *Tractatus de anima*, c. 9, 72.

30 Sometimes the animal in the example changes, but the overall idea remains the same: "[...] and a wolf would never feel compassion for its offspring, unless it cognized [1] that particular individual, and [2] that this individual is its offspring." (Albertus Magnus, *De anima* 3.1.2, 317).
31 Roger Bacon, *Perspectiva* 1.1.4, 13–15. The translations of Bacon's work are by Lindberg, although I have occasionally amended them.
32 John Duns Scotus, *Ordinatio* 1.3.1.1–2, n. 62 (2014, 144).
33 The only case in which intention may be apprehended without perceiving an object is when one imagines or remembers an object with an intention.
34 Alexander of Hales, *Summa Theologica* II-1.4, tract. 1, sect. 2, q. 2.1.2, c. 3, 436.
35 John of la Rochelle, *Summa de anima* 2.101, 248.
36 A useful discussion and references can be found in Oelze 2018.
37 Roger Bacon, *Perspectiva*, 2.3.9, 246–247. Albertus Magnus seems to presuppose a similar ability when he explains what kind of abstraction the estimative power makes: "Et tale est quod accepimus hunc esse filium leonis, et esse agnum, vel hominem: alium autem esse lupum, vel leonem, secundum quod substantiales formae mediantibus sensibus et non separatae ab ipsis, apprehenduntur" (Albertus Magnus, *De anima* 2.3.4, 237).
38 Smith 2010, 342.
39 Roger Bacon, *Perspectiva*, 1.10.3, 159.
40 Another often repeated example was perception of yellow wax-like substance as honey. See, e.g., Dominicus Gundissalinus, *Tractatus de anima*, c. 9, 73.
41 For an overview, see Owens 1982, Hasse 2010, 318–319.
42 Thomas Aquinas, *Sentencia Libri De Anima*, 2.13, 121b–122b.
43 Peter Olivi, *Summa* II q. 73, 99.
44 Avicenna, *De anima* 1.5, 88–89; John of la Rochelle, *Summa de anima* 2.97, 241.
45 This interpretation is tentative and requires further research. We may note, however, that Albertus Magnus argues that judgments such as "this white is sweet" take place in an instant, because they belong to the common sense (*De anima* 2.4.10, 309–310).
46 For a discussion, see Yrjönsuuri 2007, 141–152.
47 See, e.g., Peter Olivi, *Summa* II q. 59, 553–554 and q. 63, 599–600.
48 Scarpelli Cory 2013, 134–137.
49 Peter Olivi, "Impugnatio quorundam articulorum Arnaldi Galliardi, articulus 19," in Piron 2010, 457–458.
50 For Olivi's complex theory of self-reflexivity, see Toivanen 2013, 281–292.
51 See, e.g., Albertus Magnus, *De anima* 3.1.3, 318–319. Matthew Boyle 2016 dubs this the transformative model of rationality.
52 Dominicus Gundissalinus, *Tractatus de anima*, c. 9, p. 77.
53 This research has been funded by the Academy of Finland and Riksbankens Jubileumsfond.

Bibliography

Primary sources

Albertus Magnus (1890). *De anima*, ed. A. Borgnet, *Alberti Magni Opera Omnia* 5, Paris: Vivès.

Albertus Magnus (1890). *De somno et vigilia*, ed. A. Borgnet, *Alberti Magni Opera Omnia* 9, Paris: Vivès.

Alexander of Hales (1928). *Summa Theologica*, Florence: Collegium S. Bonaventurae.

Averroes (2009). *Long Commentary on the De anima of Aristotle*, trans. R. C. Taylor, New Haven: Yale UP.

Avicenna (1952). *Avicenna's Psychology: An English Translation of Kitāb al-najāt, Book II, Chapter VI With Historico-philosophical Notes and Textual Improvements on the Cairo Edition*, trans. F. Rahman, London: Oxford University Press.

Avicenna (1968/72). *Avicenna latinus. Liber de anima seu Sextus de naturalibus*, 2 vols., ed. S. van Riet, Vol. I, Louvain/Leiden: E. Peeters/E.J. Brill; Vol. 2, Louvain/Leiden: Éditions orientalistes/E.J. Brill. (= *De anima*).

Dominicus Gundissalinus (1940). *Tractatus de anima*, ed. J. T. Muckle, in "The Treatise De Anima of Dominicus Gundissalinus," *Mediaeval Studies* 2, 23–103. (= *Tractatus de anima*).

John Duns Scotus (2014). "*Ordinatio* 1.3.1.1–2, n. 62," in (eds.) S. Knuuttila and J. Sihvola, *Sourcebook for the History of the Philosophy of Mind*, Dordrecht: Springer.

John of la Rochelle (1995). *Summa de anima*, ed. J. G. Bougerol, *Textes philosophiques du Moyen Age* 19, Paris: Librairie Philosophique J. Vrin.

Peter Olivi (1922–26). *Quaestiones in secundum librum Sententiarum*, 3 vols, ed. B. Jansen, *Bibliotheca Franciscana Scholastica Medii Aevi* 4–6, Florence: Collegium S. Bonaventurae. (= *Summa* II).

Peter Olivi (2010). "Impugnatio quorundam articulorum Arnaldi Galliardi, articulus 19," ed. S. Piron, in (ed.) C. König-Pralong, O. Ribordy and T. Suarez-Nani, *Pierre de Jean Olivi – Philosophe et théologien*, Berlin: De Gruyter, 453–462.

Roger Bacon (1996). *Perspectiva*, ed. and trans. D. C. Lindberg, *Roger Bacon and the Origins of Perspectiva in the Middle Ages*, Oxford: Clarendon Press.

Thomas Aquinas (1948–50). *Summa Theologiae*, ed. P. Caramello, Turin: Marietti. (= *ST*).

Thomas Aquinas (1984). *Sentencia Libri De Anima*, Sancti Thomae de Aquino Opera Omnia Iussu Leonis XIII P.M. Edita 45.1, Rome/Paris: Commissio Leonina/Les Éditions du Cerf.

Thomas Aquinas (1996). *Quaestiones disputatae de anima*, ed. B.-C. Bazán, *Sancti Thomae de Aquino Opera omnia iussu Leonis XIII P.M. edita* 24.1, Rome/Paris: Commissio Leonina/Les Éditions du Cerf.

William of Auvergne (1963). *De anima*, ed. F. Hotot, *Opera omnia*, vol. 2, Orléans-Paris, 1674; reprinted Frankfurt am Main.

William of Auvergne (2000). *The Soul*, trans. R. J. Teske, Milwaukee, WI: Marquette University Press.

Secondary sources

Black, D. (2000). "Imagination and Estimation. Arabic Paradigms and Western Transformations," *Topoi* 19, 59–75.

Bloch, D. (2007). *Aristotle on Memory and Recollection: Text, Translation, Interpretation, and Reception in Western Scholasticism*, Leiden: E.J. Brill.

Boyle, M. "Additive Theories of Rationality: A Critique," *European Journal of Philosophy* 24, 527–555.

Burnyeat, M. (2001). "Aquinas on 'Spiritual Change' in Perception," in (ed.) D. Perler, *Ancient and Medieval Theories of Intentionality*, Studien und Texte zur Geistesgeschichte des Mittelalters 76, Leiden: E.J. Brill, 129–153.

Cory, T. (2013). *Aquinas on Human Self-Knowledge*, Cambridge: Cambridge University Press.

De Leemans, P. and Klemm, M. (2007). "Animals and Anthropology in Medieval Philosophy," in (ed.) B. Resl, *A Cultural History of Animals in the Medieval Age*, Oxford/New York: Berg, 153–177.

Hasse, D. N. (2010). "The Soul's Faculties," in (ed.) R. Pasnau, *The Cambridge History of Medieval Philosophy*, vol. 1, Cambridge: Cambridge University Press, 305–319.

Kaukua. J. (2014). "The Problem of Intentionality in Avicenna," *Documenti e studi sulla tradizione filosofica medievale* 25, 215–242.

Kemp, S. and Fletcher, G. (1993). "The Medieval Theory of the Internal Senses," *The American Journal of Psychology* 106/4, 559–576.

Knuuttila, S. (2004). Emotions in Ancient and Medieval Philosophy, Oxford: Oxford University Press.

Knuuttila, S. (2008). "Aristotle's Theory of Perception and Medieval Aristotelianism," in (ed.) S. Knuuttila and P. Kärkkäinen, *Theories of Perception in Medieval and Early Modern Philosophy*, Dordrecht: Springer, 1–22.

Lindberg, D.C. (1976). *Theories of Vision from al-Kindi to Kepler*, Chicago: University of Chicago Press.

Oelze, A. (2018). *Animal Rationality: Later Medieval Theories 1250–1350*, Investigating Medieval Philosophy, Leiden/Boston: E.J. Brill.

Owens, J. (1982). "Faith, Ideas, Illumination, and Experience," in (ed.) N. Kretzmann, A. Kenny and J. Pinborg, *The Cambridge History of Later Medieval Philosophy*, Cambridge: Cambridge University Press, 440–459.

Perler, D. (2012). "Why Is the Sheep Afraid of the Wolf? Medieval Debates on Animal Passions," in (ed.) M. Pickavé and L. Shapiro, *Emotion and Cognitive Life in Medieval and Early Modern Philosophy*, Oxford: Oxford University Press, 32–51.

Silva, J. F. and Toivanen, J. (2010). "The Active Nature of the Soul in Sense Perception. Robert Kilwardby and Peter Olivi," *Vivarium* 48, 245–278.

Silva, J. F. and Yrjönsuuri, M., eds. (2014). *Active Perception in the History of Philosophy: From Plato to Modern Philosophy*. Studies in the History of Philosophy of Mind 14, Dordrecht: Springer.

Smith, A. M. (2010). "Perception," in (ed.) R. Pasnau and C. van Dyke, *The Cambridge History of Medieval Philosophy*, vol. 1, Cambridge: Cambridge University Press, 334–345.

Toivanen, J. (2013). *Perception and the Internal Senses: Peter of John Olivi on the Cognitive Functions of the Sensitive Soul*, Leiden: E.J. Brill.

Wood, R. (2007). "Imagination and Experience in the Sensory Soul and Beyond. Richard Rufus, Roger Bacon and Their Contemporaries," in (ed.) H. Lagerlund, *Forming the Mind: Essays on the Internal Senses and the Mind/Body Problem From Avicenna to the Medical Enlightenment*, Studies in the History of Philosophy of Mind 5, Dordrecht: Springer, 27–57.

Yrjönsuuri, M. (2007). "The Structure of Self-Consciousness: A Fourteenth-Century Debate," in (ed.) S. Heinämaa, V. Lähteenmäki and P. Remes, *Consciousness: From Perception to Reflection in the History of Philosophy*, Studies in the History of Philosophy of Mind 4, Dordrecht: Springer, 141–152.

7

THE SYSTEMATIZATION OF THE PASSIONS IN THE THIRTEENTH CENTURY

Henrik Lagerlund

1 Introduction

Passions play a central role in medieval philosophical psychology both as part of a purely descriptive psychological theory of human nature and as a key aspect of a normative theory of behaviour and moral action. It was clear to most philosophers at this time that passions play an important part in any theoretical understanding of human nature, and they hence devoted a lot of space in various treatises to understand them as well as to lay down a theory that could not only explain our behaviour, but also find ways in which to control the passions. Controlling the passionate side of our nature was seen as key to a good and moral life.

The thirteenth century stands out as the time of a few great attempts to systematize a theory of passions and present what one could perhaps call a more scientific account. There are a few famous classifications at this time, which will be the centerpiece of this chapter, but there is also an attempt to give a naturalistic or natural philosophical account of the passions. This is perhaps best seen in Thomas Aquinas (1225–1274). He also gives by far the most comprehensive treatment of the passions in the whole medieval tradition.

The philosophers of the thirteenth century were presented with a great ancient and Arabic background that they seek to unify in their efforts to find a new theory. I will here present some of the most important aspects of this background. As with everybody else who studies the passions in the medieval tradition, I am greatly indebted to the work of Simo Knuuttila. His monumental book *Emotions in Ancient and Medieval Philosophy* from 2004 includes a detailed account of the developments of the passions.[1] I can only here draw out some of my own thoughts on the same material that he has so eloquently presented for us.

I begin this chapter with a short treatment of the background to the thirteenth-century discussions of the passions. I there draw the reader's attention to Plato,

Aristotle, the Stoics, Augustine and Avicenna. I then turn to the great systematizer, namely John of La Rochelle (*ca.* 1200–1245). He presents the most extensive classification of the passions in the medieval tradition, and he was very influential. I then turn to Aquinas, and I try to be fairly exhaustive in discussing his argument from the definition of the passions to the role they play in morality.

2   Background to the thirteenth-century discussions of passions

As with many concepts discussed in the thirteenth century, the concept of the passions – especially as developed by John of La Rochelle and Thomas Aquinas – is also a mix of Platonic and Aristotelian elements, but in this particular discussion we can also find Stoic ideas as well as ideas developed from Augustine and Avicenna. It is a rich and complex background that is not easy to sort out.

In the Platonic division of the soul into three parts (*Republic* IV), the two lower parts are called the appetitive (*epithumetikon*) and the spirited (*thumoeides*), respectively. The appetitive part seeks pleasure and avoids pain while the spirited part is associated with aggression. In the Latin philosophical tradition, these became known as the concupiscible and the irascible parts of the soul, but through the years they were associated with Aristotelian *powers* of the soul instead of actual *parts* of souls.

This basic classification was combined in some early medieval texts with the Stoic idea that there are four basic passions. The medieval tradition knew the Stoic theory, as well as a lot of Plato and Aristotle, from Augustine's *De civitate Dei*, but they also read Cicero's *Tusculan Disputations* and Seneca's *Letters* independently. This particular Stoic view of the four basic passions was also reported by Nemesius of Emesa and John Damascene.[2] Here is Cicero's presentation in the *Tusculan Disputations*:[3]

> They hold furthermore that there are divisions of disorder originating in two kinds of expected good and two of expected evil, with the result that there are four in all: pleasure (*libidinem*) and appetite (*laetitiam*), in the sense of delight in present good and lust of future good, originate in what is good; fear (*metum*) and pain (*aegritudinem*), they consider, originate in what is evil, fear in the future and distress in present evil. For events whose coming is feared also cause distress by their presence.
>
> (4.11–12)

On this view, pleasure and pain are seen as related to the present while appetite and fear are related to the future. Other passions were thought to sort under these.

The early medieval thinkers did not always think the four basic passions were the same, however, but the principle they relied on is certainly Stoic. An example can be found in Isaac of Stella (1100–1170). Although he was not original, he was rather influential, since his view was taken up by the twelfth-century anonymous author of *Liber de Spiritu et anima*. Certainly most of the elements of this view could be found in Augustine. Isaac of Stella writes:

> Affects are fourfold: as for things which we love, we either enjoy them as present or hope for them as future, while with respect to things which we hate we already have distress about them or else are in fear of having it. And joy and hope arise from the concupiscible power, while distress and fear arise from the irascible power.[4]

The analysis given here makes passions with a present or expected pleasure a concupiscible power and passions with a present or feared distress an irascible power. Love is hence a present or future pleasure while anger or hate is present or future distresses. The similarity to the Stoics is obvious. Their division is also based on whether something is seen or taken to be a present or future good or evil. For them, of course, the object is judged to be good or evil, while for Isaac of Stella the object gives rise to a pleasure or a pain/distress. On the Stoic view, a passion (or, perhaps better in their case, an emotion)[5] is a result of an act of the mind, but the medieval view is Aristotelian at core and love or anger are passions, that is, passive. This is an important distinction, and it will be clear that the thirteenth-century view is heavily indebted to Aristotle, as one might assume.

The Stoic view is well known and has been studied by many scholars.[6] There is a three-stage development of an emotion, in their view. Seneca explains in *On Anger* (Seneca here speaks about anger in particular, but the general theory is the same for all emotions):

> That you may know, further, how the emotions (*adfectus*) begin, grow, and run riot, I may say that the first movement is involuntary, a preparation for emotion, as it were, and a sort of menace; the next is combined with an act of volition, although not an unruly one, which assumes that it is right for me to avenge myself because I have been injured, or that it is right for the other person to be punished because she has committed a crime; the third movement is now beyond control in that it wishes to take vengeance, not if it is right to do so, but whether or not, and has utterly vanquished reason.
>
> (II.4.1–2)

The first movement (*pro-patheia* in Greek and *primus motus* in Latin) is an involuntary movement of the body that gives rise to a judgment that the thing causing the motion is good or evil. The emotion does not exist, however, until this judgment is accepted or assented to, but, as Seneca says, by that time it is too late, and the emotion has taken control of us. On this three-stage theory, emotions are put under our control, or under the control of the will, and we cannot be said to have an emotion, or suffer the emotion as the Stoics would put it, unless we have assented to the proposition at the second stage. It is clear that this is a very different theory from the ones presented in the early medieval period.

Augustine is not the only reason this particular theory cannot be found in the early medieval tradition, but he surely played an important role. He had his own particular take on Seneca's theory that did not preserve the three-stage developmental view of the emotions. In a recent analysis of Augustine's view, Sorabji[7] claims that Augustine misunderstood the Stoic theory or misread a story from Aulus Gellius's *Attic Nights* (19.1.15–21). In the relevant part, Augustine writes the following:

> Aulus Gellius says that he read in this work that the Stoics believed in mental visions, which they called phantasies, and no one can prevent their impact on the mind or choose the time thereof. When these sensations arise from terrifying and awe-inspiring circumstances, the mind of even the wise person must unavoidably be moved, so that for a little while she either gets the jitters with fear or shrinks with sadness, inasmuch as these passions inhibit the proper activity of mind and reason. Yet this does not cause the mind to form an opinion of evil, nor to give assent nor to yield to them. For this assent, they maintain, is within the power of someone to grant or withhold, and they think the difference between the mind of the wise and that of the foolish is just this, that the mind of the foolish yields to these same passions and subordinates its mental assent to them, while the wise, though obliged to experience them, preserves with mind unshaken a true and steadfast opinion regarding the things that she ought rationally to pursue or avoid. I have described as well as I could, not, it is true, more attractively than Aulus Gellius, but certainly more briefly and, to my mind, more clearly, what he relates that he read, in a book by Epictetus, of that philosopher's utterance and opinion, which follow the tenets of the Stoics.
> (IX.4)

As is clear from this quotation, Augustine equates the first motion with the actual emotions, or passions, as he calls them. It is, of course, significant that he calls them passions (*passiones*), since that is what the first motion is, that is, something that *happens to us*, and by misunderstanding the Stoic theory of the three-stages of an emotion, Augustine can identify the first movement with the passion itself. It is only at a later stage that the passion comes under the control of the will, or, to use Stoic language, becomes a matter of assent or not. We already have the passion; however, it is now a matter of controlling it or being overcome by it. On Augustine's view we cannot avoid the passion just as we cannot avoid a first motion, according to the Stoics, but the will can at a later stage take back control. This view fits much better with Augustine's view of human nature and original sin. How would you even make lust an original sin on the Stoic view, where having it in the first place is in our control? That is not the world after the fall. By misunderstanding the Stoic theory, as Sorabji will have it, or by simply using his version of the theory for his own purpose, Augustine makes the emotions, or better the first motions, of the Stoics into the passions of the medieval tradition.

As is already well known, thirteenth-century psychology was indebted to Avicenna for the faculty psychology, and this naturally had an effect on how medieval thinkers dealt with the passions.[8] This will become evident later, but Avicenna also influenced the discussion in another way, namely in thinking about passions as movements or as something that moves an agent to action. In this sense, Avicenna is also closer to the Stoic view of thinking about passions as acts. This is the source of the complicated and confusing medieval view that passions are also actions. We will see this more closely in Aquinas. In the part of the *Book of Healing* (*Kitab al-Shifa*) that deals with the soul and became known as Avicenna's *De anima* in the Latin tradition, he writes:

> There are two modes of action of the motive power, for it may move either by commanding a movement or by causing movement to take place. As far as it commands a movement, it is an appetitive and desiderative power, which commands other moving powers to move when the imagination, of which we shall speak later, imagines a desirable or repugnant form. It is divided into two parts. One is called the concupiscible power, and this commands the movements which bring one near to things which are regarded as necessary or useful for a pleasurable appetite. The second is called the irascible, and this commands the movements, which repel things which are regarded as harmful or destructive for the desire for overcoming things.[9]

A passion for Avicenna is part of the sensitive moving power. He divides such a power in two, namely into a commanding and an executive moving power. Passions are commanding powers and hence function as motivations for action, but they only result in actions if they are accompanied by an actualized executive moving power. This distinction allows animals to control their passions, but in humans the executive moving powers are also under the control of the will. The commanding moving power is divided into a concupiscible and irascible power. As with Isaac of Stella the concupiscible power draws one towards an imagined object while the irascible power makes one avoid objects.[10] This way of setting up the psychological treatment of passions was very influential and can be seen throughout the thirteenth century.

3   John of La Rochelle's classification of the passions

John of La Rochelle (1200–1245) was a Franciscan and a student of Alexander of Hales (1185–1245). He plays an important role in this story because of his influence on Aquinas, but he was very important for the developing Franciscan school and, for example, influenced Bonaventure (1221–1274) greatly. La Rochelle initiates the considerable systematization of the passions that takes place in the thirteenth century. He had a considerable influence on Aquinas and wrote several important works on the soul, but the most important was probably *Summa de anima*, from 1235. In any case that is the work in which we find his extensive treatment of the passions.

La Rochelle was heavily influenced by Avicenna. His treatment of the passions is set up in the same way. He also, for example, distinguishes the commanding power into concupiscible and irascible powers. Objects are presented to these powers by the imagination or by the estimation, and we are moved to act on these by the concupiscible or the irascible powers. We are naturally inclined to act in certain ways, and objects elicit different kinds of reactions in us. In this way, La Rochelle thinks, the concupiscible power commands acts by which we acquire things that are related to pleasure. The irascible power, however, commands acts that have to do with honor and victory.[11]

The original part of La Rochelle's classification comes as he claims that both these powers can be effected in different ways or, as he puts it, two kinds of dispositions can arise in the power. The concupiscible power can be disposed positively or negatively. La Rochelle talks about these as a liking (*placentia*) and a disliking (*displacentia*).[12] The irascible power can, on the other hand, be disposed strongly (*corroboratio*) or weakly (*debilitas*). He here introduces the idea that the passions are classified as contrary pairs, for example, joy and pain, love and hate, and so on, for the concupiscible power, and for example ambition and poverty of spirit for the irascible. A defining feature of the irascible power is that its objects are arduous or difficult. This obviously also distinguishes it from the concupiscible passions, for which the object is more straightforward.

The classification La Rochelle presents is very extensive and certainly more comprehensive than anything else presented in the medieval period (see Figure 7.1).

Appetite is, according to La Rochelle, a simple liking of an object perceived to be good for me, while desire, although a liking as well, is a more intense appetite for an object. He proceeds in a similar way to explain all the passions in the division. The liking that is generated by an object appearing pleasant is called joy or delight, and similarly the liking that comes, if the object is perceived to be good for someone else, is called love. On the other hand, if the object is an evil, it can only be liked as far as it is directed towards someone else,[13] and then the passion is hate.

Dislike can be towards what is good and evil as well as for oneself and towards others. For example, dislike for what is good for oneself generates disgust or aversion, but if it is towards someone else then it generates envy. If we have a dislike for an evil directed to ourselves, then the passion is pain or distress, and, if the same thing is directed to someone else, then we have pity.

Irascible passions are directed towards different objects, and they mainly divide into two dispositions, namely, strength and weakness. They are also directed towards good and against evil. By 'good' he means the good associated with excellence and honor; strong such passions are ambition, hope, pride, lust for

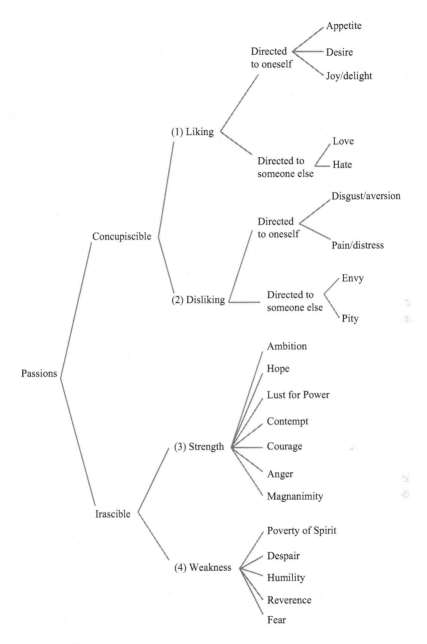

Figure 7.1 La Rochelle's division.
(1) and (2) are contrary sets of passions as well as (3) and (4).

power and contempt. The strong passions against evil are courage and anger. The irascible passions in accordance with weakness are poverty of spirit, despair, humility and reverence.[14]

4 Aquinas on the passions

The most comprehensive treatment of the passions in the Middle Ages can be found in Aquinas's *Summa Theologiae* (ST) II-1, 22–48, but comments on the passions can be found throughout Aquinas's very large body of work. Quite a bit has also already been written about Aquinas's theory of the passions.[15] I will here present my own understanding of Aquinas. I will hence foremost interact with Aquinas's own text and only refer to the secondary literature on occasion.

Aquinas presents a thoroughly naturalistic view of the passions. On his view, a passion is a physical change or movement of the body, and it is "found in an act of the sensitive appetite". He clearly distinguishes it from an intellective appetite, which does not require a bodily transformation. Hence, Aquinas distances himself from La Rochelle when he says that a passion is a movement. He writes:

> A passion is a kind of movement, as stated in [Aristotle's] *Physics* III. Therefore the contrariety of passions should be treated as contrariety of movements or change.
>
> (ST II-1, 23, 2)

This is further spelled out in familiar Aristotelian terms when he explains the name 'passion'. He says the name captures how "a patient is drawn to that which is the agent" (ST II-1, 22, 2). This expresses the way in which a passion is truly something passive that is activated by some cause. It also stresses how the passion is not to be identified by the power or capacity that is the appetitive power but by the movement from passive power to active power. It is, hence, this change or movement that is the passion.[16]

In describing passions as movements, Aquinas is distancing himself not only from La Rochelle but also from Albert the Great (*ca.* 1200–1280) and explicitly endorsing the view of John Damascene (675 or 676–749). John Damascene, also known as John of Damascus, was a Syrian priest most known for his work *De fide orthodoxia* (*On the Orthodox Faith*). Consider this quotation from Albert the Great:

> John Damascene says that "a passion is a movement of the appetitive sensible power caused by the imagination of something good or evil" and, differently, that "a passion is a movement of the irrational soul caused by an assumption about good or evil" and, differently, that "a passion is a movement from something to something". . . . One has to say that a passion is not, in truth, a movement, although it does not occur without a movement. Damascene mistakenly equates what is left from a movement with a movement, for a moving thing is a subject of passion through a movement.[17]

On Albert's view a passion is instead a qualitative state of a moving power and is hence identified with the actualized state of the appetitive power – not the motion itself. He thinks this view is supported by Aristotle in *Categories* 8.

Aquinas on the other hand accepts Damascene's view (ST II-1, 22, 3). In the final analysis a passion will hence be a motion towards or away from something.[18] What kind of passion it is is determined by the direction of the movement and the object. Let us first look closer at the cause of a passion. As the earlier quotation from Damascene, as reported by Albert the Great, suggests, the cause of the passion is an imagination or perception of something as good or evil. Aquinas explains in the following way:

> The soul is more drawn to a thing by the appetitive power than by the apprehensive power. For by the appetitive power the soul is ordered to things, such as they are themselves, and as the Philosopher[19] says, in *Metaphysics* VI, that good and evil, which are the objects of the appetitive power, are in the objects themselves.
> (ST II-1, 22, 2)

The movement that is the passion and is in the appetitive power is a motion caused by an object appearing good or evil to us. What moves the appetitive power is on Aquinas' view hence the same as on Damascene's view.

It is important to realize that although the appetitive power is moved by what is apprehended to be good/desirable or evil/repulsive, this does not mean that the passions themselves are good or evil. Moral good or evil involves reason for Aquinas, and as Aristotle says in the *Nicomachean Ethics* II.5, we are not praised or blamed for our passions. Aquinas certainly agrees with this. But let us return to the morality of the passions a little later and now instead turn to the object of the passions.

As is traditional, Aquinas also distinguishes the appetitive power into concupiscible and irascible powers. The passions fall into these divisions based on their objects. He writes:

> The passions that are in the irascible and concupiscible [powers] differ in species. For since different powers have different objects, . . . the passions of different powers must of necessity be referred to different objects. . . . To know therefore which passions are in the irascible [power] and which are in the concupiscible, we must take the object of both these powers. For it was said in the first part that the object of the concupiscible power is sensible good or evil, simply apprehended as such, which is pleasurable or painful. But since the soul necessarily experiences difficulty or struggle at times, in acquiring some such good, or in avoiding some such evil, in so far as such good and evil is more than our animal nature can easily acquire or avoid; therefore, this good and evil, inasmuch as it is arduous or difficult, is the object of the irascible [power]. Hence any passion that is about good or evil absolutely pertains to the concupiscible

[power], such as joy, sorrow, love, and similar. Whereas those passions that are about good or evil as arduous, through being difficult to acquire or avoid, belong to the irascible [power], such as courage, fear, hope, and similar.

(ST II-1, 23, 1)

Aquinas argues elsewhere that powers are individuated by their objects (ST I, 77, 3) and causes or activating principle. As is clear from this quotation, not only do the good and the evil distinguish the concupiscible from the irascible but also the way or manner in which the good and the evil is sought and avoided. An irascible passion is hard to avoid or hard to acquire. Courage requires a lot from a person to acquire and fear requires a lot to avoid, while love and joy come more easily to humans, and pain, for example, which is a concupiscible passion, takes very little effort to avoid. We do it instinctively as it is felt. Notice also that the object and the cause is the same thing, namely the good or evil apprehended. It is not the object or thing in itself that moves the appetitive powers, but the objects perceived as good or evil by us.

Obviously the classification of the passions starts with the distinction between concupiscible and irascible powers and then further into the distinction between those moved by what is good and evil, but Aquinas also thinks passions come in contrary pairs, as La Rochelle. Given that passions are motions, the criteria for contrasting two passions will be the same as the criteria stated by Aristotle in *Physics* V.5 for contrasting motions in general. The first contrariety is between an access to a terminus and a recess from the same terminus. This primarily pertains to the contrariety between generation and corruption, that is, something's coming into being and going out of being. The second contrariety is based on the contrariety of the terminus and pertains to processes; thus bleaching, the motion from black to white, is the contrary of blackening, the motion from white to black. In applying this distinction Aquinas writes:

Therefore, there are two kinds of contraries in the passions – one according to the contrariety of objects, that is, of good and evil, and another is according to approach to or withdrawal from the same terminus. In concupiscible passions there is only the former contrariety, whereas both forms are found in irascible passions. The reason for this is that the object of the irascible power is the sensible good or evil, not as such but as arduous. The good which is arduous or difficult is such that one may tend to it as good, as in hope, or one may turn from it as arduous and difficult, as in despair. Similarly the evil which is arduous is such that one may avoid it as evil, as in fear, or one may tend to it as arduous in order to avoid something evil, as in courage. Therefore the irascible passions may be contraries according to the contrariety between good and evil, as hope and fear, or according to approach and withdrawal, as courage and fear.

(ST II-1, 23, 2)

Passions sort into two groups based on their objects being good or evil for us. These are contrary objects and they divide the concupiscible passions, but the irascible also divide based on the second contrariety, which is motion on a scale from one terminus, namely leading away from something or towards something. We may be avoiding an evil in the sense of running away from it, as we do when we fear something, or by facing it and moving towards it as we do in courage.

Aquinas seems to have thought that the passions were in need of a scientific grounding in the thirteenth century. He constantly brings the discussion back to Aristotle's *Physics* and wants to give a natural philosophical underpinning of the passions. Aquinas notes this in particular in question 23, article 4, when he explains that every mover in some sense can be said to draw a patient to it or to repel it. He points out that a mover does three things to the patient. First (1), it gives the patient an inclination to tend towards the mover or to move away from it. Second (2), it moves the patient towards its proper place, if it is not already there. Third (3), it makes the patient rest in its proper place. These are general principles that apply to any motion. Having pointed these out he goes on to apply them to the passions.

He explains that objects that are good work on the appetitive power through an attractive force (*virtus attractiva*), while objects that are evil correspondingly work through a repulsive force (*virtus repulsiva*). Following (1), the perceived good object causes a certain inclination for it in the appetitive power. This 'aptitude', as he also calls it, is a movement towards the object. It is what we have named the passion of love. Correspondingly, evil causes an inclination to move away from the evil object. This is what we call hate. Now, if the good is not possessed, then, in accordance with (2), the good causes a motion to acquire the object, which is desire. Contrariwise, an evil object causes the motion to stay away from the object, which is called aversion. Finally, as far as the concupiscible passions are concerned, when the object is obtained, it causes, in accordance with (3), a motion to rest in that place. This is delight or joy, while the opposite of this is sorrow, since if we have a perceived evil, we have what we do not want.

Aquinas thinks these three principles governing motion also apply to the irascible passions. The irascible passions have their origin in the concupiscible passions, since, according to (1), a motion in the concupiscible power is presupposed. Hence, there is a motion towards the good already, and if the object is not obtained, as in (2), then we have hope, which is an irascible passion since its object is not easily obtainable. On the other hand, if the object is some good, but not obtained, and there is a motion away from it, we are in despair. If the object is evil, but not obtained, and we are moving away from it, then we have fear. On the other hand, in the same situation, but we are moving towards the object, we have courage. These are two ways of overcoming an evil. If we then apply (3) in the same way and the object is obtained and good, then we see that there cannot be such an irascible passion. There is then just joy, which is a concupiscible passion. If the object is evil, however, and obtained there is only one irascible passion, namely anger. Aquinas' natural philosophical way of approaching the passions of the soul in terms of their objects and motions away from and towards these objects results in a certain set of passions. Aquinas thus thinks these are the basic passions. He writes:

> Accordingly it is clear that in the concupiscible power there are three pairs of passions, namely, love and hate, desire and aversion, joy and sorrow. In a similar manner there are three groups in the irascible power, namely, hope and despair, fear and courage, and anger, which has no contrary passion. Consequently there are altogether eleven passions differing specifically; six in the concuspiscible power and five in the irascible; and under these all the passions of the soul are contained.
>
> (ST II-1, 23, 4)

I have summarized this in the division presented as Figure 7.2. As one clearly sees, it is a great simplification from what we saw in Figure 7.1, which presented La Rochelle's division.

In the picture Aquinas paints for us, love, and its contrary passion, hate, are given a very special status, and all passions are said to start with love or hate towards the object. When I perceive an object that appears good to me, there is a movement towards the object, and, on this view, this is love. Only later does the passion become more nuanced or more complicated and difficult. He states this special status of love by saying that it is the 'principle' of the sensitive appetite's motion towards a perceived object (ST II-1.26.1). This might strike someone as an unusual notion of love for a Christian, since it construes love as physical attraction. Aquinas obviously distinguishes this notion of love from the more Christian idea of friendly love (*amor amicitiae*), derived from Augustine (ST II-1.26.4).

Anger also stands out in this division, since it does not have a contrary passion. Aquinas explains this in the following way:

> The passion of anger is peculiar in this, that is cannot have a contrary, either according to approach or withdrawal, or according to the contrariety of good and evil. For anger is caused by a difficult evil already present, and when such an evil is present, the appetite must either succumb, so that is does not go beyond the limits of sadness, which is a concupiscible passion, or else it has a movement of attack on the hurtful evil, which movement is that of anger. But it cannot have a movement of withdrawal, because the evil is supposed to be already present or past. Thus, no passion is contrary to anger according to contrariety of approach or withdrawal.
>
> (ST II-1, 23, 3)

Let us consider an example. According to Aquinas, anger is caused by a present evil. If we succumb to this, let us say someone has intentionally or unintentionally hurt us, we are only sad. But in many people the evil that is present

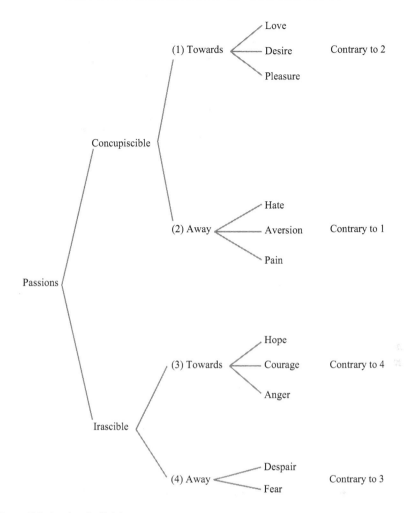

Figure 7.2 Aquinas's division.

causes a reaction, even if only temporarily, to *overcome* the one or the thing that causes the pain. This is anger on Aquinas' analysis – a counter-movement to the object. Obviously there cannot be an irascible contrary passion, since accepting a pain or a hurt is only sadness, which is a concupiscible passion. The example also nicely shows how concupiscible passions must precede the irascible passions.

The analysis of the passion of the soul outlined so far applies to animals as well as humans. On several occasions Aquinas describes the movements of the appetitive power for humans and animals in the same way as he describes the movements of inanimate objects. He, for example, says that inanimate objects have a natural appetite towards their proper place. Aquinas even calls this 'natural love' (ST II-1, 26, 1–2). This is obviously not something they have through their apprehension of other things but something that is given to them through God's providential plan. In this way, animals and humans are not different, but God's plan is realized in a different way for them. He, for example, thinks that the concupiscible passions are ordered towards the preservation of the species and the individual. The irascible powers have been given to animals to overcome hindrances that may stand in the way of the concupiscible powers to fulfill their goals, since some good might be difficult to obtain or some evil difficult to avoid. In this way we all, humans and animals, conform to natural teleology. Humans are different from animals, but the difference is a matter of degree. Aquinas writes:

> Natural things desire the things that accord with their nature, not through their own apprehension of them but through the apprehension by the author of their nature, as we have shown in the first book. A second sort of appetite does follow apprehension by its own subject, but as a matter of necessity, not from free choice. The sensitive appetite of dumb animals is like this. In human beings there is something of freedom about it, to the extent that it is subject to rational control. Further, there is the appetite which arises both through apprehension and free judgment. This is the rational or intellective appetite, commonly called the will.
> (ST II-1, 26, 1)[20]

As far as the passions are concerned they are subject to the motions and laws of natural bodies. They, of course, can stand in relation to reason and hence take on a moral dimension, but as I have already stated, they are in themselves neither good nor bad. Aquinas writes:

> We may consider the passions in two ways: in themselves or as subject to the control of reason and will. Now in themselves the passions are simply movements of the non-rational appetite; thus there is no moral good or evil in them, since this involves reason, as we have shown. But if they are considered as subject to the control of reason and will, then moral good and evil are in them. For the sensitive appetite is much more intimately linked to reason and will than are the bodily members. Yet the movements and actions of our bodily members are morally good or evil in so far as they are voluntary. Much more, therefore, may the passions, in so far as they are voluntary, be called morally good or evil. And they are said to be voluntary, either because they are commanded by the will or because the will does not check them.
> (ST II-1, 24, 1)

The passions can, hence, be morally good or evil, but only in so far as they involve reason or are in some way voluntary.[21] It is only when the passions are under the control of reason that they are distinctly human; otherwise they are the same in us as in all other animals (ST II-1, 24, 1).

Aquinas had a clear view of the Stoic view of the passions. In his view, they held that "every passion of the soul is evil" (ST II-1, 24, 3). This view is true, he thinks, if we take the passions only by themselves as "the inordinate movements of the sensitive appetite" (ibid). This can also happen suddenly as a surprise to reason. He writes:

> A movement of the sensory appetite is sometimes aroused suddenly, in response to imagination or sensory cognition. And in that case, such a movement occurs without the command of reason, although it could have been presented by reason if it had been foreseen.
> (ST II-1, 17, 7)

The Stoics are generally wrong, however, Aquinas thinks, since the passions can be moderated by reason and, hence, be controlled. Taken in that way, the passions are good and can be of great help. The relation of the passions to reason is complicated, however. He explains:

> There are two ways in which passion may be related to rational judgment: antecedently and subsequently. In the former case, it will cloud the rational judgment on which the goodness of the moral act depends, and so diminishes the goodness of the act. An act of charity is more praiseworthy when done from the judgment of reason than simply from a feeling of pity. But when passion is subsequent to rational judgment, there are two possibilities. First, it may take the form of a kind of overflow: the higher part of the soul is moved to anything so intensively that the lower part also follows it. In that case, the passion that results in consequence, in the sensitive appetite, is a sign of the intensity of the will, and so indicates greater moral goodness. Secondly, it may be the outcome of choice, that is, a man may make a deliberate choice to be affected by a passion so that he will act more promptly, thanks to the stimulus of the sensitive appetite. In this case too the passion increases the goodness of an action.
> (ST II-1, 23, 3)

Passions are not always an aid to us, since they can come before reason, as he puts it, and overwhelm it. This frequently happens in akratic behaviour. In that scenario, we are overcome by a given passion and our reason is, due to the strength of that passion, temporarily clouded. In these cases we act viciously or morally wrong because of our passions, but as he points out we can act for the good in such cases as well; however, the goodness of the act is always lesser than if we had acted from reason. If passion, however, comes after rational judgment, then it can enhance the goodness of the act, on account of the great intensity that the passion brings to the action. Interestingly, Aquinas also thinks we can choose to have a passion. Obviously, the passions then also follow reason. Aquinas is outlining this two-way interaction between passion and reason (or will) that gives him a powerful theory to explain various complicated aspects of human behaviour.

One might also ask, as a follow up to this, in what way does reason control the passions? Aquinas explains this too. He writes:

> The rule is called despotic whereby a man rules his slaves, who have not the means to resist ... the orders of the one that commands them, since they have nothing of their own. But that rule is called political by which a man rules over free subjects who, though subject to the government of the ruler, have nevertheless something of their own, by reason of which they can resist the orders of him who commands. And so, the soul is said to rule the body by despotic rule.... But the reason is said to govern the passions by political rule.
>
> (ST I, 81, 3, ad 2)

Reason, hence, rules passion by political rule, as he puts it. Reason is, on this picture, the ruler, but passion has its own autonomy and does not always follow the ruler, or at least passion does not always follow freely without resistance. In this way of putting things, we can see a clear Platonic element in Aquinas' theory, since such rule does not work unless there is a harmonious relationship between passion and reason. A harmonious soul, hence, works better where the different parts work together and we feel the right thing in the right circumstances. Plato talks this way about the tripartite soul and about the well-functioning state in the *Republic*.[22]

This brings us to the relation between passion and virtue. Obviously Aquinas thinks virtue and passion are distinct, but he nevertheless thinks that there is a close relation between them. They are distinct since moral virtue is a habit and as such it is not a movement like a passion, but "a principle of the movement of the appetite" (ST II-1, 59, 1). As a habit it guides the movements of both the sensitive and the intellective appetites. Furthermore, passions are, as I have said, neither good nor evil in themselves, but obviously virtue is good and vice evil. A third reason for the difference between moral virtue and passion is that while virtue begins in reason and ends in appetite, a passion begins in appetite and may end in reason or rather tend toward reason.

Aquinas is in this respect concerned with the Stoic view of the passions, as he understands it, which is derived from Augustine, that the wise person or virtuous person has rid herself of the passions. He contrasts this view with his own or with what he also thinks is Aristotle's view. He writes:

> Because the Stoics, by not discriminating between the intellective appetite ... and the sensitive appetite.... did not ... distinguish the passions from the other affections of the human soul ... but only in the point of

> the passions being, . . . any affection in disaccord with reason. . . . But if the passions are taken for any movement of the sensitive appetite, they can be in a virtuous man, in so far as they are subordinate to reason.
>
> (ST II-1, 59, 2)

Following Augustine, Aquinas also quotes Aulus Gellius's *Attic Nights* and tells the story of a Stoic sage experiencing fear on board a boat in a terrible storm. Aquinas follows Augustine's take on the story and, hence, holds that the Stoic sage can be overcome by strong passions.[23] Given such a reading it looks as if there is no real difference between the Stoic view and Aquinas's own, but only a difference in words, as he himself puts it.

The moral virtues are said to perfect the appetitive part of the soul by directing them towards the good as defined by reason, but reason also directs the will, so moral virtues are not about the passions (ST II-1, 59, 4). A virtue like justice applies only to the will and is an operation that does not involve a passion. However, the will might cause joy in the sensitive appetite by overflow as a result of the act of justice, so even moral virtues that are without passions may, hence, include an element of passion.

The close connection between the moral virtues and the passions is part of the teleology of God's providence, argues Aquinas, since if it were the case that the moral virtues could be without the passions, then the passions in humans would serve no purpose.[24] He writes:

> Whereas it is not the function of virtue to deprive the powers subordinate to reason of their proper activities, but to make them execute the commands of reason, by exercising their proper acts. Wherefore just as virtue directs the bodily limbs to their external acts, so does it direct the sensitive appetite to its proper regulated movements.
>
> (ST II-1, 59, 5)

This is part of Aquinas' integrated psychology and his view of human nature as embodied being. We are not separated souls, like angels, and our psychology functions properly only as a true unity between body and soul/mind. Moral virtue can on this view be said to perfect the passions, and in this respect the virtues can also be said to be about the passions.

As noted earlier, the passions are free and cannot be fully controlled. The reason for this is that they are after all bodily motions. This point plays an absolutely crucial role in how Aquinas in the end views the moral virtues. In the *Summa Contra Gentiles* (SCG) he writes the following:

> Moreover, a human's changeableness in vice and virtue depends not a little on her changeableness in the soul's passions, because, when those passions are curbed by her reason, the human becomes and remains virtuous, whereas she becomes wicked when her reason obeys the impulse

> of her passions. Therefore, as long as the human is subject to change in her passions, she is also changeable in vice and virtue. Now the changeableness which results from the soul's passions is not removable by sacramental grace but remains in the human as long as her soul is united to a passible body.
>
> (SCG 4, 70)

It is the bodily nature of the passions that makes them not fully controllable and makes it impossible for us to reach happiness through the moral virtues. Aquinas writes:

> The purpose of the moral virtues is that through them we may observe the mean in the passions within us, and in things outside us.[25] Now it is impossible that the moderation of passions or of external things be the ultimate end of a human's life, since both passions and external things can be directed to something less. Therefore, it is not possible that the practice of moral virtue be a human's final happiness.
>
> (SCG 3a, 34)

Not only are acts of moral virtue not our final end or happiness, we cannot reach beatitude on our own because of our passions and their bodily nature. This is why we need God's help in the end (SCG 3b, 147).

5 Conclusions

In this chapter, I have presented John of La Rochelle and Thomas Aquinas's systematization of the passions. Naturally, their detailed classifications are important, but another significant aspect of their treatment of the passions is their natural philosophical approach. Passions are dispositions for La Rochelle, and they are motions for Aquinas. Aquinas's account is more detailed and made explicitly with reference to Aristotle's *Physics*. Aquinas's naturalistic account of the passions is systematically applied throughout his works, and the consequences of this view can be seen in his discussion of the moral virtues. It is, he argues, because of their connection to the passions that the moral virtues cannot be our final happiness. Our final happiness instead lies in the infused theological virtues, but we cannot get those in any natural way.

Giles of Rome (d. 1316) and John of Jandun (*ca.* 1280–1328) both picked up on Aquinas's classification later in the thirteenth and fourteenth centuries, but his idea that passions are motions seems not to have been very popular. John Duns Scotus (*ca.* 1266–1308) moved the discussions of passions into a very different direction in the fourteenth century. Aquinas was obviously read and influential later on in the fifteenth and sixteenth centuries, particularly after he became Doctor of the Church in 1567. Even Descartes knew his classification of the passions.[26]

Notes

1 Knuuttila 2011 also contains a good but much shorter summary of the medieval discussions of the passions.
2 See the texts supplied in Knuuttila and Sihvola 2014, 473–478. This collection of texts is essential for anyone interested in medieval philosophical psychology from ancient times up until Kant, and it also contains a great number of texts for the study of the passions.
3 All the translations in this chapter are my own unless I specify otherwise.
4 See Isaac of Stella, *Epistola de anima*, 1878d. The translation is from Knuuttila and Sihvola 2014, 482.
5 Most scholars distinguish between passions and emotions. I use passions throughout this chapter to capture the Latin '*passio*', which is what the authors I talk about here use, but for an account like the Stoics it is more appropriate to use the term 'emotion', since it will involve an active aspect and is under the control of the will.
6 See, for example, Knuuttila 2004 and Sorabji 2000. There are many other studies of the Stoic theory, but please consult these books for further references.
7 Sorabji 2000.
8 On Avicenna's psychological theory, see the chapters by Richardson (Chapter 8) and Taylor (Chapter 3) in this volume.
9 See Avicenna, *Liber de anima seu Sextus de naturalibus*, I.5 (82.42–83.55). For the translation see Knuuttila and Sihvola 2014, 479.
10 Avicenna's psychological story was combined with a compelling medical or physiological story as well. He writes:

> But in so far as the motive power causes a movement, it is distributed through the nerves and muscles and contracts the tendons and ligaments which are connected to the organs towards the starting point of the movement or, in an opposite way, it relaxes and stretches the tendons and ligaments away from the starting point.
>
> (ibid.)

11 For the details of this see Knuuttila 2004, 230–232.
12 Bonaventure used the same terminology to talk about the motivations or inclinations of the will. See Knuuttila 2004, 232. This became very important in the later fourteenth-century voluntaristic tradition.
13 Most medieval philosophers thought that we cannot like or be attracted to what is evil to ourselves. This was mostly discussed in terms of whether we can will evil for the sake of evil. Plato rejected this in *Meno*. See Matthews 2005, Chapter 13, for Augustine's take on the argument in *Meno*.
14 A translation of a relevant passage can be found in Knuuttila and Sihvola 2014, 482–483. See also John of La Rochelle, *Summa de anima*, II.107.
15 The main treatments of this topic are King 1999, Knuuttila 2004, and Miner 2009. See either of these for further references.
16 King 1999 identifies the passion with the passive power, but this is technically not quite right. Knuuttila 2004 has it right.
17 Albert the Great, *De bono* V (195.11–6, 197.5–9). The translation is from Knuuttila and Sihvola 2014, 482.
18 There is an interesting debate about whether a passion can consistently be described as a motion. Aquinas himself raises this objection (ST II-1.26.2.arg. 3), and it is commented on by Knuuttila 2004, 249 and Miner 2009, 38–45.
19 Aristotle was referred to simply as 'the Philosopher' throughout the medieval tradition.
20 The translation is from Knuuttila 2004, 247.

21 See also the following passage: "Passions do not belong to the will, either as commanding or as eliciting them, for the principle of passions as such is not in our power. But things are called voluntary because they are in our power" (*Quaestiones disputatae de veritate*, 26, 6).
22 See chapter 5 of Volume I in this series.
23 See Sorabji 2000, 375–384. As mentioned in the beginning of this chapter, Sorabji thinks Augustine misunderstood the Stoic theory and as a consequence led Christianity astray.
24 See the chapter by Eardley (chapter 11) in this volume.
25 'The mean' is a reference to Aristotle's Doctrine of the Mean, presented most famously in *Nicomachean Ethics*.
26 See Knuuttila 2004, chapter 4 and King 2002.

Bibliography

Primary sources

Albert the Great (1951). "*De bono*," (ed.) H. Kuhle et al., *Opera Omnia*, vol. XXVIII, Munster: Aschendorff.

Aristotle (1984). *The Complete Works of Aristotle*, ed. J. Barnes, Princeton: Princeton University Press.

Avicenna (1972). *Liber de anima seu Sextus de naturalibus*, ed. S. van Riet, Avicenna Latinus I–III, Louvain: Peeters.

Augustine (1981). *De civitate Dei*, eds. D. Dombart and A. Kalb, Corpus Christianorum Series Latina 27, Turnhout: Brepols.

Aulus Gellius (1990). *Noctes Atticae*, ed. P. K. Marshall, Oxford: Clarendon Press.

Cicero (1960). *Tusculan Disputations*, trans. J. E. King, The Loeb Classical Library, Cambridge, MA: Harvard University Press.

Isaac of Stella (1977). "*Epistola de anima*, PL 194, trans. B. McGinn," in (ed.) B. McGinn, *Three Treatises on Man: A Cistercian Anthropology*, The Cistercian Fathers Series 24, Kalamazoo, MI: Cistercian Publications, 155–177.

John of La Rochelle (1995). "*Summa de anima*," in (ed.) J. G. Bougerol, *Textes philosophique du moyen âge* 19, Paris: Vrin.

Plato (1997). *Complete Works*, ed. J. Cooper, Indianapolis: Hackett.

Thomas Aquinas (1948–1950). *Summa theologiae*, ed. P. Caramello, Turin: Marietti.

Thomas Aquinas (1961). *Summa contra Gentiles*, ed. P. Marc et al., Turin: Marietti.

Thomas Aquinas (1970–1976). *Quaestiones disputatae de veritate*, cura et studio Fratrum Praedicatorum in Opera Omnia iussu Leonis XIII P.M. edita, vol. XXII.1–3, Rome: Editori di San Tommaso.

Secondary sources

King, P. (1999). "Aquinas on the Passions," in (eds.) S. MacDonald and E. Stump, *Aquinas's Moral Theory: Essays in Honor of Norman Kretzmann*, Ithaca/London: Cornell University Press, 101–132.

King, P. (2002). "Late Scholastic Theories of the Passions," in (eds.) H. Lagerlund and M. Yrjönsuuri, *Emotions and Choice from Boethius to Descartes*, Dordrecht: Springer.

Knuuttila, S. (2004). *Emotions in Ancient and Medieval Philosophy*, Oxford: Oxford University Press.

Knuuttila, S. (2011). "Emotions," in (ed.) H. Lagerlund, *Encyclopedia of Medieval Philosophy*, Dordrecht: Springer, 290–294.

Knuuttila, S. and Sihvola, J. (eds.) (2014). *Sourcebook for the History of the Philosophy of Mind: Philosophical Psychology From Plato to Kant*, Dordrecht: Springer.

Matthews, G. (2005). *Augustine*, Oxford: Blackwell.

Miner, R. (2009). *Thomas Aquinas on the Passions: A Study of Summa Theologiae Ia2ae 22–48*, Cambridge: Cambridge University Press.

Sorabji, R. (2000). *Emotions and the Peace of Mind: From Stoic Agitations to Christian Temptations*, Oxford: Oxford University Press.

8

SOUL AND AGENT INTELLECT
Avicenna and Aquinas

Kara Richardson

1 Introduction

Avicenna (Ibn Sīnā, d. 1037) was the most prominent of the Aristotelian philosophers who flourished in Islamic lands in the ninth–twelfth centuries. His doctrine of the agent intellect interprets Aristotle's account of understanding in Book III of the *De anima*. According to Aristotle, understanding involves a receptive factor and an active factor. Ancient and medieval interpreters of Aristotle call the receptive factor "material" or "possible" intellect and the active factor "agent" intellect.[1] Like most Greek and Islamic Aristotelians, Avicenna sees the agent intellect as a singular separate substance, not a power of the human soul. His doctrine of the agent intellect concerns its causal contribution to human understanding.[2]

According to Avicenna, the agent intellect plays an efficient causal role in our acquisition of concepts or "intelligible forms". When a potential knower is considering phenomena to which a concept applies and she is adequately prepared to grasp the relevant concept, she receives that concept, which is said to emanate from the agent intellect. On the traditional reading, Avicenna's doctrine of the agent intellect denies that concepts are derived from images of particulars. Rather, concepts exist permanently in the singular and separate agent intellect, which provides them to us (section 8.2).

Avicenna's medieval interpreters tend to assume the traditional reading of his doctrine of the agent intellect. Several Latin theologians embrace a modified version of this view: one that retains its account of the causal role played by a singular separate agent intellect in human understanding but that identifies the separate agent intellect with the divine intellect. By contrast, Thomas Aquinas touts his own doctrine of the agent intellect as superior to Avicenna's. According to Aquinas, we must posit in the human soul an active power for understanding. So the agent intellect is a power of the human soul (section 3). This chapter examines two arguments for this position which feature in several of Aquinas' discussions of the agent intellect.[3] I consider how Avicenna would respond to these arguments.

The first argument appeals to a version of Aristotelian naturalism. It involves two main claims: that sublunary substances operate by means of intrinsic powers and that humanity is the most perfect type of sublunary substance. I argue that Avicenna's account of human understanding is compatible with both of these claims (sections 4–5). I also argue that Aquinas misconstrues Avicenna's singular separate agent intellect as a supernatural cause (section 5).

The second argument appeals to the evidence of introspective observation: we perceive that we abstract concepts from images of particulars. I argue that the evidence in question is compatible with Avicenna's doctrine of the agent intellect as traditionally interpreted. I also argue that Aquinas' argument from experience distorts Avicenna's account of human cognition and diverts attention from some of his important contributions to philosophy of mind (section 6).

2 Avicenna's separate agent intellect

Avicenna's most detailed and systematic discussion of the agent intellect occurs in the *Psychology* of his masterwork, *The Book of Healing*. It achieves two main objectives: to describe our cognitive powers and their interrelations and to explain how we acquire concepts. The account is guided by the idea that human perfection consists in intellectual understanding and the related idea that our "lower" cognitive powers of sensation, imagination and estimation serve our "highest" cognitive power, intellect. Although the account is permeated by these ideas of hierarchy, Avicenna gives due philosophical attention to the "lower" cognitive powers. Indeed, many of his most innovative contributions to the philosophy of mind are found in his discussion of the internal sense powers of imagination and estimation.[4] Still, Avicenna considers these "lower" powers as insufficient for concept acquisition. This requires, in addition, two intellectual powers: the material or possible intellect, which he counts among the powers of the human soul, and the agent intellect, which he sees as a singular separate substance. In this section, I will sketch Avicenna's account of the role of the agent intellect in human understanding.

Following Aristotle, Avicenna analyzes cognition, including concept acquisition, through the lens of a general theory of potentiality or power, which he defines as a principle of change.[5] A power may be receptive; for example, a cool body has a receptive power to be heated. Or a power may be active; for example, a warm body has an active power to heat. Receptive powers are actualized by active powers whenever the conditions for their actualization obtain. For example, a cool body's power to be heated is actualized whenever it comes into contact with a warm body, assuming the absence of impediments. Under these conditions, the cool body undergoes a change: it becomes actually warm, or, in other words, it is brought from potentiality to actuality with respect to heat. Again following Aristotle, Avicenna regards the cool body as the material cause of the change: it is the substratum that endures the change. And he regards the warm body as the efficient cause of the change.

This general theory of powers is applied in the following passage from *Psychology* V.5, which introduces the agent intellect as a cause of human understanding. The passage builds on several ideas established in earlier parts of the *Psychology*: To understand is to acquire a concept or "intelligible form". Concept acquisition is an instance of change. Prior to the change, the human soul is that which can understand φ. As a result of the change, it actually does understand φ. To explain the change, we must posit a receptive power and an active power. The receptive power, called "material" or "possible" intellect, is a power of the human soul. The term "material" reflects the idea that the receptive intellectual power serves as the substratum of the change. Interpreting Aristotle's *De Anima* 3.4, Avicenna argues that to receive concepts, which are abstract entities, "material" or "possible" intellect must be incorporeal.[6] In the following passage, Avicenna begins to describe the active power, called "agent intellect":

> We say that the human soul is at one time something understanding potentially and thereafter becomes something actually understanding. Now, whatever is brought from potency to act is so brought only on account of a cause in act that brings it out. So, there is a cause that brings our souls from potency to act with regard to the intelligibles. Since it is the cause with respect to providing the intelligible forms, it is nothing but an actual intellect in whom the principles of the intelligible forms are separate (*mujarrada*) [from matter], and whose relation to our souls is the relation of the Sun to our vision.[7]

In this passage, Avicenna describes the "cause in act" of human understanding as an intellect that "provides" intelligible forms. Furthermore, he claims that, in order to play its causal role, it must be "an actual intellect in whom the principles of the intelligible forms are separate (*mujarrada*)". By "separate" Avicenna means wholly abstract from, or entirely stripped of, matter. So, in this passage, Avicenna derives his doctrine of the agent intellect from its efficient causal role in concept acquisition. Roughly speaking, he appears to reason that, in order to play its causal role, a cause that "provides" an intelligible form φ must itself possess φ. So, the agent intellect must possess concepts in actuality.

Implicit in this discussion is the view that this intellect is a separate substance, not a power of the human soul. Avicenna has been said simply to assume this view, which was widely held by his Greek and Islamic predecessors.[8] No doubt the influence of tradition partly explains his view. Still, Avicenna's conclusion that the agent intellect must possess concepts in actuality provides philosophical support for his view that the agent intellect is a separate substance. Given that it must possess concepts in actuality, were the agent intellect a part or power of the human soul, each of us would have a complete set of concepts in actuality. But this is contrary to fact. So, the agent intellect cannot be a part or power of the human soul. This reasoning supports the view that the agent intellect is separate substance. (It does not show that the agent intellect is a *singular* separate substance, however. The latter claim requires, in addition, a principle of simplicity.)

Avicenna's claims that the agent intellect "provides" concepts to us and that it must possess concepts in actuality have traditionally been interpreted to indicate that he rejects the view that concepts are derived from images of particulars.[9] Thus interpreted, his doctrine of the agent intellect raises two main questions: Why does he reject the view that concepts are derived from images of particulars? How does he account for the evident relationship between our consideration of images of particulars and our acquisition of concepts? To some extent, these questions are addressed as the previous passage continues:

> Just as the Sun is actually visible in itself and through its light it makes actually visible what is not actually visible, so likewise is the state of this intellect vis-à-vis our souls; for when the understanding faculty reviews the particulars that are in the imagination, and the Active Intellect sheds light into us upon them (which we discussed), things abstracted from matter and its attachments are altered and impressed upon the rational soul not in the sense that they themselves are transferred from the imagination to our intellect, nor in the sense that the intention immersed in the attachments (which in itself and with regard to its very being is separate [*mujarrada*]) makes something like itself. Quite the contrary, [the alteration and being impressed] is in the sense that reviewing them prepares the soul in order that the thing separate from matter [coming] from the Active Intellect [i.e., the intellectual forms] flows down upon them; for acts of cogitation [*afkār*] and reflection are certain motions that prepare the soul in a way to receive what flows down just as middle terms prepare [the soul] to receive the conclusion in the most convincing way, although the first is according to one way and the second according to another, as you will come to know.[10]

In this passage, Avicenna attempts to clarify his account of concept acquisition. One major goal of the discussion is to delimit the role of images of particulars in concept acquisition. He first denies that images of particulars are transferred from the imagination to our (material or possible) intellect. He also denies that images of particulars produce a likeness of themselves, which is then impressed in our (material or possible) intellect.[11] He then contrasts the view that concepts are derived from images of particulars with the view that concepts "flow down" (or emanate) from the agent intellect. So, in this passage, Avicenna appears to consider and reject the view that concepts are derived from images of particulars: he suggests that images of particulars are unable to produce concepts. In this way, he presents additional support for his claim that the agent intellect "provides" our concepts and for his claim that the agent intellect must possess concepts in actuality in order to cause human understanding.

In the passage just quoted, Avicenna seems to reject the view that concepts are derived from images of particulars on the ground that the latter are unable to produce concepts. Still, he affirms that cognitive operations involving images of particulars play some role in concept acquisition. First, he suggests that our receipt of concepts from the agent intellect occurs when we review images of particulars. Second, he mentions cogitation and reflection as "motions that prepare the soul in a way to receive what flows down". In describing these cognitive operations involving images as playing a preparatory role in concept acquisition, Avicenna alludes to a distinction between two types of efficient causes elaborated in his *Physics* and *Metaphysics*: preparers and perfecters.[12] The former prepare a subject for the receipt of some form ϕ, while the latter "give" ϕ.[13] So Avicenna affirms a causal relationship between our consideration of images of particulars and our being prepared to acquire a certain concept. Such preparation is necessary for the receipt of concepts from the agent intellect.

In sum, Avicenna's discussion of concept acquisition in the above passages is the main basis for the traditional reading of his doctrine of the agent intellect: According to Avicenna, the agent intellect "provides" our concepts, which it possesses in actuality. It is a separate substance, not a power of the human soul. Avicenna denies that concepts are derived from images of particulars but affirms that cognitive operations involving images function as preparing efficient causes of concept acquisition. Avicenna's medieval interpreters tend to assume the traditional reading of his doctrine of the agent intellect.

3 Aquinas on the agent intellect as a power of the soul

The *Psychology* of Avicenna's *Book of Healing* was translated into Latin in the twelfth century. Several Latin theologians in the twelfth and thirteenth centuries embrace a modified version of the doctrine of the agent intellect described in *Psychology* V.5: they accept Avicenna's account of the causal role of a singular separate intellect in human understanding, but they identify the separate intellect with the divine intellect.[14] Some saw this modified version of Avicenna's doctrine of the agent intellect as indicating the harmony of Aristotle with Augustinian illumination theory.[15] Aquinas takes a different approach. Against Avicenna, he argues that the agent intellect is a power of the human soul.[16] (It is perhaps worth noting that, though Aquinas sees the agent intellect as a power of the human soul, he also sees it as incorporeal and separable from the human body.) In this section, I introduce Aquinas' doctrine of the agent intellect as illustrated in *Summa Theologiae* I q. 79 a. 4.

In *Summa Theologiae* I q. 79 a. 4, Aquinas treats the question whether the agent intellect is something in the human soul. To begin, he acknowledges that we must posit some superior intellect "from which the [human] soul acquires the power of understanding". He indicates a bit later that this superior intellect is God. He also acknowledges that some identify this superior intellect as the agent intellect of which Aristotle speaks in *De anima* 3, but he rejects this position. He writes:

> But, even supposing the existence of such a separate agent intellect, it would still be necessary to assign to the human soul some power participating in that superior intellect, by which power the soul makes things to be actually intelligible. Such is also the case in other perfect natural things, among which, besides the universal active causes, each one is endowed with its proper powers derived from those universal agents. For the sun alone does not generate man, but in man himself there is the power of begetting man; and in like manner with other complete animals. Now among these sublunary things nothing is more perfect than the human soul. Therefore it must be said that there is in the soul a power derived from a higher intellect, whereby it is able to illumine the sense representations. And we know this by experience, since we perceive that we abstract universal forms from their particular conditions; which is to make them actually intelligible. Now no action belongs to anything except through some principle formally inherent in it, as we have said above, of the possible intellect. Therefore the power which is the principle of this action must be something in the soul.[17]

In this passage, Aquinas attempts to show that we must posit in the human soul a power to make things actually intelligible. Such a power is what is meant by the term "agent" intellect. So, the agent intellect is a power of the human soul. On this ground, he rejects Avicenna's position that "the agent intellect is one in all", as well as the position of some of Avicenna's Latin followers, who identify the singular and separate agent intellect with the divine intellect.[18] He then offers two arguments for the position that the agent intellect is a power of the human soul. He clearly sees these arguments as mutually supporting. Still, each argument presents an independent line of reasoning in support of the conclusion that the agent intellect is a power of the human soul.

The first argument appeals to a version of Aristotelian naturalism. Aquinas observes that, even though perfect or complete natural things are in some way aided in their operations by a superior, universal cause, they nevertheless possess "proper powers" by which they operate. He echoes Aristotle's claim in *Physics* 2 that "man is begotten by man and by the sun as well", which he presumably sees as evidence that his position accords with Aristotle's.[19] He then argues that, because the human soul is the most perfect of perfect natural things, it must possess a power by which it makes things actually intelligible, namely, the agent intellect. In sections 4–5, I address this argument in light of a different version of it found in *Summa Contra Gentiles*.

The second argument appeals to experience: Aquinas says, "[W]e perceive that we abstract universal forms from their particular conditions."[20] He asserts that to perform this action is to make things actually intelligible. So he concludes that we must posit in the human soul a power to make things actually intelligible, namely, an agent intellect. In section 6, I examine this argument in light of a more detailed version of it found in *Disputed Questions on Spiritual Creatures*.

4 Naturalism and the sufficiency tenet

In his first argument in *Summa Theologiae* I q. 79 a. 4, Aquinas suggests that his position on the agent intellect is superior to Avicenna's in that it better reflects the truth of Aristotelian naturalism. This line of argument is puzzling for a number of reasons.[21] For our purposes, the most important of these is Avicenna's own commitment to Aristotelian naturalism. As we have seen in section 2, he explains change, including concept acquisition, in terms of powers possessed by created substances. And he posits in the human soul a receptive power for understanding. Furthermore, many interpreters of Aristotle, including several recent ones, find him to posit a singular and separate agent intellect in *De Anima* 3.5.[22] So it is far from clear that a commitment to Aristotelian naturalism leads to the position that the human soul includes both an active and a receptive power for understanding. Aquinas appears to address this objection in a somewhat different version of his argument from Aristotelian naturalism, which he gives in *Summa Contra Gentiles*.

In *Summa Contra Gentiles* II q. 76 §16, Aquinas writes,

> In the nature of every mover is a principle sufficient for its natural operation. If this operation consists in an action, then the nature contains an active principle; for instance, the powers of the nutritive soul of plants. But, if this operation is a passion, the nature contains a passive principle, as appears in the sensitive powers in animals. Now, man is the most perfect of all lower movers, and his proper and natural operation is understanding, which is not completed without a certain passion, in that the intellect is affected by the intelligible; nor again, without action, in that the intellect makes things intelligible in potency to be intelligible in actuality. Therefore, the proper principles of both [the action and the passion], namely, the agent and possible intellects, must be in man's nature; and neither are separate in being from the soul of man.[23]

In this passage, Aquinas offers an argument for the claim that the agent intellect is a power of the human soul that is similar to his argument from Aristotelian naturalism in *Summa Theologiae* I q. 79 a. 4. This version of the argument also relies on two main claims: (1) In the nature of every mover is a principle sufficient for its natural operation. I will call this claim the "sufficiency tenet". This tenet is similar to the claim in *Summa Theologiae* I q. 79 a. 4 that perfect or complete natural things possess "proper powers", a claim attributed to Aristotle. (2) "[M]an is the most perfect of the lower movers". I will call this claim the "perfection tenet". This tenet is similar to the claim in *Summa Theologiae* I q. 79 a. 4 that the human soul is the most perfect of perfect natural things.

This version of the argument differs from the one in *Summa Theologiae* in that it also compares understanding, the operation distinctive of the rational soul, to nutrition and sensation, the operations distinctive of the nutritive and sensitive souls. Aquinas suggests that this comparative analysis, together with the sufficiency tenet and the perfection tenet, yields the conclusion that the human soul includes both an active and a passive power for understanding and so yields the conclusion that the agent intellect is a power of the human soul. In this section, I examine the sufficiency tenet and its application to understanding, nutrition and sensation. In the next section, I turn to the perfection tenet.

The sufficiency tenet states that in the nature of every mover is a principle sufficient for its natural operation. It assumes a view about the relationship between the nature of a substance and its causal powers, which Aquinas adopts from Aristotle and his followers. On this view, a substance is first and foremost a species-member. Members of the same natural species share the same kind of nature. In the terms of Aquinas' hylomorphic account of substance, a nature is roughly equivalent to a substantial form. Moreover, where a substance is a living thing, a plant or an animal, its substantial form is a soul. Now, to each natural substance belongs a set of principles of operation, an array of active and passive powers common to members of its species. According to Aquinas, these powers "follow" or "flow" from its nature or substantial form.[24] In short, Aquinas' sufficiency tenet assumes this view of the relationship between a nature or substantial form and the set of causal powers common to members of a natural species: The latter are in the former in the sense that they "follow" or "flow" from the former. In addition, the sufficiency tenet asserts that the nature of a substance contains a principle sufficient (*sufficiens*) for its natural operation. So, what is meant by "a *sufficient principle*"?

Aquinas elaborates the sufficiency tenet through two examples of natural operations, nutrition and sensation. He claims that, because nutrition consists in an action, the nutritive soul must contain an active principle for nutrition. Likewise, he claims that, because sensation consists in a passion, the animal soul must contain a passive principle for sensation. To these points we must add, for the sake of clarification, that neither an active nor a passive principle is sufficient unto itself for the occurrence of a natural operation. The exercise of an active principle (an action) requires the exercise of a correlated passive principle. Likewise, the exercise of a passive principle (a passion) requires the exercise of a correlated active principle. In many cases, the correlated active and passive principles required for a natural operation are contained in different bodies. The natural operation occurs when the bodies come into contact, assuming the absence of impediments. For example, in sensation, which is said to consist in a passion, the correlated active principle belongs to an external body, such as a sunflower, whose yellowness is perceived by the animal via its passive power for sight.[25]

In light of Aquinas' examples of nutrition and sensation, it seems that we may interpret the notion of "a *sufficient* principle" as follows: The nature of a mover has a sufficient principle for its natural operation if it contains a power whose actualization is that natural operation. Put another way, where the natural operation of a mover consists in an action, the nature of the mover has a sufficient principle for its natural operation if the nature contains an active power whose actualization is that action. Likewise, where the natural operation of a mover consists in a passion, the nature of the mover has a sufficient principle for its natural operation if the nature contains a passive power whose actualization is that passion.

The implications of my interpretation of the notion of "a sufficient principle" for Aquinas' disagreement with Avicenna are surprising. To repeat, I have argued that, according to Aquinas, the nature of a mover has a sufficient principle for its natural operation if it contains a power whose actualization is that natural operation. Now, as we have seen in section 2, Avicenna considers understanding, the operation distinctive of the rational soul, to consist in a passion, i.e., the reception of concepts, and he also holds that the human soul contains a passive principle, "material" or "possible" intellect, whose actualization is that passion. So, if I interpret Aquinas' sufficiency tenet correctly, it follows that Avicenna attributes to the rational soul a principle sufficient for understanding. Furthermore, it follows that the sufficiency tenet does not help show that we should reject Avicenna's doctrine of a separate agent intellect in favor of Aquinas' view that the agent intellect is a power of the human soul.

It is perhaps worth noting that Aquinas' sufficiency tenet, together with the claim that human understanding *consists in* both an action and a passion, would yield the conclusion that the human soul contains both an active and a passive principle for understanding and so that the agent intellect is a power of the human soul. Aquinas, however, does not assert that human understanding consists in both an action and a passion: he says, instead, that human understanding is not completed without an action and a passion.[26] Furthermore, in the context of the argument, the claim that human understanding consists in both an action and a passion would beg the question against Avicenna: for in the context of the argument, to say that the natural operation of human understanding consists in both an action and passion is just to assert that the human soul contains both an active and a passive principle for understanding. In order to avoid circularity, Aquinas must prove the latter claim.

In sum, on my interpretation of Aquinas' sufficiency tenet, that tenet is compatible with Avicenna's view that the human soul contains only a receptive power for understanding, as well as with Aquinas' view that the human soul contains both active and receptive powers for understanding. So, the sufficiency tenet is compatible with Avicenna's doctrine of a separate agent intellect and with Aquinas' position that the agent intellect is a power of the human soul. In the next section, I consider whether the second main claim in *Summa Contra Gentiles* II q. 76 §16 – namely, the perfection tenet – helps Aquinas make his case against Avicenna.

5 Naturalism and the perfection tenet

The perfection tenet states that man is the most perfect of the lower movers. It assumes that perfection admits of degree and asserts that, of the lower movers, humanity has the highest degree of perfection. By "lower movers", Aquinas presumably means sublunary substances as compared to heavenly ones. No doubt Aquinas considers our status as the most perfect of the lower movers to have various implications. For the purposes of this argument, however, the salient implication has to do with power. In the context of the argument, the perfection tenet suggests that, of the lower movers, humanity has the highest degree of power.

Since the perfection tenet compares humanity to the rest of the "lower movers", I will analyze its role in Aquinas' argument against Avicenna by comparing the human power for understanding to the animal power for sensing, as Avicenna construes these powers.

According to Avicenna, the human power for understanding is similar to the animal power for sensing in being a receptive power, whose actualization depends on an active power possessed by an external thing. In the case of sensation, the external thing is a body, whereas in the case of human understanding, the external thing is an intellect (namely, the agent intellect). But the claim that both powers are receptive does not entail that both involve the same degree of power. On the contrary, according to Avicenna, the human power for understanding is "higher" than the animal power for sensing because it has a "superior" object. His hierarchy of cognitive powers ranks them according to the degree of abstractness of their objects. For example, the power for imagining is higher than the power for sensing because its object is more abstract from matter: this is shown by the fact that the power for imagining does not require for its actualization the presence of the imagined body, whereas the power for sensing does require for its actualization the presence of the sensed body. According to this hierarchy, the power to understand is the highest cognitive power because its object is wholly separate from matter.[27] In sum, while Avicenna sees the human power for understanding as similar to the animal power for sensing in being a receptive power, this similarity seems compatible with the perfection tenet because the former has a more perfect object than the latter.

According to Avicenna, the human power for understanding differs from the animal power for sensing in that it requires for its actualization an active power in a separate intellect. By contrast, the animal power for sensing requires for its actualization an active power in a natural body. This difference does not obviously run afoul of the perfection tenet. Still, I contend that this difference may seem to

Aquinas to run afoul of the perfection tenet when it is considered together with his conception of Avicenna's separate agent intellect. According to Aquinas, if we see the agent intellect as a separate substance, we must see it as a supernatural substance: he says, in *Summa Contra Gentiles* II, a. 76, §17, "[I]f the agent intellect is a separate substance, it is manifest that it is above man's nature." He also suggests that operations that occur by a power possessed by a supernatural substance are akin to miracles and other events that occur "by God's favor [*munus*]".[28] So, by Aquinas' lights, Avicenna sees the human power for understanding to depend for its actualization on an active power in a supernatural substance, and this implies that human understanding is akin to a miracle. From this claim, it follows that Avicenna sees the human power for understanding as different from the animal power for sensing in that the former requires for its actualization a type of supernatural aid that the latter does not require. This view does seem to accord humanity less power than the other animals and so does seem to contravene the perfection tenet. By contrast, Aquinas' own position, that the human soul contains both an active and a passive power for understanding, avoids this problem.

So, perhaps Aquinas' perfection tenet helps support the claim that the human soul contains both an active and a passive power for understanding when this tenet is conjoined with the claim that to posit a separate agent intellect is to posit a supernatural cause of human understanding. Still, there remains a problem with the argument insofar as it targets Avicenna: Aquinas misconstrues Avicenna's agent intellect as a supernatural cause whose effects are akin to miracles.

It is important to emphasize that Avicenna's separate agent intellect is described as exercising its causality without discretion. There is no suggestion that the agent intellect might withhold a concept from a fully prepared human knower. On the contrary, Avicenna claims that, whenever we perform the cognitive operations involving images which prepare us to receive a concept, we receive that concept from the agent intellect as a matter of course. Now, Avicenna does hold that there exist a few human beings who are exceptional in their ability to acquire concepts: they acquire them faster than others and acquire more of them than others. But he does not explain this phenomenon as the result of favor on the part of the agent intellect. Rather, he sees it as the result of differences in cognitive ability across human beings. In short, Avicenna does not consider the separate agent to act with discretion. Rather, he indicates that it always acts in the same way.[29] In connection with this point, it is important to note that, by Avicenna's lights, the acts of any separate intellect, including God, are no more discretionary than the acts of natural bodies, such as fire. This is one reason his views are attacked by Islamic theologians, such as al-Ghazālī, who aim to safeguard belief in miracles.[30]

In sum, Aquinas' perfection tenet, taken by itself, does not support the conclusion that the agent intellect is a power of the human soul. The perfection tenet, together with the claim that a separate agent intellect is a supernatural cause whose effects are akin to miracles, does help support the conclusion that the agent intellect is a power of the human soul. But Avicenna's separate agent intellect is not a supernatural cause whose effects are akin to miracles. So, the line of argument related to the perfection tenet does not succeed against Avicenna's doctrine of the separate agent intellect.[31]

6 Evidence from introspection

As we have seen, in *Summa Theologiae* I q. 79 a. 4, Aquinas also appeals to experience as support for his view that the agent intellect is a power of the human soul: he says that we perceive ourselves to perform the action of abstraction, an action by which we make things actually intelligible. It seems that the type of experience to which Aquinas appeals is introspective observation. He says a bit more about the relevant content of the experience in other versions of the argument. For example, in *Disputed Questions on Spiritual Creatures*, he writes "it is clear from experience" that the human soul has a power to make things actually intelligible:

> For each particular man, whether Socrates or Plato, makes things intelligible in act when he wishes by apprehending a universal from particular things, while he discerns what is common to all individual men from those things that are proper to particular men. So, therefore, the action of the agent intellect, which is to abstract the universal, is the action of this man, as is also to consider or judge with respect to the common nature, which is the action of the possible intellect.[32]

In this discussion, Aquinas identifies the feature of experience to which he appeals as support for his position on the agent intellect: we experience that we distinguish traits common to all members of a kind from those peculiar to one or some. Aquinas glosses this action as that of abstracting the universal and as that of making things intelligible in act. On these grounds, he suggests that experience supports his view of the agent intellect as a power of the human soul.

How might Avicenna respond to this argument from experience? Since his account of the rational soul relies in part on the evidence of introspective observation, we may assume that he considers introspective observation a legitimate source of information about our psychology. Furthermore, in his account of our cognitive powers and their interrelations, Avicenna also mentions that we distinguish the common from the special, and he links this cognitive operation to concept acquisition.[33] It seems, then, that Avicenna accepts Aquinas' evidence and considers it relevant to concept acquisition. But he provides a different explanation of the evidence. After expounding Avicenna's explanation, I will argue that it is compatible with Avicenna's doctrine of the agent intellect as traditionally interpreted.

In *Psychology* V.3, Avicenna mentions our distinguishing the common from the special in the course of a discussion of how the lower cognitive powers aid the rational soul. The lower powers are said to enable us to perform certain cognitive operations because they convey images of particulars to the rational soul. To distinguish the common from the special is one of these cognitive operations.

This discussion follows upon a lengthy account of our various cognitive powers, which is derived from detailed observation of our cognitive acts. In light of that account, we may infer that, according to Avicenna, to distinguish the common from the special involves two powers of the human soul: (i) intellect and (ii) compositive imagination, a brain-based internal sense power. Intellect is a two-sided cognitive power. On the one hand, it functions as the receptive power in concept acquisition, as described in section 8.2. On the other hand, it functions in concert with "lower" cognitive powers. Compositive imagination combines and divides images of particulars acquired through sensation and estimation.[34] While each of these powers operates independently from the other, they also have a joint activity: Compositive imagination operates under control of intellect. As Deborah Black has shown, Avicenna uses the terms "cogitation" (*fikr*) and the "cogitative power" (*al-quwwah al-mufakkirah*) to capture the joint activity of these two powers of the human soul.[35] In light of Avicenna's account of our various cognitive powers, we may infer that to distinguish the common from the special is an act of the cogitative power.

Avicenna links the act of distinguishing the common from the special to conception acquisition. In *Psychology* V.3, he says that, as result of this act, "the principles of conceptualization come about in the soul".[36] This raises the question of how the act in question contributes to concept acquisition.[37] As we have seen, in *Psychology* V.5, Avicenna claims that cognitive operations involving images of particulars are preparing causes of concept acquisition. Given that the act of distinguishing the common from the special is a cognitive operation of this type, it seems likely that Avicenna considers this act to be a preparing cause of concept acquisition. This interpretation is strengthened by the fact that, in *Psychology* V.5, Avicenna specially mentions cogitation (*fikr*) as a preparing cause of concept acquisition. And it seems clear that the act of distinguishing the common from the special is an act of the cogitative power and so an instance of cogitation. As we have also seen, in *Psychology* V.5, Avicenna appears to consider and reject the view that concepts are derived from images of particulars on the ground that images of particulars cannot produce concepts. His conclusion, if sound, helps supports his claim that, although cognitive operations involving images of particulars are preparing causes of concept acquisition, a separate agent intellect "provides" our concepts.

In sum, Avicenna sees the act of distinguishing the common from the special as a preparing cause of concept acquisition. As such, this act is not the cause that brings us from potency to act with respect to understanding. So, by Avicenna's lights, the fact that we perform this act would not count as evidence for the claim that the agent intellect is a power of the human soul. Aquinas, by contrast, considers our performance of this act to make things intelligible in actuality. So, by his lights, it does count as evidence for the claim that the agent intellect is a power of the human soul. It is important to note that both philosophers attempt to explain the evidence in a similar way. Both attribute the act of distinguishing the common from the special to a power of the human soul. In this respect, their explanations are equally satisfactory (or unsatisfactory). It is also important to note that the evidence in question does not help us determine which explanation is superior: it is compatible with both explanations. That is, the evidence in question is compatible with Aquinas' claim that the agent intellect is a power of the human soul, but it is insufficient to establish this claim; we must also determine how the act of distinguishing the common from the special contributes to concept acquisition. Likewise, the evidence in question is compatible with Avicenna's doctrine of the agent intellect as traditionally interpreted, but it is also insufficient to establish this doctrine; again, we must determine how the act of distinguishing the common from the special contributes to concept acquisition.

On my analysis of Aquinas' argument from experience for the claim that the agent intellect is a power of the human soul, it does not succeed against Avicenna, since the argument adduces evidence that is compatible with Avicenna's doctrine of the agent intellect as traditionally interpreted. In addition, it distorts Avicenna's account of human cognition and diverts attention from some of his important contributions to philosophy of mind. When Aquinas asserts that introspective observation tells against Avicenna's doctrine of the agent intellect, he suggests that Avicenna gives short shrift to the evidence of experience in developing his psychology. This suggestion is very misleading. As mentioned earlier, Avicenna's account of our various cognitive powers is derived from detailed observation of our cognitive acts. This suggestion also diverts attention from Avicenna's account of the hybrid cogitative power, which is perhaps among his most original and interesting contributions to philosophy of mind. Furthermore, Aquinas' argument from experience suggests that Avicenna overlooks the contribution of cognitive operations involving images to concept acquisition. This suggestion is taken up by some of Aquinas' interpreters, who consider him to succeed where Avicenna failed in developing a theory of abstraction.[38] I hope to have shown that this reckoning is, at best, premature. To be in a position to adjudicate the dispute, we must first examine Avicenna's account of cognitive operations involving images of particulars, including the act of distinguishing the common from the special, as well as his reasons for denying that such operations are sufficient to produce concepts.

Notes

1 Their disputes about the material or possible intellect are perhaps better known than those about the agent intellect. Most ancient and medieval interpreters of Aristotle consider the material or possible intellect a faculty of the human soul that receives concepts or 'intelligible forms'. So they see the material or possible intellect as multiplied in accordance with the number of human souls. Furthermore, most of these interpreters, including Avicenna and Thomas Aquinas, consider the material or possible intellect as incorporeal. Because this account ascribes to the human soul an incorporeal part or power, it seems to allow for personal immortality. On the other side are the Late Ancient commentator Alexander of Aphrodisias and the twelfth-century Islamic philosopher Averroes (Ibn Rushd). Alexander considers the material or possible intellect as corporeal. Averroes considers it as incorporeal but also maintains that it is a unique, separate substance. According to Averroes, then, neither the material or possible

intellect nor the agent intellect is a part or power of the human soul. Both Alexander and Averroes adopt positions on the material or possible intellect that seem to preclude personal immortality. Alexander's position, however, is more difficult to reconcile with Aristotle's claims in *De anima* 3.4: this text suggests that a receptive intellectual power must be incorporeal in order to play its cognitive role. In contrast to Alexander, Averroes is better able to defend his view as the correct interpretation of Aristotle. Partly for this reason, Averroes' position was the subject of intense controversy in the Latin West, where the correct interpretation of Aristotle was a subject of great interest and where Averroes' commentaries on Aristotle were widely consulted.

2 Following al-Fārābī, Avicenna identifies the agent intellect (the active factor in human understanding described by Aristotle) and the "giver of forms", the lowest of the created intellects in his emanationist theory of creation. The giver of forms is said to beget the rational souls of human beings, as well as the matter and forms of the sublunary world; Davidson 1992, Janssens 2006.

3 Other aspects of Aquinas' reception of Avicenna's doctrine of the agent intellect are discussed in Lee 1981, Weisheipl 1982, Hasse 2000, Taylor 2013.

4 Black 1993, 2000, 2013, Hasse 2000.

5 See Aristotle, *Metaph.* IX 1046a 10–11, Avicenna, *Metaph.* 4.2, Marmura 2005, 131.

6 Avicenna, *Psychology of the Healing*, V.2, Rahman 1952, 209–216.

7 Avicenna, *Psychology of the Healing*, McGinnis and Reisman 2007, 199–200 (trans. slightly modified), Rahman 1952, 234.

8 Hasse 2001, 41.

9 Hasse 2001 challenges the traditional reading on the ground that Avicenna develops a theory of abstraction to explain concept acquisition. See also Hasse 2013. Of course, this view is difficult to reconcile with Avicenna's discussion of the role of the agent intellect in human understanding in *Psychology* V.5. Still, some scholars accept aspects of Hasse's interpretation: Adamson 2004, McGinnis 2006; D'Ancona 2008. On the other hand, Black 2014 argues, decisively in my view, that we should accept the traditional reading. I discuss a key part of this interpretive debate in more detail at notes 33 and 37.

10 Avicenna, *Psychology of the Healing*, McGinnis and Reisman 2007, 199–200 (trans. slightly modified), Rahman 1952, 234.

11 Black 2014, 134–135 explains his reasoning in more detail.

12 Richardson 2013 explains this type of efficient causality.

13 Black 2014, 129–130, 134–135 explains the role of preparatory efficient causes in concept acquisition in more detail.

14 I restrict my account to this Latin variant of Avicenna's doctrine of the agent intellect because it appears to play a role in Aquinas' discussion. Hasse 2000 provides a more comprehensive account of the Latin reception of the doctrine.

15 Hasse 2000, 205 gives four "indisputable examples" of Latin authors who take this view: Roger Bacon, Roger Marston, John Pecham, Vital du Four (Hasse 2000, 205). Gilson 1929 calls this 'Avicennized Augustinianism'.

16 Though Aquinas recognizes that Aristotelians prior to Avicenna held the agent intellect to be a separate substance; he tends to associate this position with Avicenna in particular, presumably because Avicenna's version of the position was influential among his contemporaries.

17 Aquinas, *Summa Theologiae* I q. 79 a. 4.

18 Aquinas, *Summa Theologiae* I q. 79 a. 5.

19 Aristotle, *Physics* II 194b13.

20 Aquinas appeals to introspective observation to support his claim that the agent intellect is a part of the human soul in several texts. In addition to the ones I discuss from

Summa Theologiae I and *Disputed Questions on Spiritual Creatures*, see also *Summa Contra Gentiles*, lib. 2 cap. 76 n. 18.
21 In addition, Aquinas himself acknowledges that God makes some contribution to the operations of natural things, as we have seen in *Summa Theologiae* I q. 79 a. 4. So it seems that Aquinas' own commitment to Aristotelian naturalism is not absolute. On the other hand, in his discussion of Aquinas' *Treatise on Human Nature*, Pasnau 2002, 305–307 suggests that Aquinas may limit God's contribution to natural operations to that of giving us the powers by which we operate.
22 Frede 1996, Caston 1999, Gerson 2004, Burnyeat 2008.
23 *Summa Contra Gentiles*, Book 2, 76.16, Anderson 2001a (trans. modified).
24 Aquinas, *Summa Theologiae* I q. 77 a. 5.
25 I pass over media in sensation for the sake of simplicity.
26 The claim that understanding *is not completed without* an action and a passion does not help show that the human soul contains both an active and a passive power for understanding. This is easily seen from my discussion of the example of sensation. Sensation requires for its completion a passion in the animal and an action by an external body. Yet, according to Aquinas, the sufficient principle for sensation is the passive power contained in the animal soul.
27 Avicenna, *Psychology of the Healing*, II 2, Rahman 1952, 33–34.
28 He says that "an operation which man performs solely by the power of a supernatural substance is a supernatural operation; for instance, the working of miracles, prophesying, and other like things of this kind that men do by God's favor [*munus*]" (*Summa Contra Gentiles* II, a. 76, 17). The force of this claim against Avicenna and his Latin followers is unclear, since they see human understanding as an operation we perform through a receptive power of the human soul. (So they deny that it is an operation we perform *solely* by the power of a supernatural substance.) Against these opponents, a more apt claim would be that, where an operation is performed through a receptive power whose actualization requires an active power in a supernatural agent, the operation is akin to a miracle.
29 It is perhaps worth noting that, according to Avicenna, separate intellects, such as the agent intellect and God, cannot know particulars (Marmura 1962; Adamson 2005). This is another reason Avicenna's agent intellect cannot function as a supernatural cause whose effects are akin to miracles, given that performing a miracle appears to require knowledge of particular events.
30 Al-Ghazālī 2000, 165.
31 On the other hand, it might succeed against those of Avicenna's Latin interpreters who identify the separate intellect with the divine intellect.
32 Aquinas, *Disputed Questions on Spiritual Creatures*, a. 10, my translation.
33

> The mind extracts the simple universals from the particulars by abstracting their intentions from matter and its appendages and accidents, and noting what is common and what unique, what is essential and what accidental. As a result of this, the principles of conceptualization come about in the soul and that [takes place] with the aid of its use of imagination and estimation.
> (Avicenna, *Psychology of the Healing*, McGinnis and Reisman 2007, 192 [trans. slightly modified], Rahman 1952, 221–222)

This passage is among those presented by Hasse 2001 to show that Avicenna considers us to abstract concepts from images of particulars. I maintain, following Black 2014, that this interpretation of the passage cannot be rendered consistent with Avicenna's

claims in *Psychology* V.5 that concepts emanate from the agent intellect and that cognitive operations involving images function as preparing causes. See note 37.
34 Avicenna, *Psychology of the Healing*, Rahman 1952, 169–176.
35 Black 2013.
36 Avicenna, *Psychology of the Healing*, McGinnis and Reisman 2007, 192 (trans. slightly modified), Rahman 1952, 221–222.
37 This is the subject of debate amongst recent interpreters. According to Hasse 2001, Avicenna's discussion of cognitive operations such as distinguishing the common from the special in connection with concept acquisition show him to develop a theory of abstraction to explain concept acquisition. Against Hasse, Black 2014 argues that only the traditional reading can make sense of both Avicenna's claim that cognitive operations involving images of particulars contribute to concept acquisition and his claim that concepts emanate from a separate agent intellect. As we have seen in §2, on the traditional reading, cognitive operations involving images of particulars function as preparing causes of concept acquisition, but the separate agent intellect "provides" concepts to us.
38 Weisheipl 1982, 150, Haldane 1992, 205.

Bibliography

Primary sources

Avicenna (1952). *Avicenna's Psychology: An English Translation of Kitāb al-najāt, Book II, Chapter VI With Historico-Philosophical Notes and Textual Improvements on the Cairo Edition*, trans. F. Rahman, London: Oxford University Press.

Avicenna (2005). *The Metaphysics of the Healing*, trans. M. Marmura, Provo, UT: Brigham Young University Press.

Avicenna (2009). *The Physics of the Healing*, trans. J. McGinnis, Provo, UT: Brigham Young University Press.

Aristotle (1984). *The Complete Works of Aristotle*, ed. J. Barnes, Princeton: Princeton University Press.

Al-Ghazālī (2000). *The Incoherence of the Philosophers*, trans. M. Marmura, Provo, UT: Brigham Young University Press.

Thomas Aquinas (1953). *Quaestiones Disputatae*, 9th rev. ed., Rome: Marietti.

Thomas Aquinas (1997). "Summa Theologiae, Part One," in (ed.) A. Pegis, *Basic Writings of Saint Thomas Aquinas*, Indianapolis: Hackett.

Thomas Aquinas (2001a). *Summa Contra Gentiles, Book Two: Creation*, trans. J. F. Anderson, Notre Dame, IN: University of Notre Dame Press.

Thomas Aquinas (2001b). *Summa Contra Gentiles, Book Three: Providence, Part 1*, trans. V. J. Bourke, Notre Dame, IN: University of Notre Dame Press.

Secondary sources

Adamson, P. (2004). "Non-Discursive Thought in Avicenna's Commentary on the *Theology of Aristotle*," in (eds.) J. McGinnis and D. C. Reisman, *Interpreting Avicenna: Science and Philosophy in Medieval Islam*, Proceedings of the Second Conference of the Avicenna Study Group, Leiden/Boston: Brill.

Adamson, P. (2005). "On Knowledge of Particulars," *Proceedings of the Aristotelian Society* 105, 257–278.

Black, D. L. (1993). "Estimation in Avicenna: The Logical and Psychological Dimensions," *Dialogue* 32, 219–258.

Black, D. L. (2000). "Imagination and Estimation: Arabic Paradigms and Western Transformations," *Topoi* 19, 59–75.

Black, D. L. (2013). "Rational Imagination: Avicenna on the Cogitative Power," in (eds.) L. X. López-Farjeat and J. A. Tellkamp, *Philosophical Psychology in Arabic Thought and the Latin Aristotelianism of the 13th Century*, Paris: Vrin, 59–81.

Black, D. L. (2014). "How Do We Acquire Concepts? Avicenna on Emanation and Abstraction," in (ed.) J. Hause, *Debates in Medieval Philosophy*, New York/London: Routledge.

Burnyeat, M. F. (2008). *Aristotle's Divine Intellect*, Milwaukee: Marquette University Press.

Caston, V. (1999). "Aristotle's Two Intellects: A Modest Proposal," *Phronesis* 44, 199–227.

D'Ancona, C. (2008). "Degrees of Abstraction in Avicenna: How to Combine Aristotle's De Anima and the Enneads in Theories of Perception," in (eds.) S. Knuuttila and P. Karkkainen, *Medieval and Early Modern Philosophy*, Dordrecht: Springer, 47–71.

Davidson, H. (1992). *Alfarabi, Avicenna, and Averroes on Intellect: Their Cosmologies, Theories of the Active Intellect, and Theories of Human Intellect*, New York: Oxford University Press.

Druart, T.-A. (2000). "The Human Soul's Individuation and Its Survival After the Body's Death: Avicenna on the Causal Relation Between Body and Soul," *Arabic Sciences and Philosophy* 10, 259–273.

Freddoso, A. (1988). "Medieval Aristotelianism and the Case Against Secondary Causation in Nature," in (ed.) T. V. Morris, *Divine and Human Action: Essays in the Metaphysics of Theism*, Ithaca: Cornell University Press, 74–118.

Frede, M. (1996). "La théorie aristotélicienne de l'intellect agent," in (eds.) G. Romeyer Dherbey and C. Viano, *Corps et âme. Sur le De Anima d'Aristote*, Paris: Vrin, 377–390.

Gerson, L. (2004). "The Unity of Intellect in Aristotle's *De Anima*," *Phronesis* 49, 348–373.

Gilson, É. (1929). "Les sources greco-arabes de l'Augustinisme avicennisant," *Archives d'Histoire Doctrinale et Littéraire du Moyen Âge* 4, 5–149.

Haldane, J. (1992). "Aquinas and the Active Intellect," *Philosophy* 67/260, 199–210.

Hasse, D. N. (2000). *Avicenna's De Anima in the Latin West: The Formation of a Peripatetic Philosophy of the Soul 1160–1300*, London: The Warburg Institute.

Hasse, D. N. (2001). "Avicenna on Abstraction," in (ed.) R. Wisnovsky, *Aspects of Avicenna*, Princeton, NJ: Markus Wiener Publishers, 39–72.

Hasse, D. N. (2013). "Avicenna's Epistemological Optimism," in (ed.) P. Adamson, *Interpreting Avicenna: Critical Essays*, Cambridge: Cambridge University Press, 109–119.

Janssens, J. (2006). "The Notions of *Wāhib al-Suwar* (Giver of Forms) and *Wāhib al-'Aql* (Bestower of Intelligence) in Ibn Sīnā," in (eds.) M. Pacheco and J. Meirinhos, *Actes du XIe Congrès International de Philosophie Médiévale de S.I.E.P.M., 2002*, Turnhout: Brepols, 551–562.

Lee, P. (1981). "St. Thomas and Avicenna on the Agent Intellect," *Thomist* 45/1, 41–61.

Marmura, M. (1962). "Some Aspects of Avicenna's Theory of God's Knowledge of Particulars," *Journal of the American Oriental Society* 82, 299–312.

Marmura, M. (1981). "Avicenna on Causal Priority," in (ed.) P. Morewedge, *Islamic Philosophy and Mysticism*, Delmar, NY: Caravan Books, 65–83.

Marmura, M. (1984). "The Metaphysics of Efficient Causality in Avicenna (Ibn Sina)," in (ed.) M. Marmura, *Islamic Theology and Philosophy*, Albany: SUNY Press, 172–187.

McGinnis, J. (2006). "Making Abstraction Less Abstract: The Logical, Psychological, and Metaphysical Dimensions of Avicenna's Theory of Abstraction," *Proceedings of the American Catholic Philosophical Association* 80, 169–183.

McGinnis, J. and Reisman, D. (2007). *Classical Arabic Philosophy: An Anthology of Sources*, Indianapolis: Hackett.

Pasnau, R. (2002). *Thomas Aquinas on Human Nature*, Cambridge: Cambridge University Press.

Perler, D. and Rudolph, U. (2000). *Occasionalismus: Theorien der Kausalität im arabisch-islamischen und im europäischen Denken*, Göttingen: Vandenhoeck and Ruprecht.

Richardson, K. (2013). "Avicenna's Conception of the Efficient Cause," *British Journal for the History of Philosophy* 21/2, 220–239.

Taylor, R. (2013). "Aquinas and the Arabs: Aquinas's First Critical Encounter with the Doctrine of Averroes on the Intellect, *In 2 Sent*. d. 17, q. 2, a. 1," in (eds.) L. X. López-Farjeat and J. A. Tellkamp, *Philosophical Psychology in Arabic Thought and the Latin Aristotelianism of the 13th Century*, Paris: Vrin, 59–81.

Weisheipl, J. A. (1982). "Aristotle's Concept of Nature: Avicenna and Aquinas," in (ed.) L. D. Roberts, *Approaches to Nature in the Middle Ages*, Binghamton/New York: Centre for Medieval & Early Renaissance Studies, 137–160.

9

THE COMPLEXITY OF THE SOUL AND THE PROBLEM OF UNITY IN THIRTEENTH-CENTURY PHILOSOPHY

Andrew Arlig

1 Introduction

Medieval thinkers hold that a human soul is simple. This, they think, must be so because the human soul is incorruptible and anything that has parts is corruptible.[1] Yet it is also maintained that there is a vast ontological divide between God and His creation. Only God can be absolutely simple. Created beings, including so-called "simple substances" such as angels, must have some sort of complexity. But where there is complexity, there are parts. Hence, human souls ought to have parts.

However, mereological complexity presents a problem. One job that the soul has is to be the principle of unity for the animate substance. If the soul itself has parts, these parts apparently will need their own principle of unity. How could something that itself needs glue be the glue for something else? This last argument is especially pressing if one thinks, as the majority of medieval Aristotelians do, that the human soul is the principle of unity because it is a form. How can a *form* have parts?

In what follows we will consider several Aristotelian strategies for walking this fine line between simplicity and complexity. We will focus on the thirteenth century because this was a time when Western arts masters and theologians were introduced to the full Aristotelian corpus in Latin translation, along with some treatises (also in translation) from Arabic philosophers such as Avicenna (d. 1037). It is during this period, as Western thinkers attempted to assimilate this new material, that the full range of options begins to appear. By focusing on this period, we will also be able to identify some of the underlying assumptions at work, and in particular, propositions that contemporary philosophers who are otherwise attracted to hylomorphism might not want to take on board.

2 Parameters and obstacles

It is almost universally accepted in medieval disputations at Paris and Oxford that a soul is a substantial *form*. There was nothing inevitable about this, since other authorities, such as Augustine and Boethius, subscribed to the view one finds in Plato's *Phaedo*, namely, that a human soul is a separable substance that is like a form in many respects, but strictly speaking it is not a form. Philosophers would have also encountered this Platonic position in a Latin translation of Avicenna's major treatment of the soul. Avicenna concedes that a soul can be thought of as a form in that it is the *active* part that perfects, or completes, the body and makes the composite human being what it is.[2] However, Avicenna makes it eminently clear that the soul is not a form in the strictest sense of the term; it is only a form in an extended, analogical sense. Avicenna prefers to characterize the soul as the perfecting constitutive part of the whole human being.

This form of Platonism stresses the *per se* subsistence of the soul, and in particular, the notion that at least some souls – namely, intellects – are separable and can exist on their own. Platonism is compatible with one of the central tenets of orthodox theism. Indeed, this is one of the major desiderata for a theory of soul, at least from the perspective of philosophers in our period of focus.

Theological Desideratum: The soul should itself be a self-subsisting thing so that it can survive the separation from the body and persist without being unified with a body.

With respect to this desideratum the Platonic theory seems to have an advantage over the competing Aristotelian proposal that the soul is a substantial form of the individual. For it would seem that a form is not the sort of thing that can exist on its own. Here is how an early reader of Avicenna, John Blund (d. 1248), puts the point.

> The form provides the being, whereas the matter is intrinsically (*in se*) imperfect. Hence, every perfection is a form. Therefore, given that the soul is the perfection of an organic body possessing life potentially, the soul is a form. But no form is a thing that exists *per se* when separated from the substance. Thus, since the soul is a form, the soul cannot be said to be a thing existing *per se* when separated from the substance. Therefore, the soul cannot be separated from the body; it perishes along with the body.[3]

Blund sees this as a reductio of the assumption that the soul is a form. Others in our period took a different lesson from this sort of argument; for they rejected the premise that no form can exist *per se* when separated from the substance that it perfected. Thomas Aquinas (d. 1274) is perhaps the most well-known proponent of this position. His argument for the self-subsistence of the human soul draws upon a notion that is a commonplace in the thirteenth century, namely, that the soul has an operation – specifically, thinking – that does not require the body as an instrument. We will not attempt to evaluate Aquinas's arguments in this chapter.[4] However, in due course, we will explore some of the implications of the notion that a form can be self-subsistent (see section 5).

The soul is not only responsible for personal survival after death; the soul is also responsible for making the animate substance a *hoc aliquid* (lit. "this something"), that is, a unified, individual thing that falls under one of the established kinds of substantial beings.

Metaphysical Desideratum: The soul should be the sort of thing capable of making the ensouled thing a *hoc aliquid*.

Here, the Aristotelian proposal seems to have a distinct advantage over the Platonist. For despite all of Avicenna's clever arguments in the defense of the position that a soul is like a form of the body, he is nonetheless forced to concede that the soul's union with the body is strictly speaking accidental.[5] Even though the soul at the time of its creation is created in a body, and it has a tendency toward its specific body,[6] once it has been created, the soul does not require a body in order to exist.[7] The concession that the Platonic soul would be accidentally tied to the body seems to be a fatal move, as we are then left with the conclusion that the degree of unity found in a composite of a body and a soul is no greater than that which we find in a heap of stones or, perhaps, a sailor in a boat.[8] The problem with accidental unities is that, while there is a form associated with the composite, this form is merely the byproduct of the arrangements and ordering of the material components. These forms don't fuse the material components together and make them into a single substance.

To get this fusion, it seems that one needs a special ingredient, an ingredient that is itself substantial – but substantial in a radically different sense from the substantiality of the material components. Only the infusion of this distinct substantial ingredient into a collection of material parts will suffice in order to get a being that is metaphysically glued together in the right way.[9] It is for this reason, at least in part, that in recent years there has been a renewed interest in hylomorphism as an account for the unity of things.[10] For a form seems to be precisely the sort of thing that can glue the material parts together and make them a *hoc aliquid*.

A form can be the glue required because, as it is often said, a form is a "principle", not a part of an individual substance.[11] What is meant by this slogan is at the very least the idea that a form *qua* principle is not a stand-alone or self-subsisting thing. Matter and form are not like the more familiar parts that one finds in, for instance, a box from Ikea. Unlike the wood, pins, and screws in the box, which one then puts together to get a bookcase, one does not take a form and the material components and then put them all together to make a whole.[12]

Here, then, we have hit upon a tension between two major desiderata. On the one hand, according to the Theological Desideratum, the soul should be a stand-alone thing. But in order to address the Metaphysical Desideratum, it appears that the soul should not be stand-alone or self-subsisting in any robust way.

There is an additional obstacle to the proposition that a soul is a substantial form. It appears that the soul itself is the subject of numerous properties, passions, and activities. I seem to think specific thoughts – say, about the Pythagorean theorem – and I have these thoughts at one time, but not another. Indeed, there appears to have been a time when I was not able to think about the Pythagorean theorem. I had to *learn* it. I also have desires, often of a higher ordered sort, such as the desire to be a better husband or to vote Green whenever possible. Some of these properties and passions might be attributable to the composite human, viz. the soul and the body, but others seem to be properly in the soul alone. Indeed, it is a commonplace in the thirteenth century, one inherited from Aristotle, that thought *cannot* take place in or make use of a bodily organ. We thus have another desideratum, which, because it comes in part from subjective experiences, I will call the Empirical Desideratum:

Empirical Desideratum: The soul itself should be the subject for at least some properties and actions – e.g. thoughts, appetites, and actions of will.

The reason that the Empirical Desideratum puts pressure precisely on the Aristotelian theory is that many, if not most, of the properties, passions, and actions of the soul are accidental forms. But, as we will see later (section 4), it would seem that a form cannot be the subject for other forms.

Of course, merely pointing out that there is a tension between, on the one hand, the Metaphysical Desideratum and, on the other, the Theological along with the Empirical Desiderata does not by itself imply that the Aristotelian project is doomed. Some distinctions, clarifications, and even the occasional innovation might suffice to put Aristotelian hylomorphic doctrine on a firm footing. However, there will be costs, and we might arrive at the position that the costs for doing this are too high.

One issue that will be hounding the Aristotelian as he attempts to negotiate between the three desiderata identified is that the soul is not absolutely simple. It cannot be simple, if it is to perform all the duties ascribed to it. But if the soul has parts, care must be taken to ensure that one does not run afoul of what I will call the Unity Argument. The Unity Argument was well known to medieval philosophers – although, to my knowledge, they never gave it this label – for it appears in Aristotle's *De Anima*.[13] Here is a paraphrase.

The Unity Argument (version 1): Suppose X is constituted by a set of parts P^X. P^X will need something external to it to unify it. Call this Y. But now suppose that Y also has parts, P^Y. P^Y too will need something external to it to unify Y. Call this Z. Z will either be partless or it too will have parts. If Z is partless, then we have found our principle of unity, and Z ought to be the form, not Y. But if not, the argument will run again. And so it might go to infinity. Therefore, if Y had parts, Y cannot be the form.

If the argument is sound, then, assuming that a soul is responsible for the unity of the substance, it would seem that no soul can have parts, or, if it has "parts", it does so in a very loose sense of the term. Yet even though Aristotle sometimes seems hesitant to attribute parts to the soul, there are a host of passages in the psychological corpus where Aristotle claims that the soul is complex without any hint of equivocation.[14] Accordingly, medieval Aristotelians generally do not question *whether* the soul has parts; rather, they are interested in the *way* that a soul has parts. Thus, a more charitable construal of the Unity Argument might be the following:

The Unity Argument (version 2): Suppose X is unified to degree D and that X is constituted by a set of parts P^X. P^X will need something external to it to unify it, namely, Y. But now suppose that Y has a degree of unity that is on the same par as or weaker than X. If that were true, Y would be unable to unify P^X to degree D.

For example, if X and Y were both substances (in the same sense of "substance"), then Y would not be unified to the degree required in order to make P^X into the one substance, X. At best, Y could combine with P^X to form an aggregate.[15]

If we construe the Unity Argument in this second way, the soul could be divided into parts, so long as this division is compatible with the soul being unified to a greater degree than the composite that it unifies. But it should be immediately observed just how high the bar is being set. It is a commonplace that a substance is the best sort of unity,[16] and thus, that a substance's cause of being one should be, if not a fundamental and irreducible principle of unity, a principle of unity that is tighter than the unity that it must impose on the composite. The challenge, then, is to show that none of the divisions of the soul leaves us with a principle of unity that is too weak to meet the Metaphysical Desideratum. We will also need to be constantly on the lookout for places where the soul considered as a form cannot meet either the Theological Desideratum or the Empirical Desideratum.

3 Divisibility in virtue of being in a body

Aristotle begins partitioning the soul by attending to the faculties, or powers, of the soul. This is a strategy that is reinforced by Boethius in his highly influential treatise on division, where he observes that, in addition to familiar wholes, such as quantities, aggregates, artifacts, and animals, we also find that there is the division of the soul into its powers.[17]

Several points are worth emphasizing. First, as we have already noted in the previous section, the default assumption should be that the soul – in some real sense of "part" – has parts. Second, the parts that the soul has are powers. And, third, these parts of the soul are not like other parts. Indeed, the parts of soul may not be anything more than *analogously* like the parts of a line, the parts of a flock, the parts of a house, or the parts of an animal. Indeed, given the Metaphysical Desideratum and the Unity Argument, we should hope that the parts of the soul are not like the parts of more familiar objects. If they were, this would seem to entail that the soul does not have the kind of intrinsic unity that it needs in order to be the principle of unity for the composite human.

Partitioning the soul, then, begins with the soul's powers. But many of the soul's powers only manifest themselves in a body, and then only in specific parts of the body. The power of sight, for example, only appears to manifest in the eye, not in the foot. Most medieval thinkers denied that something could act upon another from a distance. The soul, then, must be present in the body. Yet, if the soul is literally present in the body, where is it? Is it in one part? If so, how can it enliven and perfect all the other parts? If it is in every part, does the soul imbue the body by being partially in one portion and partially in another, or does the soul somehow have the capacity to be "holenmerically" present in the body – that is, to be not only wholly in the whole body, but also wholly in each part?[18]

Let us start with the thought that different powers manifest in different parts of the body because one part of the soul is here and another part of the soul is there. For example, the seeing part is in the eyes and touching part is in the skin. There is even, perhaps, a part of the soul that has no place in the body at all, since it does not require any part of the body to perform its distinctive activity. This would be the intellect.

Medieval commentators associate the view just presented with Plato,[19] and they interpret the Unity Argument as it appears at the end of *De Anima* 1.5 to be a definitive refutation of this Platonic position. It is easy to see why, since it is unclear how a soul composed of spatially discrete parts can have the kind of unity required to then unify the composite human being.[20]

It is interesting, then, to note that there is a minority position in the thirteenth century which *does* propose that the soul is composite in something like this "Platonic" way. Siger of Brabant (d. *ca.* 1283) thinks that there are good reasons to reject the view that the rational soul imbues the human body as its substantial form. A form can either perfect a thing by being its substantial form, or it might perfect a body or a bodily part by operating through it. If a form operates through something, there is no need to posit that this form's essence is *in* that part through which it operates.[21] Siger acknowledges that the mode of thinking that humans typically engage in requires images (*phantasia*), and these do require a bodily instrument. But pure intellection is not a perfection of any body, nor does intellection need any part of a body to operate. If the intellect neither perfects nor operates in the whole body or any of its parts, there is no reason to posit that the intellective soul is the substantial form of the human body.[22]

Siger believes that the human animal has a substantial form. He merely refuses to identify this form with the intellective soul. Hence, he is committed to there being a *composite soul* in a human being.[23]

Siger's position has many affinities to the view that a human is composed of prime matter plus a plurality of substantial forms. This "pluralist" thesis was quite popular in the thirteenth and fourteenth centuries.[24] But here we must tread carefully. The pluralist position defended by most thirteenth- and fourteenth-century masters is not the position that a human is composed of many *souls*.[25] It is the view that a human being is a composite of matter plus a soul *plus additional substantial forms*, where these additional substantial forms are not souls but rather *incomplete* substantial forms. These subordinate substantial forms require the arrival of the final substantial form, the rational soul, in order that there be a complete human being.[26] The reason for this maneuver is that there is a powerful argument in the unitarian's quiver, which draws upon the Aristotelian dictum that the soul is supposed to be the actuality or perfection of the organic body and animal.[27] The basic idea is simple and compelling: once something has been completed, there is no need to have anything else come along to further complete it. Indeed, it is logically impossible to complete something that is already completed. Hence, if one soul is a perfection of the body, any additional souls would have nothing to do. They would be ontologically gratuitous. I call this the **Redundancy Argument**. It is a close cousin of the Unity Argument, and it is one that appears over and over in our chosen period whenever there are disputes about the number of substantial forms in a thing.[28]

In contrast to pluralism, Siger does not posit incomplete forms that stand in relation to superior substantial forms as potencies to some higher actuality. And he seems to do this precisely because of the force of the Redundancy Argument. Thus, he asserts that there is only one substantial form of the body, as the unitarian does. This still leaves Siger with the challenge posed by the Unity Argument. To this, Siger says something quite intriguing:

> One should consider, as the Philosopher says in the second book of the *Politics* [1261a15–22], that if Socrates tries too hard to unify the city, he will destroy it. For a multitude of different parts pertains to the account of a completed composite. And given that a human is a natural composite more perfect than all other [natural composites] – as a certain kind of city [is the most perfect] – it is not absurd or all that remarkable that it is less of a unity than other natural composites which might have only one simple form or perfection.[29]

Siger is challenging one of the key premises that had been pushing us toward finding a way to guarantee the simplicity and unity of the soul. It is an intriguing counterpoint to the unitarian's obsession with ever more perfect unities, but since Siger more or less gives away the game, we will not pursue his position any further. Instead, let us turn to the unitarian position, since this position is attempting to capture all the desiderata without giving up on the unity of the soul.

Let us assume that the soul is one substantial form and that this substantial form is somehow responsible for all the activities of the human organism. This appears to leave us with only two live options: (1) holenmerism or (2) the soul is present in one part, but somehow has the capacity to act upon the rest of the body. Aquinas can be counted among the advocates for the former position. His teacher Albert the Great (d. 1280) is an advocate for the second.

Albert claims that holenmerism is unintelligible; instead, he insists that the soul is in the heart but somehow is able to radiate its powers out from the center to all the limbs.[30] Albert doesn't offer any reasons why holenmerism is unintelligible. But it is not too hard to see why the view is troubling. To propose that a soul is holenmerically in the organism is to posit that a particular can be wholly present in more than one place at the same time. In short, a particular thing has the property associated traditionally with a universal thing.[31]

Holenmerism also appears to have this troubling consequence: by hypothesis, the entire soul is in the foot, and the soul as a whole perfects the body and makes it an animal. Hence, the foot should be an animal. John Blund uses this line of reasoning to demonstrate that the human soul cannot be split into an incorporeal (i.e. rational) part and a corporeal (sensitive and vegetative) part. For our purposes, we can overlook the context, as we are not interested in Blund's particular target. Rather, we should focus on the reason why a soul – whether itself corporeal or incorporeal – cannot be "spread out through", that is wholly present in, each part of the body.

> Let one pick out some peripheral part of the vegetating, sensing body, such as a finger. Then, proceed as follows: This body is animate and capable of sensation, since it is made to vegetate and it is made use of by a sense, namely, touch. "Animate body capable of sensing" is convertible with "animal". Therefore, since this [finger] is a body that is animate and capable of sensing, it will be an animal, as this just is the definition of animal: an animal is an animate body capable of sensing. Yet this is a finger of a human being. Therefore, a finger of a human being is an animal. And in the same manner one can point to an indefinite number of human parts [and say] that they are animals.[32]

This argument, which we might call the Problem of Too Many Animals, is quite popular. One can find it being alluded to in the middle of the twelfth century, and it is all over the literature in the thirteenth and fourteenth century.[33] While we cannot trace the history of this argument here, it is worth pointing out that it does put pressure on the holenmerist to explain why the soul does not in fact perfect each part in such a way that each is an animal.

The proponent of holenmerism might be in a position to answer these worries, and there is a good reason to see whether this is possible. For holenmerism seems to help the Aristotelian to answer the demands of the Metaphysical Desideratum. As Aquinas observes, a soul must be wholly present in each part in order to make that part a part *of a substance*. If the human soul were to leave the body, the material thing left over would be a human body only in name. Likewise, unless the form were present in each part of the body – e.g. the hand or bone – these things would be hands or bone in name only.[34]

Aquinas's argument to this point still leaves open the possibility that the soul might wholly inform each part by splitting up the task – that is, that the soul will inform both the whole and each part of the body by having one soul-part informing the hand and another, distinct soul-part informing the eye. To block this move, Aquinas must demonstrate that a soul cannot be divided into distinct soul-parts, or partial forms. This is precisely what Aquinas now tries to do by observing that there are three kinds of wholeness: (1) There is the kind of whole that is divided into quantitative parts. (2) There is the kind of whole that is divided into parts of a definition or essence. Finally, (3) there is the power whole, which is divided into power-parts. To get a form to inform its whole in a part-by-part manner, one would have to be able to divide the soul quantitatively. But Aquinas insists that this not possible. Quantitative divisibility fails to apply to forms, save in some cases, when it does so accidentally. What Aquinas has in mind is the case of the whiteness in a white wall, which can be divided accidentally by attending to the whiteness in this half-wall and the whiteness in the other half. Both halves, taken individually, are white things. Such a phenomenon, however, is not available in the case of a soul.[35] If we combine the fact that the soul cannot be cut up into partial souls – in any relevant sense – with the fact that the soul must be the substantial form of the body, then it follows that the soul must inform the whole body as a whole and each part of the body as a whole.

Given that a substantial form must be holenmerically in the body in order to make the animal one substance, Aquinas must address the worry about the Problem of Too Many Animals. Aquinas is indeed aware of the problem; he quotes the argument as one of the objections that he needs to reply to in order to establish that holenmerism is true. He replies by first conceding that the soul is wholly *in* each part in terms of its essence and perfection. The reason why we do not end up with barbarous assertions such as that a foot is an animal or, even, that an eye is a foot, is due to the fact that the soul is not wholly present in each part with respect to the totality of its power.[36] The soul requires a diverse array of parts, each with its own specific configuration and structure, to do all that the soul does. An eye cannot be a foot, because the eye is specially configured to receive visual forms and, thus, it is not configured to run or walk. Since a foot is configured in such a way that the animal can run, walk, and stand, it cannot receive visual forms. Furthermore, even though the whole essence of the soul is there in the foot or eye, no one part can do everything that the animal does.[37] Hence, neither the foot nor the eye can be an animal. Finally, and this seems to be the most crucial point for Aquinas, the whole animal is ontologically prior to the parts of the animal. The definition of the eye (or foot) includes the definition of the animal, and hence the essence of the eye requires the essence of the animal. One can have an animal without a left eye, but there cannot be a left eye without the animal. It is ultimately these facts about the way in which the soul perfects the body and the ontological subordination of the parts to the whole that explain why our barbarous sentences are false.

We are now in a position to see that our Aristotelian must assert that the soul is able to perfect and operate on the whole body either by being situated in one part but radiating its powers out to the other parts (Albert's view), or by being wholly present in each part of the body (holenmerism). We can also now see that holenmerism works best if one subscribes to the Aristotelian principle that the organic parts of the animate substance are ontologically dependent upon the whole. Finally, we have seen that to preserve the unity of the soul, one must posit either that some forms are incomplete or that there is only one substantial form. This is already an impressive list of commitments that someone flirting with Aristotelian theories of the soul must consider taking on board.

But before we move on, one more cost must be noticed. The unitarian, it seems, will need to revise our understanding of embryology. When building his case for the composite soul, Siger leans on the fact that the vegetative and sensitive powers of the soul are something that are "educed", or derived, from the matter in the mother's womb. Sometimes this is asserted by an appeal to Aristotle's authority.[38] But there is some plausible empirical evidence for this as well. For it seems that the human embryo metabolizes and senses well before it has the power to think. A unitarian, therefore, will need to either posit that thinking is also educed from the matter, or that embryonic development involves a lot more substantial changes than one might think. Aquinas famously goes for the latter view, and he takes on all the attendant worries that this position entails.[39] Specifically, Aquinas will need to concede that there is not one moment of substantial generation, which occurs at conception, but rather several moments of substantial generation in embryological development.

Whether this sort of unitarian view is worth the costs that the system incurs will depend, again, on whether the system as a whole provides a satisfactory account of human nature. But we need to get several more things in place before we should dare to enter into that sort of appraisal.

4 Powers and collections of powers

Now that we have found ways to ensure that the manifestation of powers in the body do not compromise the unity of the soul, we are in a position to look at the soul proper and to examine once more Boethius's claim that the soul is a whole divisible into its powers. For this remark by Boethius would, at least at first blush, seem to compromise the unity of the soul.

It would seem that a part of some whole along with all the other parts constitutes the whole – i.e. makes it exist. Indeed, Boethius claimed that the "substance of the soul is combined out of these powers".[40] So, if the powers are parts, we need to be very clear about what precisely is constituted by them. If, as Boethius's dictum suggests, the soul *qua* substance is constituted by the powers, this would seem to imply that the soul is a complex item that is itself in need of an external principle of unity. The Unity Argument, accordingly, is lurking just around the corner.

One way out of this mess would be what was proposed by Ockham and other fourteenth-century thinkers, namely, that the powers of the soul are merely ways of considering and talking about the soul. In other words, there was merely a conceptual distinction between the powers and the soul *qua* substance.[41] Several prominent thirteenth-century masters also collapsed the divide between the powers of the soul and the soul itself by asserting that the soul is essentially the same as its powers and that their diversity is explained by the diversity of their acts only.[42] They seem to have held this position not so much because they had a sophisticated reductivist agenda (as Ockham did) but rather because of some claims by Augustine that were collated and presented in Peter Lombard's (d. 1160) *Sentences*, which was the standard theology textbook in the Middle Ages. In particular, Augustine claimed that memory, the will, and the intellect are one life, one mind, and one essence.[43] Many thirteenth-century philosophers and theologians took Augustine's remark to be an assertion of the identity of the soul with its powers.

But many masters were resistant to identifying the soul with its powers.[44] A little reflection will reveal why there was resistance to tightening the unity of the soul to the extent that a soul's powers are not distinct from its essence. Powers seem to be properties of a substance, whereas the soul is supposed to be a substance, in the sense of substance *qua* form, or substance *qua* subject, or both. As it happens, our Aristotelians tend to assert that the soul is a substance in both senses. We have already noted the oddity of suggesting that a form can itself have properties. However, this is something that our Aristotelians are willing say; it is a part of the framework that we will consider purchasing later on. If a soul is a subject of the powers it has, there seems to be no way to avoid the conclusion that each power is really distinct from the substance that is the soul.[45]

Once forced to concede that a power must be really distinct from the soul, the next best position appears to be one in which the power is nevertheless inextricably tied to the soul's substance; that it be, in other words, an essential property or quality of the soul. For if a power were merely accidental, it would seem that we could have in principle a naked soul. But what would such a thing be?

> Again, memory and the others are either in the soul accidentally or essentially. If accidentally, then *soul* can be understood without this. And the same argument applies to intelligence and will. Therefore, *soul* can be understood without *rational*.[46] But this is false.[47]

It would be difficult to pinpoint the soul's essence and definition if one cannot make reference to the soul's acts and powers. And there is another problem with the notion that the powers are accidents. Accidents do not sort things into distinct kinds of substances. Hence, if the powers were accidents, a rational soul would not differ substantially from an irrational soul.

If the powers of the soul were essential properties of the soul, it would seem that they nevertheless ought to be essential qualities, since powers are one kind of quality. This would not have been too hard on a thirteenth-century ear, since this would suggest that powers are the *differentiae* of the soul.[48] *Differentiae* are *essential* qualities. This is an innovation, but it was perhaps a necessary innovation precisely because the *differentiae* seemed to need a place within the substance-accident framework introduced by Aristotle. And it was an innovation that was eagerly accepted by medieval thinkers and employed in contexts precisely like the present one.

One attractive feature of considering the powers as *differentiae* is that they would be in a sense "internal" structural features of the soul, not properties inhering in the soul as a subject.[49] That is, they would be parts of the soul's definition, and hence essence, not parts in the sense of ingredients out of which a soul is constructed. For this reason, we will return to the idea that the soul is complex only in the sense that it has definitional parts in section 5. For the present, however, we will only suggest that this ought to be how thirteenth-century philosophers should think of powers *qua* essential qualities. Any other paradigm would quickly turn the soul *qua* substance into an integral whole consisting of properties. This in turn would quickly invite in the troubles raised by the Unity Argument.

Other thirteenth-century masters, however, thought that positing powers as essential properties of the soul was too tenuous a position. The powers had to be accidental properties, although accidental properties of a special sort. One especially powerful reason behind this position was that, in the natural order of things, agents cannot be the immediate origins of accidental *effects*.[50] The effects of thinking, sensing, and metabolic processes are accidental; hence, it must be the case that the immediate source of these effects is also an accident.

But it seems odd to assert that an animal's sensitive capacity is accidental, since that seems to imply that it is a contingent feature of the animal. If an animal failed to sense, wouldn't it fail to be an animal? If I were to permanently lose my capacity to think, wouldn't there be legitimate sense in which I have ceased to be a human? The solution is to help oneself to the Aristotelian notion of a *proprium*, that is, an accident which is, nevertheless, always found along with the substance that possesses it.[51]

> I say that some accidents belong to the species, and some to the individual. Some of the accidents that belong to the individual are separable, and others are inseparable. Accidents in the first sense, that is, that belong to the species, are not found without that whose accidents they are. [. . .] With this in view, I say that the accidents of the soul, the ones that are its powers, are accidents that belong to the species, and thus, they cannot *not* exist, even though they do not belong to the essence of the soul.[52]

Although, this author does not use the term "proprium", clearly it is behind the notion that he does appeal to, namely, the sort of accident that is possessed by the species, and hence, inseparable from things belonging to that species.

One might wonder whether the difference between this position and the position that the powers are essential properties of the soul trades on a terminological dispute. I suspect that it does not. Proponents of the view that the powers are essential properties of the soul tend to focus on the idea that the powers in some real sense complete the being of the soul. The soul could not be understood, or even be, without its powers. The position that a soul's powers are accidents, albeit inseparable ones, does not carry with it this commitment.[53] And there might indeed be theoretical advantages to drawing the line between substance and accident in this manner. For example, it will allow the soul to have incompatible properties, such as both active and passive capacities. If this means that the soul's "naked" substance is unintelligible to a human mind, so be it. In fact, it was a relatively common scholastic position that the naked substance was unintelligible to the unaided human intellect.[54]

But there is a sense in which it does not matter whether the powers are accidents or essential properties of the soul. Either way, we seem to be stuck with the surprising thesis that a form can be the subject for other forms. Forms, however, do not seem to be the right sort of thing for being subjects of inherence; that is a role played by either matter or a hylomorphic composite. There is not only the weight of authority behind such a restriction,[55] there is also a conceptual reason. Form's natural correlate is something that is in need of perfection; for it is the form that does the perfecting. To suggest that a form itself is a subject for forms is thus tantamount to the view that a form itself has some potentiality in it. If we did not like the pluralist's "incomplete" forms, surely we now should resist the thought that any form can be the subject of another form.

It appears that our Aristotelian has two options: fall back on the Ockhamist reductive strategy mentioned earlier, or innovate. It is, thus, interesting to see that some Aristotelians in our period picked the latter.

> In opposition to the first, one should reply that some accidents are real. Examples of these are the white, the dark, and things of this sort, and for these kinds of accidents it cannot be the case that a simple substance is their subject. But other accidents are intentional, and for these kinds a simple substance can very well be a subject.[56]

While it might at first glance appear that an "intentional" accident is some sort of logical construction, I don't think that this can be the meaning of the distinction. This author is clearly concerned with the phenomena epitomized by our Empirical Desideratum, and hence, the accidents in question cannot be merely logical abstractions. They must answer to something out there in the world. (It should also be remembered that when medievals talk about something being "real", they often have a much more restricted notion in mind than our English word connotes.) Hence, I think that what we are seeing here is an attempt to distinguish between two kinds of forms that things can have, and one kind is precisely such that it can inhere in a simple substance. I won't press whether this is a promising strategy. Instead, I merely note that this is one more commitment that the Aristotelian might need to take on board to meet the Empirical Desideratum.

There is one more issue that needs to be addressed when it comes to the powers of the soul and their relation to the soul *qua* substance. Unless one has a view whereby the powers are merely ways of talking about the substance itself, these powers are real. Since no collection of accidents can be a substance, there must be a sense in which the soul *qua* substance and the *collection* of its powers must be really distinct things. This seems to be behind Albert the Great's interpretation of Boethius's cryptic remark (mentioned at the beginning of this section) that the "substance of the soul is combined out of these powers". When glossing this passage, Albert carefully distinguishes between the soul *qua* substance and a "whole of powers" (*totum potestativum*).[57] Boethius's comments about the division of the soul, he insists, are only about the latter.

> The substance of the soul is combined or composed out of these potencies or powers with respect to that which it is, because it is in this sense the principle of life and motion. Yet, "principle of life and motion" names a potential whole, not an absolute substance.[58]

In order to appreciate Albert's solution, it is helpful to see how he introduces the notion of the whole of powers.

> There is something called a whole which is something like an intermediary between these two [viz. the integral whole and the genus]; this is the whole of powers, which is composed out of certain faculties or powers, in the way that a soul, in so far as it is a whole of powers, is composed out of power for thinking (that is, the rational power) and out of the power for sensing and out of the power for performing basic life functions (*vegetandi*). The whole of the soul, in so far as it is the principle of life and change, consists of these powers. And again a regime (*regnum*) is a whole of this kind, given that it consists of its powers, namely, the king, the prefect, the superintendent, and others of this sort.[59]

Albert is thinking of the regime in terms of an act or role, which is analyzable and hence consists in smaller roles and their associated powers.[60] The complete list of the roles in regimes would give a full account of *being a regime*. But while a particular regime will require some of these roles and their attendant powers, it need not possess all of them. The same is true of souls. A complete list of all the powers that go into something being alive and self-moving will provide the whole account of what it is for something to have a soul. Nevertheless, it is still true that not all souls will possess the power to reason, and many will even lack the sensitive powers.

The example of the regime also helps us to see why the whole of powers is not the substance itself, even though it does give us a complete account of what the substance does. A regime might need an executive, a judiciary, and a legislature. But it does not follow from this fact that there are three really distinct things. One thing could play all three roles. Likewise, the fact that the whole consisting of psychological powers is multiplex does not imply that the soul itself is a composite of many things. In Albert's view, then, powers are in some respects like the parts one finds in more familiar objects, which he calls "integral wholes". But they do not combine in such a way as to constitute the soul itself; rather they combine to constitute a complex property that is distinct from the substance that this complex property points to and fully characterizes.

5 Self-subsistence and structure

We have been counting up the propositions that the Aristotelian must take on board if she wants to maintain that the human soul is a substantial form. So far, the burden is perhaps not too great. But as we noted in section 2, we need to consider what the Aristotelian must take on board in order to meet the demand of the Theological Desideratum.

Recall that the human soul must be able to subsist in its own right. Yet it would appear that any self-subsisting thing – even a self-subsisting form – must have something analogous to hylomorphic structure. This position, well known by the name of "universal hylomorphism", can be traced back to the twelfth-century Andalusian philosopher Solomon ibn Gabirol. It was endorsed by a number of both major and lesser thinkers in the thirteenth century. Perhaps the most prominent of these was Bonaventure (d. 1274).[61]

Bonaventure's argument pertains to angels, but it should be clear how his line of reasoning also will apply to a human soul, assuming that it too is self-subsistent and capable of being the subject of accidents. Bonaventure first observes that there are numerous kinds of composition. Some of these kinds of composition are unquestionably applicable to angels and *a fortiori* human souls. An angel, for example, is "composite" when considered in relation to its principle, or causal, origin. An angel is also composed out of its substance, or actuality, and potency, for if there were no potency in an angel, it would be absolutely actual – i.e. a god. Parallel to this metaphysical structure, an angel has a logical composition, namely, a composition of genus and differentia. Finally, all created substances, including angels, are composed of their being and their essence. Therefore, even though an angel is said to be simple, it is not absolutely simple, since it exhibits these aforementioned modes of composition. At the same time, Bonaventure acknowledges that angels lack some forms of composition. They are not composed out of quantitative parts, and they are not composed out of "a corporeal and a spiritual nature", by which he means a soul and a body.

This much, Bonaventure takes to be agreed upon by all comers. Where he breaks ranks with his opponents is on the question of whether angels have hylomorphic composition. Bonaventure identifies four phenomena that, he believes, will force us to concede that angels and rational substances in general must have hylomorphic structure:

(1) Rational substances are changeable, which means that there must be the proper internal structural features to accommodate change, namely, an active ("formal") part and a passive ("material") part.
(2) Rational substances both act and suffer; there must be the proper internal structural features to accommodate, namely, an active ("formal") part and a passive ("material") part.
(3) Rational substances are individuals. All individuals must have a principle of individuation. The only principle of individuation available is the combination of a formal element with a material element.
(4) Rational substances have an essence and a definition, which requires that there be both a part that is responsible for the substance belonging to a general class (the genus) and a part that is responsible for the substance belonging to its most specific class. The former is a "material" element, the latter a "formal" element.

Bonaventure's opponent must concede that all created substances, including angels, exhibit these phenomena. The challenge is thus to explain the metaphysical grounding of these phenomena. Bonaventure insists that there is no intelligible option for explaining these phenomena other than to posit that the metaphysical parts that make these phenomena possible are a material nature and a formal nature. Bonaventure even concludes that while spiritual matter and corporeal matter differ with respect to how they exist, when it comes to their essence, they are the same.[62]

If Bonaventure were right, the results would be quite remarkable. First and foremost, if a soul were a form, then a *form* would itself have hylomorphic structure. It would also seem that the soul would be corruptible. Substantial generation is the "arrival" (*advenere*) of a substantial form into some matter. This idea is clearly at the root of Bonaventure's thought. In order to be a created substance, there must be substantial generation. Hence, a created substance must have hylomorphic parts. But anything that can be put together can be taken apart. If something can be substantially generated, it can also be substantially corrupted. Thus, if an angel or a human soul has hylomorphic structure, it must be corruptible. But this is not compatible with either theistic doctrine or even secular authority. Aristotle and Avicenna, for instance, both claim that an intellect is impassible and incorruptible. Therefore, no intellect – angelic or human – can have matter as one of its parts.[63]

It should be obvious why an Aristotelian would want to resist universal hylomorphism. It is interesting to note, then, that many opponents of universal hylomorphism concede that there is something *analogous* in structure to hylomorphic composition in immaterial created things.[64] Bonaventure insists on the need for metaphysical elements that explain the generation as well as the operations and properties of intellects. Many of his opponents not only agree but even acknowledge that one of these metaphysical elements must be a passive principle or nature. One could perhaps forgive a Bonaventure if he expressed some exasperation at this point: Isn't a passive metaphysical part matter? In other words, does the difference between Bonaventure and the Aristotelian rest on a terminological dispute?

Perhaps it does, but we will not pursue that possibility. Rather, let us grant that these active and passive metaphysical parts are not form and matter. The more fundamental issue is whether these metaphysical parts of the soul are real. It turns out that many Aristotelians conceded that they are.[65] Assuming that they are, we are once again left with the awkward thought that a form has quasi-hylomorphic metaphysical structure. It also seems that the Unity Argument is once more lying in wait. As we noted at the beginning of this chapter, parts imply decomposability and dependence. Worse, and more to the point at issue, the existence of parts entails the existence of an external principle of unity. Is the glue that holds these quasi-formal and quasi-material parts together going to be good enough to thereby guarantee the unity of the composite human being?

Our thirteenth-century Aristotelians thought that they had an answer to this challenge: Not every kind of composition entails decomposability. For example, consider the definitional parts of a substance. All substances have a definition, which means that in some sense they are "composed" out of a genus and substantial *differentiae*. There is much discussion in this period, as well as the periods prior to the thirteenth century, as to whether the parts of a thing's definition are merely logical abstractions or whether they indicate some structural features in the thing itself. Even many of those who settled on the latter view thought that the resulting compound was only in a distant sense like a hylomorphic composite.[66] The Aristotelian, by the way, was not alone in resorting to this maneuver. For example, when Avicenna attempts to demonstrate that the human soul is incorruptible, he does not deny that the soul lacks any parts, he only argues that the soul lacks the kinds of parts that would entail that it is corruptible.[67]

6 Conclusions

We have examined some of the challenges to the unity of the soul that a thirteenth-century advocate of the thesis that a soul is a form must address. It would seem that none of these challenges is insurmountable. But what this exercise does reveal is that there are a number of assumptions and principles that the thirteenth-century Aristotelian must take on board in order to maintain that a human soul is the substantial form of the body. Here are a few of them that we have encountered:

(1) Either the soul is not in every part of the body, but somehow radiates out and perfects all of them, or the soul is holenmerically in the body. (Section 3)
(2) The ontological priority of the whole to its organic parts and the Aristotelian principle of homonymy. (Section 3)

(3) A commitment to either pluralism, and hence "incomplete" forms, or unitarianism, which seems to entail that substantial generation occurs more often than it would at first seem. (Section 3)
(4) That there are necessary accidents. (Section 4)
(5) That a form can be the subject of other forms, which seems to require two distinct kinds of forms. (Section 4).
(6) That at least one kind of substantial form can be analyzed into an active element and a potential element. (Section 5)
(7) That some modes of composition, while real, do not imply decomposability, let alone the dependence of the composite upon these components. (Section 5)

None of these alone or in combination appears to entail any absurdity. But, as I already mentioned, metaphysical systems are often best evaluated holistically. The elements just identified seem to be what one must take on to get this particular thirteenth-century Aristotelian system off the ground. Whether contemporary metaphysicists or psychologists are willing to buy this total package is something that I will leave for them to decide.

Of course, another option is to disown one or more of the fundamental desiderata that pushed our thirteenth-century Aristotelian in this particular direction. Clearly, many contemporary philosophers will not feel the pull of the Theological Desideratum. Many might also be willing to disown the Empirical Desideratum as well and instead embrace something akin to functionalism. Such philosophers would then be free to fall back on the primary Aristotelian thought that a form is not a thing, but rather a principle. But if they do so, it should be appreciated just how distant a cousin their theory is to the Aristotelian systems examined here.[68]

Notes

1 The link between complexity and corruptibility is commonly asserted in discussions of Divine Simplicity. See, e.g., Thomas Aquinas *Summa Theologiae* 1.3.7. For the application of this assumption in the specific case of the human soul, see Avicenna *De Anima* 5.4 (esp. 121–124) and also his *Kitab al-Najat*, 2.6.13 (English translation of the Arabic: Rahman 1952, 58–63). All translations from Greek and Latin originals are mine.
2 Avicenna *De Anima* 1.1.
3 John Blund *Tractatus de Anima* II.i.15; 1970, 5.
4 See Thomas Aquinas *Summa Theologiae* 1.75.2, and the discussion in Pasnau 2002, 48–57.
5 Avicenna *De Anima* 1.1, 5.4, 5.7; *Najat* 2.6.12–13. See also John Blund, *Tractatus de anima* II.i, 15–16.
6 Avicenna denies that souls pre-exist the body and that they can migrate from one body to another: *De Anima* 5.3–4; *Najat* 2.6.12 and 14 (Rahman 1952, 56–58 and 63–64).
7 *Najat* 2.6.12; Rahman 1952, 58.
8 See, e.g., Pasnau 2002, 79–88.
9 The locus classicus for this sort of argument is Aristotle's *Metaphysics* 7.17, 1041b18–28.

10 Johnston 2006 and Koslicki 2008.
11 Johnston 2006, 672–675.
12 Indeed, for Aquinas, *both* the matter and the substantial form are merely principles.
13 *De Anima* 1.5, 411b5–14.
14 Here is a partial list: *De Anima* 2.2, 413b5–9, 413b13–16, 413b27–414a1; 3.4, 429a10–18; *On Memory* 450a16–18; *On Sleep and Waking* 454a11–14. See also the discussion in Johansen 2012, 49 sqq. and Corcilius and Gregoric 2010, 82–85.
15 Medieval thinkers are aware of an Aristotelian dictum that no substance can be composed out of parts that are themselves actually substances. (See Aristotle *Metaphysics* 7.13, 1039a3–11; and Aquinas *Sententia Metaphysicae* loc. cit., as well as ibid., book 5, lectio 21 nn. 18–19.) It would seem that the thought process at work in the Unity Argument is behind this Aristotelian dictum as well.
16 See Aristotle *De Anima* 2.1, 412b6–9.
17 Boethius *De div.* 887d-888a.
18 This formulation is attributed to Augustine (*De Trin.* 6.6; cf. Aquinas *Summa Theologiae* 1.76.8 sed contra). On holenmerism, see Pasnau 2011, 337–349.
19 See Albert the Great *De Anima*, Book 2, tract. 1, cap. 7 (1968, 75). The attribution is not wildly off the mark. One could easily interpret Plato's *Timaeus* 69c sqq. in this manner (cf. *Republic* 434–441).
20 This is true even if the parts of the soul were homogenous. The thought that the parts of the soul – if there are any – are homogenous is taken from Aristotle's observation about what happens when one cuts a plant or a worm in two (*De Anima* 1.5, 411b24–27; 2.2, 413b18–19; cf. *On Length of Life* 6, 467a18–23; *On Youth* 468a23–b12). Some plants, when cut into spatially distinct parts, will yield two plants. Likewise, when a worm is cut into two, both parts will wriggle and respond to pokes and prods (at least for some time). This suggests that at least some powers are inseparably bundled together.
21 Siger of Brabant *Quaestiones in tertium De Anima* 8; 1972, 25.
22 Aquinas and indeed most Aristotelians acknowledge that the act of intellection does not require a bodily organ. This puts tremendous pressure on Aquinas to explain why the intellective soul is nevertheless the substantial form of the human body, which he attempts to do in *Summa Theologiae* 1.76.1. See also Pasnau 2002, 48–57 and 361–366.
23 *Quaestiones in tertium De Anima* 1; 1972, 3.
24 See Pasnau 2002, 126–130 and Pasnau 2011, 574–578. For John Duns Scotus's (d. 1308) distinctive form of pluralism see Ward 2012.
25 Although William Ockham (d. 1347) might have thought that a human has two *souls* (see Perler 2015, 119–123, and the texts cited therein).
26 See, e.g., Richard of Middleton (d. *ca.* 1302) *Questiones Disputatae* 39 (2014, 242).
27 Roland of Cremone (d. *ca.* 1230) *Liber de pura bonitate* (MS Paris Maz. 795, f. 34va); quoted in Lottin 1957, p. 465. See also Richard of Middleton, *Ques. Disp. 39*, argument # 26 (2014, 72).
28 For a rehearsal of the redundancy argument and Richard of Middleton's response, see his *Ques. Disp. 39*, p. 82 and pp. 266–268, respectively.
29 Siger of Brabant *De Anima Intellectiva* 8; 1972, 110.
30 Albert the Great *De Anima*, Book 2, tract. 1, cap. 7 (1968, 75). Strictly speaking, it would seem that Albert cannot assert that the soul is *in* the heart. For the heart is divisible into parts. Accordingly, the same question about whether the soul holenmerically occupies the parts of the heart arises. Given Albert's allergy to holenmerism, it would seem that he really ought to say that the soul is not literally in the heart; although we can associate the substance of the soul with the heart because that is where the soul's core, vital powers operate and then radiate out from.
31 This is effectively one of Henry More's (1614–1687) central criticisms. See Pasnau 2011, 339–345 for citations and discussion.

32 *Tractatus de Anima* 12.311; 1970, 84.
33 See Arlig 2015, section 4.1.
34 Aquinas *Summa Theologiae* 1.76.8. Cf. his *Quaestiones disp. de Anima* 10 corpus.
35 Aquinas *Summa Theol.* 1.76.8 corpus.
36 *Idem.* Cf. *Ques. de Anima* 10 corpus.
37 See esp. *Ques. de Anima* 10 ad 7.
38 See Aristotle *On the Generation of Animals* 2.3.
39 See Pasnau 2002, 120–125.
40 Boethius *De div.* 888d.
41 See King 2008 and Perler 2015, 115–117.
42 See Bieniak 2010, 97–123 and Lottin 1957, 483–502, for citations and discussion.
43 Augustine *De Trinitate* book 10, ch. 11, 18. See Peter Lombard *Libri IV Sententiarum*, book 1, dist. 3, ch. 2.
44 King 2008 asserts that the dominant position in the scholastic period was to draw a real distinction between the soul and its powers.
45 A formulation by Philip the Chancellor in his *Summa de bono* provides the thin edge of the wedge that would pry a soul's power apart from the substance that is the soul. For in this work, Philip asserts that memory, intellect, and will are "said to be *in* the soul substantially" (quoted in Lottin 1957, 489). But it is possible to distinguish between *being the soul* and *being substantially in the soul*. This idea forms the core of a common Franciscan position, which is that while a power is not strictly identical to the soul, there is a sense in which it is either substantially or even "essentially" the same as the soul given that it is an inextricable element from the soul (Lottin 1957, 492–496).
46 That is, one could think of a soul that is neither rational nor irrational; one could have an intellectual grasp of a "naked" soul.
47 Hughes of Saint-Cher (d. 1235), from Lottin 1957, 487.
48 William of Auxerre *Summa aurea* (Paris 1500, f.63va; quoted in Lottin 1957, 486).
49 This seems to be William of Auvergne's view – that is, to predicate a power of the soul is to reveal something about the soul's essence; it is not a claim that something inheres in the soul (see Perler 2015, 102 sqq.).
50 See "Semi-Averroist" *Ques. in de An.* 2.8. Aquinas offers two primary reasons (*Summa Theol.* 1.77.1). The first is akin to the Semi-Averroist's argument. An operation of the soul is not a substance, hence the soul's power to operate cannot be a substance. The second is that if a power were the soul, then the power should always be in act. But this is false.
51 See Aquinas *Summa Theol.* 1.77.1; *Ques. de Anima* 12 ad 7; and discussion in Perler 2015, 108–110.
52 "Semi-Averroist" *Ques. in de An.* 2.8 (Giele et al. 1971, 211).
53 Indeed, some who defend the idea that the powers are essential properties of the soul might ultimately be committed to the notion that the powers are *identical* to the soul. This is how Perler suggests that we interpret William of Auvergne's position (2015, 104). Hugh of St-Cher also seems to endorse this view. His exact formulation is that the powers are the "same in essence" as the soul (*In 1 Sent.* d. 3, 2; in Bieniak 2010, 189–190). But others, including William of Auxerre, Alexander of Hales, and possibly Philip the Chancellor, rejected the identity thesis, even though they did concede that the soul's powers are not accidents (see Bieniak 2010, 99–123; Lottin 1957, 484–493).
54 See Pasnau 2011, 119–132 and 634–641. For Aquinas's somewhat more optimistic view about our capacity to know the essence of the soul, see Pasnau 2002, 164–170.
55 For instance, Boethius *De Trin.* 2, and Averroes *De Substantia Orbis* 1.
56 "Semi-Averroist" *Ques. in de An.* 3.2 (Giele et al. 1971, 304).
57 As Dominik Perler and others have pointed out to me, "potential whole" suggests the wrong connotations to a modern philosopher's ear.
58 Albertus Magnus *In de Div.* 4.2; 1913, 78.

59 Albertus Magnus *In de Div.* 4.1; 1913, 75.
60 Political analogies seem to be quite popular. William of Auvergne and later on Ockham describe powers as "offices", and Aquinas appeals to the notion of a constitution. See Perler 2015, 103, 116, and 114 (respectively), for references and discussion.
61 Bonaventure *In II Sent.*, dist. 3, pars 1, art. 1, q. 1.
62 Ibid., dist. 3, pars 1, art. 1, q. 2.
63 For a rehearsal of this argument as well as more technical objections to universal hylomorphism, see e.g. Siger of Brabant's *Quaestiones in tertium De Anima* 6 (1972, 17–22).
64 See, e.g.,"Semi-Averroist" *Ques. in de An.* 3.2 (Giele et al. 1971, 304), and Siger of Brabant *Quaestiones in tertium De Anima* 6 (1972, 17–22). Aquinas concedes that there is a composition of act and potency, but that this is not a composition of form and matter, but rather "of form and participated being" (*Summa Theol.* 1.75.5 ad 4).
65 See Wippel 2010, 625–628.
66 What these philosophers had in the back of their minds was a famous dictum by Porphyry that the structure of a definition was analogous – but only analogous – to that of a hylomorphic composite. If one merely gives the genus of X – say, *animal* – it is still underdetermined what sort of animal X is. The *differentiae*, therefore, are required to "perfect" the genus, that is, to make it determinate what sort of animal something is (*Isagoge* 11.12–17; Aristoteles Latinus 1.6–7, 18).
67 Avicenna *De Anima* 5.4 (1968, 121–124); and *Najat* 2.6.13 (Rahman 1952, 58).
68 Many thanks to Christina Van Dyke, the scholars at the 2015 NEH Summer Institute (held at CU-Boulder), and the editor for comments on earlier versions of this chapter.

Bibliography

Primary sources

Albertus Magnus. 1913. *Commentarii in librum Boethii de Divisione*. Edited by Paulus Maria de Loë, Bonn: P. Hanstein.
Albertus Magnus. 1968. "*De Anima*," in (ed.) C. Stroick, *Alberti Magni Opera Omnia*, VII, Part 1, Aschendorff: Monasterii Westfalorum.
Avicenna. 1968. *Liber de Anima seu Sextus de Naturalibus*, IV–V. Edited by S. van Riet, Louvain/Leiden: Éditions Orientalistes/E. J. Brill.
Avicenna. 1972. *Liber de Anima seu Sextus de Naturalibus*, I–III. Edited by S. van Riet, Louvain/Leiden: E. Peeters/E. J. Brill.
Johannes Blund. 1970. *Tractatus de Anima*. Edited by D. A. Callus and R. W. Hunt, London: For the British Academy by Oxford University Press.
Richard de Mediavilla [Richard of Middleton]. 2014. *Questions Disputées. Tome VI: 38–45. L'homme*. Edited and translated by Alain Boureau, Paris: Les Belles Lettres.
Siger de Brabant. 1972. *Quaestiones in tertium De Anima. De Anima Intellectiva. De Aeternitate Mundi*. Edited by Bernardo Bazán. Philosophes Médiévaux 13, Louvain: Publications Universitaires.

Secondary sources

Arlig, A. 2015. "Medieval Mereology," *The Stanford Encyclopedia of Philosophy* (online): https://plato.stanford.edu/archives/fall2015/entries/mereology-medieval/
. Originally published 2006, substantially revised June 2015.

Bieniak, M. 2010. *The Soul-Body Problem at Paris, ca. 1200–1250: Hugh of St-Cher and His Contemporaries*, Leuven: Leuven University Press.

Corcilius, K. and Gregoric, P. 2010. "Separability and Difference: Parts and Capacities of the Soul in Aristotle," *Oxford Studies in Ancient Philosophy* 39, 81–120.

Giele, M., van Steenberghen, F. and Bazán, B. 1971. *Trois Commentaires Anonymes sur le Traité de l'Ame D'Aristote*. Philosophes Médiévaux 11, Louvain: Publications Universitaires.

Johansen, T. K. 2012. *The Powers of Aristotle's Soul*, Oxford: Oxford University Press.

Johnston, M. 2006. "Hylomorphism," *Journal of Philosophy* 103, 652–698.

King, P. 2008. "The Inner Cathedral: Mental Architecture in High Scholasticism," *Vivarium* 46, 253–274.

Koslicki, K. 2008. *The Structure of Objects*, Oxford: Oxford University Press.

Lottin, D. O. 1957. *Psychologie et Morale aux XIIe et XIIIe Siècles. Tome 1: Problèmes de Psychologie*. 2nd edition, Gembloux, Belgium: J. Duculot.

Pasnau, R. 2002. *Thomas Aquinas on Human Nature: A Philosophical Study of Summa theologiae Ia75–89*, Cambridge: Cambridge University Press.

Pasnau, R. 2011. *Metaphysical Themes, 1274–1671*, Oxford: Clarendon Press.

Perler, D. 2015. "Faculties in Medieval Philosophy," in (ed.) D. Perler, *The Faculties: A History*, New York: Oxford University Press, 97–139.

Rahman, F. 1952. *Avicenna's Psychology: An English Translation of Kitab al-Najat, Book II, Chapter VI With Historico-Philosophical Notes and Textual Improvements on the Cairo Edition*, London: Oxford University Press.

Ward, T. 2012. "Animals, Animal Parts, and Hylomorphism: John Duns Scotus's Pluralism about Substantial Form," *Journal of the History of Philosophy* 50, 531–557.

Wippel, J. F. 2010. "Essence and Existence," in (ed.) R. Pasnau with (assoc. ed.) C. van Dyke, *The Cambridge History of Medieval Philosophy*. 2 volumes, Cambridge: Cambridge University Press, volume 2, 622–634.

10

THE PHENOMENOLOGY OF IMMORTALITY (1200–1400)

Christina Van Dyke[1]

Discussions of immortality in the Middles Ages tend to focus on the nature of the rational soul and its prospects for surviving the death of the body. The question of how medieval figures expected to *experience* everlasting life – what I will be calling the phenomenology of immortality – receives far less attention. Yet expectations for immortal existence speak volumes about a whole nest of important philosophical issues, including views about God, embodiment, happiness, and love. Examining medieval positions on this topic provides important insight not just into ideas about unending existence but about what it means to be human.

In this paper, I explore the range of these expectations during a relatively narrow but intensely rich temporal and geographical slice of the Middle Ages (the thirteenth and fourteenth centuries in the 'Latin Christian West'). Scholastic and mystical/contemplative traditions during this time share a common focus on the final or ultimate end for human beings, although they differ with respect to methodology. Scholastics tend to address human expectations of immortality in discussions of the bodily resurrection, of perfect happiness (which we attain only in the life to come), and of Scriptural passages that were taken to refer to/ discuss the afterlife;[2] these discussions tend to be entirely theoretical (as opposed to experiential), but they often display a lively curiosity about what our immortal experience will be like, speculating about questions such as how long our hair will be and how old we will appear.[3] Contemplative and mystical works, by contrast, contain a wealth of first-person reports of union with God, many of which relate these unitive experiences to what the blessed will experience in the life to come.[4] Some figures, such as Meister Eckhart (*ca.* 1260–1328) and Marguerite Porete (1250–1310), portray our final goal as a transcendent merging with the divine that includes "phenomenological de-emphasis, blurring, or eradication of multiplicity".[5] Other figures, such as Hadewijch of Brabant (*ca.* thirteenth century), Angela of Foligno (1248–1309), and Mechtild of Magdeburg (*ca.* 1207–*ca.* 1282), tend to portray our final end as a deeply intimate experience that nevertheless preserves a sense of self. The picture of medieval accounts of immortality that emerges from these diverse discussions is too complex to be comprehensively covered in one chapter, but my contention is that it offers a more accurate framework for future discussions of this topic.

To that end, in section 10.1, I sketch the two central accounts of the rational soul and human nature (inspired by the Platonist and Aristotelian traditions) that set the metaphysical parameters for medieval discussions of our experience of the afterlife. In section 10.2, I address accounts that involve transcending the soul's experiences of itself as an individual. In section 10.3, I turn to views that emphasize the embodied aspect of human existence and depict our unending union with God in affective and physical terms. In section 10.4, I argue that the views discussed in 10.2 and 10.3 form endpoints of an 'experiential continuum of immortality' that provides important context for scholastic accounts of immortality as well as expanding the traditional narrative of medieval philosophy.

1   The metaphysics of immortality

Questions of the 'how' and 'what' of immortality in the Middle Ages revolve around the relation of rational soul to human body.[6] It was generally assumed that non-rational animals did not survive their death and that intellective, immaterial beings such as angels were necessarily immortal (since their lack of connection to matter meant that they were in no danger of corruption).[7] The case of human beings was complicated by the fact that we are both animals whose bodies suffer corruption and rational beings capable of intellective cognition. Our ability to transcend matter via intellection indicates that our existence itself might transcend our death;[8] at the same time, the fact that we die at all – unlike other intellective beings – raises worries about both how and what might persist. These worries are compounded by the Christian doctrine of the resurrection of the body. Philosophical traditions arguing for the immortality of the soul stretch back before Plato, but the insistence the soul would not only continue to exist but also be rejoined with an incorruptible body[9] puts serious pressure on medieval accounts of our postmortem possibilities.

To vastly oversimplify matters in ways that will be helpful for what follows, the main problem for Platonists – who tended to understand the soul as a *substance in its own right* – lay not in accounting for the survival of our souls but in providing any motivation for their continued connection to material bodies. The main problem for Aristotelians, in contrast, lay in explaining how the rational soul – which they understood in hylomorphic terms as *the substantial form of a material body* – could survive the death of that body (in a way that would also allow for its being reunited with that body again later).

If the soul is understood primarily as a substance in its own right, accounting for the soul's persistence at the death of the human body poses no real problem. Substances are exactly the sorts of things that have independent existence, and both the soul's immateriality and its intellective nature put it in the same category as incorruptible and immortal substances such as the angels. This view also avoids worries about the continued identity of the human person through death and resurrection, since the person is identified with the soul that persists through these changes. The main problem for Platonic traditions arises from the doctrine of the bodily resurrection and its implication that the unity of soul and body is somehow essential for our continued survival in the afterlife. The doctrine states that our bodies will be raised incorruptible and that we will continue forever as physical and not merely spiritual beings, but (to put it bluntly) why bother with bodies if we survive in virtue of our souls? Bodies seem at the very least to be an unnecessary addition and (as the *Phaedo* famously argues) might even endanger our proper intellective and volitional functioning. If the soul is a substance in its own right, it's unclear how soul and body together would make up a human being that is a genuine unity, or what role our bodies would play in our continued existence in the afterlife.[10]

If the soul is understood primarily as the substantial form of the body, on the other hand, explaining the unity of the human being doesn't pose a serious problem. On this view, popular among Aristotelian-influenced figures (most notably, Thomas Aquinas [1225–1274]), human beings are composites of matter and form. The rational soul functions as the substantial form that structures matter and makes the human being the thing that it is, but there is only one substance on the table, so to speak: the human being.[11] This view also provides philosophical motivation for the doctrine of the bodily resurrection, since the body is an essential component of the human being and needs to be present for *you* to be present in the afterlife. The importance of the body raises issues of persistence and identity for this view, however. For one thing, how can a substantial form continue to exist in separation from the matter/body of which it is the form?[12] For another, even if we grant that the rational soul persists at the death of the body (in virtue of its intellective nature), this account faces further puzzles about personal identity through death and the bodily resurrection. Either the human being ceases to exist at the death of the body, in which case it's difficult to explain how the human being who is resurrected can be numerically the same as the one who dies, or the human being persists in virtue of the persistence of the rational soul, in which case this view picks up the problems associated with Platonism that are mentioned earlier.[13]

For the purposes of this chapter, we can grant that the soul survives the death of the body and that there is a coherent story to tell about both the unity and the continued identity of the resurrected human being. The reason to sketch these views and highlight these puzzles is to provide the general framework – complete with internal and external tensions – within which medieval figures speculate about the phenomenology of immortality. As we will see, some accounts of the experience of immortality exemplify the Platonic focus on the soul as complete and as 'us' (with a corresponding de-emphasis on affect and the body), while other accounts display the pull of the Aristotelian tradition between our intellective similarity to

God and our status as rational animals whose physicality forms an integral part of human experience.

2 Transcending matter, becoming God

The majority of extant medieval contemplative literature originates from outside the university system and remains largely overlooked by contemporary philosophers.[14] The one exception to this has been the work of Meister Eckhart, a late-thirteenth/early fourteenth-century Dominican and proponent of 'apophatic mysticism'. Apophaticism is the view that human language and thought cannot capture Divine Truth in any deep or meaningful way; apophatic mysticism applies this belief to unmediated experiences of the Divine.[15] As the fourteenth-century Franciscan tertiary Angela of Foligno complains,

> When I return to myself after perceiving these divine secrets ... [and] speak entirely from outside the experience, I say words that come nowhere near describing the divine workings that are produced in my soul. My statements about them ruin the reality they represent.[16]

If we characterize mysticism generally as involving experiences that are inherently *phenomenological* ("concerning individual felt experience in addition to systems of knowledge or belief")[17] and *transcendent* ("involving an encounter – whether direct or mediated, transformatively powerful or paradoxically everyday – with God"),[18] then we can think of the apophatic tradition as further characterizing the content of those experiences as inherently inexpressible.

This characterization might make apophatic texts seem like a non-starter for medieval views of immortality, but in fact they frequently contain detailed instructions for attaining the highest state available to human beings – namely, this ineffable and unending union that they can talk *around* if not *about*. Apophatic mysticism has roots reaching back to Platonism, and typically uses language of 'ascent' and 'stages' to describe the mystical life as progressing in natural degrees to a final end that we attain eternally in the afterlife.

One central theme in apophatic mysticism is the necessity of self-loss. Eckhart, for instance, repeatedly counsels his disciples to strive for detachment, not just from worldly goods but also from any sort of attachment to self. This process is portrayed as both ongoing and essential:

> You should know that there was never any man in this life who forsook himself so much that he could not still find more in himself to forsake.... But as much as you go out in forsaking all things, by so much, neither less nor more, does God go in.[19]

Emptying oneself allows God to fill the void and, thus, facilitates mystic union.

In her *Mirror of Simple Souls*, Marguerite Porete describes the final end of this process in terms of radical self-annihilation:

> All things are one for her [the Soul], without an explanation (*propter quid*), and she is nothing in a One of this sort. Thus the Soul has nothing more to do for God than God does for her. Why? Because He is, and she is not. She retains nothing more of herself in nothingness, because He is sufficient of Himself, because He is and she is not. Thus she is stripped of all things because she is without existence, where she was before she was created.
>
> (chapter 135)[20]

The desire to merge with God so absolutely that it is as though the individual person never existed is not unique to Porete. After detachment is complete, Eckhart says, "There is still one work that remains proper and his own, and that is annihilation of self."[21]

What proceeds from this total self-abnegation is a state in which the human being's will becomes identical with that of God's and in which no sense of individuality remains in which the person could take pride, or for which she could claim responsibility.[22] The climax of the *Sister Catherine* treatise (written by an anonymous follower of Eckhart in the fourteenth century) is the startling moment at which Catherine announces: "Rejoice with me, I am become God!" In the context of this tradition, however, Catherine is not claiming divinity for herself; rather, the claim is that God is there because 'she' no longer exists.[23] Whether or not the self-annihilation these figures advocate is actually ontological – something impossible to determine from the texts themselves, which so frequently appeal to the inadequacy of words to express the realities involved – we are at least called to conform our knowledge and love of God to the point where our *experience* of those states is indistinguishable from God's. Whatever 'our' experience of immortality is, then, it is nothing more or less than God's own experience of eternity.

On this version of apophatic mysticism, the divine union which we seek is one that falls outside Christian orthodoxy. Indeed, both Porete and Eckhart's views underwent extensive doctrinal examination by the Inquisition, and both figures were condemned: Porete to the flames on June 1, 1310, and Eckhart posthumously (on March 27, 1329). The mere fact that the Pope took the trouble to issue a bull against Eckhart's views after his death indicates the level of official concern about this sort of 'mystical heresy', often referred to as the Free Spirit movement.[24]

Other versions of apophatic mysticism were less extreme, but they all share an emphasis on transcending individual human experience, especially ones involving affective and physical sensations. Strongly influenced by Platonist prejudices against matter, apophatic texts like the anonymous fourteenth-century English *Cloud of Unknowing* and Walter Hilton's *The Scale of Perfection* (*ca.* 1340–1396) lay out detailed procedures for dealing with and overcoming attachment to the body – including embodied mystical experiences such as "sounding of the ear, or savoring in the mouth, or smelling at the nose, or else any perceptible heat as if it were fire, glowing and warming the breast".[25] In this, they join Eckhart, who repeatedly counseled his disciples that part of the essential process of detachment from self was detachment from sensible experiences, "tartly condemning those who want to see God with the same eyes with which they behold a cow".[26]

This push towards selfless union with God as the final end of human life constitutes one end of the medieval 'experiential continuum of immortality': immortality as endless undifferentiated experience of the divine (or loss of any sort of conscious experience whatsoever). In the next section, I lay out the other end of this continuum: union with God that involves not self-annihilation but self-*fulfillment*, and where the self is taken to include body as well as soul.

3 Embodied immortal experience

As I mentioned in section 1, the doctrine of the bodily resurrection constitutes a central constraint for medieval accounts of immortality. Not only were the souls of human beings to persist at death, but they were to be rejoined to new and improved bodies that were, nevertheless, numerically identical to their earthly bodies. Although this doctrine creates any number of problems for metaphysical accounts of identity, it undergirds a picture of the afterlife that resonated deeply with a number of thirteenth- to fourteenth-century contemplatives who viewed the urge to permanently transcend our bodies as ignoring the importance of the Incarnation. After all, according to Christian doctrine, Christ did not just *become* human; Christ *remains* human. In this tradition, Christ's resurrected body was taken up into heaven, where its physical presence assures us that our immortal existence will not be that of disembodied angels but that of flesh and blood – albeit flesh and blood that have been transformed into incorruptibility. Thus, Mechtild of Magdeburg (a thirteenth-century beguine) rejoices in *The Flowing Light of the Godhead* that

> When I reflect that divine nature now includes bone and flesh, body and soul, then I become elated in great joy, far beyond what I am worth. . . . The soul with its flesh is mistress of the house in heaven, sits next to the eternal Master of the house, and is most like him.[27]

When Mechtild goes on to describe our immortal existence in both spiritual and bodily terms ("There, eye reflects in eye, spirit flows in spirit, there, hand touches hand, there, mouth speaks to mouth, and there, heart greets heart"), she is not speaking metaphorically.

Reference to Christ's resurrected body and its implications for our own experience of the afterlife appears in any number of contemplative texts at this time, crossing geographical regions and religious orders. In her late fourteenth-century *Dialogue*, for instance, the Dominican-affiliated Catherine of Siena

(1347–1380) describes in colorful terms how the damned will react to seeing Christ in heaven:

> When the wicked are reunited with their bodies, their suffering at the sight of my Son will be renewed and increased. What a reproach to their miserable indecent sensuality, to see their own nature, this clay of Adam, exalted above all the choirs of angels in the humanity of Christ joined with the purity of my Godhead![28]

The problem here is not human individuality or union with matter – both of those things are specifically listed here as causes for celebration in the case of Christ. Rather, the problem is how the wicked used those bodies and exploited their 'sensuality'.[29] Their experience of immortality will be one of embodied suffering, while the experience of the blessed will be that of embodied bliss. In his *Fire of Love*, the influential fourteenth-century English mystic Richard Rolle (*ca.* 1290–1349) also describes affective and physical experiences of mystic union which he portrays as a foretaste of the life to come and which include a 'glowing' or warmth in the breast, a taste of unimaginable sweetness, and the sound of celestial music in addition to intellective and volitional fulfilment.

Angela of Foligno, a late-thirteenth century Franciscan tertiary and influential mystic, speaks often of the 'God-man' as a way of emphasizing both aspects of the second person of the Trinity and intimately connects Christ's humanity with her union with God. After one experience where, upon looking at the cross, she "saw and felt that Christ was within me, embracing my soul with the very arm with which he was crucified", she is filled with joy and understands "what this man, namely Christ, is like in heaven, that is to say, how we will see that through him our flesh is made one with God".[30] Again, it is our *flesh* that is made one with God in the life to come, not just our souls.

There is no thought here that our experience of immortality will be one of self-annihilation or transcendence of physicality. As Catherine of Siena puts it,

> When my Son was lifted up on the wood of the most holy cross, he did not cut off his divinity from the lowly earth of your humanity. . . . In fact, his divinity is kneaded into the clay of your humanity like one bread.[31]

In this tradition, Christ's status as fully human and fully divine both removes the need for any other intermediary between the human subject of experience and the triune God and offers us a way of understanding how our experience of immortality can involve embodied spirituality.

The affective movement (the tradition that considers affective and embodied states as well as apophatic states to be properly mystical) regularly employed the imagination in addition to the intellect and the will. In a popular devotional exercise of the time, contemplatives were encouraged to imagine themselves present at key moments of Christ's life in order to "construct an inner space that creates affectively embodied access to the divine".[32] That is, rather than counseling practitioners to withdraw increasingly from one's attachment to the self and its experiences (as Eckhart and Porete did), this tradition advocated facilitating certain affective and physical experiences as a way of developing an appropriate sense of self in relation to God. In general, strong emotion was seen as opening the subject to the divine presence, as were visions, auditions, smellings, and tastings. The 'inner' and 'outer' body were intrinsically connected, and the language of medieval mystics often moves seamlessly from the one to the other, as when Mecthild of Magdeburg writes: "I do not know how to write, nor can I, unless I see with the eyes of my soul and hear with the ears of my eternal spirit and feel in all the parts of my body the power of the Holy Spirit."[33]

Many of the contemplatives in this movement also frequently describe mystic union in terms of self-loss and dissolution, but unlike figures in the apophatic movement they do so without downplaying or denigrating the significance of affective and embodied unitive experiences. This acceptance of embodied mystical states, I would argue, actually constitutes the most important distinction between the apophatic and affective mindset. Figures like Porete, Eckhart, and Walter Hilton and texts such as the anonymous *Cloud of Unknowing* acknowledge that unusual embodied states such as visions and auditions regularly occur in the contemplative life, but they portray them as experiences to be ignored, suspicious of, and/or as part of an early stage that needs to be moved past. In contrast, other figures such as Angela of Foligno and Hadewijch (a thirteenth-century beguine from Brabant or Antwerp), both of whom are sometimes referred to as apophatics, regularly speak both of self-loss and self-fulfillment in depictions of mystical union.

In a letter to a fellow beguine, for instance, Hadewijch describes union simultaneously in terms of a loss of self via complete interpenetrability *and* in terms of an eternal self-awareness that includes physicality as well as spirituality:

> Where the abyss of his wisdom is, God will teach you what he is, and with what wondrous sweetness the loved one and the Beloved dwell one in the other, and how they penetrate each other in a way that neither of the two distinguishes himself from the other. But they abide in one another in fruition, mouth in mouth, heart in heart, body in body, and soul in soul, while one sweet divine nature flows through both and they are both one thing through each other, but at the same time remain two different selves – yes, and remain so forever.[34]

The portrayal of the Scriptural metaphor "one flesh" for marriage here is striking; in speaking of God and the human being (God's Beloved) in these intimate terms, Hadewijch stresses the beauty of both spiritual and physical union.

Importantly, this sort of unitive experience is also what we are told we will enjoy in the life to come. There is sometimes self-loss or being 'taken out of' oneself, but there is also a return to oneself. Angela of Foligno, for instance, describes alternating between profoundly apophatic experiences and deeply personal experiences that involve the embodied Christ. In the following passage, she explains how as an experience of unspeakable 'darkness' and indistinguishable union ebbs away, she remains intimately connected with the God-man:

> When I am in that darkness I do not remember anything about anything human, or the God-man, or anything which has a form. Nevertheless, I see all and I see nothing. As what I have spoken of withdraws and stays with me, I see the God-man. He draws my soul with great gentleness, and he sometimes says to me: "You are I, and I am you." I see, then, those eyes and that face so gracious and attractive as he leans to embrace me.

Here again we see the sort of mystical identification of human person with God discussed in section 10.2: "You are I, and I am you." Yet here it appears in a setting in which the second person of the Trinity is speaking those words to Angela with a human mouth and looking at her with human eyes, *after* her experience of darkness, not *during* it.

Angela immediately goes on to explain how her two sorts of mystical experiences are related to each other:

> In short, what proceeds from those eyes and that face is what I said that I saw in that previous darkness which comes from within, and which delights me so that I can say nothing about it. When I am in the God-man my soul is alive. And I am in the God-man much more than in the other vision of seeing God with darkness. The soul is alive in that vision concerning the God-man. The vision with darkness, however, draws me so much more that there is no comparison. On the other hand, I am in the God-man almost continually. It began in this continual fashion on a certain occasion when I was given the assurance that there was no intermediary between God and myself. Since this time there has not been a day or night in which I did not continually experience this joy of the humanity of Christ.[35]

It is hardly obvious how to read the claims made here – and, indeed, Angela herself often exclaims at how poorly words capture her experiences. At the same time, although she says that she vastly prefers her experience of God's inexpressible darkness, her union with the God-man is already unmediated, and there is no indication that her experience of Christ's humanity is anything but an appropriate source of delight.

One reason this point is worth stressing is that the primary motivation for focusing on Christ's humanity within the affective tradition was precisely to counter the sort of gnostic tendencies which run through apophaticism. Rather than hoping to move beyond contemplation of Christ's humanity to an experience of divinity, the affective movement saw human beings as most closely joined with Christ's divinity *through* his corporeity.

This 'both/and' approach has been all-too-frequently overlooked in philosophical discussions of mysticism, but it proves crucial for understanding medieval expectations for immortality. The following vision reported by Hadewijch, for instance, first describes the Man-Christ satisfying the "desire of my heart and my humanity" via a physical embrace during the celebration of the Eucharist:

> With that he came in the form and clothing of a Man, as he was on the day when he gave us his Body for the first time; looking like a Human Being and a Man, wonderful and beautiful, and with glorious face, he came to me as humbly as anyone who wholly belongs to another. Then he gave himself to me in the shape of the Sacrament, in its outward form, as the custom is; and then he gave me to drink from the chalice, in form and taste, as the custom is. After that he came himself to me, took me entirely in his arms, and pressed me to him; and all my members felt his in full felicity, in accordance with the desire of my heart and my humanity. So I was outwardly satisfied and fully transported.[36]

Here, Christ is repeatedly referred to as a Man, and as such speaks to Hadewijch's human nature.

After this, however, Christ "dissolves" so that they became "one without difference" – an experience Hadewijch relates to the physical mystery of the Eucharist (via the metaphor of digestion): "So can the Beloved, with the loved one, each wholly receive the other in full satisfaction of the sight, the hearing, and the passing away of the one in the other." This 'passing away' then turns into an apophatic experience of complete self-loss: "After that I remained in a passing away in my Beloved, so that I wholly melted away in him and nothing any longer remained of myself; and I was changed and taken up in spirit, and there it was shown me concerning such hours."[37] As with Angela of Foligno and Catherine of Siena, embodied experience of Christ's humanity forms a crucial component of Hadewijch's mystical union with God. It's not self-annihilation *as opposed to* affective experience on this view, but something much more complex – and complex in a way that recognizes the importance of body as well as soul.

In general, the thirteenth- and fourteenth-century emphasis on the Incarnation and Christ's permanently assumed human body (which was thought to be physically present in heaven, together with his mother, Mary) provided an embodied model of union with God that was enthusiastically explored by contemplatives from a wide variety of backgrounds. If we think of apophaticism's emphasis on phenomenological de-emphasis or erasure as one endpoint of the experiential continuum of immortality, then affectivism's emphasis on embodied fulfilment can be seen as the other endpoint. In section 4, I discuss how scholastic views map onto this continuum; in general, the most relevant factor is not religious affiliation (that is, whether the author is Dominican or Franciscan, etc.) but rather whether the body is seen more as hindering or helping connect us with God.

4 Intellective union and the scholastic tradition

As we saw in sections 2 and 3, medieval expectations of immortality range widely, from loss of individual experience in union with an unknowable God to a deeply personal connection with God (via the Incarnate Christ) that includes affective and sensory as well as intellective and volitional experiences. To demonstrate the breadth of this range, I have drawn on contemplative literature from a variety of literary genres and languages. In what follows, I turn back to the Latin scholastic tradition. One common way of distinguishing scholastic views of the afterlife is by whether they stress the primacy of intellect or the primacy of will in our final end – that is, whether we will be united with God first and foremost via knowledge or via love. When it comes to the phenomenology of the afterlife, however, this distinction proves much less helpful. Although many figures do emphasize either intellective or volitional aspects of eternal union (often depending on whether they are Dominican or Franciscan), this turns out not to map neatly onto the experiential continuum discussed earlier. Instead, attitudes towards the Otherness of God and the material world correspond much more closely to what people expect the afterlife to be like from a first-person perspective.

We have, in fact, already seen wildly diverse portrayals of love as the primary experience of mystical union. Marguerite Porete stresses the importance of love for self-abnegation: the stage at which one "is stripped of all things because she is without existence, where she was before she was created" is reached by complete conformity of one's will with God and motivated by increasingly selfless love. Hadewijch also emphasizes love as the central act of mystical union, but in such a manner that God and the Beloved "at the same time remain two different selves – yes, and remain so forever". Mechtild of Magdeburg centers her attention on the unitive power of love as well, but in extreme contrast to Porete, she rejoices in the thought that the soul "with its flesh" will literally sit next to the "eternal Master of the house" (i.e., the resurrected Christ). Emphasis on the will (and love as the proper act of the will) thus does not incline towards one particular view of immortal experience.

In the remainder of this section, I use two 'intellectivist' accounts of union with God from within the scholastic tradition – that of Robert Grosseteste (*ca.* 1175–1253) and that of Thomas Aquinas – to show that an emphasis on the intellect (and knowing as the proper act of the intellect) also allows for a range of different expectations of immortality.

The centrality of the human desire for knowledge runs throughout medieval discussions of immortality. In fact, the 'naturalness' of our desire for both abstract knowledge and immortality was appealed to by Augustinian illuminationists, Neoplatonists, and Aristotelians alike as an indication that human beings are meant for more than just material existence. In addition, one thing on which both the apophatic and affective contemplatives agree is that knowledge of one's self is the starting point for one's journey towards divine union.[38] This is often intimately linked with the will and its love, as when Catherine of Siena gives voice to Supreme Truth:

> You ask for the will to know and love me. . . . Here is the way, if you would come to perfect knowledge and enjoyment of me, eternal Life: Never leave the knowledge of yourself. Then, put down as you are in the valley of humiliation you will know me in yourself, and from this knowledge you will draw all that you need.[39]

A closer connection to God is always portrayed as the ultimate end of self-knowledge, but medieval intuitions vary widely with respect to the results of introspection, and in ways that we have already seen. Are we immaterial souls who need to transcend our corrupt bodies, or are those bodies an integral part of who we are?

An important early thirteenth-century response to these questions appears in Robert Grosseteste's commentary on Aristotle's *Posterior Analytics* – a work that is especially significant because it represents the Latin university system's first attempt to address Aristotle's system in what had been largely a Platonic world. Interestingly, Grosseteste avoids taking sides in what becomes an acrimonious debate, preferring instead to incorporate Platonic Ideas, Neoplatonic emanation, Aristotelian universals, *and* divine illumination into his complex framework. Although how best to understand details of the resulting framework remains controversial, what is clear is that on his view, ideal cognition is completely removed from matter.[40] In his own words: "Knowledge is most complete in these things that lack senses."[41]

Grosseteste generally applies an Aristotelian epistemic framework to human cognition here on earth. His discussions of the levels of cognition, however, emphasize that this sort of cognition, which depends on sense perception and phantasms (essentially, mental images that we store in our imaginations), is the lowest sort. The higher the intellect, the less dependent on the senses and phantasms it is. Employing Platonist language of purity, Grosseteste explains that

> for the intellect that is pure and separated from phantasms – able to contemplate the first light, which is the first cause – the principles of cognizing are the uncreated ideas (*rationes*) of things that exist from eternity in the first cause.[42]

In fact,

> when the pure intellect is able to fix its sight on them, it cognizes created things in them as truly and clearly as possible – and not only created things, but also the first light itself in which it cognizes other things.[43]

As becomes clear through the commentary, Grosseteste believes that we can gain true knowledge of God only when we have separated our intellects completely from their dependence on the body and its phantasms – that is, only after death.

There is no mention of a positive role for the body here. Indeed, although we appear to retain a sense of individuality in the afterlife on this view, it is not because we are essentially embodied. We must draw our mental gaze away from corporeal matters, for "divine things are more visible to the mind's vision that is healthy and not clouded by phantasms". Grosseteste goes so far as to refer to the mind's vision "while we are burdened by the weight of the corrupt body and the love of corporeal things" *unhealthy*.[44] Our love for the material world and corresponding reliance on phantasms is a sickness that actively interferes with our ability to know God:

> The reason why the soul's sight is clouded by the weight of the corrupt body is that the affection and vision (*affectus et aspectus*) of the soul are not distinct, and it attains its vision only by means of that by which it attains its affection or its love.[45]

So long as the soul loves the body and its 'enticements', the soul's vision is turned away from the source of its natural light. Our goal as human beings is to turn our love (*affectus*) towards God, so that our minds can follow suit, and we can spend eternity cognizing things through our cognition of the First Light.

The vision of immortality that emerges from Grosseteste, then, is one in which our connection with physicality is tenuous at best. If (as Christian doctrine insists) we are joined to incorruptible bodies, those bodies appear to play no role in our experience of our final end. Grosseteste's afterlife in one of intellective fulfilment, intrinsically linked with volitional fulfilment. We may retain individual existence, but our primary experience of that individuality will be come via our experience of God as our First and Final Cause.

Robert Grosseteste's view is significant because it represents an early attempt in the Latin West to reconcile Aristotelian with Platonic intuitions; the resulting account, however, takes a decidedly Platonist perspective on the body. Thomas Aquinas, on the other hand, is known for advocating a thoroughly hylomorphic, Aristotelian conception of human nature. On his view, the human being is a composite of form and matter, and cognition is an activity that requires us to use our bodies as well as our rational capacities. To make an extremely complicated story short, human beings have the weakest intellects in the hierarchy of being,[46] and so the typical process of human cognition moves first from sense experience to phantasms and then from phantasms to intelligible species (the proper objects of abstract thought). Furthermore, in this life, any time we are thinking, our intellects must refer back to the phantasms that ground the intelligible species that serve as the objects of our thought.

This general account of cognition makes it look as though Aquinas's account of immortality should be robustly embodied, with us drawing on our glorified sense perception to better know and love God. Aquinas's actual depiction of our final end emphasizes its intellectual, contemplative nature, however, and explicitly denies that sense perception plays a role in that act of contemplation: "In that perfect happiness in heaven to which we look forward . . . the operation by which the human mind is joined to God will not depend on the senses."[47] The reason for this is that Aquinas believes that the primary activity of the life to come is direct (unmediated) contemplation of God's essence – an activity we share with God and the angels, who are wholly immaterial. In this life, we require mutable bodies for gathering information from the world around us; in the life to come, we will still have sense perception, but there will be no *need* for it.[48] Human beings attain the beatific vision only when God gives us his essence as intelligible form and then illuminates our intellects so we are capable of cognizing it to the degree that we love it.[49] God is the First and the Final Cause in this cognitive story: "In such a vision, the divine essence must be both *what is seen* and *that by which* it is seen."[50]

Our experience of immortality on Aquinas's view differs radically from our experience of mortal life, for it also involves a drastic shift in our experience of time. In this life, human beings employ discursive reasoning, moving from premise to premise to conclusion, rather than instantly comprehending an argument in its entirety. Aquinas argues that in the life to come, however, we will exist in a state of perfection in which motion ceases:

> Each thing rests when it reaches its ultimate end, since all motion is for the sake of acquiring that end, and the ultimate end of the intellect is vision of the divine substance, as was shown above. Therefore, the intellect which is seeing the divine substance does not move from one intelligible thing to another.[51]

Our contemplation of God's eternal and unchanging essence is "one continuous and sempiternal activity".[52]

Our rational souls will be joined to resurrected material bodies, which will be "brighter, more firmly impassible, much more agile, and with a more perfect dignity of nature".[53] These bodies are glorified by sharing in the perfect happiness our souls receive from their contemplation of God's essence. In fact, Aquinas claims, "there will be such an outflow to the body and the bodily senses from the happiness of the soul that they will be perfected in their operations".[54] Yet the beatific vision is everlasting and unchanging, and our experience of it will be likewise. Whatever information the sense might provide us with will at best enhance that vision.

Aquinas's view of phenomenology of immortality, then, significantly downplays the role of our bodies and our senses. At the same time, our bodies are not portrayed as weighing down our intellects or as a burden we need to transcend, as they are in Grosseteste's account. Intellectivist accounts of union with God thus also fall on different points along the experiential continuum. Although the spread is not as wide as that among the volitional accounts of union we observed, the close relation between the will and affect in medieval philosophical psychology should, perhaps, make that to be expected. In any event, it seems clear that what's most relevant for medieval expectations of immortality is not a stress on love versus knowledge but rather attitudes towards the body and its connection (or lack thereof) to experiences of God. Platonist inclinations push towards self-abnegation in union with a God beyond being itself; emphasis on our connection to God via Christ's humanity inclines towards mystical union with physical and emotional as well as intellective and volitional components.

5 Conclusion

Traditionally, philosophical discussions of immortality in the Middle Ages have focused on scholastic arguments for and against the survival of the rational soul and questions of personal identity through death and the bodily resurrection. These views are important and certainly worthy of attention, but this focus fails to engage the full range of medieval perspectives on immortality and the afterlife (even just in the thirteenth–fifteenth centuries, as I have shown here). There is a wealth of material in the contemplative tradition that has remained overlooked by philosophers but that is vital for an accurate understanding of these issues – material that is particularly relevant to the history of the philosophy of mind.

I close by reiterating the general need for philosophers to look outside the scholastic tradition for an accurate sense of the range of medieval perspectives on classical philosophical questions. As I have argued elsewhere, engagement with these contemplative texts both facilitates interdisciplinary conversations and corrects serious misimpressions about who 'did philosophy' in the Middle Ages and how they did it.[55] In this chapter, I have been able only to highlight a few of the figures and ideas that deserve contemporary philosophical attention; I hope that it proves sufficient to inspire others to continue the work of bringing these marginalized voices more fully into medieval discussions.

Notes

1 I owe many people thanks for helpful comments and questions on this project, especially participants at the *Longing, Suffering, and Love in Mystical Theory and Practice* workshop at the University of Konstanz in July 2015 and the workshop in Analytical Existentialism at Boğaziçi University in November 2015, as well as audiences at L'Abri Fellowship International (Switzerland), the University of Leeds Center for Philosophy of Religion seminar, and Lingnan University. Various parts of this chapter have benefitted from discussions at a number of other venues as well, and particularly from conversations with Andrew Arlig, Natalie Hart, Christia Mercer, Bob Pasnau, Laurie Paul, Mike Rea, Eric Schliesser, Irem Krustal Steen, and so many other wonderful people that I leave the following space blank for you to write your name if I should have mentioned you: _____. This publication was made possible in part through the support of the Immortality Project (UC-Riverside) and the Experience

Project, both of which were funded in part by a grant from the John Templeton Foundation. The opinions expressed in this publication are those of the author and do not necessarily reflect the views of the John Templeton Foundation.
2. Whether describing heaven's bliss or hell's eternal torments, medieval figures were clear that Scriptural descriptions of these states are to be taken literally, not metaphorically. Aquinas, for instance, argues explicitly in his *Questions on the Soul* 20 that the separated souls of the damned suffer from not just mental anguish but also physical fire.
3. There are far more scholastic texts dealing with our embodied resurrected state than most people realize: each candidate for a master's in theology at the University of Paris in the Middle Ages had to lecture on the four books of Peter Lombard's *Sentences*, the final book of which concludes with a substantial discussion of the bodily resurrection. Because many of the masters revised their initial theses into independent treatises later in their careers, this means we find detailed discussions of the bodily resurrection in a huge number of medieval works. For a book-length history of this tradition (and its predecessors), see Bynum 1995.
4. See, e.g., Angela of Foligno, who reports after an experience of 'unspeakable good' that

> This is the same good and none other than that which the saints enjoy in eternal life, but there the experience of it is different. In eternal life, the least saint has more of it than can be given to a soul in this life before the death of the body.
>
> (*Memorial IX*, p. 217)

5. Gellmann 2014. For a discussion and critique of the definition of mystical experience offered in this entry, see Van Dyke forthcoming.
6. For an excellent book-length discussion of the status of the rational soul at this time, see Dales 1995. Pegis 1934 is a classic treatment of the topic with special attention on Thomas Aquinas.
7. The question of celestial intelligences – the incorruptible 'heavenly bodies' – was trickier. See, e.g., see Marrone 2006 and Dales 1980.
8. For Augustine and later adherents of increasingly complex illuminationist theories, the soul's ability to grasp eternal, unchanging truths indicates that, like other intellective beings (such as angels and the celestial bodies spheres), human souls exist forever once they are created by God. See Marrone 2001 for a comprehensive (if slightly idiosyncratic) study of the development and decline of theories of illumination. Aristotelians disagreed about the mechanics of human cognition, but they agreed that the soul's ability to grasp immaterial truths demonstrated that the soul itself was the sort of being whose existence (*esse*) transcended matter and thus *could* continue to exist in separation from the matter of which it was the form. See Pegis 1934.
9. The moment of body being reunited with soul was said to happen at the Final Judgment, when God would confirm each person's everlasting status in either hell or heaven.
10. See Andrew Arlig's chapter in this volume (Chapter 9) on the parts of souls for a discussion of different medieval attempts to solve the puzzle of the unity of the human being.
11. For secondary sources that argue forcefully for this position, see Van Steenberghen 1980 and Van Dyke 2009.
12. This has been a heated subject of debate since Aristotle's *De Anima* 3.5 suggested that if any part of the soul persisted through the death of the organism of which it was the substantial form, it would be the intellective part. In the Islamic tradition, this claim famously inspired the doctrine of the Agent Intellect. See chapters 3 and 8 on the agent intellect.
13. This problem has received particular attention in Aquinas's treatment of it. Brower 2014 and Stump 2003 both lay out and defend complicated (and different) views on

which the soul's survival is sufficient for the survival of the human being without being numerically identical to the human being; Toner 2012 allows that the human being ceases to exist at death on this view but argues for a view on which gappy existence doesn't pose an insurmountable problem for diachronic identity. I argue (Van Dyke 2014a) that Aquinas's account of the separated soul is nonetheless insufficient.
14 There are a number of other complicating factors here as well, including political debates over what constitutes 'mysticism', both in general and specifically what constitutes the sort of mystical experience of interest to philosophers. See section 1 of my Van Dyke forthcoming.
15 For a detailed treatment of this topic, see Turner 1995.
16 Angela of Foligno 1993, *Memorial* IX, p. 214.
17 See Watson 2011, 1.
18 Ibid.
19 Council 4 of *Counsels*, in Eckhart 1981, 250.
20 Marguerite Porete 1993, 218, translation slightly modified. As Newman 2003, 203 notes in her discussion of Porete's theory of self-abnegation: "In this dissolution of the ego no room remains for the body: even the physical humanity of Christ is no longer cherished by the free soul." Porete explicitly addresses the need to move past consideration of Christ's humanity in chapter 79. See also Hollywood 1995.
21 Counsel 23, Meister Eckhart 1981, 280.
22 As Meister Eckhart 1981, 286 writes in 'On Detachment': "Perfect humility proceeds from annihilation of self."
23 See 'The "Sister Catherine" Treatise' in McGinn 1981, 358. For further discussion of this treatise and also this general tradition, see McGinn 2005. For a book-length treatment of this topic (that focuses particularly on Meister Eckhart), see Morgan 2013.
24 Much of church officials' concerns about this movement, of course, stemmed less from the thought that God (and, eventually, we) transcends existence itself and more from the fact that it appeared to undermine church authority by claiming that lay people could have a relationship with God unmediated by priests. Despite official attempts to stamp this idea out, it became one of the cornerstones of the Protestant Reformation, with its emphasis on Sola Scriptura and Sola Gratia.
25 *The Scale of Perfection.*
26 Meister Eckhart 1981, 61. The sermon referenced is *Sermon* 16b in Meister Eckhart 1936, 272.
27 Mechtild of Magdeburg 1998, IV.14.
28 Catherine of Siena 1980, *Dialogue* 42.
29 Catherine consistently talks about 'sensuality' when she is referring to the inappropriate use of the senses, not as a blanket terms condemning the senses themselves.
30 Chapter VI, 4th Supplemental Step from the *Memorial*, in Angela of Foligno 1993, 175.
31 Catherine of Siena 1980, *Dialogue* 26.
32 Largier 2003. For further discussion of this meditation and its use of the imagination, see Matter 2012. For a close examination of the use of this meditation in one particular medieval religious community, see Flora 2009.
33 Mechtild of Magdeburg 1998, IV.13.
34 Hadewijck of Brabant 1980, Letter 9.
35 Angela of Foligno 1993, *Memorial* IX, 7th Supplemental Step, 205.
36 Hadewijch of Brabant 1980, Vision Seven, 281.
37 Ibid., 282.
38 It is generally characteristic of the medieval tradition at this time that people are counseled to look for knowledge of God via introspection. For a fuller discussion of the importance of self-knowledge in the contemplative tradition, see Van Dyke 2016.
39 Catherine of Siena 1980, Prologue, *Dialogue* 4.

40 For discussion of both the controversies involved in interpreting Grosseteste's position on universals (with extensive bibliography) and my own interpretation, see Van Dyke 2010a.
41 *Commentary on the Posterior Analytics* I.14; translation mine. References are to Robert Grosseteste 1981.
42 Robert Grosseteste 1981, I.7, 100–106.
43 Ibid., I.7, 106–111.
44 Ibid., I.17, 353–363.
45 Ibid., I.14, 279–286. See chapter 18, conclusion 28 for further discussion about love and desire moving the soul.
46 See, e.g., the extended discussions of human cognition in comparison to other intellects in Aquinas, *Summa theologiae* Ia 84–89, *Summa contra gentiles* II 94–101, III 37–60, *Quaestiones de anima*, and *De veritate* VIII-X.
47 Aquinas, *Summa theologiae* IaIIae 3.3.co. In his early *Sentences Commentary*, Aquinas mentions our seeing Christ's resurrected body and the glorified bodies of the martyrs as enhancing our experience of the beatific vision, but in his works, he removes any reference to this and claims that our vision of God's essence will be entirely intellective, rather than also including a literal component.
48 See also Ibid. III.62, 8, where Aquinas explains that the enjoyment of the beatific vision never ends; our intellects will not tire in their contemplation (with God's assistance), "and no act which is carried out through a physical organ coincides with this vision". Aquinas is careful in all his discussions of the beatific vision to make it clear that this vision is purely intellective and not physical.
49 This vision is given passionate voice by the later Dominican-affiliated Catherine of Siena 1980, *Dialogue* 85:

> I have told you this, my dearest daughter, to let you know the perfection of this unitive state in which souls are carried off by the fire of my charity. In that charity, they receive supernatural light, and in that light they love me. For love follows upon understanding. The more they know, the more they love, and the more they love, the more they know. Thus each nourishes the other. By this light they reach the eternal vision of me in which they see and taste me in truth when soul is separated from body. . . . This is that superb state in which the soul even while still mortal shares the enjoyment of the immortals.

50 Aquinas, *Summa Contra Gentiles* III.51.
51 Ibid. III.60. Aquinas reiterates this point at length in his discussion of peace in his commentary on the Sermon on the Mount.
52 Aquinas, *Summa theologiae* IaIIae 3.2.ad4.
53 Aquinas, *Summa Contra Gentiles* IV.86. These qualities are possessed only by the bodies of the blessed, however. The bodies of the damned Aquinas describes as dark, heavy, suffering, and degraded. Aquinas discusses the bodies of the resurrected at length in *Summa Contra Gentiles* IV.83–89; unfortunately, the corresponding discussion in *Summa theologiae* is contained in the Supplement compiled after Aquinas's death by his followers, primarily from his much earlier *Sentences* commentary.
54 Aquinas, *Summa theologiae* IaIIae 3.3.co. Although we will have bodies and sense perception, "All the occupations of the active life (which seem ordered to the use of food and sex and those other things that are necessary for corruptible life) will cease. Only the activity of the contemplative life will remain after the resurrection." Aquinas, *Summa Contra Gentiles,* IV.83.
55 Van Dyke 2018, section 4.

Bibliography

Primary sources

Angela of Foligno (1993). *Angela of Foligno: Complete Works*, trans. P. Lachance, O.F.M., Mahwah: Paulist Press.
Catherine of Siena (1980). *Catherine of Siena: The Dialogue*, trans. S. Noffke, O.P., Mahwah: Paulist Press.
Hadewijch of Brabant (1980). *Hadewijch: The Complete Works*, ed. and trans. Mother C. Hart, O.S.B., Mahwah: Paulist Press.
Marguerite Porete (1993). *Marguerite Porete: The Mirror of Simple Souls*, trans. E. L. Babinsky, Mahwah: Paulist Press.
Mechtild of Magdeburg (1998). *Mechtild of Magdeburg: The Flowing Light of the Godhead*, trans. F. Tobin, Mahwah: Paulist Press.
Meister Eckhart (1936). *Meister Eckhart. Die deutschen Werke, Vol. 1. Herausgegeben in Auftrage der Deutschen Forschungsgmeinschaft*, Stuttgart and Berlin: W. Kohlhammer.
Meister Eckhart (1981). *Meister Eckhart: The Essential Sermons, Commentaries, Treatises, and Defense*, eds. E. Colledge, O.S.A. and B. McGinn, Mahwah: Paulist Press.
Robert Grosseteste (1981). *Commentarius in Posteriorum Analyticorum Libros*, ed. P. Rossi, Firenze, Italy: Leo S. Olschki.
"Sister Catherine" (1986). "The 'Sister Catherine' Treatise," trans. Elvira Borgstädt, in (ed.) B. McGinn, *Meister Eckhart: Teacher and Preacher*, New York: Paulist Press.

Secondary sources

Beckwith, S. (1993). *Christ's Body: Identity, Culture, and Society in Late Medieval Writings*, London: Routledge.
Brower, J. (2014). *Aquinas's Ontology of the Material World: Change, Hylomorphism, and Material Objects*, Oxford: Oxford University Press.
Bynum, C. W. (1987). *Holy Feast and Holy Fast: The Religious Significance of Food to Medieval Women*, Berkeley: University of California Press.
Bynum, C. W. (1992). *Fragmentation and Redemption: Essays on Gender and the Human Body in Medieval Religion*, New York: Zone Books.
Bynum, C. W. (1995). *The Resurrection of the Body in Western Christianity, 200–1336*, New York: Columbia University Press.
Caciola, N. (2003). *Discerning Spirits, Divine and Demonic Possession in the Middle Ages*, Ithaca: Cornell University Press.
Dales, R. (1980). "The De-Animation of the Heavens in the Middle Ages," *Journal of the History of Ideas* 41:4, 531–550.
Dales, R. (1995). *The Problem of the Rational Soul in the Thirteenth Century*, Leiden: Brill.
Flora, H. (2009). *The Devout Belief of the Imagination: The Paris Meditationes Vitae Christi and Female Franciscan Spirituality in Trecento Italy*. Disciplina Monastica, volume 6, Turnhout: Brepols.
Furlong, M. (2013). *Visions & Longings, Medieval Women Mystics*, Boston: Shambhala Publications.
Gellmann, J. (2014). "Mysticism," in (ed.) E. N. Zalta, *The Stanford Encyclopedia of Philosophy*, <http://plato.stanford.edu/archives/spr2014/entries/mysticism/>.

Hilton, W. (1994). "The Scale of Perfection," in (ed.) B. Windeatt, *English Mystics of the Middle Ages*, Cambridge: Cambridge University Press.

Hollywood, A. and P. Dailey (eds.) (2012). *The Cambridge Companion to Christian Mysticism*, Cambridge: Cambridge University Press.

Hughes, A. (2004). *The Texture of the Divine: Imagination in Medieval Islamic and Jewish Thought*, Bloomington, IN: Indiana University Press.

Idel, M. and B. McGinn (eds.) (1999). *Mystical Union in Judaism, Christianity, and Islam: An Ecumenical Dialogue*, New York: Continuum.

Jantzen, G. (1995). *Power, Gender, and Christian Mysticism*, Cambridge: Cambridge University Press.

Largier, N. (2003). "Inner Senses – Outer Senses: The Practice of Emotions in Medieval Mysticism," in (eds.) C. Jaeger and I. Kasten, *Emotions and Sensibilities in the Middle Ages*, Berlin and New York: de Gruyter, 3–15.

Lerner, R. (1972). *The Heresy of the Free Spirit in the Later Middle Ages*, Berkeley: University of California Press.

Marrone, S. (2001). *The Light of Thy Countenance: Science and Knowledge of God in the Thirteenth Century*, 2 volumes, Leiden: Brill.

Marrone, S. (2006). "From Gundisalvus to Bonaventure: Intellect and Intelligences in the Late Twelfth and Early Thirteenth Centuries," in (eds.) M. C. Pacheco and J. F. Meirinhos, *Intellect and imagination dans la philosophie médiévale*, volume 2, Brepols: Turnhout, 1071–1081.

Matter, E. A. (2012). "*Lectio Divina*," in (eds.) A. Hollywood and P. Dailey, *The Cambridge Companion to Christian Mysticism*, Cambridge: Cambridge University Press, 147–156.

McGinn, B. (1981). "Introduction," in (eds.) E. Colledge, O.S.A. and B. McGinn, *Meister Eckhart: The Essential Sermons, Commentaries, Treatises, and Defense*, Mahwah: Paulist Press.

McGinn, B. (1991, 1994, 1998, 2005, 2013, 2017). *The Presence of God: A History of Western Christian Mysticism*, New York: Crossroad.

Mooney, C. (ed.) (1999). *Gendered Voices: Medieval Saints and Their Interpreters*, Philadelphia: University of Pennsylvania Press.

Morgan, B. (2013). *On Becoming God: Late Medieval Mysticism and the Modern Western Self*, New York: Fordham University Press.

Newman, B. (2003). *God and the Goddesses: Vision, Poetry, and Belief in the Middle Ages*, Philadelphia: University of Pennsylvania Press.

Pegis, A. (1934). *St. Thomas and the Problem of the Soul in the Thirteenth Century*, Toronto: Pontifical Institute of Mediaeval Studies.

Stump, E. (2003). *Aquinas*, New York: Routledge.

Toner, P. (2012). "St. Thomas Aquinas on the Problem of Too Many Thinkers," *The Modern Schoolman* 89, 209–222.

Turner, D. (1995). *The Darkness of God: Negativity in Christian Mysticism*, Cambridge: Cambridge University Press.

Underhill, E. (1920). *The Essentials of Mysticism and Other Essays*, New York: Dutton.

Van Dyke, C. (2009). "Not Properly a Person: The Rational Soul and 'Thomistic Substance Dualism'," *Faith and Philosophy* 26:2, 186–204.

Van Dyke, C. (2010a). "The Truth, the Whole Truth, and Nothing But the Truth: Robert Grosseteste on Universals (and the *Posterior Analytics*)," *Journal of the History of Philosophy* 48:2, 153–170.

Van Dyke, C. (2010b). "Mysticism," in (eds.) R. Pasnau and C. Van Dyke, *The Cambridge History of Medieval Philosophy*, Cambridge: Cambridge University Press, 720–734.

Van Dyke, C. (2014a). "I See Dead People: Disembodied Souls and Aquinas's 'Two-Person' Problem," *Oxford Studies in Medieval Philosophy* 2, 25–45.

Van Dyke, C. (2014b). "Aquinas's Shiny Happy People: Perfect Happiness and the Limits of Human Nature," *Oxford Studies in the Philosophy of Religion* 6, 269–291.

Van Dyke, C. (2016). "Self-Knowledge, Abnegation, and Fulfillment in Medieval Mysticism," in (ed.) U. Renz, *Self-Knowledge*, Oxford Philosophical Concepts Series, Oxford: Oxford University Press, 131–145.

Van Dyke, C. (2018). "What Has History to Do With Philosophy? Insights From the Medieval Contemplative Tradition," in (ed.) M. Van Ackeren, *Philosophy and the Historical Perspective*, Proceedings of the British Academy, Oxford: Oxford University Press, 155–170.

Van Steenberghen, F. (1980). *Thomas Aquinas and Radical Aristotelianism*, Washington, DC: Catholic University Press.

Watson, N. (2011). "Introduction," in (eds.) S. Fanous and V. Gillespie, *The Cambridge Companion to Medieval English Mysticism*, Cambridge: Cambridge University Press, 1–28.

11

MORALITY

Peter S. Eardley

1 Introduction

You are offered the choice between a gift of twenty dollars, no strings attached, and one hundred dollars, also no strings attached. You take the twenty. Could a rational, not to say a *sane* person, make such a choice, all things being equal? No. But suppose that the twenty came with a free trip to Disneyland, while the hundred did not: that might well affect your deliberations, particularly if you had a weakness for the thrill of fast rides. If you were the sort of person for whom roller coasters were a source of anxiety, by contrast, you would likely take the hundred and be done with it. Of course there need be nothing particularly moral or immoral about choosing either of these options, and typically both will be equally rational or irrational depending on one's preferences with respect to one's leisure time.

But suppose that your choice to take the twenty and go to Disneyland was rooted in the conscious decision to lead a hedonistic lifestyle. You made most if not all of your decisions on the basis of the principle: *pleasure is always to be pursued*. Furthermore, suppose that the adoption of such a principle along with the choices that derived from it disqualified you from achieving eternal bliss, the existence of which you accepted, and that you appeared to be fully aware of that fact. Would your choice still be rational? Would it even be possible in the absence of some sort of ignorance on your part? Were you really, we might wonder, aware of what was at stake in making such a choice? And, if so, might we not be justified in thinking that there was something perverse about your psychological make up – something 'satanic' perhaps – that accounted for why you might deliberately choose to forgo eternal bliss, the reality of which you acknowledged, in exchange for such a transitory, worldly good as pleasure (or fame or power or wealth)? But what if this perversity was innate? How responsible would you ultimately be for the choices that sprang from it? This is the problem of deliberate wrongdoing (*malitia*) or knowingly choosing the lesser good that was so foreign to the Greek tradition but that was taken for granted in the Judeo-Christian one. As with so much else, thirteenth-century moral psychology represents an attempt to reconcile these two traditions: the Greek and the biblical.

Perhaps more than any other dilemma, the problem that flummoxed Greek moral psychology was the problem of moral weakness (*akrasia*), or whether it is possible to act against one's better judgment with respect to such objects of the sense appetite as food, drink and sex. Being generally intellectualistic in orientation, Greek thinkers tended to discern a strong connection between reason and action, making it difficult for them to see how it could be possible for rational agents to know what is best from a practical point of view and yet still be able to act against such knowledge under the influence of passion.[1] Socrates, as is well known, argued that akratic behaviour was in fact impossible since it would be 'strange if such a fine thing as knowledge (*epistêmê*) were nothing other than a slave that could be dragged about by all the other affections'.[2] All bad actions were therefore reducible to some lack of knowledge, since if the wrongdoer knew better, according to Socrates, he would do better.[3]

Aristotle held a slightly different view. For him akratic behaviour was an apparently all too common phenomenon.[4] He acknowledged that it was indeed possible for someone to know what they ought to do and yet fail to do it, against his better judgment. How so? In cases where passion is a factor, it temporarily clouds the akratic's judgment, leading him to do what he later realises he ought not to have done. Moral weakness, in short, represents a passing failure to actualise general knowledge about right and wrong, which is ordinarily possessed by the akratic agent when confronted with objects of the sense appetite. At the time that he acts, in other words, the akratic acts in ignorance. The result is that, as D.S. Hutchinson puts it, 'Aristotle manages to find an explanation of moral weakness that disturbs the Socratic position as little as possible.'[5] As a general rule, then, the Greek tradition leaves little room for the possibility of clear-eyed, non-passionate akrasia, which is to say, wrongdoing that is not ultimately reducible to some sort of ignorance.

As with Aristotle, the possibility that human beings can act from weakness due to the influence of passion was simply taken for granted in the Christian tradition, the most famous example of incontinence undoubtedly being St. Paul's description of his own moral failure in Romans 7: 'I see a different law in my members, warring against the law of my mind, and bringing me into captivity under the law of sin which is in my members. What a wretched man I am! Who will deliver me out of the body of this death?'[6] Human beings have corporeal desires that often, as it were, lead them into temptation, despite possessing habitual knowledge to the contrary, as St. Augustine was apt to point out. Indeed, from his *Confessions* we know that Augustine, like Paul, was all too familiar with the phenomenon of incontinence:

> Clouds of muddy carnal concupiscence filled the air. The bubbling impulses of puberty befogged and obscured my heart so that it could not see the difference between love's serenity and lust's darkness. Confusion of the two things boiled within me. It seized hold of my youthful weakness, sweeping me through the precipitous rocks of desire to submerge me in a whirlpool of vice.[7]

Acting against one's better judgment under the influence of 'carnal concupiscence' was therefore recognised as a distinct possibility within the medieval tradition, as it was for Aristotle. Indeed, according to some thinkers within the tradition, temptation even provided the opportunity for moral struggle and therefore virtue, and to that extent was welcome.[8] However, what is absent from even Aristotle's works, as Gosling and Pasnau have correctly observed, is the question of whether one can deliberately choose evil, or the worse course, in the absence of passion to obscure one's judgment.[9] Foreign to the Greek tradition, this form of wrongdoing – acting from deliberate malice – was distinctive to the Christian one, the most famous example of such a phenomenon within the latter being the fall of Satan.

Now, it is important to be clear about the terms that we are using. When we say that malice involves the deliberate choice of evil that is independent of passion, we are not denying that sexual desire, for example, can be associated with malice, for clearly it can. Indeed for the hedonist in our previous example, sexual gratification will probably be one of his goals in life, and perhaps even his primary one. What makes him different from the akratic or incontinent agent who commits adultery is that his desire for sexual gratification is ultimately rooted in a settled disposition to do what he apparently knows to be wrong. Malice, then, refers to any sort of wrongdoing that is done deliberately and consistently rather than, say, occasionally, out of passing weakness and under diminished judgment. As Gregory Reichberg puts it in reference to Thomas Aquinas's understanding of malice:

> We should not be misled into thinking that malice signifies a particular sort of sin, one freed from all passion, for example, or one involving especially cruel behaviour towards others. Malice refers not to a kind of sin (sins of the flesh can be done from malice); rather, it denotes a special way that sin, any kind of sin, can be carried out. When the sinner chooses to do what is gravely wrong, knowing that it is wrong, he sins from malice. Far from being a momentary lapse into vice, this agent's misdeed represents his firm and settled conviction about how his life ought to be lived.[10]

In this chapter I shall look at some of the key developments in the concept of *malitia* in medieval philosophy, and specifically during the late thirteenth and early fourteenth centuries when, as Bonnie Kent has put it, a 'transformation of ethics' was taking place.[11] I shall begin with the views of Thomas Aquinas (*ca.* 1225–1274) on the topic of how it is possible to choose the lesser option before turning to those of Henry of Ghent (*ca.* 1217–1293), a prominent voluntarist, or defender of the autonomy of the will, in the generation after Aquinas, and one of the latter's most vocal critics. I shall conclude with the interesting test case of the fall of the angels. Angels do not have bodies and therefore lack passions that might distract or otherwise corrupt their ability to clearly apprehend and apply the dictates of right reason. They are therefore, unlike human beings, incapable of sinning either from passion or from ignorance. How then did they fall from grace? The official account is that they must have acted from *malitia*. But this account, as we shall see, was fraught with philosophical problems, as we will see in the famous account of the fall of Lucifer defended by John Duns Scotus (*ca.* 1265–1308). Ultimately, such discussions are illuminating for the light that they shed on the psychological motives of wrongdoing, not to mention the question of moral responsibility.

2   Thomas Aquinas on deliberate malice

Like Aristotle, and indeed most thinkers within the ancient and medieval traditions, Thomas Aquinas was a eudaimonist.[12] He thought that human beings were psychologically predisposed towards the achievement of happiness (*beatitudo*): their highest good or ultimate end.[13] Again, like Aristotle, Aquinas thought that happiness consisted in the perfection of the rational part of the soul.[14] Unlike Aristotle, however, Thomas thought that such perfection could only be achieved in the experience of the beatific vision, which is to say, in the hereafter. Strictly speaking, then, our ultimate end can be thought of in a twofold sense: as both (1) an object, which is the cause of happiness, and (2) as the possession or enjoyment of that object.[15] The first Aquinas identifies with God, the second with the perfect actualisation of the intellect, which is attained in the next life when the beatified soul comes to know the essence of God who, as First Cause, is the ultimate explanation of all that exists. Once this is achieved, not only will the intellect of the rational creature be perfected but so too will his will (*voluntas*), since the possession of the divine essence will leave nothing further for the agent to rationally desire.[16]

Another reason that ultimate happiness cannot be had in the present life is due to the fragility of earthly existence. Happiness is 'a perfect and sufficient good <that> excludes every evil and fulfils every desire'.[17] The present life, however, contains too many evils (*mala*) that are incompatible with the experience of perfect happiness, such as ignorance, temptation and suffering.[18] Rational agents desire the good, and they desire it to be everlasting, as is evidenced from the fact that they shun death and take great pains to avoid it for as long as possible. All of this, so Thomas thinks, points to the existence of a more perfect state in the hereafter.[19] That the intellect is capable of taking on the forms of all things without their matter is testimony to the fact that the human soul is by definition immaterial and therefore incorruptible.[20]

Needless to say, if happiness consists in the perfect actualisation of the intellect which brings desire to rest, and this cannot be had in the present life for the aforementioned reasons, then neither can any created good comprise an adequate object of happiness. All the usual candidates – wealth, honour, fame, pleasure or power – are, in one respect or another, unable to answer to the foregoing definition, since none are completely satisfying, permanent nor immune from being abused.[21] Every single one of these goods, for example, can be used as a tool to exploit others in the hands of an unscrupulous person. Indeed, that the possession of such goods can be acquired by both the virtuous and the wicked alike suggests that none of them can, by definition, constitute perfect happiness, since happiness is a reward for virtue and is therefore incompatible with vice.[22]

Although external goods such as health, wealth, power, pleasure and so on cannot comprise the highest good as such, they are still constituents of the virtuous life in the present state and therefore legitimate objects of choice.[23] One's life does not go well if one is one is poor, friendless, powerless or in chronic pain. Indeed, external goods are often crucial to moral virtue. To practise the virtue of generosity, for example, it is clear that one must have some disposable income. Many of the other virtues similarly require the possession of such goods.[24] The problem is when the desire for such temporal, transitory goods becomes disordered, which happens when they come to be seen, not seen as constituents or means to the objective end for humans, but as ends in themselves and deliberately chosen to the exclusion of the true good. This is the form of wrongdoing that Aquinas calls *certa malitia* or deliberate malice.

Aquinas's account of malice comprises part and parcel of his general account of sin (*peccatum*), which represents, in its most basic form, a failure of the will to be properly ordered to its true good.

> The will lacking the direction of the rule of reason and of the Divine Law, and intent on some mutable good, causes the act of sin directly, and the inordinateness of the act, indirectly, and beside the intention: for the lack of order in the act results from the lack of direction in the will.[25]

The will is the rational appetite, which is to say, an appetite for the good as apprehended by reason.[26] It is naturally suited to follow the conclusions of practical deliberation. However, practical reason itself can be influenced by appetite, both sensitive and rational.[27] There are therefore three 'principles of human action' or three faculties of the soul that are relevant to moral activity according to Aquinas: intellect, will and sense appetite.[28] When they are all functioning properly, there is order in the soul. When any one of them becomes disordered, there is sin.

According to Aquinas, then, there are three sources of sin, which correspond to the three principles of human action when any one of them becomes defective. First of all, rational agents can sin out of ignorance, which corresponds to a defect in the intellect; second, they can sin from passion or weakness when there is a defect in the sense appetite; and finally, they can sin from malice, which corresponds to a defect in the will. Now it is important to be clear about what this defect in the will amounts to in the case of malice. This is because *all* immoral actions, whatever their source, involve a disordered will to some degree or another. Thus the will can be said to incline to evil when there is a defect in the reason, whose judgments the will is naturally suited to follow.[29] However, in that case the agent will sin not from malice, but from ignorance (*ex ignorantia*). At other times, the will inclines to evil as the result of a disorder in the concupiscible appetite, which derails the agent's judgment about what is best in a particular situation. Since the will is naturally suited to follow reason, such an obscuring of the intellect will in turn lead to a disordered will and, in turn, to a bad choice.[30] But in that case the agent sins through passion (*ex passione*) as opposed to ignorance. It is only when it is moved to evil of 'its own accord' (*ex seipsa*), rather than under the influence of passion or ignorance, that the will it is said to sin through malice as such.[31]

How precisely does Aquinas understand such a defect in the will? Malice arises in the will when it loves a lesser, transitory good – riches or pleasure are the examples Thomas uses in the *Summa* – more than the 'order of reason or divine law or divine charity or some such thing'.[32] The malicious agent is aware that his inordinate love for some transitory good runs contrary to the dictates of right reason and the divine law but seems to attach little value to that fact. He is accordingly willing to forgo the greater good, which would be achieved by following the dictates of right reason and the divine law, in return for the lesser good which can only be had by choosing contrary to these.[33] He prefers in short to profit from whatever benefits attach to sinning than to do what he knows to be right.

This is Aquinas's basic account of how rational agents can do wrong deliberately. As one can see, there is no possibility of the sinner choosing evil as such since whatever we will we will under the aspect of the good.[34] Evil is a privation, which cannot therefore be directly chosen. Rather, the principal object of volition is a *good*, albeit a temporal one. The problem for the agent who acts from malice is that he cannot enjoy the temporal good, which is the lesser one, without sinning. Still, he accepts this as a cost worth incurring. In this sense he can be said to both choose the lesser good as well as the deformity, or evil, associated with it. The difference is that the first he wills directly or principally, and the latter, indirectly or secondarily.

Take Thomas's example of adultery, which is a sin. The agent who deliberately commits adultery does not choose in the first instance to incur the fault of doing something sinful. Rather, the principal object of his volition is the good of pleasure that is attached to the adulterous act. But because he knows that he cannot enjoy the pleasure without sinning, he may be said to will not just the pleasure associated with the act, but also the deformity. He deliberately chooses, in other words, to sin, albeit in return for the pleasure of fornication, which is his primary end. As Aquinas puts it in the *De malo*:

> If then a person should wish so much to enjoy some pleasure, say, adultery, or some desirable thing of this kind, that he does not shrink from incurring the deformity of sin which he perceives to be conjoined to what he wills, not only will he be said to will that good he principally wills, but even that very deformity, which he chooses to incur, to avoid being deprived of the desired good. Hence the adulterer both wills principally the pleasure and wills secondarily the deformity.[35]

Now for Thomas the will can move toward wickedness 'of its own accord' (*ex seipsa*), or act from malice, in two ways. First, it can do so when the agent possesses a corrupt disposition, which is acquired either through habituation or through congenital defect. For such an agent, evil things – i.e., temporal goods desired in a disordered way – are naturally suitable to his disposition, and so they appear objectively good to him. And because they appear good, he is able to choose them, for Thomas insists that the will can only select what the intellect regards as good in some sense, as mentioned a moment ago.[36] Having acquired such a corrupt disposition, the agent now sees morality, at least as it applies to him, in a distorted manner.

The second way in which the will can tend to evil of its own accord is when an agent, who previously avoided sin for extrinsic reasons only, is no longer motivated by those reasons. According to Thomas, some rational agents avoid sin not because they find it repugnant – quite to the contrary – but in order to avoid punishment, for example. Once such motives are removed, they will inevitably sin. As Aquinas puts it:

> the will, of its own accord, may tend to an evil through the removal of some obstacle: for instance, if a man be prevented from sinning, not through sin being in itself displeasing to him, but through hope of eternal life, or fear of hell, if hope give place to despair, or fear to presumption, he will end in sinning through certain malice, being freed from the bridle, as it were.[37]

What should we make of Aquinas's account? When an agent acts from malice is he in fact engaged in clear-eyed wrongdoing? On the face of it, the answer is yes. The second type of malice, in particular, looks like an unambiguous case of such wrongdoing. For whatever reason, the rational agent regards himself as no longer eligible for salvation and therefore decides that he may as well indulge his appetites before he shuffles off his mortal coil. Although previously self-restrained and responsive to the dictates of right reason and the divine law for their promise of eternal salvation, he once gave into temptation, say, and engaged in an adulterous affair out of weakness. The result is that he has, rightly or wrongly, now given up all hope of salvation. He therefore decides to make the pursuit of pleasure his life's goal. What, after all, does he have to lose? So he carries on committing sins knowing that this goes against God's will – acting from deliberate malice, in other words.

Still, a potential problem for Aquinas remains. If we – and this includes the agent who sins from the second type of malice just mentioned – only ever choose anything under the aspect of the good, never being able to will evil as such, then when we act out of *malitia* it would seem that we are choosing what is in fact bad to do *as if it were* good. And this looks an awful lot like an outcome that is caused by a defect in the intellect rather than in the will. Indeed Aquinas is prepared to admit that when an agent sins from malice there is ignorance associated with his action, namely, ignorance of the general principle that evil ought not to be endured for the sake of acquiring a lesser good.[38] In point of fact Aquinas frequently argues that *all* bad acts of the will can ultimately be traced to some error in the reason, which is a natural consequence of the denial that rational beings can choose evil *qua* evil. When we do will what is objectively evil, so Thomas thinks, this is because of some antecedent error in the intellect presenting the object to the will as 'good' and therefore choiceworthy. Thomas states this quite explicitly in the *De veritate*:

> The will naturally tends to good as its object. That it sometimes tends to evil happens only because the evil is presented to it under the aspect of a good. But evil is involuntary, as Dionysius says. Consequently there cannot be any sin in the motion of the will so that it tends to evil unless there previously exists some deficiency in the apprehensive power, as a result of which something evil is presented as good.[39]

Of course, such ignorance need not let the wrongdoer off the hook, as it were. Aquinas leaves ample room in his account of moral responsibility for ignorance that is culpable, and in the case of the malicious agent this is surely the case. Such an agent ought to know or at least take care to find out that there is a principle of morality that states that evil ought not to be endured for the sake of achieving some temporal good. Either he is negligent in finding out about this principle or simply ignores it: in either case, his ignorance is voluntary and therefore entirely culpable.[40] The only type of ignorance that might potentially render the act involuntary is ignorance of particulars. Ignorance of or negligence with respect to the principles of the moral law is never excusable.[41] The reason for this is that – although this is not made explicit in his discussion of malice – Aquinas believes that all human beings, regardless of how perverse their wills have become or how corrupted their moral beliefs, retain a native habitual knowledge of the principles of morality. For Thomas this is rooted in their possession of *synderesis*, which 'can never be extinguished'.[42]

Still, Aquinas repeatedly insisted that the will never inclines to evil (*malum*) unless there is some sort of ignorance or error in the reason.[43] Sentiments such as these became a cause for concern in the generation after Aquinas, for they suggested that rational agents cannot ultimately act against their own better judgment and do wrong deliberately, despite Thomas's claims to the contrary. They implied, in short, a defense of cognitive determinism, which was regarded by some as a threat to moral responsibility, not to mention Catholic teaching.

3 Henry of Ghent on voluntarily choosing the lesser good

Regent master of theology at Paris from 1276–1293, Henry of Ghent was one of the most influential thinkers of the late thirteenth century. He was also a trenchant critic of Thomas Aquinas. Indeed, Thomas's views on moral psychology were particularly anathema to Henry, since he regarded Thomas as a soft determinist on the question of human freedom. As Henry puts it, citing Aquinas's *Summa theologiae*:

> away with the claim of some persons that 'the root of liberty, as a cause, is reason, or intellect,' though 'its subject is the will,' so that 'the will can freely be carried to different things only because reason can have different conceptions of the good.' We have elsewhere shown that this is impossible. Indeed the will (*voluntas*) is both the subject and first root of liberty.[44]

Whether Aquinas was an intellectual determinist or not is beyond the scope of the present chapter.[45] What is clear is that he was regarded as such by several of his contemporaries and near contemporaries. We now know, for example, that Thomas's teachings on human freedom were implicated in the infamous condemnations of 1277 at the University of Paris, on which commission Henry served as a member.[46] Two of the condemned articles on the will in particular were believed to have been derived from or at least associated with Aquinas's works: (1) article 129: 'that the will, while desire and particular knowledge remain in act, cannot act contrary to that knowledge (*Quod voluntas, manente passione et scientia particulari in actu, non potest agere contra eam*)', and (2) article 130: 'that if reason is correct, then the will is correct (*Quod si ratio recta, et voluntas recta*)'.[47]

In the wake of the condemnations, to hold or even to teach either of these propositions at Paris was considered grounds for excommunication.[48] The worry was clearly that any defense of such heterodox opinions diminished moral responsibility since they seemed to deny that human beings could act from deliberate malice. Rather, they implied that the ultimate cause of sin was ignorance or error, the corrective for which was not punishment, but education.[49] What then was the correct account of wrongdoing? Since Henry of Ghent was one of the theologians responsible for drafting the list of condemned articles, we must turn to his writings to answer this question.

In his first quodlibet Henry addressed the question of whether, when the intellect presents the will with two goods, one greater and one lesser, the will is able to choose the lesser.[50] According to Henry, this question can be reframed in terms of whether the will possesses the freedom to act either in accordance with the judgment of right reason or against it, or whether, to the contrary, it must always follow such a judgment, whether correct or erroneous.[51] Those who adhered to the first possibility we might term 'voluntarists'. Those who held that the will always follows the judgment of practical reason, on the other hand, we might call 'intellectualists'. Henry was a staunch defender of the former position as against the latter.

As Henry characterises the intellectualist view, human freedom is ultimately rooted in practical reason's ability to compare alternative courses of action during deliberation. Out of this process comes an intellectual judgment – that may or may not be correct – that *x* or *y* option would be best to pursue. The will duly follows this judgment and the agent makes, on that basis, his or her choice. I have just completed a bachelor's degree in philosophy and am presently trying to decide between going to law school and pursuing my Ph.D. in the subject. Although I am attracted to the idea of teaching and doing research in medieval philosophy, there are simply no jobs in the area, which is an important consideration for me. I decide against graduate school and opt to go to law school instead. Note that, on this view, the will cannot deviate from the intellect's considered judgment that going to law school ought, on balance, to be preferred.[52] Henry strongly objects to this account. For him, such a picture of human action reduces the will to the level of the natural appetite, which necessarily follows its own form, whether that form be natural in the case of things without cognition or pleasurable in the case of the animals who possess sense cognition. For Henry, to reduce the will to the level of the sense appetite or the natural appetite is effectively to say that it acts necessarily rather than freely.[53]

Henry concedes of course that the will is a rational appetite that depends on the intellect for its objects. To claim that the will can make choices entirely independently of reason would be to make human action random and unintelligible. The key for Henry then is to ensure that the will is sufficiently influenced by practical reason to make human action intelligible, while granting the will sufficient autonomy from the judgments of the intellect to preserve moral responsibility. How does Henry achieve this balancing act? In the act of choice there is a concurrence of two operations. The first occurs on the part of the intellect, which proposes two objects of choice, one better and one worse, and the second on the part of the will, which has the power to choose one over the other. If the will opts for the object that reason judges better, then the resulting choice is virtuous.[54] In a later quodlibetal question Henry will reiterate this point, namely that the will, alone amongst the powers of the soul, is fully autonomous with respect to everything except the last end, which cannot be refused when clearly intuited. With respect to all other objects, the will is radically free to accept or to reject them. To assume any other view is to deny human freedom and therefore moral responsibility.[55]

In short, while Henry's adversary Thomas Aquinas thought of the will as a moved mover that must be reduced to act by the intelligible object, Henry regards the will as a self-moving power that reduces *itself* from potency to act – a free power, in other words. The intellect, by contrast, is not similarly free since it is, amongst other things, necessitated by the rules of logic. It is for this reason that it is pointless to try to ground human freedom in the indeterminacy of the intellect since, to the extent that the intellect possesses any freedom at all, this is derived from the will, which has the power of command over it:

> If we want to speak of freedom of decision in the proper and strict sense, it is in the will alone and not at all in reason, except insofar as reason is freely moved by the will to investigate different things. Cognitive reason

as such is in fact not free. For it is moved by the simple objects of cognition necessarily, and it is not in its power not to apprehend these. Nor is it in its power not to assent to the connection of the [terms in] self-evident first principles and to the [demonstrative] connection [between the principles and] the conclusions. In fact, when a conclusion presents itself to reason by way of a necessary proof, it assents of necessity; when the proof is relatively manifest, it necessarily opines accordingly.[56]

It follows from Henry's account that when it comes to doing evil the will can choose the lesser good – act from malice in other words – entirely at its own discretion.[57] Interestingly, Henry acknowledges that the will can only choose an object under the aspect of the good, whether real or apparent.[58] But does this not suggest that when there is malice in the will there must be some ignorance in the intellect and, if so, is this not ultimately similar Aquinas's (intellectualistic) position? In the next question of his first quodlibet, Henry addresses this very issue, namely, 'whether a disorder (*deordinatio*) in the will is caused by a disorder in the reason, or vice versa'.[59] The ostensible topic of this quodlibet is incontinence: sins associated with passion to which there is always some error or clouding of the intellect attached. Is such error the cause of a malicious will or rather an effect?

According to Henry, some theologians (again, the target here is almost certainly Thomas Aquinas) argue that a disorder in the will is always caused by a prior disorder in the intellect. For such thinkers, some antecedent determination on the part of the intellect is always required in order to reduce the will from potency to act. In the case of sinning from passion the incontinent actually possesses the correct (though highly abstract) moral principle that, say, fornication is immoral. Sexual desire for the flesh and blood acquaintance that is in her presence, however, clouds her awareness of that principle, causing her reason to err and to judge the pleasurable option as the best of the alternatives at that moment. Her will then necessarily follows in accordance with this wrong judgment, ushering in the adulterous, sinful act.[60] The ultimate cause of the act is passion although the proximate cause is ignorance.

Henry, by contrast, argues that it is the *will* that is the ultimate cause of wrongdoing in this case and, for that matter, any other. Where incontinence is concerned there is obviously passion involved, which in turn clouds the judgment of the intellect and leads it into error. But Henry is emphatic that the disordered state of the intellect comes *after* the will has dispassionately, as it were, consented to passion. Unlike Thomas, for whom passion can obscure reason directly, Henry thinks that this can only happen with the will's consent. Although, then, Henry agrees with Aquinas that the will only ever chooses under the aspect of the good – that there is never malice in the will unless there is some error in the reason – the will and the will alone is the power that is ultimately responsible for controlling how the object is evaluated by the practical intellect. Whatever ignorance is associated with wrongdoing is therefore, so Henry thinks, voluntary. It is in this sense that the will can be said to act against right reason. As Henry puts it:

> if a vicious disorder arises in the will this is due to its own depraved delight or from a consent to the enjoyment of an apparent good with one's senses, so that it is <the will> *itself* that is the first cause of its own disorder . . . and not some ignorance or disorder in the reason.[61]

To hold any other view would make it impossible to make sense of Adam's sin, not to mention that of Lucifer.

4 Duns Scotus on the fall of the angels

For the medievals, the fall of Lucifer was the test case par excellence of how the will of a rational creature might become disordered. According to the standard account, as Hoffman has succinctly put it, 'Lucifer sinned first, then other angels, then Adam and Eve, and finally the human race born from them.'[62] Angels do not have bodies and are therefore not subject to the temptation of passion, nor are they prone to ignorance nor, prior to their fall, could any of them have had wills that were in any way inclined to evil. The sin of the demons must therefore have been a case of non-passionate, clear-eyed akrasia. But why would such beings – virtually perfect, for all intents and purposes – have acted in such an obviously irrational way? If there was ever a case of sinning from malice – that is, deliberately acting against what one knows to be best, free from passion or ignorance – then the fall of Lucifer and the demons would seem to be it. Working out how this was possible naturally led medieval thinkers to speculation about the ultimate foundations of freedom and the relation of the will to the intellect.

Both Thomas Aquinas and Henry of Ghent devoted serious attention to the question of angelic sin. For both, the angels fell, not from desiring evil as such, but from desiring a good object – happiness – in a disordered way. The difference between the two thinkers was that Henry attributed the moral failure of Lucifer ultimately to his will, while Aquinas did not.[63] Perhaps the most famous use of the test case of angelic sin, however, was that of John Duns Scotus, who invoked the theory of Anselm (*ca.* 1033–1109) of the two affections of the will in an effort to show how Lucifer's fall could have been both free and deliberate.[64] Like Henry, Scotus was a voluntarist who traced the ultimate cause of Lucifer's sin to his will.

There are two acts of the will: liking or wanting (*velle*) and disliking or aversion (*nolle*), the latter being parasitic, as it were, on the former.[65] We only dislike something, according to Scotus, because it interferes with the acquisition of something we like and value.[66] We dislike sickness because it interferes with health, which we desire, and we dislike poverty because it interferes with our comfortable self-preservation, which we also desire. There are two acts of liking or wanting in a volitional sense: love of friendship (*velle amicitiae*) and love of concupiscence (*velle concupiscentiae*). These wants or loves are good, but they can become disordered.

Because a friend is one towards whom we wish well, to the extent that we want what is best for ourselves, love of friendship can be self-reflexive. There are three possible objects of friendship-love: God, other people and ourselves. Because it is impossible to love God inordinately and because our love of others is derivative of our love for ourselves, it must be the case that the very first sin of Lucifer was an act of inordinate love for himself that was rooted in the love of friendship:

> And this is what Augustine says in *The City of God*, Bk. XIV: 'Two loves created two cities; the love of God to the contempt of self created the city of God and the love of self to the contempt of God created the city of the devil.' The first source from which the city of the devil stems, then, is inordinate friendship-love, which root germinates until it yields contempt of God, in which malice (*malitia*) reaches its peak. It is clear, then, that the initial disorder in an unqualified sense consists in that inordinate <self> love that was simply first.[67]

Now according to Scotus the result of Lucifer's inordinate love of friendship (*amicitia*) towards himself was that it generated another disordered love: that of concupiscence (*concupiscentia*) by which Lucifer, according to Scotus, immoderately desired happiness for himself. Like all rational agents, humans included, Lucifer's will consisted of two inclinations: the 'affection for the advantageous' (*affectio commodi*) and the 'affection for justice' (*affectio iustitiae*).[68] The first *affectio* refers to the will's inclination towards personal happiness or self-actualisation, and Scotus associates it with the rational or intellective appetite. The latter *affectio*, by contrast, refers to the will's ability to incline to the good for its own sake, independent of whether such a volition contributes to personal happiness, and which Scotus associates with the 'freedom that is innate to the will'.[69] This is because the affection for justice acts, according to Scotus, as a 'checkrein' (*moderatrix*) on the affection for the advantageous, in the absence of whose moderating influence we would desire our own advantage both necessarily and in a disordered fashion.[70] And this is exactly how Lucifer fell. He failed, according to Scotus, to moderate his desire for his own happiness, which he had an obligation to do according to the rule of justice that is rooted in the divine will, which is a higher will than his own.[71] Lucifer acted, in other words, in an insubordinate way.

Now notice that both the affection for the advantageous and the affection for justice are inclinations toward *goods*. To follow either inclination in pursuit of its respective good – personal happiness or the good for its own sake – is therefore to act for a reason. The problem, however, is that the choice over whether to act in accordance with one inclination over the other, or one as moderated by the other, remains entirely unexplained and therefore, in an ultimate sense, arbitrary. Although we are choosing goods, in other words, our choices themselves ultimately seem to have no rational basis. The radical freedom of the will seems to trump the rationality of choice, leaving all of our actions ultimately mysterious. Of course, if the preservation of moral responsibility were achieved in such an account, then sacrificing the rationality of choice might be worth the trade off. But this is not obviously the case. For on such an account of freedom the will cannot be determined by causes or reasons outside of itself, which includes, presumably, me. My will, and therefore all of my choices, are no more under my control than the will of anyone else. So much for moral responsibility.

5 Conclusion

In the end, the situation is perhaps not so dire for humans as it was for Lucifer and the demons. Once the demons made their bad choice their wills became obstinately malicious and their fall from grace irrevocable. It is difficult to see how Lucifer's primal sin could have been anything but irrational. Human beings, by contrast, even if they have committed the most extreme of mortal sins, are eligible according to Christian theology for redemption, provided that they are willing to repent of their sins. Given this, many people might well be tempted to pray, with Augustine, 'O Lord, give me chastity and continence, but not yet.' One could both enjoy the sin, as it were, as well as eternal life, so long as one played one's cards right. Indeed, such a sentiment would be quite rational.

Notes

1 Charleton 1988, 4.
2 Plato, *Protagoras* 352B.
3 Idem. *Protagoras* 352A-358D. See also, *Meno* 77C-79D and *Gorgias* 468A-469A.
4 Aristotle, *Nicomachean Ethics* 1145b28. There is a significant literature on the topic of moral weakness in Aristotle. See, however, Charles 2007 and Pickavé and Whiting 2008.
5 Hutchinson 1995, 217.
6 See Kretzmann 1998. Recent literature on the question of moral weakness in the medieval tradition is quite substantial. Good places to start, however, are: Saarinen 1994 and Hoffmann, Müller and Perkams 2006.
7 Augustine, *Confessions* 2.2. (Trans. Chadwick 1991, 24).
8 In the twelfth century, for example, Peter Abelard argued exactly this. See his *Ethics or 'Know Yourself'* 1.22.
9 Gosling 1990, 71 and Pasnau 2002, 249, 442n16.
10 Reichberg 2002, 778.
11 Kent 1995.
12 On this, see Eardley 2006a and Eardley 2013.
13 Thomas Aquinas, *Summa theologiae* 1a.2ae, q. 1, a. 7, corp.: 'all agree is desiring the last end since all desire the fulfilment of their perfection, and it is precisely this fulfilment in which the last end consists.'
14 Ibid., 1a-2ae, q. 5, a. 1, corp.
15 Ibid., 1a2ae, q. 3, a. 1, corp.
16 Ibid., 1a2ae, q. 3, aa. 4 and 8.
17 Ibid., 1a2ae, q. 5. a. 3, corp.
18 Aquinas is of course following Augustine here, as he tells us explicitly. See Augustine's *City of God*, 19.4 on all of the ills of earthly existence.

19 Thomas Aquinas, *Summa theologiae* 1a2ae, q. 5, a. 3, corp.
20 Ibid., 1a, q. 75, a. 2, corp.
21 Ibid., 1a2ae, q. 2, a. 4, corp.
22 Ibid.
23 On this, see for example, Bradley 1997, 401–403.
24 Thomas Aquinas, *Commentary on Aristotle's* Nicomachean Ethics, 1.16.
25 Ibid., *Summa theologiae* 1a2ae, q. 75, a. 1, corp.
26 Ibid., 1a2ae, q. 8, a. 1, corp.
27 Ibid., 1a2ae, q. 77, a. 1, corp.
28 Ibid., 1a2ae, q. 78, a. 1, corp.
29 Ibid., 1a, q. 83, a. 3, ad 2.
30 Ibid., 1a2ae, q. 75, a. 2, corp.
31 Ibid., 1a2ae, q. 78, a. 3, corp.
32 Ibid., 1a2ae, q. 78, a. 1.
33 Ibid.:

> when an inordinate will loves some temporal good, e.g. riches or pleasure, more than the order of reason or Divine law, or Divine charity, or some such thing, it follows that it is willing to suffer the loss of some spiritual good, so that it may obtain possession of some temporal good.

34 Ibid., 1a2ae, q. 77, a. 2, corp.
35 Thomas Aquinas, *Disputed Questions on Evil*, q. 3, a. 12, corp.
36 Idem, *Summa theologiae* 1a2ae, q. 78, a. 3, corp.
37 Ibid.
38 Ibid., 1a2ae, q. 78, a. 1, ad 1.
39 Aquinas, *Disputed Questions on Truth*, q. 24, a. 8, corp.
40 Ibid., *Summa theologiae* 1a2ae, q. 19, a. 6, corp.
41 Ibid.
42 Thomas Aquinas, *Disputed Questions on Truth*, q. 16, a. 3, corp.
43 Ibid., 1a2ae, q. 77, a. 2, corp.
44 Henry of Ghent, *Quodlibet* 9.6. (trans. Teske 1993, 72). Henry is citing Thomas's *Summa theologiae* I–II, q. 17, a. 1, ad 2.
45 But see, for example, Gallagher 1994, 247–277 and Hoffmann 2007, 122–156.
46 There is a rather large literature on the condemnations. Some standard works, however, are Aertsen et al., 2001, Hissette 1977, Thijssen 1998, 40–56, and Wippel 1977.
47 Piché 1999, 118.
48 See Tempier's letter attached to the list of condemned articles in Piché 1999, 72–77.
49 On the condemnations as they touched on the questions of human freedom and moral responsibility, see for example, Kent 1995, 76–79, Putallaz 1995, 65–91, and Eardley 2006b.
50 Henry of Ghent, *Quodlibet* 1.16, 5: 94. For a detailed discussion of this and other relevant texts, see Hoffmann 2008.
51 Ibid., 5: 96.
52 Ibid., 5: 98–101.
53 Ibid.
54 Ibid., 5: 104.
55 Ibid., 9.5. (trans. Teske 1993, 58–59).
56 Ibid., *Quodlibet* 1.16, 5: 107–108 (trans. Hoffmann 2008, 121).
57 Ibid., 5: 111.
58 Ibid., 5: 110.
59 Ibid., *Quodlibet* 1.17, 5: 115.

60 Ibid., 5: 124.
61 Ibid., 5: 140.
62 Hoffmann 2012, 286.
63 Hoffmann 2012, 286–293.
64 The locus classicus for Scotus's treatment of angelic sin can be found in his *Ordinatio* 2.6.2. An English translation of this text can be found in Wolter 1986, 463–477.
65 Note that 'like' and 'dislike' are Wolter's terms for the Latin *velle* and *nolle*. Gosling, on the other hand, refers to them as 'wanting' and 'aversion'. See Wolter 1986, 462–463 and Gosling 1990, 82.
66 Scotus, *Ordinatio* 2.6.2 (trans. Wolter 1986), 462–463.
67 Ibid., 465.
68 Scotus derives this theory from Anselm's *De casu diaboli*. For an overview of the theory as Scotus employs it, see Ingham and Dreyer 2004, 156–162.
69 Ibid., 470–471.
70 Ibid., 464–469.
71 Ibid.

Bibliography

Primary sources

Augustine (1991). *Confessions*, trans. H. Chadwick, Oxford: Oxford University Press.

Henry of Ghent (1979–). "*Quodlibeta*," in (ed.) R. Macken, *Henrici de Gandavo Opera Omnia*, Leuven: Leuven University Press.

Henry of Ghent (1993). "Quodlibetal Questions on Free Will," trans. R.J. Teske, *Mediaeval Philosophical Texts in Translation, Vol. 32*. Milwaukee: Marquette University Press.

Peter Abelard (1995). *Ethics, or Know Thyself*, trans. P. V. Spade, Indianapolis: Hackett Publishing Company.

Plato (1997). *Plato Complete Works*, ed. J. Cooper, Indianapolis/Cambridge: Hackett Publishing.

Secondary sources

Aertsen, J. A. et al., eds. (2001). *Nach der Verurteilung von 1277: Philosophie und Theologie an der Universität von Paris im letzten Viertel des 13. Jahrhunderts*. Studien und Texte. Miscellanea Mediaevalia 28, Berlin: De Gruyter.

Bradley, D. J. M. (1997). *Aquinas on the Twofold Human Good: Reason and Human Happiness in Aquinas's Moral Science*, Washington, DC: The Catholic University of America Press.

Charles, D. (2007). "Aristotle's Weak Akrates: What Does Her Ignorance Consist In?," in (eds.) C. Bobonich and P. Destree, *Akrasia in Greek Philosophy*, Leiden: Brill, 193–214.

Charleton, W. (1988). *Weakness of Will*, Oxford: Basil Blackwell.

Eardley, P. S. (2006a). "Conceptions of Happiness and Human Destiny in the Late Thirteenth Century," *Vivarium* 44, 276–304.

Eardley, P. S. (2006b). "The Problem of Moral Weakness, the *Propositio Magistralis* and the Condemnation of 1277," *Mediaeval Studies* 68, 161–203.

Eardley, P. S. (2013). "Happiness," in (eds.) K. Pollmann and W. Otten, *The Oxford Guide to the Historical Reception of Augustine*, Oxford: Oxford University Press, 605–609.

Gallagher, D. (1994). "Free Choice and Free Judgment in Thomas Aquinas," *Archiv für Geschichte der Philosophie* 76, 247–277.

Gosling, J. (1990). *Weakness of the Will*, London and New York: Routledge.

Hissette, R. (1977). *Enquête sur les 219 articles condamnés à Paris le 7 mars 1277*, Louvain: Publications Universitaires.

Hoffmann, T. (2007). "Aquinas and Intellectual Determinism: The Test Case of Angelic Sin," *Archiv für Geschichte der Philosophie* 89, 122–156.

Hoffmann, T. (2008). "Henry of Ghent's Voluntarist Account of Weakness of Will," in (ed.) T. Hoffmann, *Weakness of Will From Plato to the Present Day*, Washington, DC: The Catholic University of America Press, 115–137.

Hoffmann, T. (2012). "Theories of Angelic Sin From Aquinas to Ockham," in (ed.) T. Hoffmann, *A Companion to Angels in Medieval Philosophy*, Leiden: Brill, 283–316.

Hoffmann, T., Müller, J. and Perkams, M. (2006). *Das Problem der Willensschwäche in der mittelalterlichen Philosophie: The Problem of Weakness of Will in Medieval Philosophy*, Bibliotheca 8, Leuven: Peeters.

Hutchinson, D. S. (1995). "Ethics," in (ed.) J. Barnes, *The Cambridge Companion to Aristotle*, Cambridge: Cambridge University Press, 195–232.

Ingham, M. B. and Dreyer, M. (2004). *The Philosophical Vision of John Duns Scotus: An Introduction*, Washington, DC: The Catholic University of America Press.

Kent, B. (1995). *Virtues of the Will: The Transformation of Ethics in the Late Thirteenth Century*, Washington, DC: The Catholic University of America Press.

Kretzmann, N. (1998). "Warring Against the Law of My Mind: Aquinas on Romans 7," in (ed.) T. V. Morris, *Philosophy and the Christian Faith*, Notre Dame, IN: University of Notre Dame Press, 172–195.

Pasnau, R. (2002). *Thomas Aquinas on Human Nature: A Philosophical Study of Summa theologiae Ia 75–89*, Cambridge: Cambridge University Press.

Piché, D. ed. (1999). *La condamnation parisienne de 1277: Texte latin, traduction et commentaire*, Paris: Vrin.

Pickavé, M. and Whiting, J. (2008). "Nicomachean Ethics 7.3 on Akratic Ignorance," *Oxford Studies in Ancient Philosophy* 34, 323–372.

Putallaz, F.-X. (1995). *Insolente liberté: Controverses et condamnations au XIIIe siècle*, Fribourg: Editions Universitaires.

Reichberg, G. M. (2002). "Beyond Privation: Moral Evil in Aquinas's *De Malo*," *The Review of Metaphysics* 55, 751–784.

Saarinen, R. (1994). *Weakness of the Will in Medieval Thought: From Augustine to Buridan*, Leiden: E.J. Brill.

Thijssen, J. M. M. H. (1998). *Censure and Heresy at the University of Paris, 1200–1400*, Philadelphia: The University of Pennsylvania Press.

Wippel, J. F. (1977). "The Condemnations of 1270 and 1277 at Paris," *The Journal of Medieval and Renaissance Studies* 7, 169–201.

Wolter, A. B. (1986). *Duns Scotus on the Will and Morality: Selected and Translated With an Introduction*, Washington, DC: The Catholic University of America Press.

12

THE SELF

John Marenbon

1 Introduction: the self, knowledge of the self and subjectivity

A fuller title for this chapter would be: 'The self without subjectivity'.

That title might seem a contradiction in terms. Most reflection on the self today is about subjectivity and its importance – the idea that we each have experiences that are *ours*, a first-personal perspective on the world, and that it matters that it is so. Such reflection begins from the self as the subject of experiences – of thoughts, feelings, images and pains. This self is conceived as something present to each of us: we are each aware of it, some believe, all the time, or at least whenever we wish. Such awareness is bare and inarticulate and, in itself, thin and momentary: an awareness of what has been described as "the ultimate private object, apparently lacking logical connections to anything else, mental or physical ... which cannot be defined as a kind of object, either physical or non-physical, but must be understood as some subjective consciousness" (Nagel 1986, 32–33).

From this bare self-consciousness we can work towards a self-knowledge based on our subjectivity. To take a famous example: Descartes (*Meditation* II) puts the bare self we encounter whenever we introspect at the foundation of his system of knowledge. From awareness of the bare self, the meditator quickly discovers, by reflection, what he is – a thinking thing, where 'thinking' (*cogitans*) means having experiences: not just understanding, affirming, denying, but also willing, imagining and feeling. Although such self-knowledge is not personal, in the sense of being about the peculiarities of Descartes's or some other meditator's character, or the particular contents of his mental world, it is subjective – an account in general terms of what I am from within. Such an account can also be developed in another direction. Although we encounter our subjective consciousness moment by moment, most theorists (there are some exceptions, such as Hume) hold that there is a unified self that underlies these moments and makes them belong together.

A rather dated, but still widespread, misconception is that such notions of the self and subjectivity are modern ones, anticipated perhaps in late antiquity, but with little purchase on the following centuries until the time of Descartes.

Foucault's *The Order of Things* (*Les mots et les choses*), published a half-century ago, and Charles Taylor's *Sources of the Self* (1989) were especially influential sources for the view.[1] Scholars of medieval philosophy, who before then had hardly considered the self, reacted to this exclusion of their period. Whereas specialists in ancient philosophy questioned the framework imposed on study of the self by this modernity-centred historiography (e.g. Sorabji 2006; Remes 2007), the medievalists accepted the terms of those they were setting out to correct and sought to show that subjectivity is not a modern discovery by finding it in accounts of self-knowledge from centuries earlier. They have been remarkably successful. Augustine's theory of self-knowledge has been shown to be – as Taylor himself had, indeed, anticipated (1989, 127–142) – a landmark in the theory of subjectivity (Cary 2000). From the late thirteenth century onwards, university theologians – especially the Franciscans, who were very open to Augustine's influence – developed sophisticated theories of self-knowledge, which often were based on the idea of the subjective self; according to some historians, even Aquinas was among their number (see section 12.6). And, recently, specialists in Islamic thought have pointed out that subjectivity is central to the thinking of the Avicenna (d. 1037) and of a whole series of thinkers who followed him, from Suhrawardī in the twelfth century to Mulla Ṣadrā in the seventeenth (see section 12.5). It might still be objected that, although self-knowledge is treated by many medieval writers, the self, as a theoretical concept, is modern; a chapter on 'The Self' in a volume on the period 500–1300 is a blatant anachronism. No doubt: but is it a useful anachronism? The following pages aim to show that it is, and the Conclusion (section 12.7) returns to this methodological point.

If the aim of the chapters in this collection were to synthesize and present the findings of current scholarship, then the subject of the following pages would be the material just described, in so far as it falls between 500 and 1300. But contributors have been asked, rather, to provide new research. The focus chosen is, therefore, a different one, which puts the elements usually in the historiographical mainstream at the edges so as to look in detail at aspects of the topic that have been neglected. The self is far wider as a topic than subjectivity. On the one hand, rather than being seen as the centre of our subjectivity, the self can be conceived as that which, for each of us, remains as we change – what grounds our personal identity. Some theories of this sort do, indeed, urge that it is our continuity as subjects of experience that gives us identity, but some look in a quite different direction, even to the extent of leaving anything distinctively mental out of their account. On the other hand, there are theories of self-knowledge which do not involve subjectivity much or at all. They are orientated mainly to a knowledge of the self that is not subjective. Although derived from introspection, this knowledge is not about how it looks from within. These two areas will be the main concern of this chapter – especially the second of them, since much in the first falls outside the philosophy of mind. Not only does this focus allow for a new approach and give the chance to question some of the assumptions of current scholarship, it also fits the whole period far better, since there are almost no texts dealing with the self in terms of subjectivity from the Latin tradition between Augustine and the thirteenth century.

A single chapter can offer only case studies. The first one is about Boethius's *Consolation of Philosophy*, written in the early sixth century, which provides a dense and perhaps far from straightforward example of a common ancient and early medieval approach to self-knowledge without subjectivity, in which the true self, so far from being ever present to each of us, is hidden, an ideal that can only with difficulty be discovered or rediscovered. The second case study looks at the ninth-century philosopher John Scottus Eriugena, who approaches the self in terms of continuity between life on earth and after death and also from the point of view of self-knowledge, and in both cases arrives at theories which have no place for the self of subjective experience. The next section uses Anselm's *Monologion* to illustrate how early medieval theologians, unlike their thirteenth-century successors, did not derive a theory of self-knowledge from Augustine's *On the Trinity*, although it was a widely read text, but did use it to develop an equally Augustinian but non-subjective idea of the self. There follows a glimpse at philosophy in Arabic which looks very briefly at Avicenna's idea of the self before turning to Ibn Ṭufayl, a twelfth-century philosopher who takes the Avicennian self but adapts and, perhaps, ultimately rejects it. The final section before the conclusion rejoins the bulk of current writing on the area by looking at the theories of self-knowledge and subjectivity in late thirteenth-century Franciscan theology. But the central question it poses is whether Aquinas also had such a theory, or whether he too conceived a form of self-knowledge without subjectivity.

2   Boethius: the self as an ideal

Boethius's *Consolation of Philosophy* does not seem to be a discussion of the self. Set in circumstances taken directly from its author's own life, it presents Boethius imprisoned and awaiting execution on trumped-up charges of treason.[2] He is visited in his cell by Philosophy, a personification of the wisdom he had learned through his studies but has forgotten in the shock of his sudden downfall. Philosophy treats Boethius as a sick man, whom she sets out to cure. One aspect of his sickness is his failure to recognize how God rules the world (I.6.7–8). In the dialogue which follows, Philosophy provides a cure by showing Boethius that, despite appearances, he has lost nothing of value, the wicked neither prosper nor have power and humans are encompassed in divine providence along with all creation. But, when she is diagnosing his illness, Philosophy judges that it has another, more fundamental cause – Boethius's ignorance of himself.

After Boethius has acknowledged that he is a man, she asks him what a man is. He responds with the classic Aristotelian definition, 'a mortal, rational animal', and is unable to add anything further (I.6.14–16). "Now," she says, "I know another cause of your illness – the greatest one. You have stopped knowing what you are. And so I have completely discovered both the reason for your sickness and the way to restore you to health" (I.6.17). Already, almost immediately after her first appearance, Philosophy had identified Boethius's sickness as that of having "forgotten himself" (I.2.5: "he is suffering from a lethargy, the common illness of deceived minds. He has forgotten himself for a little"). The theme is taken up again, in the next book, when Philosophy is showing Boethius why none of the transitory goods of fortune, which he has complained about losing, are true goods. She summarizes her point in terms of a contrast between what is inner and proper to humans and what is external to them. "Is there then no good which is your own and within you, so that you seek your goods in things that are external and set apart from you?" asks Philosophy sarcastically (II.5.24). She goes on to complain about how man, a "divine animal because of his reason", "similar to God in his mind", is not content with himself. "Human nature," she concludes,

> has the condition that, when it knows itself, it excels other things, but it is brought lower than the beasts if it ceases to know itself, because it is natural for other animals not to know themselves, but for humans it is a vice.
> (II.5. 29)

But what is it that humans know when they know themselves, and which Boethius the character, despairing in his prison cell, had forgotten? What are humans beyond being, as Boethius had recognized, rational, mortal animals? The answer Philosophy will imply sounds shocking, although it is a view which was accepted by both pagans and Christians in late antiquity (Boethius 1925, 88; Gruber 2006, 293–294). They are gods. Happiness and divinity itself, Philosophy has established, are identical; and so, given that humans become happy by gaining happiness, they must gain divinity when they become happy. But, in the same way that gaining justice or wisdom makes someone just or wise, gaining divinity makes those who gain it gods. Therefore "every happy person is a god" – though Philosophy hastily adds that by nature God is one, "but nothing prevents his being many by participation" (III.10.22–25). Although Philosophy does not connect her comments here with Boethius's ignorance of himself, the verse section which follows asserts that we gain true knowledge by looking into ourselves: "what the mind strives for outside it possesses concealed in its own treasure-chests: what the black cloud of error long concealed will shine more clearly than Phoebus himself" (III, m. xi, lines 5–8).

My self, then, for Boethius is anything but the bare subject which I might encounter at any moment of introspection, although I do need to introspect in order to discover it. My self is what I am potentially and what I can become in actuality through self-knowledge. This self-knowledge has nothing to do with my individual characteristics: it is simply that of what I am, as a human, beyond being just a rational, mortal animal, as Boethius had believed in his self-forgetfulness when Philosophy first entered his cell. But, just as through self-knowledge I can become what I truly am, a god, so, through a more complete forgetfulness of myself than the prisoner's I can cease altogether to be human. "Whatever falls away from the good," insists Philosophy (IV.3.15),

> ceases to be. And so it happens that the wicked cease to be what they were. The fact that the appearance of the human body remains shows that they once were humans: because they have turned to evil, they have lost even their human nature.

Philosophy goes on to compare wicked people to various animals – the greedy to wolves, the irate to lions and so on, and ends (IV.3.21) by suggesting that those humans who fail to find their true selves as gods will turn in this way into beasts. She is not pointing merely to metaphorical likenesses (cf. Dougherty 2004; Van den Meeren 2012, 157–185). The poem she goes on to incant (IV m. iii) brings out her point very clearly. She tells the story of Ulysses's crew enchanted by Circe and given the physical appearance of lions, wolves and tigers. But the enchantress is unable to affect their minds: they are the very opposite of the wicked, who keep their human shape but have really become lower than humans.

As in his presentation of many of the individual themes in the *Consolation*, Boethius is deeply unoriginal. His idea of an inner human self that is more-than-human is a tradition that goes back to Plotinus and ultimately to Plato himself (cf. Remes 2007), and the opposite transformation, of wicked humans into beasts, was a common theme, found in Cicero, Stoic and Platonic writers (see Gruber 2006, 331). Yet, arguably, the overall structure of the *Consolation* adds a layer of complexity to what Boethius takes from his sources. Philosophy gives the Prisoner two different sorts of answer to his complaints that he has suffered unjustly, that the wicked prosper and that God has omitted humans from his providential plan, the first plausible, the second strenuously argued but counter-intuitive. The plausible set of answers rests on a varied conception of the good and on a view of God as an efficient cause, arranging the universe for the best. They are intended to show the Prisoner that the goods he has lost are not true goods but only the false goods of fortune and that his trials have a purpose in a divinely ordered universe. The counter-intuitive set of answers depends on a monolithic conception of the good, in which only the supreme good, which is God, should be sought, and on a view of God as only a final cause: the good are rewarded simply by doing good, and the evil punish themselves whenever they do evil (Marenbon 2003, 96–121). One reason why the Prisoner's ignorance of himself, although diagnosed as the fundamental cause of his illness, receives only passing treatment as the dialogue progresses may be that Philosophy's solution as to what he really is, a god, and what the wicked have become, beasts, makes sense only in connection with the counter-intuitive set of answers, along with which it is indeed presented. Many interpreters consider that Philosophy intends the counter-intuitive answers as the correct ones, and the plausible ones are given merely as a preparation, a gentler remedy before the stronger medicine. But this interpretation is at odds with the way in which the debate between Philosophy and the Prisoner actually unfolds.

Philosophy is forced to return (IV.6.32–56) to the plausible answers in order to respond to the Prisoner's objections. Boethius may, then, have intended to put a question-mark over the counter-intuitive arguments and, along with them, the conception of the true human self as divine.

Such complications are absent from the way most Latin authors in the period up to 1200 thought about self-knowledge as an ideal. Pierre Courcelle (1974, 232–291) has traced a whole tradition, found especially among the twelfth-century Victorines (Hugh, Achard and Richard of St Victor) and Cistercians such as Bernard of Clairvaux and William of St Thierry, of how the injunction to 'Know yourself' was treated. The maxim was treated as a call to focus on one's inner self rather than the external world, but the result was neither the discovery of subjectivity nor an abstract knowledge about the nature of the self nor, as for Boethius, the discovery that one is a god, but rather the discovery of God. What is called self-knowledge here is really a call to a type of interiority that leads to the abandonment of the self for an ideal that lies beyond it.

3   Eriugena: the unknowable self

John Scottus Eriugena, who finished his masterpiece, a five-book dialogue between student and master called the *Periphyseon*, in the 860s at the court of Charles the Bald, is a fascinating thinker because he takes not just Augustine but, even more, the Greek Christian Platonic tradition (Gregory of Nyssa, pseudo-Dionysius, Maximus the Confessor) as his starting point and subjects their ideas to his idiosyncratic, bold and systematic rethinking. He is one of the only Latin thinkers between Augustine and the thirteenth century to elaborate a theory of self-knowledge. But he also looks at the self when he is thinking about personal identity from earthly life through to the hereafter, and his views on this area make his stance on self-knowledge more comprehensible.

Christian thinkers faced the problem of explaining how a human being could remain the same self when passing from embodied existence during this life to disembodied existence as a separate soul in the period between death and the Last Judgement, when the body would be resurrected. Eriugena gave detailed attention to the nature of this disembodied post-mortem existence, both in the *Periphyseon* and in an earlier work, *De praedestinatione* (early 850s), mainly because he wished to argue against the generally held views about eternal punishment.

In *De praedestinatione*, he made a distinction, in the case of the souls of the damned, between their human nature and their wills. Human nature, he insists, will not be punished, but merely the movement of the sinners' wills:

> <Human> nature is punished in nothing, because it is from God and does not sin. But the voluntary movement of the will, using the good of its nature according to wrongly-directed desire, is punished: deservedly so, because it transgresses the law of nature, which without doubt it would not transgress were it a substance created by God.
>
> (420A)[3]

On its own, this passage might be taken as saying no more than that the universal nature of humanity will not be punished. But Eriugena makes it clear that he is also talking about single instances of human nature – individual human beings – since he says that "no nature" will be punished (418B), and in the passage quoted he makes it clear that no substance at all, and so no individual substance, will transgress and therefore be punished (cf. Marenbon 2016). Is he then, so far from trying to preserve the identity of sinners, their selves, from mortal life to the hereafter, splitting it into two: in each case, the substance, which is human nature, and the voluntary movements of the will? Not exactly, since people are not at all distinguished from each other with regard to human nature, and so there is an important sense in which Eriugena's theory does indeed explain the survival of the self. It survives as just the other element: the movements of wrongly directed desire, which remain in existence only so as to be subjects of punishment, or rather of self-punishment, since they are tortured by being prevented from fulfilling their evil aim, which would be their own entire non-existence. In this work, Eriugena does not discuss the condition of the blessed, but it is hard to see how, on his theory, they could persist as selves; rather, they would survive only as identical instances of human nature.

The *Periphyseon* makes clear that this is, indeed, his outlook. Here he does also discuss the condition of the blessed, introducing the idea of *theōsis*, which he had learned from his Greek writers. It is, as the name suggests, a state of becoming Godlike: those so favoured not only lose their individual but even their human identity, since their nature is transformed into something more-than-human. As for sinners, Eriugena maintains his view that it is "the wicked and unlawful movements of a rational and intellectual creature's own will" which are the objects of punishment (Book 5; 959C). But he adds an extraordinary and daring suggestion, which throws into even sharper relief the contrast between loss of self for the blessed, and its continuance for the others. He evokes (Book 5; 1014AB) the state of many, content with purely earthly goods – nobility of birth and an influential family, a sturdy body and good health, a penetrating minds and quick tongue, a beautiful and attentive wife, numerous offspring, riches in goods and lands along with various honours and marks of dignity. It is to this state, he declares, that at the end of time all those who are not deified will return (cf. Marenbon 1990, 322).

It would be wrong to conclude that Eriugena has failed to provide an adequate theory about the survival of the self in the case of the blessed. Rather, the self, in so far as it stands for something absolutely distinctive to me, or to you – whether because it is each person's subjectivity, or what as a whole we each are – is of no concern to Eriugena in his extravagantly optimistic account of human potentiality. Even in this life, the highest of the soul's three motions, that of intellect, is around God and beyond the nature of the soul itself (Book 2; 572C-79A).

The question of self-knowledge shows even more strikingly how Eriugena leaves subjectivity out of the picture. His thought about the topic rests on two of his characteristic positions.[4] First, he considers that individuation of substances by accidents is merely superficial – they are all really universal.[5] (For this reason, in considering Eriugena, *homo* needs to be translated as 'Man', rather than 'a person' or 'a human being', in order to capture this understanding of the universal indistinguishable from its singulars.) Second, Eriugena believes that things originate from their intellectual notions (rather than vice versa). Indeed, although he is not a straightforward idealist monist, since he allows that there are bodies, produced by a concourse of accidents, Eriugena considers that these individual accidents too are not distinct from their universals (Cf. Marenbon 2014, 362–364). Moreover, these intellectual notions are not, at least not directly, separately existing Platonic Ideas, or Ideas in the mind of God: they are in Man's intellect – the incorporeal natures of things subsist "in their notions, in the soul of one who is wise" (Book 4; 769D). Man is the "workshop of all things" (*officina omnium* – Book 5; 893C): all things are contained in him and created in him (Book 4; 763D-64C; cf. 760A and Moran 1986).[6]

All things do not just *happen* to be in Man's intellect. Eriugena explains that the human mind, *disciplina* (by which he means the art which encompasses the notions of created things) and skill in *disciplina* are a triad, all sharing the same essence (Book 4; 766C–67D; cf. Gracia 1978, 161). Although, because of sin, we seem to be born lacking this skill and so ignorant, we can recover it (Book 4; 767C). This knowing is therefore – as Eriugena's own language makes clear (Book 4; 770AB) – self-knowledge. Yet Eriugena also holds that Man cannot be known by any created thing, including himself. He has made this position clear in the *Periphyseon* long before his discussion of self-knowledge. It derives from Eriugena's views about God, what it is to know something, and Man as the image of God. Like all Christians, Eriugena holds that God is infinite, but he takes this position very literally. If God is infinite, he reasons, then God is entirely unbounded. But to know what something is involves defining it – that is to say, placing it within bounds. And so even if only God could know what he is, God would have to be in some way bounded. What God is must remain unknown, therefore, even to God himself (Book 2; 586B–98C). But Man is created in the image of God: if our intellect "understood in any way what it is, it would necessarily deviate from the likeness of its creator", and so "what it is in essence is not known by itself nor by anything other than God" (Book 2; 585B).

Eriugena faces up directly to the apparent contradiction. "How is it," the pupil asks,

> that you already said earlier that the human mind has a notion, by which it knows itself, and a discipline by which it learns about itself, and now in turn you assert that it is known neither by itself nor by any other created thing?
>
> (Book 4; 771B)

The Master's answer is that the human mind both knows itself and does not: it knows that it is, but not what it is. In this way it is able most fully to be the image of God, who is comprehensible to his creatures because they know that he is, but incomprehensible because "what he is is understood neither by any human nor angelic intellect, nor by himself, because he is not a what." By this strange phrasing, Eriugena indicates that we cannot answer the question, "What is God?" – not because we lack the ability but because it is an ill-formed question. But this still leaves the question of how every creature can be made in the knowledge of Man, when Man does not know what he is (Book 4; 771D–72A). The Master answers by bringing up an idea that already had been raised far earlier (Book 1; 443B, 487A): what he there calls '*ousia*' – essence – and here refers to as the 'substance' of all the things that exist cannot be defined as to what it is. Eriugena's idea seems to be that the specific identity of created things other than Man is always a matter of definition, which must be added on by limiting and circumscribing, through accidents, that on account of which it exists, which remains indefinable. Man and God alone have an identity not just as they can be circumscribed, but also in their incircumscribability. Eriugena has, therefore, a rich theory of self-knowledge, in which subjectivity plays no part.[7]

4 Anselm's *Monologion*: avoiding Augustinian self-knowledge

No Christian author was better known in the early Middle Ages than Augustine, and among his works *On the Trinity* appealed especially to philosophically minded theologians from Alcuin (who abridged and adapted it) onwards – and to Anselm perhaps more than anyone. In the prologue to his *Monologion* (1075–76), Anselm claims that there is nothing in his work that is inconsistent with Augustine and refers those who accuse him of asserting novelties or falsehoods specifically to that author's *On the Trinity* (Anselm 1946, 8:13). Especially in the later sections, where he discusses the Trinity, he makes extensive use of this work of Augustine's. But he almost entirely leaves out the discussion there of self-knowledge.

Augustine himself does not set out to discuss human self-knowledge for its own sake. *On the Trinity* is, as the name suggests, a work of Trinitarian theology. Augustine considers the human mind because he finds analogies in its processes and their relations – in particular, the mind, its knowledge and its love, and remembering, understanding and loving – to the persons of the Trinity. But in doing so he focuses on self-knowledge and, with his characteristic inability either to leave philosophical insights aside or to draw them together into a finished theory, ends by sketching a suggestive position, which some later medieval theologians would develop into theories of self-knowledge and subjectivity. Unless the soul knows itself, it cannot love itself, and because it is incorporeal, it must know itself through itself (IX.3.3). The soul "does not seek to make itself out as if it were something absent, but carefully scrutinizes itself as something present" (X.9.12) – and Augustine goes on to argue that all people know they think, exist and live (X.10.13) and, in his pre-Cartesian *cogito*, that if anyone doubts he or she lives, thinks, knows, judges or wills, then it follows from the very act of doubting that the person does indeed live, think, know, judge and will (X.10.14). Augustine puts the point in the third person, but it would go more neatly in the first, since what he has in mind is essentially subjective.

Even when, in a short passage, the *Monologion* discusses self-knowledge explicitly, Anselm leaves this side of Augustine's thinking aside and proposes a very different account. In this work, Anselm sets out to show, by reason alone, not merely that one, all powerful, eternal, immutable and supremely good and wise God exists, but that also he is triune. One move towards this conclusion is to say (Chapter 32; Anselm 1946, 50–51) that, because God is wise, he must understand, and, if he understands, he must understand something, and that which he understands can be called his Word. But what if there were to be no creatures? It cannot be that God would have no Word, and so not understand and so not be wise. The solution is that God must understand himself. In order to make this solution clearer (cf. Visser and Williams 2009, 139–140), Anselm turns to human self-knowledge. "How can we even think that there is any time when the highest wisdom does not understand itself, when the rational mind can remember not only itself but also the highest wisdom, and understand itself and it?" (Chapter 32; Anselm 1946, 51:7–9). Anselm thus insists that we are capable of self-understanding but immediately links to it our ability to understand God.

In the next chapter, in order to explain how God, in understanding himself, begets a likeness or Word that shares his substance, Anselm again uses the comparison with human self-understanding and gives more detail about what he takes the process to be. The rational mind understands itself by giving rise to an image of itself in thought – it is "a likeness as if formed by an impression of it" (Chapter 33; Anselm 1946, 52:15). The process, says Anselm, is exactly the same as when the mind tries to think about anything truly, and it is most evident when it is thinking about things other than itself, especially bodies. If I wish to think about a man who is absent, the gaze of my thought (*acies cogitationis meae*) is formed into the image which I stored in my memory as a result of seeing him: this image is the 'word' of this man in my thought, and the image and the thought can be distinguished only by reason, not in reality. The implications as an analogy for the Father and Son are obvious. But it is striking that the mechanism of self-knowledge underlying it is so un-Augustinian: rather than direct knowledge, the process of cognition requires an image; and so far from being seen as a special type of basic knowledge, self-knowledge is obtained by the same process as any other type of knowledge – a process which is seen more clearly in the cognition of bodily things.

In later chapters (especially 48–61), Anselm makes use of Augustine's analogy of understanding, memory and love to help understand the Trinity, but without drawing out the theme of self-knowledge. But he finally returns to it (Chapters 66–67; Anselm 1946, 184–185). We can see God in this life only "in a glass darkly" (*per speculum in aenigmate*: I Corinthians xiii, 12): that mirror, says Anselm, is our own mind, because alone of all things that are made, it can remember, know and love itself. The more carefully, therefore, each rational mind seeks to learn about itself, the more successfully it rises to cognition of

God. The self's subjectivity has much less interest for Anselm than for Augustine, but both thinkers were equally keen to explore a different model of the self, as an analogical structure, allowing us to understand the Trinity through understanding ourselves.

5 Extinguishing the Avicennian self: Ibn Ṭufayl

As recent scholarship has revealed, a century before Anselm and three thousand miles to the East, Avicenna put an idea of the self founded on self-awareness at the centre of his thought (Black 2008; Kaukua 2015). His often repeated example of the 'flying man' lends itself to this reading. A human is created instantly and with a fully developed intellect but is without input from the senses, floating in a void with eyes veiled. Such a flying man affirms the existence of his self, but not of any part of his body or any external thing (Marmura 1986 – for the various texts; Kaukua 2015, 30–42). Although some have interpreted this so-called thought experiment differently (Hasse 2000, 80–87), passages from the *Ta'līqāt* (Kaukua 2015, 51–54) show beyond doubt that Avicenna championed a notion of the self, based on self-awareness, unlike anything found in the thought of Latin authors between Augustine and the thirteenth century. Self-awareness individuates selves; indeed, "self-awareness is innate to the self, it is [the self's] very existence; so nothing external is needed by means of which to apprehend the self – rather, the self is that which apprehends itself" (*Ta'līqāt* 161, transl. Kaukua 2015, 53).[8] Avicenna's approach to the self was taken up and further developed by later Arabic thinkers, such as Suhrawardī (d. 1191).

Not everyone in the Arabic tradition followed this side of Avicenna's thought, however. Al-Ghazālī (d. 1111), who introduced many Avicennian ideas into theology, rejected it (Black 2008, 20–21). Ibn Ṭufayl (d. 1185), who worked in Islamic Spain, seems at first to embrace it but turns out to have a rather different view. His only surviving work, *Ḥayy ibn Yaqẓān*, is a philosophical novel about a baby, Ḥayy, who grows up in an island on his own, suckled by a deer. Ḥayy gradually, through careful observation and deduction, teaches himself what contemporaries would have recognized as a sophisticated, scientific view of the world. Then, going beyond the visible, he deduces the existence of a God who corresponds both to Quranic teaching and that of Avicenna, a being "the existence of which there is no cause, and it is the cause of the existence of everything" (Ibn Ṭufayl 1936, 90 [translation 68]). Ḥayy then turns his attention inwards, asking how he gained his knowledge of this necessary being. It could not be from any of his bodily senses, he reasons, because they cognize only bodily things, whereas the necessary being is entirely incorporeal. Ḥayy decides that he must know it because of a notion in his own self or essence (*thāt*) and that this self itself must therefore be incorporeal. He further infers that, being incorporeal, his self must be incorruptible, and he concludes that it is supremely happy when its contemplation is of God, and that if he can keep himself in contemplation of God, then, when his body dies, his self will remain forever in this blissful state.

The next stage, therefore, of Ḥayy's spiritual journey is to seek how, through ascetic practices and exercises in contemplation, he can come to a grasp of God himself. Gradually he manages to clear his mind of every image, since none of them applies to God, but even when he has cleared from his thought and his memory everything else, his self remains. Finally, however, Ḥayy achieves "the extinction of his self" (*al-fanā 'an nafsihi*) (Ibn Ṭufayl 1936, 120 [translation 86]), and only then can he enjoy this indescribable vision of the divine.

The self of *Ḥayy* is as obviously Avicenna's as the necessary being. But it plays a quite different role in Ibn Ṭufayl's novel than for Avicenna. The story of Ḥayy's self-education suggests that, so far from being the object of constant and immediate awareness, the self is something we discover only after long-drawn enquiry or instruction, and only through our knowledge of God, just as we understand its incorporeality through understanding God's. There is also another, less obvious difference. Avicenna's idea of the self fits with his views about the character of survival after death, in which he put himself at odds with Islamic tradition by insisting on the immortality of the immaterial soul in place of the doctrine of bodily resurrection.[9] Ḥayy seems to adopt this Avicennian view when, from the immateriality of his self, he concludes that it is incorruptible and seeks to ensure that it – he himself – remains after death forever in a state of blissful contemplation of God. But, if extinction of the self is to be taken seriously, then this Avicennian view of personal immortality is one that Ḥayy finally learns to reject. Reaching God should not be seen, Ibn Ṭufayl is apparently arguing, as a meeting between the self and the divinity, but as an encounter in which there is no room for the self at all, entirely beyond the register of subjective experience.[10]

6 Aquinas and the thirteenth century: self-knowledge without the self

The striking development in thinking about the self in the Latin tradition in the years after 1250 was the beginning of a sustained discussion of self-knowledge. In the work of some Franciscan thinkers, this discussion allowed them to develop an idea of subjectivity and subjective knowledge. According to a number of recent specialists, Aquinas too developed a theory on these lines. But did he?

Thirteenth-century accounts of self-knowledge began from an encounter between two new sources. One of them was Aristotle's *On the Soul*, which had started to become available shortly after 1200. In this treatise, Aristotle distinguishes between sensory cognition, which is of particulars, and intellectual cognition, which is of universals. As most interpreters understood him, each human has a 'possible' or 'potential' intellect: just as formless matter is in potency to the particular forms which make it into some sort of a thing (a tree, a horse, a human), so the potential intellect is in potency to universal forms: when it grasps, for instance, the universal form of horse, it is changed from potency to act, actually understanding what it is to be a horse. On this model, the intellect does not seem as if it has the power to know itself. Yet Aristotle says (430a3) that "it is itself an object of thought, just like <other> objects of thought" and goes on to explain that, since the intellect is without matter, what thinks and what is thought are the same. For Aristotle, then, the intellect knows that it knows, but only when it knows something other than itself.

The second new source was, in a sense, anything but new. Augustine's works had been widely read ever since he wrote them. Books 9 and 10 of *On the Trinity* were, as already discussed, texts that had been carefully read and taken over by writers such as Anselm (and, in the twelfth century, Richard of St Victor), but they had not been mined, as they now were, for a theory of self-knowledge. Perhaps the thirteenth-century theologians were led to see them in this light through having studied Aristotle's *On the Soul*, although Augustine provided them with a theory of self-knowledge that contrasted sharply with the one found there. The soul, he says, knows not just its own acts, but itself, and it does so directly. Rather than its self-knowledge depending upon knowing other things, the starting point for the soul's knowledge is itself (Perler and Schierbaum 2014, 37–38). This idea of direct self-knowledge was complemented by a more obviously new source, Avicenna. Although the *Taʿlīqāt* were unknown, the flying man argument was often discussed (Toivanen 2015).

The late thirteenth-century theologians who argued about self-knowledge usually tried to harmonize the apparently conflicting views of Aristotle and Augustine, but often leaned more towards one than the other. The Franciscans favoured Augustine's account. For example, Roger Marston, writing in the early 1280s, contends that the soul knows itself through a combination of deduction, based on its acts, and more directly, by seeing its own nature "in the eternal light" (in the same way, he considers, as it grasps the principles of justice) (*Disputed Questions on the Soul*, q. 1; Perler and Schierbaum 2014, 177–217). Another Franciscan, Matthew of Aquasparta, writing in 1277–78, allows for the soul to know itself in three ways. Two of them, which fit the Aristotelian picture, are, he says uncontroversial: first, I can come to understand in general what souls are; and, second, my soul can know itself in particular and its dispositions by a process of argumentative reasoning starting from my acts. But he insists that there is also a third sort of self-knowledge: it depends on the second sort in order to become possible, but it is quite different from it, consisting in a direct, spiritual vision of one's own soul and its dispositions (*Disputed Questions. On Cognition*, q. 5; Matthew of Aquasparta 1903, 317–341; cf. Perler 2017, 122–123).

Both of these theories definitely imply quite extensive knowledge of the self, not merely in general terms but seen from the inside. But the dissident Franciscan, Peter John Olivi, goes further in developing a notion of subjectivity (*On the 'Sentences' Book II*, q. 76; Peter John Olivi 1926, 145–149). Like Matthew, he believes that the soul can have a direct grasp of itself (he calls it an "experiential, quasi-tactile" sort of knowing), and he distinguishes it from the grasp of what the soul is in general and how it differs from other things – universal, scientific knowledge. But he does not think any other sort of indirect knowledge is needed to make the direct sort possible. On the contrary, universal knowledge of the soul must be founded on this direct experiential knowledge, otherwise it will be "false and bestial". Olivi, much more clearly than his two colleagues, envisages the self as a centre of subjective knowledge. Describing the experiential sort of knowing, he says:

> In this way <the soul> indubitably perceives (*sentit*) that it exists and lives and thinks and wills and sees and hears and that it moves the body, and so with regard to its other acts, of which it knows and perceives that it is the principle and the subject. So much is this so that it cannot actively know or contemplate any object or act without always perceiving and knowing itself as the foundation (*suppositum*) for the act by which it knows and considers these things. It is for this reason that always in its thinking the proposition to which it gives force is "*I* know or *I* believe this or *I* am doubtful about this".
>
> (Peter John Olivi 1926, 146)

Olivi goes out of his way to stress here that the self which is known in this direct self-knowledge is not just the intellect but the soul in its many aspects: rational (thinking and willing), sensitive (seeing and hearing) and also as the principle of motion. Working from our subjective consciousness, Olivi tries to construct a solid concept of the self, which plays an important part throughout his writings.[11]

All three of these Franciscans developed their theories of self-knowledge in explicit conflict with the view proposed by a thinker of the preceding generation: the Dominican, Thomas Aquinas. Their main reproach is that Aquinas does not allow the soul any direct knowledge of itself – a position adopted because of his wish to follow Aristotle closely. Looking at Aquinas's mature theory (anticipated in Sentences commentary III, d. 23, q. 1, a. 2, ad3; put forward in detail in *On Truth*, q. 10, a. 8 and *Summa Theologiae* I, q., 87; cf. *Summa contra Gentiles*, III.46; Commentary on *On the Soul* III, lectio 9 on 429b22–430a9), the Franciscans' characterization seems to be accurate.

Intellect does indeed, Aquinas believes, grasp itself intellectually in a direct way, through its essence, as can be seen in the case of God's and the angels' self-knowledge. But humans, although endowed with intellect, have it only in a limited way. In its embodied state, the human intellective soul remains a pure potency until it is made actual by receiving an 'intelligible species' – a form that has been abstracted from material things. Aquinas points out that only what is actual, not merely potential, is known, and so the embodied human intellect cannot, like other intellects, know itself through its essence, since it is in essence potential. Could it, however, know itself in the way it knows other things, not in essence but still directly? When the intellect receives an intelligible species, it grasps through it the universal quiddity of the material thing from which the quiddity has been abstracted. So, for example, through the intelligible species abstracted from sense impressions of Socrates, the intellect grasps the quiddity of human beings – it knows what is essential for something to be a human. But the intellect itself is not material, and so it is not the sort of thing that can be known directly through an intelligible species abstracted from matter. It can, however, be known indirectly, not through its own intelligible species (of which there could be none) but through any of the intelligible species by which it grasps other things.

Aquinas distinguishes two ways in which a human intellect knows itself in this way, through its act of understanding something else. It can do so, as he puts it in the *Summa Theologiae*, (a) "particularly, in the way that Socrates or Plato perceives himself to have an intellective soul, because he perceives himself to understand" (*intelligere*), or (b) "in another way, universally, in the way that we consider the nature of the human mind from the act of the intellect". The longer account in *On Truth* describes (a) as a cognition "by which any person's soul knows just what is particular (*proprium*) to it": through this cognition, Aquinas explains, "it is known whether the soul exists, as when someone perceives that he has a soul". He explains further: "Someone perceives that he has a soul, and lives and exists by perceiving that he has sense impressions and thinks of universals (*intelligere*), and that he performs other life activities of this sort." Whereas everyone can have this sort of particular cognition – (a), by contrast the universal sort – (b) – requires "careful and subtle enquiry"; many people, indeed, do not have knowledge of the nature of the soul but rather mistaken beliefs about it. The argument leading to this universal knowledge is described in *On Truth*: since our soul cognizes universal natures, the species by which they are understood must be immaterial, so as not to be individuated, and so the intellect must be something not depending on matter. Aquinas also recognizes that we have a dispositional version of (a), and he divides (b) into the process of apprehending the truth, which is described, and that of judging that it is true.

From this description, it would seem that Aquinas wants to give, especially, an account of self-knowledge in the sense of knowledge of its nature in general – (b). There is, in a sense, a subjective element in discovering this knowledge, since we need to begin from our ability to know our intellectual acts. But even here there is no notion of knowing from the inside. It is simply that we can think about our own acts of thought. From this beginning, through a difficult intellectual process in which many go wrong, an understanding can be gained, not of ourselves, but of the nature of one type of item in the world, the human intellective soul – in particular, its immateriality. Aquinas has, however, to take account of texts from Augustine (such as *On the Trinity* IX.6.9) which speak of an everyday ability of each soul to know itself – (a). Though rejecting any type of direct self-knowledge, Aquinas finds a way in which it can indeed be said that we have everyday knowledge of ourselves – one which is cashed out not in terms of our being aware of or knowing a self, but of knowing a fact: that, in the case of each of us, I have soul.

But this way of reading Aquinas is not favoured by many of his recent interpreters, although some readings (Pasnau 2002, 330–360; Perler and Schierbaum 2014, 70–77) would be at least compatible with it. Most of the other interpreters put the emphasis on (a), the everyday ability, and insist that, according to Aquinas, every time the intellect grasps something in understanding, it is also aware of itself. They thus put an idea of the self at the centre of Aquinas's theory of self-knowledge. But they differ over how Aquinas conceived this self. According to Chris Martin (2007, 99), what is involved is "an undifferentiated self-awareness" and, he adds, "nothing that Aquinas says shows how my awareness of my act of understanding can be either an awareness that the act is *my* act or that it is an act of *understanding*." By contrast, Putallaz (1991a) presents what Alain de Libera (2014, 569) calls a "quasi-Sartrean" reading of Aquinas's self-awareness, whilst de Libera himself, in a long and nuanced discussion of the texts (2014, 511–577), takes a middle course. In the most recent and thorough treatment of the whole question, Thérèse Cory (2014; 2016) goes perhaps even further than Putallaz in providing Aquinas with an elaborate theory of the self and our awareness of it. Like Putallaz, she claims that in one and the same act as we grasp anything intellectually we also have an awareness of our self. For Aquinas, she explains (2014, 104), "to perceive an act is necessarily to perceive the agent directly in itself". What, therefore, we perceive in direct awareness is "not a bare "I" or "self", but a first-person principle of action: 'I thinking'". (2014, 105). Cory goes on to argue that Aquinas thickens this 'I' into a developed concept of psychological personhood, using his ideas of habitual self-awareness, implicit self-awareness and intellectual memory to provide an account of diachronically unified consciousness (2012; 2014, 207–214). Cory sums up her reading in a brilliantly pithy sentence: according to Aquinas, "the mind merely needs to be 'lit up' by its act in order to perceive itself from the inside" (2014, 216).

Cory and her precursors have constructed an impressive theoretical edifice, taking remarks (often in isolation) from all over Aquinas's corpus and elaborating arguments to see them as making a coherent whole. An interpretation along their lines, in which Aquinas becomes a champion of the concept of the self and subjectivity, is therefore an attractive possibility, one that should be accepted according to the canons of charitable interpretation.[12] But some objections can be raised against it. The view held by some of these theorists that in one and the same act the intellect understands some object and its own act of understanding is explicitly rejected by Aquinas: "there is one act by which the intellect understands a stone, and another act by which it understands that it understands the stone, and so on" (*Summa Theologiae* I, 1. 87, a. 4, ad2) – and Aquinas accepts that this process can be reiterated in a potential infinity of *distinct* acts.[13] This argument does not rule out interpreting Aquinas as providing an account of subjectivity grounded in a self-consciousness that grasps one act in terms of a higher-order act – but that interpretation has not yet been developed.[14]

Those who wish to present Aquinas as the champion of the subjective self must also accept that he was drastically misunderstood by his early Franciscan opponents, despite their care in citing him and that their view corresponds to what is ostensibly stated in the texts explicitly on the subject. Why would Aquinas go to such trouble to hide his thinking? But Cory can reply that Aquinas's meaning is not always obvious from the surface, and some of his underlying ideas, about intellectual being, for instance, need to be reconstructed. Moreover, we sometimes lack the conceptual framework to make sense of his remarks, which is why his real views might seem to be hidden.

If, nonetheless, a more straightforward interpretation is accepted, it might seem that Aquinas does put forward a theory of the self in his account of self-knowledge, but of a self – as in the case of many of his early medieval Latin predecessors – without subjectivity. This theory would be found in the cognition, (b), Aquinas says is gained, with enquiry, of the universal nature of the soul. Aquinas's theory of the self would thus be of the same sort as Boethius's. The knowledge about the self which the character Boethius lacks at the beginning of the *Consolation of Philosophy* does not concern him in particular or from inside but is about the sort of thing he is: not a rational, mortal animal, but a god.

There is, however, good reason to think that even this sort of theory of the self is not to be found here. Aquinas does, indeed, think that it is very important for us to know the nature of our intellective souls, especially their immateriality. But he does not think that we, our selves, are our souls. No theme runs more strongly through all Aquinas's thinking than that human beings in this life are hylomorphic composites of soul and body. At the end of time, they will return to this status, each soul, of the blessed or the damned, regaining its own matter (Aquinas has an elaborate theory to explain how.)[15] Aquinas accepted the Church's doctrine that, between these times, human souls existed separately. His main consideration of questions about the self falls under these problems of continuity and identity. His is a theory of self-knowledge without the self.

7 Conclusion: the subject, the self and the archaeologist

All who write today about the self and subjectivity in the Long Middle Ages do so in the light from, and under the shadow cast by, Alain de Libera's ongoing study (three volumes have appeared 2007–14; see de Libera 2015 for an introduction; de Libera 2008 is less useful), his *Archéologie du sujet*. This chapter is no exception. But 'the subject' does not name the same topic as 'the self', although the two are closely related: 'the subject' designates a field that is wider in one way, but narrower in another. The notion of the subject, as used since the seventeenth century, and in some cases before then, immediately poses the question that de Libera very rightly puts at the centre of his enquiry. How was the Aristotelian notion of subject, the bearer of properties, transformed into that of subjective consciousness, of the 'I'? This question opens up a wide field of enquiry not directly relevant to the topic of the self. But, as most of the preceding pages illustrate, the self has often been seen in terms that do not involve subjectivity. Discussions of the self come in various guises and in many different parts of philosophy. This diversity raises a problem.

Whereas the extra breadth of the topic of the subject adds an element that helps to fix and specify it, the extra diversity of the topic of the self seems merely to produce incoherence. Is it a problem of anachronism? The self is not a medieval concept. Is there any reason to think that applying it to medieval texts will lead to any valuable results? By contrast, an investigation of 'the subject' fastens clearly on to the vocabulary of medieval philosophy, avoiding anachronism by putting its focus on how the term has changed its meaning. That clarity of focus allows the archaeologist to dig deep and expose the hidden shifts in usage that underlie the language and conceptual framework available to philosophers at a given time.[16]

Such criticisms can, however, be answered, at least partially. Although the run of contemporary philosophers regards the self in terms of subjectivity, some of those who specialize on the topic today emphasize, rather, its diversity (see the range of material in, for instance, the *Oxford Handbook of the Self*). 'The self' has an imprecise but easily graspable meaning in ordinary language: our selves are what we each are, what is important and lasting (if anything is) about us. Why not try to understand this notion better by approaching it through using the whole range of philosophical, and indeed scientific, tools that promise to be useful? Despite this diversity, the topic will remain coherent, because it is based on a vague but well-understood and basic notion from everyday life. So basic, indeed, that we can assume that those in past periods shared it in some form. That is why the anachronism of investigating the self in medieval philosophy is, arguably, benign, and the diversity in the results need not mean incoherence. It is true that such investigations must remain above ground. They cannot dig down to reveal the hidden transformations which, supposedly, shape the framework of what can be thought and argued, restricted as they are to the texts written by the medieval authors, their interrelations and contexts. But perhaps it is here, on the surface, that philosophy has its history.[17]

Notes

1 The idea that the self is a modern invention set the agenda for many more detailed studies, where the authors simply chose the seventeenth century as their starting point: see, for example, Seigel 2005, Thiel 2011. Foucault's own view, certainly by the end of his life, was in fact far more nuanced.
2 The *Consolation* was written under the circumstances it describes in *ca.* 524–525, while Boethius awaited execution. For ease of reference to different editions and translations, the standard book, section, and sub-section numbers are used (for verse passages (m), the line numbers). The best edition is Boethius 2005. For background information on Boethius, see Marenbon 2009.
3 References to Eriugena's *De praedestinatione* and *Periphyseon* are to the editions cited in the bibliography John Scottus Eriugena 2003; 1996–2003, but are given using the column number and letter references from *Patrologia Latina* 122, since these are also given in the editions and are a standard way of citing this author.
4 On self-knowledge in Eriugena, see Beierwaltes 1965/66 and Moran 1989, 186–211.
5 See e.g. *Periphyseon* I, 470D–71A. Cf. Erismann 2011, 193–291.
6 Cf. *Periphyseon* Book 4; 769A: "Is it any wonder, therefore, if the notion (*notio*) of things which the human mind possesses, as it is created in it, should be understood to be the substance of the things themselves of which it is the notion . . .?"; and see Gracia 1978, n. 16 for further references. Gracia (156–157) traces the view back to Maximus the Confessor.

7 Note especially the so-called Eriugenian *'cogito'* (Book IV; 776B). As Jeauneau 1995 points out, so far from trying to use it, like Descartes, to grasp what I am, Eriugena emphasizes that the thinker in question knows that he is a rational and intellectual nature but does not know what intellect and reason are. In any case, this passage is part of a longer argument designed to show how naturally (although it is obscured by the effects of the Fall) humans are endowed with knowledge of all things: self-knowledge turns out to be complete knowledge of everything but the self (and God).
8 Thérèse Cory made this interesting suggestion to me: the way in which Avicenna describes this self-awareness, especially in the flying man example, where the protagonist has to be brought to notice the existence of his own soul, suggests that it is self-awareness *without subjectivity*. Since for Avicenna the self is self-awareness, his theory would be another instance of the self without subjectivity.
9 For standard views in Islam, see Smith and Haddad 2002, 31–61.
10 Space does not allow an investigation of this theme of immortality without the self in Ibn Ṭufayl's two famous Andalusian successors, Averroes and Maimonides. Averroes (*Incoherence of the Incoherence*: 'About the Natural Sciences' – 4th discussion) treats corporeal resurrection as a religious doctrine to be accepted by the learned, not because they think it true but because it serves the aims of religion in keeping public order. Maimonides declares the belief obligatory for Jews, but undercuts his position by stating that bodies will be regained only for a limited period (*Letter on the Resurrection of the Dead*). Both thinkers identify grasping the unchanging truths of all things as our goal, and the essentially impersonal, non-subjective character of this understanding is especially evident in Averroes, since for him individual humans are mere facilitators, through their sense faculties, of a process that takes place in a single intellect, which belongs to no human in particular.
11 See Piron 2007. For a general survey of thirteenth-century theories of self-knowledge, see Putallaz 1991b.
12 For a balanced review, appreciative of Cory's genuine achievement in this book, see Pasnau 2015.
13 Pasnau 2002, 342, n.9 cites this passage against Putallaz. Cory explains very clearly that the evidence in Aquinas seems to point in two directions, and (2014, 142–143) she lists a set of alpha-texts that support the view that we understand ourselves in numerically the same act as that in which we understand something else, and beta-texts which deny it. She resolves the contradiction by saying that the alpha-texts describe implicit and the beta-texts explicit self-awareness.
14 I am grateful to Thérèse Cory for directing me to this point.
15 A study of this side of Aquinas's thought by Antonia Fitzpatrick is forthcoming (Oxford University Press).
16 I discuss the archaeological method, as applied to philosophy by Alain de Libera, in Marenbon forthcoming.
17 I am very grateful to Christophe Grellard, who delivered a fascinating response to a shorter, oral presentation of some of this material in Geneva in 2016, and to Thérèse Cory for her detailed and perceptive comments on this chapter.

Bibliography

Primary sources

Anselm (1946). *Opera omnia* I, ed. Franciscus Schmitt, Edinburgh: Nelson.
Boethius (1925). *De consolatione Philosophiae*, ed. A. Fortescue, London: Burns, Oates and Washbourne.

Boethius (2005). *De consolatione Philosophiae. Opuscula theologica*, ed. C. Moreschini, Munich and Leipzig: Saur (revised edition).
Ibn Tufayl (1936). *Hayy ben Yaqdân*, (ed.) L. Gauthier, Beirut: Imprimerie catholique.
John Scottus Eriugena (1996–2003). *Periphyseon*, ed. E. Jeauneau, Turnhout: Brepols (Corpus Christianorum 161–165).
John Scottus Eriugena (2003). *De praedestinatione liber*, ed. Ernesto Mainoldi, Florence: edizioni dell Galluzzo (Per verba. Testi mediolatini con traduzione 18).
Matthew of Aquasparta (1903). *Quaestiones disputatae selectae I. Quaestiones de fine et de cognitione*, Quaracchi: Collegium S. Bonaventurae.
Peter John Olivi (1926). *Quaestiones in secundum librum sententiarum*, ed. Bernard Jansen, III Questiones 72–118, Quaracchi: Collegium S. Bonaventurae (Bibliotheca Franciscana Scholastica 6).

Secondary sources

Beierwaltes, W. (1965/66). "Das Problem des absoluten Selbstbewußtseins bei Johannes Scotus Eriugena," *Philosophisches Jahrbuch* 73, 264–284.
Black, D. (2008). "Avicenna on Self-Awareness and Knowing that One Knows," in (eds.) S. Rahman, T. Street, and H. Tahiri, *The Unity of Science in the Arabic Tradition: Science, Logic, Epistemology and Their Interactions*, Dordrecht: Springer, 63–87.
Boulnois, O. (ed.) (2007). *Généalogies du sujet. De Saint Anselme à Malebranche*, Paris: Vrin.
Cary, P. (2000). *Augustine's Invention of the Inner Self: The Legacy of a Christian Platonist*, New York: Oxford University Press.
Cory, T. (2012). "Diachronically Unified Consciousness in Augustine and Aquinas," *Vivarium* 50, 354–381.
Cory, T. (2014). *Aquinas on Human Self-Knowledge*, Cambridge: Cambridge University Press.
Cory, T. (2016). "The Reflexivity of Incorporeal Acts as Source of Freedom and Subjectivity in Aquinas," in (eds.) J. Kaukua and T. Ekenberg, *Subjectivity and Selfhood in Medieval and Early Modern Philosophy*, Dordrecht: Springer (Studies in the History of Philosophy of Mind 16), 125–141.
Courcelle, P. (1974). *Connais-toi toi-même de Socrate à Saint Bernard*, Paris: Études augustiniennes.
Dougherty, M. V. (2004). "The Problem of *Humana Natura* in the *Consolatio Philosophiae* of Boethius," *American Catholic Philosophical Quarterly* 78, 273–292.
Erismann, C. (2011). *L'homme commun: la genèse du réalisme ontologique durant le haut moyen âge*, Paris: Vrin.
Foucault, M. (1966). *Les mots et les choses. Une archéologie des sciences humaines*, Paris: Gallimard.
Gallagher, S. (2011). *The Oxford Handbook of the Self*, Oxford: Oxford University Press.
Gracia, J. (1978). "Ontological Characterization of the Relation between Man and Created Nature in Eriugena," *Journal of the History of Philosophy* 16, 155–166.
Gruber, J. (2006). *Kommentar zu Boethius, 'De consolatione philosophiae,'* Berlin: De Gruyter.
Hasse, D. (2000). *Avicenna's De Anima in the Latin West: The Formation of a Peripatetic Philosophy of the Soul, 1160–1300*, London: Warburg Institute.
Kaukua, J. (2015). *Self-Awareness in Islamic Philosophy: Avicenna and Beyond*, Cambridge: Cambridge University Press.

Kaukua, J. and Lähteenmäki, V. (eds.) (2014a). "Varieties of Subjectivity," *Vivarium* 52, 3–4.
Kaukua, J. and Lähteenmäki, V. (2014b). "On the Historiography of Subjectivity," in Kaukua and Lähteenmäki 2014a, 187–195.
Jeauneau, E. (1995). "Le cogito érigénien," *Traditio* 50 (1995), 95–110.
de Libera, A. (2007–14). *Archéologie du sujet* I–III, Paris: Vrin.
de Libera, A. (2008). "When Did the Modern Subject Emerge?," *American Catholic Philosophical Quarterly* 82, 181–220.
de Libera, A. (2015). *L'invention du sujet modern. Cours du Collège de France 2013–2014*, Paris: Vrin.
Marenbon, J. (1990). "John Scottus and Carolingian Theology: From the *De praedestinatione*, Its Background and Its Critics, to the *Periphyseon*," in (ed.) M. Gibson and J. Nelson, *Charles the Bald: Court and Kingdom*, Ashgate: Aldershot, 2nd edition, 303–325 (reprinted in Marenbon, J. (2000). *Aristotelian Logic, Platonism and the Context of Early Medieval Philosophy in the West*, Aldershot and Burlington: Ashgate (Variorum Collected Studies Series 696)).
Marenbon, J. (2003). *Boethius*, New York: Oxford University Press.
Marenbon, J. (ed.) (2009). *The Cambridge Companion to Boethius*, Cambridge: Cambridge University Press.
Marenbon, J. (2014). "Eriugena, Aristotelian Logic and the Creation," in (eds.) O. Willemien and M.I. Allen, *Eriugena and Creation: Proceedings of the Eleventh International Conference on Eriugenian Studies*, held in honor of Edouard Jeauneau, Chicago, 9–12 November 2011, Turnhout: Brepols, 349–368.
Marenbon, J. (2016). "Eriugena on Damnation in *De praedestinatione*," in (ed.) I. Moulin, *Philosophie et théologie chez Jean Scot Érigène*, Paris: Vrin, 161–177.
Marenbon, J. (forthcoming). "Alain de Libera's Philosophical Archaeology," in (eds.) L. Cesalli and J.-B. Brenet, *Festschrift de Libera – 2*.
Martin, C. (2007). "Self-knowledge and Cognitive Ascent: Thomas Aquinas and Peter Olivi on the *KK-thesis*," in (ed.) H. Lagerlund, *Forming the Mind: Essays on the Internal Senses and the Mind/Body Problem From Avicenna to the Medical Enlightenment*, Dordrecht: Springer (Studies in the History of Philosophy of Mind 5), 93–108.
Moran, D. (1986). "'Officina Omnium' or 'Notio quaedam intellectualis in mente divina aeternaliter facta': The Problem of the Definition of Man in the Philosophy of John Scottus Eriugena," in (ed.) C. Wenin, *L'Homme et son univers au Moyen âge*, Louvain-la-Neuve: Éditions de l'Institut Supérieur de Philosophie (Philosophes médiévaux 26), 195–204.
Moran, D. (1989). *The Philosophy of John Scottus Eriugena: A Study of Idealism in the Middle Ages*, Cambridge: Cambridge University Press.
Nagel, T. (1986). *The View from Nowhere*, Oxford: Oxford University Press.
Pasnau, R. (2002). *Thomas Aquinas on Human Nature*, Cambridge: Cambridge University Press.
Pasnau, R. (2015). "Review of *Aquinas on Human Self – Knowledge*, by Therese Scarpelli Cory," *Mind* 124, 623–626.
Perler, D. (2017). "Self-knowledge in Scholasticism," in (ed.) U. Renz, *Self-Knowledge*, New York: Oxford University Press, 114–130.
Perler, D. and Schierbaum, S. (eds.) (2014). *Selbstbezug und Selbstwissen. Texte zu einer mittelalterlichen Debatte*, Frankfurt: Klostermann.

Piron, S. (2007). "L'expérience subjective selon Pierre de Jean Olivi," in Boulnois 2007, 43–54.
Putallaz, F.-X. (1991a). *Le sens de la reflexion chez Thomas d'Aquin*, Paris: Vrin (Études de philosophie médiévale 66).
Putallaz, F.-X. (1991b). *La connaissance de soi au XIIIe siècle. De Mathhieu d'Aquasparta à Thierry de Freiberg*, Paris: Vrin (Études de philosophie médiévale 67).
Remes, P. (2007). *Plotinus on Self: The Philosophy of the 'We'*, Cambridge: Cambridge University Press, 2007.
Schierbaum, S. (2014). "Ockham on the Possibility of Self-Knowledge: Knowing Acts Without Knowing Subjects," in Kaukua and Lähteenmäki 2014a, 220–240.
Seigel, J. (2005). *The Idea of the Self: Thought and Experience in Western Europe Since the Seventeenth Century*, Cambridge: Cambridge University Press.
Smith, J. I. and Haddad, Y. (2002). *The Islamic Understanding of Death and Resurrection*, Oxford: Oxford University Press.
Sorabji, R. (2006). *Self: Ancient and Modern Insights About Individuality, Life, and Death*, Oxford: Oxford University Press.
Taylor, C. (1989). *Sources of the Self: The Making of the Modern Identity*, Cambridge: Cambridge University Press.
Thiel, U. (2011). *The Early Modern Subject: Self-consciousness and Personal Identity From Descartes to Hume*, Oxford: Oxford University Press.
Toivanen, J. (2015). "The Fate of the Flying Man: Medieval Reception of Avicenna's Thought Experiment," *Oxford Studies in Medieval Philosophy* 3, 64–98.
Van der Meeren, S. (2012). *Lectures de Boèce. La Consolation de la Philosophie*, Rennes: Presses universitaires de Rennes.
Visser, S. and Williams, T. (2009). *Anselm* (Great Medieval Thinkers Series), Oxford: Oxford University Press.

INDEX

Page numbers in *italic* indicate a figure on the corresponding page.

Abelard, Peter 7–8, 18–31; Augustine's influence on 24–29; *Commentary on Isagoge* 30; *History of my calamities* 8; *Treatise on Understandings* 29; *Yes and No (Sic et Non)* 10
abstraction 21; cognition of singulars and 35–38, 40–44, 46; emanation and 68–69; of intelligibles 56–76; meaning in the Arabic tradition 56, 57–60
accidental perception 145
acquisition 114–115, 119, 179–182, 184, 189–191
Active Intellect 6, 56; *see also* agent intellect
active potency 85
active power 178–180, 184–188
adultery 245–246
agency, Islamic theological debate on human 114–116
agent intellect 6, 56–60, 62–75; Avicenna and 178–182; soul and 178–191; Thomas Aquinas and 178, 182–191
akratic behaviour 241
al-Ash'arī 115
Albert the Great 164–165, 204, 210–211
Alcuin 3
Alexander of Aphrodisias 2, 57, 75, 105–107
Alexander of Hales 140
al-Farabi 107–108; *Commentary on De Interpretatione* 108; intellectual abstraction of intelligibles 56–59, 61,
64, 68, 76; *Letter on the Intellect* 57–59; *Perfect State* 108
al-Ghazālī 5, 119, 121, 267
al-ikhtiyār 104–108, 110
al-irāda 104–108
al-Kindi 111–112
al-Naẓẓām, Ibrāhīm 116–117
Alpina, Tommaso 60, 69–72, *70–72*
Angela of Foligno 219, 222, 225, 226–228
angels: Bonaventure and 211–212; fall of 242–243, 251–253; immortality of 220–221
Anselm of Canterbury 2, 3–4, 83, 95, 251; *On the Fall of the Devil* 4; *On Free Will* 4; *Monologion* 259, 265–266; *Proslogion* 4; self and 259, 265–267; *On Truth* 4
anti-realist 18, 20
apophaticism 222–223, 227
appetite: as a passion 158, 162; power 164–167, 169–173; soul 105, 158, 161; will 85, 90, 244, 249
apprehension: of intelligibles 64, 67; of intentions 145–146
Arabic philosophy 2, 4–7; Avicenna and the abstraction of intelligibles 56–76; perception and 135–136; science of the soul 5; *see also specific philosophers*
Archéologie du sujet (de Libera) 273
Aristotle 1, 2, 3, 31; accidental perception 145; on akratic behaviour 241; *Categories* 20, 39, 165; *De Anima* 19,

279

56, 71–72, 109, 117, 178, 180, 183, 184, 200, 202; *De Interpretatione* 108; induction 57; influence on medieval theories of perception 135–136, 140; intellect and 268–269; intellectual abstraction 56–57; *On Interpretation* 2, 3; *Metaphysics* 85, 119; *Nicomachean Ethics* 107, 165; passions and 159; *Physics* 164, 166–167, 174, 183; *Posterior Analytics* 57, 230; prohibitions on public reading 84; sense experience 18, 56–57; sense perception 136, 139; *On the soul* 5–7, 10–12, 268–269; soul and 135–136, 201, 208; on species of a thing 36; substance-accident framework 208; translation into Arabic 4; understanding and 178; will, theory of 104
attention (attending) 22–24; Abelard and 29–31; Augustine and 26–27; mental perception as 29–31
Attic Nights (Aulus Gellius) 160
Augustine 207, 253; *City of God* 160, 252; *Confessions* 241; *De Anima* 19; *De civitate Dei* 158; emotions and 160–161; imagination and 23; influence on Abelard 24–29; passions and 158–161, 172–173; self and 259, 265–267; self-knowledge, theory of 258; superiority of the soul 139; *On the Trinity* 19, 24–28, 259, 265, 269, 271
Aulus Gellius 160
Avercentres 2
Averroes 6–7, 10, 56, 114; Divine Will 123–125; emphasis on God's ordaining laws of nature 124; intellectual abstraction of intelligibles 56–59, 64, 68, 76; *Long Commentary on the De Anima* 10, 12, 58, 109; *Longer Commentary on On the Soul* 6–7; *Middle Commentary on On the Soul* 6; on perception of senses 144; on will 109
Avicenna 2, 4–6, 10, 110; abstraction of intelligibles 56–76; agent intellect 178–182; Aquinas and 182–191; *The Book of Healing* 179, 182; concept acquisition 178–182, 184, 188–191; Dag Nikolaus Hasse and 60, 61–64, 68–69; *De anima* 146; description of God 120–121; Dimitri Gutas and 60, 64–68; internal and external senses, theories of 5–6, 138; *Isharāt* 63; *Kitāb al-Nafs* 70; on motive faculty of soul 108–109, 119; perception and 138–139, 141–142; *Proof of Prophecies* 65; *Psychology* 179, 182, 189–190; self and 259, 267–268; soul and 5, 180, 198–199; subjectivity 258; understanding and 178–182, 186–188, 190
Avicenna's De anima in the Latin West (Hasse) 61, 64

Bacon, Roger: perception and 138–139, 145–146, 148; *Perspectiva* 147
being: contingent 84; necessary 84
Bernard of Clairvaux 262
Blund, John 198, 204
Boethius 1, 2–3; *Commentary on Porphyry's Isagoge* 19–21; *Consolation of Philosophy* 3, 8, 19, 22–23, 259–261, 273; *On Division* 3; division of soul 201, 206, 210; the self as an ideal 259–262; understand 20–24, 29; universals, understanding 19–22
Bonaventure 162, 211–213
Boniface VIII, Pope 83
Book of Definitions (Israeli) 113
Book of Healing, The (Avicenna) 179, 182
Book of Spirit and Soul, The (Israeli) 113
boulesis 104–107, 122
Brentano, F. 18

Capella, Martianus 8
Categories (Aristotle) 2, 3, 20, 39, 165
Catherine of Siena 224–225, 228, 230
change, Avicenna and 179–180
Charles the Bald 262
chimera, understanding of 30
choice 103–125
Cicero 158
City of God (Augustine) 160, 252
Cloud of Unknowing (anonymous) 223, 226
cognition of material singulars 35–48
cognitive hierarchy in Boethius' *Consolation of Philosophy* 22–24

cognitive powers of the soul 136, *137*, 148
Commentary on De Interpretatione (al-Farabi) 108
Commentary on Isagoge (Abelard) 30
Commentary on Porphyry's Isagoge (Boethius) 19–21
Commentary on the De anima (Thomas Aquinas) 44
Commentary on the Mishnah (Maimonides) 123
Commentary on the Sentences (Duns Scotus) 94–95
common senses 5, 40, 61, 65–66, 137–138, 140–141, 143–146, 149–151
common sensibles 144–145
complexity of the soul 197–214
composite soul 202–203, 206
compositive imagination 190
compulsion 114, 119
concept acquisition, Avicenna and 178–182, 184, 188–191
Confessions (Augustine) 241
Consolation of Philosophy (Boethius) 3, 8, 19, 22–23, 259–261, 273
Constable, G. 7
contingency 84–88, 93–97; of free action 93–95; synchronic 87, 95–96
contingent being 84
Cory, Thérèse 272
Courcelle, Pierre 262
Cross, Richard 87

Damascene, John 158, 164–165
De Anima (Aristotle) 19, 56, 71–72, 109, 117, 178, 180, 183, 184, 200, 202
De anima (Avicenna) 146
De civitate Dei (Augustine) 158
De Interpretatione (Aristotle) 108
De malo (Thomas Aquinas) 245
De Praedestinatione (Eriugena) 262–263
De Primo Principio (Duns Scotus) 88
Descartes, René 257
desires of the rational soul 113
determination, modes of 92–93
De veritate (Thomas Aquinas) 247
Dialogue (Catherine of Siena) 224–225
Dionysius the Areopagite 3
direct intellection of the singular 38–42

dislike 162, *163*, 251
Disputed Questions on Cognition (Matthew of Acquasparta) 269
Disputed Questions on Spiritual Creatures (Thomas Aquinas) 184, 189
Disputed Questions on the Soul (Marston) 269
Divine Justice 116
Divine Truth 222
Divine Will 92, 94, 103, 105, 113–115, 117–125; as expression of pure wisdom 123–125; as "gift-giving God" and as "God, I know not what" 117–119; as pure goodness 119–123
Dragmaticon (William of Conches) 9
Duns Scotus, John 1, 41, 46, 83–98, 146; *Commentary on the Sentences* 94–95; *De Primo Principio* 88; fall of angels 243, 251–253; on freedom 83–98; *Ordinatio* 88–90, 92, 95; passions and 174; *Questions on Aristotle's Metaphysics* 86–88, 95
Duns Scotus on God (Cross) 87
Duties of the Heart (Ibn Pequda) 118

Eckhart, Meister 219, 222–223, 226
emanation 68–69
emanationist theory 6
embodied immortal experience 224–229
emotions: Augustine and 160–161; Seneca and 159–160; *see also* passions
Emotions in Ancient and Medieval Philosophy (Knuuttila) 157
Enneads (Plotinus) 120
Eriugena, John Scottus 3; *De Praedestinatione* 262–263; *On nature (Periphyseon)* 3; *Periphyseon* 262–264; self and 259, 262–265
essence 60, 115
estimation 113
estimative judgment 146
estimative power 141–142, 145–146
Eucharist 228
evil 250; Aquinas and 244–247; passions and 158–160, 162, 164–168, 170–172
experience *see* perceptual experience; sense experience
external senses 136–142, *137*, 144–146, 149

faculty psychology 134–135
fear, as a passion 158–159, *169*
Fire of Love (Rolle) 225
Flowing Light of the Godhead, The (Mechtild of Magdeburg) 224
flying man 5, 267, 269
foreknowledge, divine 22
form, soul as 197–214, 221
Foucault, Michel 258
freedom: contingency 84–88, 93–97; definition of 83, 97; Duns Scotus on 83–98; Henry of Ghent and 248–250; necessity and contingency of free action 93–95; as a pure perfection 85–86, 95–97; self-determination 92–93; of the will 88–92, 252–253; will and choice in Islamic and Jewish contexts 103–125
free power, definition of 90–91
Free Spirit movement 223
friendship, love of 251–252

Galen 4
generosity 244
Geoffroy, Marc 57
Gerard of Bologna 36, 38, 45
"gift-giving God" 117–118
Gilbert of Poitiers 9
Giles of Rome 174
good, passions and 157–159, 162, 164–168, 170–173
goodness, Divine Will as pure 119–123
goods, inclinations toward 252
grace, divine 117–118
Grosseteste, Robert 229–231
Gundissalinus, Dominicus 10, 145–146
Gutas, Dimitri 60, 64–68

Hadewijch of Brabant 219, 226, 228, 229
happiness 174, 243–244, 251–252
Hasse, Dag Nikolaus 60–64, 68–69; *Avicenna's De anima in the Latin West* 61, 64
Hayy ibn Yaqzān (Ibn Tufayl) 267–268
Henry of Ghent 45–46, 83, 88, 242, 247–251; on voluntarily choosing the lesser good 247–251
Hilton, Walter 223–224, 226

History of my calamities (Abelard) 8
history of philosophy of the mind 1–13; between Boethius and Anselm in the Latin West 2–4; development of the Arabic tradition in 4–7; thirteenth-century philosophy of the mind 10–13; twelfth century in the Latin West 7–10
holenmerism 203–206, 213
Hutchinson, D.S. 241
hylomorphism 197, 200, 211–213, 220, 231

Iamblichean principle 22
ibn Gabirol, Solomon 120–121, 211
Ibn Peqūda, Baḥya 118
ibn Safwān, Jahm 114
Ibn Tufayl 259, 267–268
ignorance, sin from 244, 246–247
imagination 137; compositive 190; internal sense of 66; perceptual experience and 143; as a storehouse 23
immortality 219–233; embodied experience 224–229; human expectations of 219, 229; metaphysics of 220–222; scholastic views of the afterlife 229; transcending matter 220, 222–224
Inciarte, Fernando 98
inclinations 116–117, 119
incontinence 107
indetermination 90–93, 97
indirect intellection of the singular 42–46
induction 57
intellect: Aquinas and 270–273; Aristotle and 268–269; doctrine of the unicity of the 7; material 6–7, 58–59, 66, 74, 75; perfect actualisation of 243; potential 72–73, 75; senses or stages of 66; universal 61–63; will and 91–92; *see also* agent intellect
intellection of singular things 35–48; direct 38–42; indirect 42–46
intellective union 229–233
intellectual abstraction: meaning in the Arabic tradition 56, 57–60; requisite for science 56–57
intellectual memory 70–71, 75
intelligible forms, Avicenna and 178, 180

intelligibles, abstraction of 56–76
intelligible species 35, 37–38, 40–41, 43–47, 270
intentions 137; apprehension of 145–146; Augustine and 25–28; Duns Scotus and 146; grasping of 6
internal senses 135, 137–143, *137*, 149–151
internationality 18
intuition, Avicenna and 64
irrational powers of the soul 135
Isaac of Stella 9, 159
Isagoge (Porphyry) 2
Isharāt (Avicenna) 63
Islam: Greek *boulesis-prohairesis* in Islamic and Jewish contexts 107–113; soul, will, and choice 103–125
Israeli, Isaac 113

James of Venice 10
John of Jandun 174
John of la Rochelle 147, 161–162
Judaism: Greek *boulesis-prohairesis* in Islamic and Jewish contexts 107–113; soul, will, and choice 103–125
judging 22–24, 29–30
judgments: estimative 146; passion related to rational 171
justice 252

Kant, Immanuel 47
Kent, Bonnie 242
Kilwardby, Robert 84
Kitāb al-Nafs (Avicenna) 70
knowledge: acquired by induction 57; self-knowledge 257–260, 262–266, 268–273
Knuuttila, Simo 157

Latin West 2–4, 7–10
Letter on the Intellect (al-Farabi) 57–59
Letters (Seneca) 158
Libera, Alain de 272, 273
light 56
liking 162, *163*, 251
Lombard, Peter 10, 207
Long Commentary on the De Anima of Aristotle (Averroes) 10, 12, 109

Longer Commentary On the Soul (Averroes) 6–7
love of concupiscence 251–252
love of friendship 251–252
Lucifer, fall of 243, 251–253

Magnus, Albertus 36, 39, 144
Maimonides 109–112, 122–123; *Commentary on the Mishnah* 123; Divine Will 123–125; "Eight Chapters" 110–111; *Guide of the Perplexed* 106
malice 242, 243–247, 250, 251–252
Marriage of Mercury and Philology, The (Capella) 8
Marston, Roger 38, 269
Martin, Chris 272
Mastri, Bartolomeo 98
material intellect 6–7, 58–59, 66, 74, 75
material singulars, cognition of 35–48
Matthew of Acquasparta 38, 40, 269
McGinnis, Jon 59–60
Mechtild of Magdeburg 219, 224, 226, 229
Meditation II (Descartes) 257
memory: Augustine and 25, 27–28; in humans *versus* animals 136; intellectual 70–71, 75; perceptual experience and 136, 143; retention of intentions 137
mental intentionality, Augustine and 25–28
mental perception 18–31; abstraction 21; as attention 29–31
Metaphysics (Aristotle) 85, 119
metaphysics of immortality 220–222
Middle Commentary on On the Soul (Averroes) 6
middle term 64, 67
mind's eye 18, 22–24, 26
miracles, belief in 188
Mirror of Simple Souls (Porete) 223
Monologion (Anselm) 259, 265–266
morality 240–253; Duns Scotus on the fall of the angels 251–253; grounded by reason 104; Henry of Ghent on voluntarily choosing the lesser good 247–251; Thomas Aquinas on deliberate malice 243–247
moral virtues, passions and 172–174
moral weakness 241

INDEX

Mulla Sadrā 258
Mutakallimûn 44
mysticism 222–223, 227–228

naturalism, Aristotelian 179, 183–184
nature: Duns Scotus and 83–88, 90–91, 94–96, 98; will different from 86–88
Nature of Body and Soul, The (William of St. Thierry) 9
necessary being 84
necessity 84–88, 92–95, 97–98
necessity of free action 93–95
Nemesius of Emesa 158
Nicomachean Ethics (Aristotle) 107, 165

Olivi, Peter John 46–47, 83, 85; perception and 142, 149, 151, 157; self and self-knowledge 269–270; self-awareness and perception 151; *On the Sentences* 269
On Anger (Seneca) 159
On Dispelling Sorrows (al-Kindi) 111–112
On Division (Boethius) 3
On Free Will (Anselm) 4
On Interpretation (Aristotle) 2, 3
On nature (Periphyseon) (Eriugena) 3
On the Fall of the Devil (Anselm) 4
On the Improvement of the Moral Qualities (Ibn Gabirol) 111
On the Intellect (Alexander of Aphrodisias) 57
On the Orthodox Faith (Damascene) 164
On the rational soul (Alcuin) 3
On the Sentences (Olivi) 269
On the soul (Aristotle) 5–7, 10–12, 268–269
On the Trinity (Augustine) 19, 24–28, 259, 265, 269, 271
On the Trinity (Richard of St. Victor) 8–9
On Truth (Anselm) 4
On Truth (Thomas Aquinas) 270–271
Order of Things, The (Foucault) 258
Ordinatio (Duns Scotus) 88–90, 92, 95

pain, as a passion 158, 169, *169*
Paraphrase of the De Anima (Themistius) 57, 60, 72–76
particularity 60, 62–63, 69
particularization 60

passions: rational judgment, relationship to 171; reason and 172; sin from 244–245, 250; stoic ideas of 158–161, 172–173; systematization of 157–174; Thomas Aquinas and 157, 164–174, *169*, 185–186; virtue and 172–174
Peckham, John 138
perception: accidental 145; active and passive theories of 139; Avicenna's interest in 6; common sense 5, 40, 61, 65–66, 137–138, 140–141, 143–146, 149–151; estimative 146–147; medieval psychology of 134–151; mental 18–31; perspectivist theories of perception 138; philosophical discussions concerning the mechanics of 138; self-awareness and 150–151; *see also* sense perception
perceptual experience 134–151; definition of 135; in humans *versus* non-human animals 136; in human *versus* non-human animals 136, 138; psychological puzzle of *137*; unified 140–143
Perfect State (al-Farabi) 108
Periphyseon (Eriugena) 262–264
Perspectiva (Bacon) 147
perspectivist theories of perception 138
Phaedo (Plato) 198–199, 221
Phaedrus (Plato) 107
phantasms 36, 38, 40, 43–46, 230–231
Philip IV of France, King 83
philosophical anthropology 1
Physics (Aristotle) 164, 166–167, 174, 183
Pines, Shlomo 106
Plato 1, 2, 4–5, 5, 8; Form of the Good above Being 120; passions and 158; *Phaedo* 198–199, 221; *Republic* 117, 158, 172; soul and 172, 202, 221
Platonic anthropology 8
Platonic cosmology 8
pleasure, as a passion 158–159, *169*
Plotinus 112; *Enneads* 120; sense of God 120–121
Porete, Martuerite 219, 223, 226, 229
Porphyry 2
possession 84–85
Posterior Analytics (Aristotle) 57, 230
potency 85
potentiality 179

power(s) 115–116, 118–119, 206–211; as accidents 207–210; active 178–180, 184–188, 185–186; appetitive 164–167, 169–173; Avicenna general theory of powers 179–180; as differentiae 208; indeterminate 91; manifest in different parts of the body 202; parts of the soul and 201; passive 185–186; as a principle of change 179; receptive 179–180, 186–187, 190; whole of 210–211
Problem of Too Many Animals 204–205
Proclus 120
prohairesis 104–107
Proof of Prophecies (Avicenna) 65
proprium 208
Proslogion (Anselm) 4
psychology, faculty 134–135
Psychology (Avicenna) 179, 182, 189–190
Punch, John 98
punishment 113
pure perfection 85–86, 95–97

Questions on Aristotle's Metaphysics (Duns Scotus) 86–88, 95

rational decision, Aristotelian theory of 103
rational powers of the soul 135–136
rational soul 136
reason: morality grounded by 104; passion and 172
receptive material intellect 66
Redundancy Argument 203
reflexio 43–46
representations 36, 38, 40, 43–46
Republic (Plato) 107, 117, 158, 172
resemblance, of a thing 36–38
resurrection, bodily 219–221, 224
reward 113
Richard of St. Victor 8–9, 89
Rolle, Richard 225

Scale of Perfection, The (Hilton) 223–224
science of the soul 5, 10
scientific knowledge 56–57, 75
self-awareness, perception and 150–151
self-consciousness 257, 272
self-determination 85–87, 91–98, 92–93

self-knowledge 257–260, 262–266, 268–273
self-loss/self-annilation 222–224
self-possession 84, 98
self-subsistent, soul as 198–199, 211–213
the self 257–274; Anselm 259, 265–267; Aquinas 259, 268–273; Augustine 259, 265–267; Avicenna 259, 267–268; Boethius 259–262; Eriugena 259, 262–265; Ibn Tufayl 259, 267–268
Seneca: *On Anger* 159; *Letters* 158; passions and 158–160
sense experience 18, 56–57; Augustine and 25–28; memory and 27–28
sense perception 57, 74, 108, 134–151, 230, 232; Abelard and 23–24; al-Farabi and 108; Avicenna and 6, 61–62, 65; Boethius and 23–24; explanation of 134; Gutas and 65–66; McGinnis and 60; storage of 23; *see also* sense experience
senses, unity of 143–144
sensory powers of the soul 136
Sentences (Lombard) 10, 207
Shahrastāni 116
Siger of Brabant 202–203, 206
sin 250, 253; Adam's 251; angelic 251; sources of 244–246
singulars: intellectual cognition of 35–48; meaning of term 47
Sister Catherine (anonymous) 223
Socrates, on akratic behaviour 241
soul: agent intellect and 182–191; al-Farabi and 57–58, 58; al-Kindi on improving 111–112; appetites of 105, 158, 161; Aristotle and 5–7, 10–12, 135–136; ascent and descent of, dynamism of 9; Averroes and 6–7, 58; Avicenna and 5, 59–68; cognition and 37–38, 42, 46–47, 136–137, *137*, 148; complexity of 197–214; concupiscible and irascible parts of the 158–159, 161; divisibility in virtue of being in a body 201–206; empirical desideratum 200–201, 209–210, 214; human being defined by his intellective 48; Islamic and Jewish contexts 103–125; metaphysical desideratum 199–202, 204; nutritive and sensitive 185–186; Plato and 5, 8, 107; potential intellect 72–7, 75; rational

and irrational powers of the 135–136; science of the 5, 10; as subsisting reality 48; theological desideratum 198–201, 211, 214; Thomas Aquinas and 182–191, 198–199, 204–206
soul return 113
Sources of the Self (Taylor) 258
species: perceptual 139; of a thing 36–38
St. Paul 241
steadfastness 93–94
stoics, passions and 158–161, 172–173
strength, passions and 162, *163*, 164
subjectivity 257–259, 262–263, 265, 267–269, 272–274
Suhrawardī 258, 267
Summa Contra Gentiles (Thomas Aquinas) 173–174, 183–184, 187–188, 270
Summa de anima (La Rochelle) 162
Summa Theologiae (Thomas Aquinas) 44, 164, 182, 184–185, 189, 248, 270–272
synchronic contingency 87, 95–96
synderesis 247
systematization of the passions in the thirteenth century 157–174; John of La Rochelle 161–164, *163*, 174, 258; Thomas Aquinas 164–174, *169*

Taylor, Charles 258
Tempier, Étienne 84
Ten Categories 4
Themistius 57, 60, 72–76
Theology of Aristotle (Plotinus) 112, 118, 120, 122
Thomas Aquinas 35, 83, 139; agent intellect 178, 182–191; Avicenna and 182–191; cognition of singulars 43–45, 48; *Commentary on the De anima* 44; on deliberate malice 243–247; *De malo* 245; *De veritate* 247; *Disputed Questions on Spiritual Creatures* 184, 189; as eudaimonist 243; hylomorphic account of substance 185; on immortality 231; malice 242; passions and 157, 164–174, *169*, 185–186; perfection tenet 184–185, 187–188; self and 259, 268–273; soul and 182–191, 198–199, 204–206; sufficiency tenet 184–187; *Summa Contra Gentiles* 173–174, 183–184, 187–188, 270; *Summa Theologiae* 44, 164, 182, 184–185, 189, 248, 270–272; systematization of passions 157, 164–174, *169*; *On Truth* 270–271; understanding and 182, 184–188; on wholeness 205; will and 244–250
transcending matter 220, 222–224
Treatise on Understandings (Abelard) 29
trinity, Christian 24–28
truth 271
Tusculan Disputations (Cicero) 158
Twesky, Isadore 106

understanding: Abelard and 18, 19, 29–31; agent intellect and 178–182; Aristotle and 178; Augustine and 25–28; Avicenna and 178–182, 186–188, 190; Boethius and 20–24, 29; determination of the soundness of 31; produced by act of intention 25–28; Thomas Aquinas and 182, 184–188
union with God 229–232
unity, principle of 197, 200–202
Unity Argument 200–203, 206, 208, 213
universal intellect 61–63
universality 60
universals: apprehension of 38–40; Boethius on 19–22; cognition of singulars and 35–43, 45–47; direct cognition of 35–36, 42–43; Henry of Ghent and 45–46; intelligible species as representation of 38; nonexistence of 18, 20; problem of 8, 19
universities, rise of 7

virtue 172–174, 244
Vital du Four 38, 47
Vitello 138
voluntarism 98

weakness: moral 241; passions and 162, *163*, 164
wholeness, kinds of 205
will 103–125; *al-ikhtiyār* and 104–108; *al-irāda* and 104–108; appetite 85, 90, 244, 249; aptness and 97, 589–90; Aristotelians' theories of 104; *boulesis* and 104–107, 122; contingency and

INDEX

85–88, 93–97; Divine Will 92, 94, 103, 105, 113–115, 117–125; evil 244–247; freedom and 252–253; Henry of Ghent and 248–251; intellect and 91–92; nature different from 86–88; *prohairesis* and 104–107; self-determination possessed by 86; Thomas Aquinas and 170; weakness of 107

William of Conches 9
William of Ockham 46, 98, 207
William of St. Thierry 9, 262
willing, act of 88–89
Wippel, John F. 84
Wisdom, Divine 123–125

Yes and No (Sic et Non) (Abelard) 10